TRANSFORMATIVE ENCOUNTERS

The Intervention of God in Christian Counseling and Pastoral Care

EDITED BY
DAVID W. APPLEBY AND
GEORGE OHLSCHLAGER

An imprint of InterVarsity Press
Downers Grove, Illinois

InterVarsity Press
P.O. Box 1400, Downers Grove, IL 60515-1426
World Wide Web: www.ivpress.com
Email: email@ivpress.com

InterVarsity Press® is the book-publishing division of InterVarsity Christian Fellowship/USA®, a movement of students and faculty active on campus at hundreds of universities, colleges and schools of nursing in the United States of America, and a member movement of the International Fellowship of Evangelical Students. For information about local and regional activities, write Public Relations Dept., InterVarsity Christian Fellowship/USA, 6400 Schroeder Rd., P.O. Box 7895, Madison, WI 53707-7895, or visit the IVCF website at www.intervarsity.org.

While all stories in this book are true, some names and identifying information in this book have been changed to protect the privacy of the individuals involved.

Cover design: Cindy Kiple
Interior design: Beth Hagenberg
Images: droplet of water: Gerard Fritz/Getty Images
drop of water: © xefstock/iStockphoto

ISBN 978-0-8308-2822-7
Digital ISBN 978-0-8308-9550-2

Printed in the United States of America ∞

green press INITIATIVE *InterVarsity Press is committed to protecting the environment and to the responsible use of natural resources. As a member of Green Press Initiative we use recycled paper whenever possible. To learn more about the Green Press Initiative, visit www.greenpressinitiative.org.*

Library of Congress Cataloging-in-Publication Data
A catalog record for this book is available from the Library of Congress.

P *21 20 19 18 17 16 15 14 13 12 11 10 9 8 7 6 5 4 3 2 1*
Y *31 30 29 28 27 26 25 24 23 22 21 20 19 18 17 16 15 14 13*

This book is dedicated to all those who have a vision, not for what God has done, but for what God can do. It is for all those who are determined to see God step into their lives, their families, and their ministries and practices, and move in a supernatural, transformative way. This book is for those who will not just settle but are willing to go where they've never been before in God.

Contents

Part Two

Transformative Paradigms for Church or Clinic

Preface

A Lesson in the School of the Holy Spirit

Most of us have gone into counseling or pastoral work because we have a genuine desire to see broken people restored. Jesus' "life verse," the statement of his reason for coming to earth, is found in Luke 4:18-19, which says:

> The Spirit of the Lord is on me,
> because he has anointed me
> to proclaim good news to the poor.
> He has sent me to proclaim freedom for the prisoners
> and recovery of sight for the blind,
> to set the oppressed free,
> to proclaim the year of the Lord's favor.

Something resonates within us when we read that verse. The Greek word here for "oppressed" is *tethrausmenous,* whose root word means literally to break into pieces and figuratively to be broken in both heart and body. Jesus declared that his mission was to mend broken hearts like pieces of broken earthenware, restoring them and making them whole. We find ourselves saying, "Lord, I want to do that too." We want to tell and show people that God's favor is truly upon them and to help them find the fruit of that favor. Throughout his earthly journey Jesus did exactly that as he healed the sick, cast out demons and raised the dead.

Merrill Unger, in his 1953 classic, *Biblical Demonology,* says that the authors of Scripture use the comprehensive term *healing* to designate the restoration of any derangement of both body and mind, whether from natural or demonic cause (Unger, 1953). While we have many examples of Jesus healing bodies and casting out demons, we have to assume that there were also many instances when Jesus shared his life and wisdom with those who were emotionally damaged as well.

When we try to walk in Jesus' footsteps in our healing ministries, particularly if we are open to the supernatural, it is very easy to confuse the means of healing with the One who gives it. We often focus on the prayer, the anointing, the gifted person, the historical evidence of miraculous change or the right measure of faith by which healing is supposed to come. We like methods and would like to package the process in a nice, neat box. Given the many ways that healing comes from the various methods outlined in this book, the reader could easily continue in this well-meaning but fallacious belief that it is the means of healing that makes healing possible, that makes all the difference.

Pastor Bill Johnson of Bethel Church in Redding, California, who has a stellar reputation in his circles of influence as a bona fide healer and all-around good guy, tells this story that is well worth reflecting upon:

> Learning to hear God's voice and follow His lead is joyful and exciting, yet I must admit it also keeps me on edge. I was at Grace Center, a great church outside Nashville, Tenn., when a woman came to me for prayer. She was afflicted with rheumatoid arthritis head to toe. As I moved to pray for her, I felt a check in my heart that I was not to pray. In this case, something was different. I could tell Jesus was going to heal her, yet it felt as if I would interfere with the work of God if I prayed or laid hands on her. I wasn't even allowed to make decrees of healing over her or pronounce her well, as Jesus did with, "Go your way; the demon has gone out of your daughter" (Mark 7:29).
>
> This woman's healing was to be a school of the Spirit for me. I asked her to close her eyes so the other ministry going on around the room wouldn't distract her. She did as I requested. Then I sensed a heat on the back of my neck, obvious but subtle. It felt like hot oil slowly flowing downward, so I told her the anointing was flowing down her neck. She said she felt it. When it reached the base, I told her the neck should be healed by now. She moved it about in ways that would have caused pain before, only to find that it was, in fact, healed.
>
> In that moment I realized what God was doing. I was a play-by-play announcer, like at a sporting event. It was my privilege to describe what God was doing in her as He showed me on my own body. He wanted to heal her without it flowing through me, whether through prayer, decree or the laying on of hands. It is important for us to understand that it is always God who heals. (Johnson, 2012)

No two miracles of Jesus recorded in Scripture were done in exactly the same way. We can't help but wonder if our tendency to get locked into patterns and principles, though they have value, might work against our need to stay connected to what the Father is doing. It's no longer a question of whether it is God's will to heal. Now it's only a question of how. Developing an ear for his voice seems to be at the heart of this issue. What we know can keep us from what we need to know if we don't stay childlike in our approach to life and ministry.

It is probably the natural bent of our organizing minds that leads to fitting these materials into workable patterns of action and principles for doing ministry. That is not the lesson that we hope you will take in reading and reviewing this book. We are not saying, don't do this for it will disserve you and your clients. We assume that you will do the mining and categorizing that comes naturally to someone in ministry and professional practice with a sharp and dissecting mind.

More than that, we are saying, don't stop your learning after you have organized these materials logically. The rational and cognitive learning you will do is the necessary start of your education. Do take the next step, however, as suggested by Johnson in the foreword: stop and yield yourself to God with the prayer to begin the deeper education of becoming like a little child and learning to listen with your "inner ear" to the whisper of God, to see with your mind's eye the kingdom of God taking shape right in front of you.

Remember the great lesson of the hammer: if that is the only tool you have, then you will try to make every job look like a nail. Don't simply learn one method of inner healing prayer and assume that such a process will apply equally well to every client or parishioner. If you have sensed God's check in your spirit, and have backed off doing something that seemed completely logical and rational, then you know how important it is to learn to listen to God and be flexible, knowing that there are a number of different ways to get the job done properly. We just have to become aware of how God wants to do it.

In part four we will further challenge you to have a personal encounter with God and to learn both the rational and emotive elements involved in Christian counseling in order to help others change in a godly direction. Just remember, when you have learned everything you can on the human, horizontal plane, then you must begin the vertical education in the school of the Spirit. Then you must learn to be still, to silence the noise that invades from all sides and hear the still small voice of God as it whispers which way to go. We need to do this first for ourselves and then for our clients.

References and Recommended Resources

Johnson, B. (2012, March). You've got the power. *Charisma.* Retrieved from <http://www.charismamag.com/site-archives/1496-312-magazine-articles/features/14932-youve-got-the-power>.

Unger, M. (1953). *Biblical demonology.* Wheaton, IL: Van Kampen Press.

Acknowledgments

There is nothing like trying to put together an edited book to make one appreciate the tremendous gift that is each of these authors. This book would literally not exist except for their willingness to share their time and expertise with us. We are especially blessed because these authors are not graduate students seeking to have their first publication. These authors are seasoned experts in their own right, many having counseled people for decades, many having taught graduate school for years and many having published multiple books of their own. These authors often undertook this project in between their classes and in between their own writing commitments in order to share their heart and experience with us. Without you this book would not exist. We would also like to give a special thanks to Eric Johnson who, early in the process, agreed to be our "ghost editor" and put us in contact with some of these authors. His belief in this project, his excellent foreword and his guidance throughout has resulted in a far better contribution to the field of Christian counseling. Thank you, Eric. Thank you all.

We would be remiss if we didn't acknowledge the sacrifice that our families made over the three years we spent readying this book for publication. Thank you Carol Appleby and Loraine Ohlschlager for releasing us to follow the dream that God gave us for this project. You are incredible.

Foreword

Counseling and Psychotherapy on a New Foundation

Eric L. Johnson

The influence of Augustine on the Christian church in the West has been enormous. One of his greatest works—*The City of God* (1958)—was an attempt to retell the story of Western civilization up to that time according to the rather sectarian perspective of the Bible. Augustine argued that there are fundamentally only two communities in the world: those who believe in Jesus Christ (the City of God) and those who do not (the City of Humanity). The former, Augustine wrote, love God and despise self, and the latter love self and despise God. Augustine, of course, did not mean that Christians should hate themselves. The issue is who is ultimate and who is subordinate, God or the self. He believed these two ultimate sets of motives differentially animate these two communities, as they coexist in every culture through the course of human history, and head toward their complete realization in the age to come.

Augustine's two-city model of humanity provides a useful interpretive framework for approaching one's culture and the Christian's place in it, especially when considering how to approach modern psychology. Writing around the time that modern psychology was being founded, Abraham Kuyper (1898)—Dutch theologian, churchman and prime minister (1904–1908)—took Augustine's framework a step further and argued that the regeneration of the Holy Spirit mediated by faith in Christ leads to the development of two versions of the human sciences, distinguished fundamentally by their assumptions or worldview. Kuyper recognized that there will be broad agreement between them where regeneration brings about no improvement in human capacities—for example, in basic observation, measurement and logical analysis. "What has been done well by one, need not be done again by you" (p. 159). Nonetheless, this regeneration leads the respective scientists "to run in opposite directions, because they have different starting-points" and "view things in a different way" (p. 155), so it inevitably brings about some substantial differences. For example, Christian versions of the human sciences will be distinguished by their reliance on Scripture. Consequently, Christian versions of the human sciences will interpret humans as currently *abnormal*—fallen and so having departed from God's design plan—and only capable of truly flourishing in union with Christ; whereas non-Christian versions will interpret humans as currently *normal* and capable of flourishing by their own powers.

Kuyper would likely have appreciated the book you hold in your hands, since it contains almost twenty specifically Christian models of counseling. Some have lately called this kind of project *Christian psychology* (Evans, 1989; Johnson, 2007; Roberts & Watson, 2010) or *transformational psychology* (Coe & Hall, 2010). Its goal is the development of the most sophisticated and comprehensive version of psychology possible (including theory, research and practice) based on a Christian worldview. As Kuyper recognized, such a project will learn from and collaborate with other communities' versions of psychology, but it will be distinguished from those versions wherever and to the extent that Christian assumptions make a difference in psychological theory, research or practice.

In contrast with a two-cities/two-sciences approach, many Christians in psychology have accepted the unified model of science assumed by modernism (the reigning worldview in the City of Humanity in the West) and the rules of scientific discourse mandated by modern psychology (e.g., the prohibition against explicit appeal to God or Scripture). As a result, such Christians have tended to concentrate on modern psychology for their main theoretical and therapeutic resources and have tended not to invest near as much time learning about the resources available in Christianity.

Modern psychology has of course compiled a remarkable treasure of psychological knowledge over the past one hundred years, and Christians in psychology must avail themselves of that knowledge. Following Augustine and Kuyper, the questions are, What is ultimate and should be our starting point? Is it adequate for Christians to begin with modern psychology and become well-educated in its knowledge and practice, and only *then* consider what Christianity has to say about a particular psychological topic? Or would it be better for Christians to first immerse themselves in the relevant theoretical and therapeutic resources of Christianity, and only then learn from modern psychology, so that it can be rightly interpreted in the light of Christian worldview assumptions?

The problem Christians face today is that we are an intellectual minority group. In order to get training and certification to practice professionally, most Christians are educated and socialized within a fundamentally secular worldview system. As a result, they are exposed to tremendous pressures to accept that the "neutral," secular approach is the only legitimate way to think about science and therapy, and to practice counseling and psychotherapy as a secularist, even when working with Christians. (Full disclosure: I received my PhD in educational psychology at Michigan State University, so I have not been immune to these influences myself.)

One of the most welcome shifts to have occurred within mainstream counseling and psychotherapy over the past twenty years from a Christian standpoint has been the remarkable opening up of the discipline to religion and spirituality. Part of this openness has resulted in significant research being published on "religion-accommodative" approaches to counseling and psychotherapy, where secular, empirically documented models are adapted to a religious orientation, including "Christian-accommodative" approaches, which adapt them to a specifically Christian orientation when working with Christians (see Worthington, Johnson, Hook & Aten, in press).

Christian-accommodative models of therapy are currently the best documented Christian models of therapy out there. The importance of this work is enormous, because it incorporates Christian content and practices into widely accepted models that have already been empirically validated and demonstrates that this kind of Christian therapy is at least as effective as secular therapy, thereby legitimating Christian therapy, broadly understood, in the eyes of consumers, licensing boards and insurance companies. This book includes some excellent examples of Christian-accommodative therapy.

However, following an Augustinian-Kuyperian vision of the human sciences, we might also expect that counseling and psychotherapy in the City of God would look substantially different from that in the City of Humanity. As a result, it is also desirable to develop models of counseling and psychotherapy for working with Christians that are what we might call "Christian-derived"—that is, models that originate from and are based on expressly Christian assumptions, beliefs and practices (see Johnson, Worthington, Aten & Hook, in press). Such models may benefit from the knowledge and legitimate insights of modern psychology, but Christianity, rather than modernism, provides their starting point. Such an agenda is most likely to lead to models that are especially and uniquely reflective of Christian distinctives and that are therefore more likely to manifest particularly potent Christian treatment and less likely to be diluted by the secular assumptions of modern models of therapy. What might characterize Christian-derived models of counseling and psychotherapy?

The Rebuilding of Counseling and Psychotherapy

Gary Collins was one of the first Christian counselors to point in this direction, in his classic text *The Rebuilding of Psychology* (1977). Though he used the term *integration* to label his approach, he argued for a psychology built on a Christian foundation rather than that of modern psychology. In the following section, his outline of a Christian foundation will be slightly updated, reorganized and elaborated, specifically with regard to counseling and psychotherapy.

In contrast to the worldview of naturalism that has dominated modern psychology, Collins wanted to rebuild psychology on a theistic worldview premise (that God exists and is the source of all truth) and a corollary (that humans can know truth, even if only in a limited way) (see chap. 8 of Collins, 1977). Following Coe and Hall (2010), we might add that knowing truth for Christians involves experiencing, living and being transformed by it. Below is a minor modification of the working assumptions of Collins's proposed "psychology on a new foundation."

Expanded empiricism.[1] The strict positivism embraced by modern psy-

[1]It made sense for Collins (1977) to include "modified reductionism" as one of the six working assumptions of the new foundation for psychology, given the remaining influence of atomism and behaviorism when he wrote. However, there is much greater appreciation for the contextual nature of both human life and knowledge, so it seems to me less unnecessary to include it today.

chology in the late 1800s continues to be largely assumed by mainstream psychologists into the present, in spite of its rejection by contemporary philosophers of science (Suppe, 1977). As a result, most modern psychologists (and even many Christians trained by them) continue to do research, theory-building and clinical work as if empirical investigation is the only legitimate (positive) source of knowledge. (Thankfully, the empirical research of positive psychology, which has utilized philosophical and religious sources of knowledge at least seminally, is undermining this traditional positivist orientation.)

The rich philosophical, theological, pastoral and spiritual resources of the Christian tradition concerning human beings and how to care for them call into question the exclusively empirical orientation of modern psychology. Also, being centered upon God makes Christians less likely to absolutize one mode of investigation. As a result, Scripture and careful reflection on it—the focus of biblical studies and theology—can be considered legitimate sources of psychological knowledge for Christians (perhaps even subdisciplines, analogous to neuroscience and statistics currently), as well as the study of the history of Christian soul-care practice. Moreover, philosophical analysis provides conceptual clarity and logical coherence that can greatly aid psychological theory, research and clinical practice. Though many modern psychologists might reject this expanded empiricism, this should not prevent Christians from holding it.

Biblical absolutism. Going a step further, Collins (1977) maintained that the Bible had priority over all other sources of knowledge. Calvin (1559/1960) called the Bible the Christians' "spectacles," enabling them to better see and interpret reality (God, the universe, others and oneself). From the Bible one also obtains ethical and spiritual absolutes and a metanarrative (see "Biblical anthropology" section below) that guide human belief, love and life, so that biblical revelation provides the "first principles" of a Christian psychology. This suggests further that Christian-derived counseling and psychotherapy will generally utilize Scripture reading and meditating as therapeutic strategies.

Christian supernaturalism. *God's centrality.* Expanding on Collins's major premise, Christian-derived counseling and psychotherapy assumes that humans cannot be properly understood apart from God and that he is central to their study and psychological care. This is so for a few reasons.

First, being made in the image of God means humans exist essentially in relation to him; second, God became a human being and revealed to humanity its perfect form; and third, humans were created by God to live for his glory (1 Cor 10:31) and to find their greatest happiness in loving, obeying and worshiping him. These considerations radically distinguish Christian psychology discourse and practice from its modern cousin.

God's relationality. Christianity differs from other religions by its belief that God is triune: one being in three persons—Father, Son and Holy Spirit (Mt 28:19). So, Christian-derived counseling and psychotherapy will promote the experience of God as Father; work with the resources provided by the believer's union with Christ in his life, death and resurrection; and rely explicitly on the power of the indwelling Spirit to bring about therapeutic change through the believer's faith. The relational nature of the triune God is also the ground of the relational nature of human beings. Individual humans are personal agents who emerge out of and are constituted by their relations with other humans.

Biblical anthropology. "Psychology should accept a model of man derived from the Bible" (Collins, 1977, p. 151). The Bible's metanarrative provides one way to organize that model. A community's metanarrative is the ultimate story within which they understand themselves and their place in the universe. Modern psychology's metanarrative is naturalistic evolution. Christianity's metanarrative can be summarized as four distinct but related perspectives on human beings.

Creation. Though Christian thinkers dispute *how* God did it, they believe he created humanity as good (Gen 1:31). The physical and psychological form, capacities and skills of human beings are therefore fundamentally good. Consequently, Christian-derived counseling and psychotherapy will eagerly work with people's created nature, along with the resources of Christ's redemption. In contrast to secular psychology, however, it will do so in dependence on God. In addition, Christian-derived counseling and psychotherapy will assume that normal adults are embodied, free, responsible agents, who are determined to some extent by biological influences and socialization.[2]

The fall. Classical Christianity also maintains that humans are now

---

[2]Collins (1977) made "determinism and free will" and "biblical anthropology" distinct working assumptions. Here the former will be subsumed under the latter.

fallen—that is, alienated from their Creator and under the dominion of Satan, having a corrupted created nature, unable to pursue the fullest good and flourish according to God's original design (Rom 3:10-23), and heading toward divine condemnation. Sin is a universal psychopathological condition that affects one's body, creates shame and guilt, disposes one to commit personal sins, and is the source of the social evils that humans experience, that altogether lead to the specific kinds of psychopathology recognized by most worldview communities, like depression and schizophrenia. Though Christian beliefs about fallenness sound too negative to modern ears, they encourage believers to take responsibility for their harmful actions and lead to a transparency and humility valuable in therapy, and research has begun documenting such benefits (Watson et al., 2007).

Human fallenness also provides a framework for interpreting human suffering and weakness. Humans understandably try to avoid them, and modern therapy rightly seeks to alleviate them. Christian-derived counseling and psychotherapy, however, also advocates the reinterpretation of suffering in light of God's loving, purposive providence and the death and resurrection of Christ, which better enables believers to face and come to terms with past suffering and that which is unavoidable in the present.

Redemption. Christianity also views Jesus Christ as God's primary intervention for healing the soul. Through Christ's life, death and resurrection, believers are reconciled to God and begin a new life in the new creation (2 Cor 5:17), which is being realized now by the Holy Spirit by means of the believer's "inward deepening" (Kierkegaard, 1990, p. 24).

This redemptive therapeutic orientation gradually redirects the attention of believers away from themselves and on to Christ, in union with whom they receive communion with God (Col 1:20), forgiveness for sin (1 Jn 1:9), adoption into God's family (Gal 4:5-6), the indwelling and empowering of the Holy Spirit (Rom 8:9), and a new self (Col 3:9-10). Such benefits create conditions in which counselees can explore and modify their internal dynamics without shame and guilt and the threat of divine condemnation. Christian counseling and psychotherapy is most distinguished from modern practice by its reliance on Christ and the Holy Spirit.

God has also instituted the church to be the social location where these changes are especially realized in mutual, upbuilding relationships with others (Eph 4:11-16). Active involvement in the local church is divinely intended to be therapeutic, and persons gifted in facilitating such changes help the church fulfill this calling (e.g., skilled Christian ministers, counselors, psychotherapists).

The Christian spiritual disciplines enable believers to avail themselves of the therapeutic resources of Christianity. Among the most relevant for this purpose are prayer, Bible study, Bible meditation, worship, love of one another and outreach, all of which contribute to the healing of the brain/soul with the help of the Spirit.

Secular counseling and psychotherapy works solely with soul-healing processes resident within the fallen creation (e.g., therapeutic alliance, empathy), which theologians would consider the fruit of *common* or *creation grace*—that is, grace available to all humans, more or less, regardless of their personal relationship with God. Christian-derived counseling and psychotherapy also makes use of these creational therapeutic processes, but when working with Christians, counselors can also work with the redemptive resources of their union with Christ.

The consummation. Christians also believe that believers ought to be future-oriented, because "God guarantees a bright and everlasting future for those who commit their lives to him" (Collins, 1977, p. 152). Focusing on a future of everlasting blessedness can give believers happiness and hope today and help them cope with past and present suffering, whereas the future according to counseling based in naturalism is ultimately tragic and meaningless.

Summary. The foregoing is only a summary of the therapeutic resources available for Christian counseling or psychotherapy, whether accommodated or derived, built "on a new foundation." (For more elaboration, see Johnson, 2007, in press; Coe & Hall, 2010). Even though we have the Bible, only God knows fully what Christian-derived counseling or psychotherapy looks like, so human efforts to describe all such models will vary considerably and necessarily fall short of God's understanding. Such variation will be seen in this book. Nevertheless, it brings together one of the most comprehensive set of models of Christian-accommodative and Christian-derived therapy ever. Each chapter offers a uniquely Christian approach to counseling with Christians, and most of them utilize Scripture, God's presence and at least some of the unique therapeutic resources that flow from Christ and union with him.

Lay and Pastoral Models of People-Helping

One more point deserves comment. One of the book's most notable features is the inclusion of a handful of what today could be called Christian lay or pastoral models of people-helping (see part one)—that is, models developed by Christian lay people or ministers untrained in contemporary psychological theory, research methods and clinical practice. As a result, some of those so trained have raised concerns about such models, including false and exaggerated claims, poor theology and training, and the possible harm caused by immature and inexperienced lay people or ministers working on problems beyond their competence. These are serious allegations and deserve investigation. At the same time, there are also a number of positive reasons to do research on these kinds of models.

1. The facts that they have arisen out of the church, tend to be Christ-centered or Holy Spirit–dependent or both, and rely on Scripture more than contemporary psychology, make it likely that they are fairly Christian-derived and reflect distinctly Christian methods of soul healing. This alone should warrant the sympathetic interest of Christians in the field. Indeed, it may be that the most Christian-derived models *had* to be developed by those who were not trained and socialized by contemporary secular psychology.
2. Some of these models have been practiced successfully (at least anecdotally) in the Christian community for decades—for example, inner healing prayer (Sanford, 1947) and biblical counseling (Adams, 1970). For that matter, aspects of these models have been practiced for centuries in some form or another.
3. There is some similarity among these models themselves, and between them and some of the models formulated by Christians trained in contemporary psychology, and this similarity exists across denominations and in all kinds of churches. Perhaps there are some common, underlying Christian therapeutic principles at work here.
4. The benefits of lay counseling are well documented. This should lead to similar hypotheses regarding Christian lay or pastoral models of people-helping, which then ought to be tested.

5. Taylor (1985) has argued that scientific psychology has to be based on lived human experience (lay psychology) for it to be valid. Otherwise, the scientific psychology risks seriously distorting human life (as happened in the heyday of behaviorism). The same logic applies to scientific models of people-helping and should foster the investigation of these lay and pastoral models.

In light of such considerations, Christians trained in contemporary psychology should generally consider the relatively less-developed Christian people-helping models that have emerged from the grassroots of the church as objects worthy of investigation. As they are subjected to empirical test, their problems will be identified and eliminated, bad models will be rejected, and increasingly sophisticated and effective, distinctly Christian techniques and models of counseling and psychotherapy will be developed.

INVESTIGATING CHRISTIAN-ACCOMMODATED AND CHRISTIAN-DERIVED COUNSELING AND PSYCHOTHERAPY

This leads to perhaps the most pressing need of Christian counseling and psychotherapy research today. To paraphrase G. K. Chesterton, Christian-derived counseling and psychotherapy has not been investigated and found wanting; it has not been investigated. In addition, more research is needed on Christian-accomodative counseling and psychotheraphy (see Worthington, Johnson, Hook & Aten, in press). Now is the time to document their value with the highest empirical standards and to see how they compare to secular models. Further down the road, it will be necessary to see which models work best with which kinds of people (differential therapies) and which kinds of disorders (specific therapies). It would be a wonderful consequence of this book if it inspires a score of researchers to investigate the effectiveness and efficacy of all the models found within these pages.

REFERENCES AND RECOMMENDED RESOURCES

Adams, J. (1970). *Competent to counsel.* Grand Rapids: Zondervan.

Augustine. (1958). *City of God* (G. G. Walsh, S. J., D. B. Zema, S. J., G. Monahan, O. S. U., & D. J. Honan, Trans.). New York: Image.

Calvin, J. (1960). *Institutes of the Christian religion* (F. L. Battles, Trans.). Philadelphia: Westminster. (Original work published 1559.)

Coe, J. H., & Hall, T. W. (2010). *Psychology in the Spirit: Contours of a transforma-*

tional psychology. Downers Grove, IL: InterVarsity Press.

Collins, G. R. (1977). *The rebuilding of psychology: An integration of psychology and Christianity*. Wheaton, IL: Tyndale.

Evans, C. S. (1989). *Wisdom and humanness in psychology: A Christian psychology approach*. Grand Rapids: Baker.

Johnson, E. L. (2007). *Foundations for soul care: A Christian psychology proposal*. Downers Grove, IL: InterVarsity Press.

Johnson, E. L. (in press). *Resurrection dialogues: The therapeutic resources of the Christian faith*. Downers Grove, IL: InterVarsity Press.

Kierkegaard, S. (1990). *For self-examination. Judge for yourselves!* (H. V. Hong & E. H. Hong, Trans.). Princeton, NJ: Princeton University Press.

Kuyper, A. (1898). *Encyclopedia of sacred theology: Its principles*. New York: Charles Scribner's Sons.

Roberts, R. C., & Watson, P. J. (2010). A Christian psychology view. In E. L. Johnson (Ed.), *Psychology and Christianity: Five views* (pp. 149-78). Downers Grove, IL: InterVarsity Press.

Sanford, A. (1947). *The healing light*. St. Paul, MN: Macalester Park.

Suppe, F. (Ed.). (1977). *The structure of scientific theories*. Urbana, IL: University of Illinois Press.

Taylor, C. (1985). *Human agency and language: Philosophical papers 1*. New York: Cambridge University Press.

Watson, P. J., Morris, R. J., Loy, T., Hamrick, M. B., & Grizzle, S. (2007). Beliefs about sin: Adaptive implications in relationships with religious orientation, self-esteem, and measures of the narcissistic, depressed and anxious self. *Edification: Journal of the Society for Christian Psychology, 1*(1), 57-65.

Worthington, E. L., Jr., Johnson, E. L., Hook, J. N., & Aten, J. D. (Eds.). (in press). *Evidence-based practices for Christian counseling and psychotherapy*. Downers Grove, IL: InterVarsity Press.

Worthington, E. L., Jr., Johnson, E. L., Hook, J. N., & Aten, J. D. (forthcoming). Evidence-based practice in light of the Christian tradition(s): Reflections and future directions. In E. L. Worthington, E. L. Johnson, J. N. Hook & J. D. Aten (Eds.). *Evidence-based practices for Christian counseling and psychotherapy*. Downers Grove, IL: InterVarsity Press.

1

Introduction

The Call to Transformational Living

David W. Appleby & George Ohlschlager

God permits what He hates in order to accomplish what He loves.
And what He loves is Christ in me, the hope of glory.
Having Christ in me is worth anything—
even a lifetime of quadriplegia.

Joni Eareckson Tada, *The Popular Encyclopedia of Christian Counseling*

Berger (2012) tells the story of a charismatic African pastor who asked an American Episcopal priest during a global missionary conference, "Why do you not raise people from the dead in your church?" At the speechless and flabbergasted response of the American cleric, the African pastor continued to bore in, "Jesus did. The apostles did. We do. Why don't you? Don't you believe in miracles? This is why we are sending so many African missionaries to America these days—no one believes any longer in a supernatural God."

Though neither of us has witnessed someone being raised from the dead, we both know people who have witnessed this miracle. Now, even after many years, they tell these stories with awe and wonder. We both believe in this miracle-working God, able to shatter death with a simple word that creates new life in its place—able, in fact, to create anything out of nothing.

By his Word, God created the entire universe and sustains it according to his good pleasure. This book, among other things, is about this all-powerful and all-loving God and the transforming miracles he works every day in those who seek out his supernatural healing touch.

A Book About Godly Transformation

Our title, *Transformative Encounters*, suggests that God himself intervenes in the ongoing counseling process. We focus on our belief that the therapist does have an active role in creating an environment where God is free to move in new and creative ways as he chooses. Is God a servant ready to do as we demand? Of course not, but at the same time, he tends not to reveal himself if he is not welcome or if the expectation that he will come is not present. God intervenes in a transformative way when we invite him to do so. Jesus emphasized that he did what he saw the Father doing. God becomes visibly active in our lives and ministry when we do what we see our Father doing in Christ (Jn 5:19).

Is God only free to move when we invite him? Of course not. Even the faith to believe flows from him (Eph 2:8-9). Is God free to move when we don't invite him to move in the counseling setting? Yes, but we believe that our faith, our attitude, our expectation increases the likelihood that he will move. Is God free to not move even when we invite him? Yes. He is, after all, sovereign God. We do know, however, that he is always working for our good, for our salvation, redemption and transformation into the image of his Son. We can always count on him to move on behalf of his children (Rom 8:28-29). He may not choose to move in a particular setting (e.g., the timing is wrong for the client); we trust God to do what he wants to do. As counselors and pastors we also have the opportunity to facilitate and become instruments of that moving.

We believe that God is more than willing to empower his servants so that they can move in supernatural ways so that his beloved children can be set free. This book, *Transformative Encounters: The Intervention of God in Christian Counseling and Pastoral Care*, demonstrates many different situations where the therapist or minister is able to cooperate with God in the accomplishment of that task (perhaps a little of doing what the Father is doing). We hold that we, as therapists and pastors, need to be much more aggressive in our pursuit of his moving in our counseling practices. We need to be ready to have a Christ-derived supernatural ministry. Stafford (2012) wrote in *Christianity Today*:

> Still, some people maintain belief in an active God. They recognize the machine-like aspect of creation, but they insist that God occasionally intervenes in the world in a supernatural way. They divide the world into "nature" and "super-nature"—between the way the world runs on its own, like a machine, and the occasional interventions of God. Newton, for example, thought that God occasionally had to step in to adjust the planets in their orbits, lest they get out of synchrony.
>
> Supernatural events, by this way of thinking, are occasions when God interferes with the natural machinery. He steps in and zaps the cancer. He turns the water into wine. He puts his finger on a gear in the machine of nature and makes it turn in a different direction.
>
> People who absolutely separate nature from super-nature call these supernatural occasions when God steps in "miracles." (p. 51)

Further on Stafford argues that dividing nature and super-nature is a mistake. He sees miracles as God walking on unusual paths, as an unusual break from the way God ordinarily works, and thus a signal of something important. We agree. God intervening in the ordinary processes of life is an instance of "when God steps in" more directly in the unbroken and seamless web of creation. In counseling it may not be of the magnitude of multiplying fish or turning water into wine, but it is nevertheless amazing to see clients transformed because of what our Father is doing in their hearts and minds. That is the focus of this book. It is about a transformative encounter with the living God—a transformative intervention. We see Christian counseling as having a divine encounter at its core. It is life wrapped around a miracle.

The counselor is plying his trade in a manner that opens the door for God to move in whatever kind of supernatural way he chooses. He might do this through deliverance, through inner healing, through the use of Christ imagery or through interventional prayer in myriad ways. We are engaging a God who is willing and desirous of transforming, encountering and engaging his children in any number of different ways. The counseling process is not the focal point; the transformative encounter with the living God is the focal point. It should be at the core of what we do.

As you read these chapters you will become aware that the authors are very intentional about the process, about creating an environment where

God can move. You will get the sense that in these God initiated moments that God is there, near, and present in a way that he wasn't earlier in the session. From these encounters comes genuine transformation.

Toward Spiritual Transformation

Transformative Encounters describes a comprehensive range of transformational spiritual encounters and interventions that have been shown to make a difference in the lives of Christian believers. This book honors and advances a distinctly Christian approach to the developing fifth force of spirituality and religious faith that is now arising in counseling and psychotherapy. The five historical forces influencing mental health care are Psychodynamic, Behaviorism, Humanism, Multiculturalism, and Religious Faith and Spirituality. We will examine spiritual encounters and interventions that, through the supernatural work of God in Jesus Christ, have produced transformative change.

This book is for clinical and pastoral practitioners and for all those interested in the ways that God comes alive by the many models of Christian counseling, formation and pastoral care revealed in this book. It shows how God is invited to heal, redeem, and form and perfect himself in the lives of those who truly seek him. In short, we will reveal how God shows up and steps into the lives of seeking believers in counseling and pastoral care, as well as in coaching, discipling and formational activities.

In this book we contend that the foundation of a believer's spiritual life—and of doing life-changing Christian counseling, spiritual formation and pastoral care—is the person of Christ, who is anointed by the Father and made alive in our hearts and minds by the Holy Spirit. Moreover, we honor the universal biblical pattern of creation, the fall, redemption and glorification rather than the evolutionary naturalism of modern psychology (we note that Eric Johnson, in his foreword to this book, refers to glorification as "consummation"). So then, when we confess our sins and weaknesses and admit our inherent limits to bring about lasting change, God is set free to indwell and transform us. He is enabled to bring about effectual, psycho-spiritual change that touches every aspect of our lives. This change is eternal in its God-promised glory, but is experienced transformatively in the here and now and results in increasing levels of spiritual maturity, relational healing and effective ministry.

We have invited some of the very best clinical practitioners, pastoral counselors, researchers, teachers and formational experts in Christian counseling, spiritual direction and pastoral ministry to share with us the caring, visible ministry of Christ as they practice it. We introduce a substantial mix of professional/clinical and pastoral/lay models for change and growth—twenty differing Christian counseling models by those who are doing high-impact and Spirit-inspired work with those in need.

We have divided these twenty-two chapters into four main sections: (1) prayer, healing and power encounters done primarily in the church; (2) helping paradigms for practice in either church or clinic; (3) the best applied models of spiritual-clinical interventions for Christian counseling professionals; and (4) the development of a spiritually-informed, strength-based metamodel (encompassing pieces from these many models) for twenty-first-century Christian caregiving. Finally, the appendix apprises the reader of recent and growing threats to Christian ministry practice and what we must do to defend and retain precious rights to religious freedom and client self-determination.

Against the Flow

We recognize that this book runs counter to the antitheistic trends and secularizing forces dominant in American culture today. We are surely swimming upstream against an ever-quickening flow in a modern and postmodern world that accepts without question an evolutionary naturalism that denies the reality of God and dismisses any reference to or evidence of supernatural intervention. Like most of our colleagues in Christian counseling and ministry, we live and work on that delicate boundary that affirms both the methods of science (while rejecting scientism and empiricism) and the God who breaks into this natural world, momentarily seizing that world and the laws by which it operates to effect supernatural change by miraculous encounter.

This ongoing, natural/supernatural relationship, and the ebb and flow that it reveals, also represents a key framing supposition of this book. We believe that Christian counseling should embrace both scientific and supernatural interventions, accepting the best findings from the clinical sciences and being willing to submit all our claims to empirical testing. Yet we also hold to the revealed truth about God in the Bible. We want the correction that true science brings without surrendering to empiricism, which asserts that only those things that can be empirically proven truly exist. We reject the presupposition that the material world is all that there is, and that God never intervenes in the lives of his children or in the midst of his creation (Clinton & Ohlschlager, 2002).

We have also been thoroughly influenced by Gary Collins's classic text *The Rebuilding of Psychology* (1977). Calling for a biblical and theistic worldview whereby "God exists and is the source of all truth," Collins argues for "a new foundation" upon which to build Christian counseling and psychology. Collins also proposes that the Bible be the basis for all model and worldview development, something that the secular fields would never accept but which should be the normative position of any Christian attempting construction of a truly God-centered model of counseling or pastoral care—especially for those doing "Christ-derived" counseling (Johnson, Worthington, Hook & Aten, in press; also see foreword).

Also pertinent to building a "lived relationship" with the God of all creation is the understanding of evangelicalism by social work educator Robert Hodge (2004) in challenging the mental health community to respect religious diversity at a far deeper level than is usually promoted by these professions. This understanding should be built not on abstract theorizing, but around the experiential communion between God and believer. He calls for an acceptance of "a worldview that allows for an experiential understanding of the sacred" (p. 252), recognizing that evangelical Christians view the world holistically, seeing the spiritual and the material worlds as being two sides of the same coin. Do you sense that we are ready to push that boundary here? We are.

You may have already concluded that we are closer to the beliefs of the African pastor in our opening story than the American cleric. Indeed, we do not merely wish to hear about miracles, we want to participate in them—to encounter God along the way. We want to know this triune God experientially so that our faith is periodically refreshed by our encounter with divine grace. We want to have heaven breaking into and transforming life and mundane existence in the here and now. As Jesus taught us in the Lord's Prayer, we want to see his kingdom come and his will be done on earth as it is in heaven (Mt 6:10).

Most of the world assumes that such "superstitions," like Santa Claus and the Easter Bunny, will fade as we age and get educated. Well, the two of us are well aged and very well educated. Nevertheless, we still believe in this God of miracles, in a God who constantly pursues relationship—a person-to-person intimacy in a sweet communion with the One who loves us beyond words.

We agree with DeMar (as cited in Bahnsen, 2007), who says that there is no common point between biblical thought and all other forms of unbelief, even when we try to discuss how we know and what we know. There are no comfortable points of intersection. Biblical thought has nothing to do with secular or postmodern thought. While we can agree on many things because of general revelation and scientific discovery (common or creation grace), when it comes to special revelation in Christ, believer and nonbeliever cannot even agree on the source or even the nature of that which is revealed.

Accepting God's grace as the unmerited and transforming gift that it is has always been the goal of working with embittered and hopeless clients (both Christians and unbelievers) who are ground down by addiction, by unrelenting craziness, by crushing grief, by selfish and deadening pursuits, or by a crazy-making, works religion with impossible standards. In ourselves we have no power to change their life situations and often find ourselves speechless, mute in the face of such horrific pain. God alone is able to accomplish that change, and he often heals and transforms as he shows up and embraces us in his supernatural love. We are hopeful that these models and tools will assist you in helping the most hopeless and exhausted sufferers find a blessed renewal in their Father's loving arms.

Mission statement. Our mission was stated succinctly on a rural church message board we saw over the holidays in central Virginia: "May you have a transforming encounter with Jesus Christ in the New Year." We would join in and extend that hope to believer and unbeliever alike, as our faith is so intimately tied to those life-changing moments we have in the presence of God. Encounters with the living God, especially if they are infrequent and unexpected, as is still so exasperatedly common in our own lives, are as necessary for sanctifying growth and maturity as they are for entrance into God's kingdom.

Nonetheless, this book was created for the sole purpose of giving counselors, pastors, church staff, clinical practitioners, academics and students-in-training the best work of those who are doing this kind of Christ-centered ministry—inviting God to step into the helping or ministry endeavor in a way that works miraculous change. We set out to find practitioners who faithfully expect God to show up in the midst of their counseling or pastoral care, helpers who rely on God to intervene in the life of the client, regardless of both their clinical theory or helping model, and whether or not God is revealed explicitly or implicitly. The faith challenge for all of us is to believe that God will intervene to heal and restore his children when he is invited to heal and will use anything offered him.

Most of the contributors to this book are very well known, including some of the best leaders of twenty-first-century ministry in the church and practice in the clinical office. Others are introducing themselves and their work to you for the first time. Some chapters are very hands-on, while others are more theoretical, theological or research oriented. Furthermore, some authors include the empirical evidence for their models, others challenge us to go and do the validating research, and still others present the most well-used and best-referred models of clinical and pastoral practice. All contributors challenge practice, development and further research by saying, “When we open the door to God the Father, to Christ and to the Holy Spirit in this manner, with this kind of client, facing these kinds of problems at this developmental stage, these amazing things happen.”

Every contributor was challenged to include one or more case studies where God was invited to show up and bring transformative change. We define transformative change as God-influenced change of beliefs, behavior or emotions that assisted a client in getting unstuck from an overwhelming dilemma or that delivered significant gains in a very short period of time—either in one session or over a few sessions. This is change that lasts, change that would have taken many months or years to effect if it could have been gained at all, but was accomplished with God’s help in a much shorter time frame. Every contributor reveals what happens when God is invited to break into our natural world and bring heavenly solace and sustenance to whipped and weary people. We hope that many of you will do yourself, and experience for yourself, what is revealed herein, and will adapt these chapters to your own interventional work.

Five truths to remember. As we begin to work through the various models that are presented in this book, there are five truths that are important for us to remember. Knowing and respecting these factors can influence how successfully these models may be used.

You can never reduce God to the methods used to know him. Choosing to worship methodologies rather than God would not be a wise move. Since many Christians want to believe in and even sense an ongoing and direct connection to God, it is easy for us to idolize methodologies that offer that possibility. Reason, "correct" theology, intense prayer and religious works are often tools that we attempt to use to leverage God. There is something in our dark sides that wants to manipulate God so that he will always remain close and do what we want him to do. So let us be doubly clear: Reducing these practices to a formula that we hope will always produce a desired response won't work and misses the whole point of this book. As Christians we tend to prefer evil that jumps out at us because it is more easily seen and challenged. A greater threat are the idols that offer us an encounter with God through perfectly practicing some preferred formula.

These idolatries that we create about God and works-centered religion have the highest risk of being embraced by seeking Christians because the difference between true religion and this manner of idolatry is so easily confused. The simple difference is that, in truth, God pursues us and we fail to pursue or be caught by him. Theologian Michael Horton (2011), in a recent article in *Christianity Today*, points out that God takes the initiative and comes down to us. We do not go up to him. "Our hearts are idol factories, in bondage to sin and spin. We look for a god we can manage rather than the God who is actually there" (p. 26).

God resists being controlled and manipulated. In order to maintain the illusion that we are in control of our own lives and the lives of others, we seek a god we can control and manage. Whatever god we find, it is *not* the God of the Bible. When God shows up as a pure act of gracious love, we may react instead as if God were the great big candy man in the sky, doling out pleasures and treasures at our beck and call on a 24/7 basis. Some of us are so arrogant that we believe that his presence is the result of our hard work and fervent prayer, that we somehow deserve his presence. Worse, when he doesn't manifest himself as we desire, we often blame him—accusing him of being uncaring and unloving.

Some people fear having an encounter with God. Never underestimate the fear or the resistance in clients around such a challenge. Those who have learned to become obsessively self-reliant, who display an avoidant attachment style, have learned that trusting others leads only to pain and sorrow. Trusting in God makes it no easier just because the object of that trust has changed (although that change is as different as night and day). It is God himself who must contend with the untrusting person to give up his or her life to him. Inviting the living God to come and show himself and his loving nature leads some to take this life-changing risk. What a delight it is to work with someone who yields and is surprised and pleased with the love and joy that God brings.

God's primary goal for us is not to make us happy. One of the more troubling truths of the way of Christ is the necessity of suffering—how suffering often provides the necessary motivation to know God as deeply as possible. Stated negatively, the experience of great pain or travail motivates us to seek God more deeply than anything else. When things are going well, we may thank him, but we so often relax and do not seek God out for anything more deeply than that. Yet when things are not going well—especially when life is at risk—we then seek out God to protect us or to release us from that which threatens us. The prayer of Psalm 25 is apt:

> Turn Yourself to me, and have mercy on me,
> For I am desolate and afflicted.
> The troubles of my heart have enlarged;
> Bring me out of my distresses!
> Look on my affliction and my pain,
> And forgive all my sins.
> Consider my enemies, for they are many;
> And they hate me with cruel hatred.
> Keep my soul, and deliver me;
> Let me not be ashamed, for I put my trust in You.
> Let integrity and uprightness preserve me,
> For I wait for You. (Ps 25:16-21 NKJV)

Sometimes God has to take us down before he can bring us up. Yielding to God in any degree focuses the great commandment and "spits in the soup" of our own selfish pursuits. And when our own hearts are exhausted and empty, we learn that God himself enables us to love him with all our hearts, minds, souls and strength; and to love others as we love ourselves (Mt 22:37-40). Regarding the overarching process of growth, John the Baptist exclaimed what is so incredible in our narcissistic age: "He [Jesus] must increase, but I must decrease" (Jn 3:30 NKJV). Peter also has his say in 1 Peter 5:5-7: "All of you, clothe yourselves with humility toward one another, because, 'God opposes the proud but shows favor to the humble.' Humble yourselves, therefore, under God's mighty hand, that he may lift you up in due time. Cast all your anxiety on him because he cares for you."

Maturing Spiritually in the Five Domains of Living

There are five primary domains by which we locate and understand human development. These include identity, cognition, affect, relationship and behavior domains. Another, earthier way of stating it is to describe *who I am, what I think, what I feel, who I love* and *what I do*. How we view these domains is reflected by our relationship with God; whether we are in his family or whether we are not. Our goal is to see all walk in kingdom life, life that is lived in the maturity of godly sanctification. This is life lived by "putting off the old man" who is dead in sin and shame, and "putting on the new man" in Christ (see Col 3:9-10). This is the abundant life that God promises all who ask.

Identity. Changed identity flows from the fact of our changed ownership. The Christian is no longer his or her own; each of us who has yielded to the call now belongs to God. "Do you not know that your bodies are temples of the Holy Spirit, who is in you, whom you have received from God? You are not your own; you were bought at a price. Therefore honor God with your bodies" (1 Cor 6:19-20). We are called to live in the "new man" or "new woman" who is redeemed by, in and for Christ, and purchased with his holy blood.

Our new identity in Christ also reflects our new citizenship. "Our citizenship is in heaven. And we eagerly await a Savior from there, the Lord Jesus Christ, who, by the power that enables him to bring everything under his control, will transform our lowly bodies so that they will be like his glorious body" (Phil 3:20-21). This heavenly citizenship is what allows us to come boldly to the throne of grace (Heb 4:16) to petition our King for the holy transformation of everything—for that which is impossible for us to do on our own.

Finally, this new identity in Christ takes precedence over any other identity. Our identity "in Christ" is more precious, more important, we dare say, than our racial or ethnic identity, or any identity based on gender or sexual orientation. Being in Christ is also more valuable, more important and eternal, than our name and family identity. Furthermore, no matter how thick our blood ties, that which is forged by the shed blood of Christ is more precious by far. Critically important is the recognition that our identity in Christ will most often bring peace and harmony and forge the healing path to maturity and integrity. By contrast, the assertion of any other identity tends to create dissension and division.

Cognition. The Christian has been set free from the bonds of sin and has been given by God a new way of viewing oneself, others and the world. He or she has been clothed with "the new self" and is "being renewed in knowledge in the image of its Creator" (Col 3:10). Thus, being renewed in their minds (Rom 12:2), Christians can rightly interpret the world that God made and the kingdom that he is making (Mt 6:9-13). The indwelling of the Spirit and freedom from sin allow the Christian to think God's thoughts after him. The Scriptures are pretty clear that at salvation a significant change in being and awareness takes place. In short, by being redeemed in, by and for Christ, we become who we weren't before, and we are headed in a very different direction, both in this life and in the eternal life to come.

The unbeliever, not having experienced the saving grace of God in the gospel, is spiritually dead in trespasses and sin (Eph 2:1). In the words of the apostle Paul, unbelievers have become "futile" in their thoughts and their "foolish hearts were darkened" (Rom 1:21). This is so because they "suppress the truth" in unrighteousness (Rom 1:18) and exchange "the truth about God for a lie" (Rom 1:25). Maturity in Christ reverses this process. A critical aspect of Christian counseling is to reveal the lies that we live by and that sabotage us, and renounce them in exchange for adopting the truths of God revealed in the Scriptures.

All this means is that God's grace not only touches our will, but also our intellect, our minds. There is no part of us that is not marred and influenced by sin; it touches every aspect of our personality. In the same way, being "saved" touches every aspect of our personality: our thought life, our relationships, our entire life. When we walked in darkness we lived without reference to God. We could only describe our life without any light present.

After salvation, God permeates everything—his light penetrates deeply into the darkness—and we are given new eyes by which to see and to seek after new life in the Spirit.

Affect. The new creaturehood that comes with salvation consists of more than an intellectual, cognitive change. It is also emotional. Ezekiel 36:26-27 says "I will give you a new heart and put a new spirit in you; I will remove from you your heart of stone and give you a heart of flesh. And I will put my Spirit in you and move you to follow my decrees and be careful to keep my laws." With a heart of stone we were not able to feel the things that God feels. Sin marred our affect as well as our minds.

However, things have changed emotionally in our new life. That which breaks his heart now breaks ours. The things that cause him to rejoice also fill us with rejoicing. The things that move him to compassion also influence compassionate responses in us. Our emotions will line up with his because this spiritual heart transplant allows our hearts to be aligned with God's heart. And our hearts are now able to empathize deeply with the hearts of our brothers and sisters the world over.

Contrary to longstanding trends in the church against emotion, viewing our emotional life as unpredictable and uncontrollable, we are strongly in favor of the affective life. In fact, we believe that one of the most important books in church history was Jonathan Edwards's classic *Treatise Concerning Religious Affections* (1746). He believed that a deeper relationship with the living God had to be motivated in large part by one's emotional life—apart from a strong emotional bond, attachments to God were altogether weak. Without a strong emotional attachment, our commitment to God is easily broken when under pressure and easily replaced by other idols that draw in and eventually enslave our affective life.

Relationship. We are hardwired for relationship, and all we are, do and become is a function of our embedded relationships. God is triune, revealing to us that he lives in relationship with himself as Father, Son and Spirit. Therefore, by redeeming us, God has also reconnected us socially with himself, and with the people who are part of his global/eternal family. Revelation 2:17 says, "Whoever has ears, let them hear what the Spirit says to the churches. To the one who is victorious, I will give some of the hidden manna. I will also give that person a white stone with a new name written on it, known only to the one who receives it."

Names in the Scripture not only speak to identity, but also speak to family relationships, the most foundational of all small group relationships, and to a deep intimacy between the namer and the named. In salvation our family of origin is stitched onto a new family that is global in scope. In Matthew 12:46-50 it is recorded that

> While Jesus was still talking to the crowd, his mother and brothers stood outside, wanting to speak to him. Someone told him, "Your mother and brothers are standing outside, wanting to speak to you." He replied to him, "Who is my mother, and who are my brothers?" Pointing to his disciples, he said, "Here are my mother and my brothers. For whoever does the will of my Father in heaven is my brother and sister and mother."

Hebrews 2:11 suggests the same thing. "Both the one who makes people holy and those who are made holy are of the same family. So Jesus is not ashamed to call them brothers and sisters." Everyone across the entire planet who receives God's salvation is grafted into the largest family on Earth—God's kingdom family, a global spiritual entity that is ruled by the Son, Jesus Christ. And this same Christ is preparing his people for his return—to a great wedding feast and his enthronement in the temple at Jerusalem. The vastness—the audacity of such a plan—contains a great mystery. Nonetheless, the Scriptures are clear in its promise of such a culmination of relationship between Christ and his bride, the worldwide church.

In joining God's family by faith, we are being reoriented socially in the most fundamental way. Our primary relationships are being shifted from ones that are founded upon flesh and blood, or mutual desires, to ones that are founded upon the transformative influence of the Holy Spirit. There is nothing of our personality that does not have the potential to be transformed, both in the experience of salvation and in every godly touch of sanctification. In our transformation to "newness of life," we are given a new identity, a new being "in Christ" and a new family in which to live that renewed life.

Behavior. Is not our behavior, including how we do therapy or ministry, also transformed? You can have your mind renewed, your heart replaced and your family of origin changed without it necessarily changing how you behave. We must soberly reflect on the parable of the sower (Mk 4:3-24), as there were many different (and some unfruitful) outcomes among those who were planted with the seeds of God. We must soberly acknowledge, especially in these "last days," that many "saved" Christians in the world will not achieve the sanctifying destiny that God would call them to if they had obeyed and persevered in that call.

Yet a changed heart should also influence changed behavior; the growing Christian must look more and more like Christ himself. We must allow God to transform us from always taking to giving, from selfish pursuits to true servanthood. For those who embrace salvation and delight in God, the spiritual transformation that accompanies conversion changes how we relate to our families, to our employers and employees, to those in our churches, and to those in our communities. Sanctification and growth in maturity does change what we do and say, as we turn from sin and "put on" our newness in Christ. Moreover, for the purpose of our discussion, it also influences how we counsel and minister to the people that God brings to us for healing and growth.

Where Is Christian Counseling Going?

We know that the Holy Spirit is ever present in genuine Christian counseling. He is omnipresent—everywhere, all the time, faithful as the transcendent One. He is also in the midst of the clinical setting—the immanent One—working in and through both the therapist and the client. When invited, the third member of the Trinity is always working mightily in the helping relationship. He desires to be the central person in the work of the therapist as he/she attempts to bring healing and freedom to the client. He is active in the ministry to the client because he loves the client and desires that the client be free from whatever has him or her in bondage (Zeiders, 2004).

Christ is Lord over all helping and healing. As Christian therapists (as opposed to secular counselors, and even Christians who do therapy without reference to God) we seek to bring the whole therapeutic process under the Lordship of Jesus Christ (Johnson, 1997). This, we believe, is central to developing and working out a genuine transformational psychology. Two major consequences follow from this redeemed worldview. First, we are diligent to approach God and to study the Scriptures to use both the content and process of God's healing designs. As an essential presupposition or first principle, let us mine and mind the Scriptures and the thoughts of God deeply, asking him to reveal his special way for this unique person that he has sent to us for help. Second, this also means that we are concerned with "placing psychological theories and interventions at the disposal of the Holy Spirit" (Zeiders, 2004, p. 15). Zeiders argues about the central question:

> Rather than ask, "How do I intellectually integrate my training in psychology and social science with Christian doctrine" the practitioner of Christian Holism asks, "How does the Holy Spirit want to use my training to help this client with these issues at this time of life?" In Christian Holism, placing social science at the disposal of the living God is the paramount concern that trumps problems of theoretical integration. (p. 15)

Only Life can produce life within us. In true Christian counseling, we are seeking God to receive his "pneuma," the breath of God that has been breathed into us, to be breathed into us once again—and again and again. We cannot grow spiritually on our own, deluding ourselves and puffing ourselves up when we try. Similarly, we cannot become whole and mature without God's continuing intervention; and we mean frequent, everyday connections. We must learn to constantly seek God to pour forth that amazing work of the Holy Spirit, to flow into our clinical settings and into the lives of those who have come for help. If that is happening in our own lives, it can then happen in the lives of our clients and parishioners.

Instead, for too many of us, our passion for God is gone and our work looks nearly identical to that of any secular therapist, apart from a perfunctory prayer at the beginning or end of our sessions. Too many of us have settled for a purely cognitive "biblical worldview" and have taken a pass on the anointing of the Holy Spirit. It's not because we don't want that in our heart of hearts; it is often because we are too afraid to give up our lives to God and seek and rely on the Holy Spirit. (Anointing often sounds so messy, so uncontrollable!) Moreover, since many of us have never seen or been mentored by anyone consistently living in and doing such transformative work, we then miss the beauty and winsomeness of such living.

Blessings unto you and those you serve. We recommend to you the reader the considerable wisdom found in every writer's contribution. Our authors represent a wide range of identities and professions and approaches to counseling. All remain true, however, to the God who is there and to some form of historic, biblical Christianity. We have contributions from many evangelicals, from orthodox believers, from the charismatic church and from the Anglo-Catholics; all have shown a passion for this subject and have graciously contributed to this book.

Our hope is that Christian therapists, pastors, directors and coaches of all stripes, those with great experience and those just beginning their careers, will have the opportunity to read about not the mere display of secular theories and methodologies but of anointed practice that flows from the throne of God and that encompasses all that he has ultimately created. We hope that you will see God coming alive in these pages, hear his still small voice speaking wondrous things in your heart and be moved to worship the One who is able to create life where death otherwise reigns. And we hope that you will be enlivened to find and adopt at least one new way, even many ways, to assist God anew in the challenge of bringing that precious life to those you serve.

References and Recommended Resources

Berger, P. (2012, January 11). Counting Christian noses. *The American Interest: Religion and Other Curiosities*. Retrieved from <http://blogs.the-american-interest.com/berger/2012/01/11/counting-christian-noses/>.

Clinton, T., & Ohlschlager, G. (2002). *Competent Christian counseling: Foundations and practice of compassionate soul care*. Colorado Springs: WaterBrook.

Collins, G. R. (1977). *The rebuilding of psychology: An integration of psychology and Christianity*. Wheaton, IL: Tyndale.

DeMar, G. (Ed.). (2007). *Pushing the antithesis: The apologetic methodology of Greg L. Bahnsen*. Powder Springs, GA: American Vision.

Edwards, J. (1746). *A treatise concerning religious affections*. Boston: S. Kneeland and T. Green.

Hodge, D. R. (2004). Spirituality and people with mental illness: Developing spiritual competency in assessment and intervention. *Families in Society, 85*, 36-44.

Horton, M. (2011, December). The good God who came down: The God revealed in Christ does what reason and morality cannot do. *Christianity Today, 55*(12), 24-29.

Johnson, E. (1997). Christ: The Lord of psychology. *Journal of Psychology and Theology, 25*(1), 11-27.

Johnson, E. (Ed.). (2010). *Psychology and Christianity: Five views*. Downers Grove, IL: InterVarsity Press.

Johnson, E. L., Worthington, E. L., Jr., Hook, J. N., & Aten, J. D. (forthcoming). Evidence-based practice in light of the Christian tradition: Reflections and future directions. In E. L. Worthington, E. L. Johnson, J. N. Hook & J. D. Aten (Eds.). *Evidence-based practices for Christian counseling and psychotherapy*. Downers Grove, IL: InterVarsity Press.

Stafford, T. (2012, September). A new age of miracles. *Christianity Today*, *56*(8), 48-52.

Tada, J. E. (2012). Faith. In *The popular encyclopedia of Christian counseling* (pp. 153-54). Eugene, OR: Harvest House.

Zeiders, C. (2004). *The clinical Christ: scientific and spiritual reflections on the transformative psychology called Christian holism.* Birdsboro, PA: Julian's House.

Part One

TRANSFORMATIVE ENCOUNTERS DONE IN CHURCH

2

The Elijah House Model of Inner Healing

Mark Sandford

The Unanswered Question

As a young pastor in the 1950s, my father, John Sandford, searched for ways to heal his flock. He found that client-centered, behavioral and cognitive counseling styles effected some changes, but they could not transform a soul at the deepest level.

Christ does transform souls, but John wondered why many Christians' lives did not fully reflect that. He realized that their view of transformation was truncated and incomplete. Yes, we are new creatures, and God has "reconciled us to himself through Christ" (2 Cor 5:18), but many ignored the following context: "be reconciled to God" (2 Cor 5:20). Christ has completed the work of saving us ("It is finished"—Jn 19:30), but we are in a process of being transformed by that saving work: "By one sacrifice he has made perfect forever those who are *being* made holy" (Heb 10:14, emphasis added). Was there a counseling strategy that could aid in that process?

Ideas came through a survey for a seminary paper John wrote on what teens were learning in local Sunday schools. Teens rated various aspects of their lives—including parents—as "valuable" or "worthless," "shallow" or "deep," "uninteresting" or "interesting," "sinful" or "wholesome," and so on. As John read the results, the commandment "Honor your father and your mother . . . that it may go well with you" (Deut 5:16 NASB) made more sense than ever! In *exactly* the areas where children had critically judged parents, their lives had not gone well! More interestingly, the same was true of the adults John counseled. John now understood the true meaning of law.

The meaning of law. Galatians 6:7 says, "Do not be deceived, God is not mocked; for whatever a man sows, this he will also reap" (NASB). Law is not just a set of rules you must follow. It is a dynamic force that acts upon your life. If you sow weed seeds, you reap weeds! The kids and adults John dealt with hadn't a clue that dishonoring parents (and others) had caused them to reap anything at all.

Lifting the curse. Malachi 4:5-6 took on new meaning: "Behold, I am going to send you Elijah the prophet before the coming of the great and terrible day of the LORD. He will restore the hearts of the fathers to their children and the hearts of the children to their fathers, so that I will not come and smite the land with a curse" (NASB). Only the cross could prevent the curse. But how could John apply the cross in counseling?

The four basic laws. Through the cross Christ reaped on our behalf what we had sown. Since Christ's sacrifice alone satisfies the requirements of the law, John realized that knowledge of the following four laws (the first two have already been mentioned) is prerequisite to effective change.

1. The law of sowing and reaping: "Do not be deceived, God is not mocked; for whatever a man sows, this he will also reap" (Gal 6:7 NASB).
2. The law of honoring father and mother: "Honor your father and your mother . . . that it may go well with you" (Deut 5:16 NASB). The inverse is also true: in exactly the areas we dishonor Mom or Dad (or others), we will reap evil—it will not go well with us.
3. The law that we reap from our judgments: "In the way you judge, you will be judged; and by your standard of measure, it will be measured to you" (Mt 7:2 NASB). We reap in two ways.

   First, *bitter root judgments* cause us to become like those we judge. I often ask audiences, "As children, did you see your father or mother doing something you hated, and you swore, 'I'll never do that'? Raise your hand." Invariably, many hands shoot skyward. Then I ask, "How many ended up doing the same thing anyway?" Sheepishly, most of the same hands go up. It happens every time! Here's how it works: whenever we judge others, we too are guilty—"For you who judge practice the same things" (Rom 2:1 NASB). Paul can say this because "whoever keeps the whole law and yet stumbles at just one point is guilty of breaking all of it" (Jas 2:10). The sin we judge others for remains in us unforgiven, for "if you do not forgive others, then your Father will not forgive your transgressions" (Mt 6:15 NASB). The law of increase (law 4) makes this sin grow, until we become just like the one we have judged.

We see this when a child becomes like his or her critical parent. Jimmy's dad ignores all his As and asks, "Why the B?" Dad's praises are few, but names like "stupid" and "numbskull" outnumber Jimmy's As. Jimmy judges Dad and becomes just like him. One day, grown Jimmy explodes at his son for leaving a spot on the car he just washed. Incredulously, Jimmy gasps, "I swore I'd never be like Dad!" Jimmy's efforts to change bear little fruit, until repenting of his judgment and forgiving Dad finally stops the cycle of sowing and reaping, and lifts the curse of Malachi 4:5-6.

Second, *bitter root expectancies* tempt others to treat us like those we have judged. Imagine peering through a red transparency. Yellow turns orange; white turns pink. In the same way, bitterness colors the way we see others. Other workers can see that Jimmy's boss is stressed and is not his usual self, so they bear with him. But through a lens of bitterness, Jimmy sees a callous drill sergeant and sends powerful signals that sorely tempt him to act like one. Jimmy quits his job, only to find this happening with the next boss . . . and the next.

4. The law of increase: what we sow is multiplied. "They sow the wind and reap the whirlwind" (Hos 8:7). God gave this law to bless—a bag of kernels yields bushels of corn! But since Adam's fall, the same law has brought harm. Jimmy becomes *increasingly* critical of his son, and has more and more run-ins with bosses.

Other types of bitter roots include the following:

Foundational lies. In his mind, Jimmy knows he is often treated fairly, but in his heart he can't help believing that life is *never* fair. Merely changing his thought processes—as in cognitive therapy—won't stop this lie. A carnal stronghold (2 Cor 10:4-6) must be reckoned dead on the cross through prayer.

Inner vows. These are promises we make in bitterness (often unconsciously) to stop the pain. Jimmy's dad doesn't let up, so Jimmy promises himself, "I'll never let anyone boss me around." (Inner vows often begin with "I'll always" or "I'll never.") The bitterness behind the vow only dares bosses to dish out more. Jimmy also vows, "I will always be perfect." This vow drives him to raise a perfect son who reflects his "perfect" fathering.

You may ask, if I don't remember judging my parents, why did I end up becoming like them? Maybe you don't remember because you tried to "honor" them falsely. Did you "forgive" by blaming yourself ("I made Daddy hit me")? Offering excuses ("He can't help it")? Ignoring the offense? Forgetting it happened? Suppressed bitterness inevitably springs back up: "See to it . . . that no root of bitterness springing up causes trouble, and by it many be defiled" (Heb 12:15 NASB).

Inner healing and deliverance. Not every sin involves a demon, but demons sometimes find access through serious or ongoing sins. For instance, Ephesians 4:26-27 admonishes, "Do not let the sun go down on your anger, and do not give the devil an opportunity" (NASB). A demon of rage energizes Jimmy's unresolved anger, transforming his tendency to berate his son into an overwhelming drive, and inciting far more defensiveness toward bosses than his own impulses can account for.

To cast away a demon, we must first remove the sin. If we only do deliverance, the demon may return to the sin that gave it access. With inner healing, demons rarely return. If one does, we look for related roots. When the roots are gone, the demon can be cast away forever.

After inner healing, Jimmy's old ways may melt away automatically. But if not, inner healing will have turned former compulsions into mere empty habits. Eliminating these will be like wading through still waters, not against a raging torrent of sowing and reaping and the demonic debris that is often swept along with it.

The Resurrection Side of Healing

How do you honor a dishonorable parent? In the same way that Jesus honors you. On his cross Jesus destroys your sin, but not your personhood; he honors you by resurrecting you: "God raised us up with Christ and seated us with him in the heavenly realms in Christ Jesus" (Eph 2:6). When Jesus first encountered Paul, he called out, "Saul, Saul, why are you persecuting Me? It is hard for you to kick against the goads" (Acts 26:14 NASB). A goad was a prod to stick in a stubborn ox's backside to keep him plowing. Jesus addressed Paul as if Paul were plowing in his service—while on his way to persecute Jesus' church! He deplored Paul's sin while honoring God's design for him. *Parents should do the same for children.* Proverbs 22:6 says:

> Train a child in the way he should go,
> and when he is old he will not turn from it. (NIV 1984)

The Hebrew conveys that we should train him to follow his own natural bent (though not his sinful inclination). Paul initially used his forceful bent to destroy the church. After meeting Jesus, he used it to build the church.

Forgiving will enable Jimmy to do what Jesus did for Paul—cherish and bless the dad God created while in no way minimizing his persecution of Jimmy. Thus, Jimmy can reap the promised blessing, "that it might go well with you" (Deut 5:16; Eph 6:2). He'll no longer see overbearing bosses or his imperfect son as the sum of their evil *deeds,* but will honor them as *persons* designed and created in God's image

Foundational Elements of Intervention

Validate emotions. Help clients recognize and talk about the pain that tempted them to form bitter roots. Suffice it to say that you must not rush this; validating feelings prepares the heart to deal with roots.

Trace from fruit to root. Inner healing can be used not only by professionals but also by any sensitive Christian. The first two of the following tools are so simple they can be used by lay persons during "altar ministry" at church. Try using the first three to trace from your own bitter fruit (negative patterns in the present) to its bitter root.

Trace from fruit to root through simple logic. Thus far, have you recognized a bitter root in yourself? If so, you have already mastered this basic tool. Quite simply, where there is a fruit, there is a root (Mt 7:16).

Trace from fruit to root through simple prayer. If you recognize a pattern of bitter fruit in your life, listen to the Holy Spirit for a few minutes. Ask him, "Is there a bitter root judgment, expectancy, foundational lie or inner vow that has caused this?"

Trace from present pain to past pain. Try the following steps:

1. Identify something to which you typically overreact ("Others' forgetting to include me").
2. Think of a specific example ("My friend forgot to invite me to a picnic").
3. Overreactions trigger a kaleidoscope of feelings. Express each one with colorful adjectives ("desolate," "humiliated") and word pictures ("locked in a dark closet and laughed at").

4. Ask the Holy Spirit to show you a memory in which a similar situation triggered the same emotions. Don't try to *think* it up; just *feel* all the feelings triggered by the present situation and let the Holy Spirit bring the memory to you ("My sisters locked me in my room and giggled as they ran off to play").
5. Ask the Lord if you have judged anyone ("My sisters"). Is there a bitter-root expectancy? ("People will shut me out and ignore my pain.") Is there an inner vow or lie?

Probably not all of these strategies worked for you, because one size does not fit all. Resist using the same formula for every situation. Formulas can miss the heart and usurp the Holy Spirit. Become adaptable. Acquire a repertoire of tools. Thus, our list continues.

Interview. Get progressively more specific about the fruit. "In what kinds of situations do you feel left out?" "Can you share a specific example?" "When you weren't invited to the picnic, what hurt the most about that?" "In childhood, what kinds of situations were similar?" "Can you share an example?" Interviewing can feel complex and unwieldy when clients take you on tangents. Taking notes can keep you on track. Review notes to catch the theme, then periodically draw the conversation back to it.

But what will most likely make you lose your way is the notion that your mind interviews, but your spirit prays and uses spiritual gifts—and that only the latter involves the Holy Spirit's leading. This is *not* biblical! Immediately after Paul said, "The things that come from the Spirit of God . . . are spiritually discerned," he said, "But we have the *mind* of Christ" (1 Cor 2:14, 16 NIV 1984). Your mind was not designed to think without the aid of your spirit! If you try to "figure out" what questions to ask, counseling will be shallow and relatively unproductive. Your mind unaided by your spirit becomes overly taxed and distracted, but your spirit, guided by the Holy Spirit, will easily keep your mind on track. At *every* step, let your spirit so infuse your mind with the Holy Spirit's guidance that you automatically know what to say and ask. Uneducated neophytes have interviewed like this with far more finesse than degreed professionals!

Quiet your mind. Mark 10:15-16 says, "'Anyone who will not receive the kingdom of God like a little child will never enter it.' And [Jesus] took the children in his arms" Do you want to receive the kingdom into your counseling? At the beginning of *every* session (and sometimes partway through), spend five minutes in God's arms quietly soaking up his love (both you and your client). It will completely change the feel of the session.

Conversation with God. The Holy Spirit may prompt you to direct questions to God instead of the client. "Lord, in what kinds of situations has ______ felt left out?" "Would you remind him/her of one?" In most cases, it is best to allow the client to hear God's answers, lest you plant suggestions.

Be led by the Spirit, not by formulas. Formulas miss the client's heart and the Holy Spirit's leading; they also keep you in your head. Ministry tools should vary from person to person and moment to moment. For instance, a person who has rarely been listened to might need to be interviewed so he/she can share his/her *own* thoughts. But a man who lives in his head might need you to ask God the questions so he can hear God and learn to relate through his spirit. Listen to God, and sense what each person and situation needs.

Additional strategies. You can use the following strategies in tandem with any tool discussed thus far.

Stop to listen to God whenever he prompts. Even in the middle of a session, if necessary, stop to reattune your heart to the Holy Spirit, to alert you to change course, to receive a word from the Lord or to intercede in prayer (praying to lift away excess pain can lighten a client's burden, enabling him to feel and share emotions).

Share what God interjects. Ask for wisdom about when to do this. A counselor received a word of knowledge that his client had undergone three abortions twenty-five years earlier and had never told a soul. When the Holy Spirit revealed she was ready to talk about it, he asked her if this word was true. Tearfully, she confessed. His gentleness enabled her to receive forgiveness, along with assurance that if she did wrong, her heavenly Father would not shame her as her earthly father had.

Ask the Lord to show the client what he was doing at the time wounding occurred. A client who was beaten as a child might "see" that Jesus took the pain upon himself until the child was ready to face it. This is biblical: "Surely our griefs He Himself bore" (Is 53:4 NASB). Or the client may "see" that Jesus absorbed the emotional force of the blows. This too is biblical: "By his wounds we are healed" (Is 53:5).

Avoid planting suggestions; urge the client to hear for himself. If the Holy Spirit reveals an answer to us, we can silently ask him to also reveal it to the client. Then we can confirm what he/she has already heard. On rare occasions when clients hear unbiblical answers (for instance, changing history: "I see my dad hugging instead of beating me"), we gently steer them back to the truth. But even a false answer can become a powerful tool, for we can look for bitter roots and unmet needs that have caused them to confuse God's voice with wishful thinking.

SUMMARY OF A COUNSELING SESSION: THE 5 RS

The following mnemonic device is not a formula. We don't always do the 5 Rs in the same order or all at the same time; we follow the Holy Spirit's leading.

Recognize the bitter fruit and its bitter root(s). Review our previous discussion for details on how to do this.

Confess and Repent of bitter root(s). Have the client pray aloud (unless he or she is too shy), for as it says in James 5:16, "Confess your sins to each other and pray for each other so that you may be healed." Since we sin against others, we need to confess to others. And Jesus said, "Where two or three have gathered together in My name, I am there in their midst" (Mt 18:20 NASB).

We assure the client he/she is forgiven, for Jesus gave us this commission: "If you forgive the sins of any, their sins have been forgiven them; if you retain the sins of any, they have been retained" (Jn 20:23 NASB). However, we do not violate the conscience of clients whose churches practice the confessional. Such churches allow lay persons to hear a "therapeutic confession," which can involve prayers to repent and forgive. But we allow them to go to their priest for absolution.

Release forgiveness. The client prays, "Lord, I forgive Dad/Mom/other for . . ."

Reckon as dead. The client prays something like: "In Jesus' name, I call this root of bitterness to death by the power of the cross." Romans 6:11 says: "Consider [in Greek, *logizomai,* "reckon"] yourselves to be dead to sin, but alive to God in Christ Jesus" (NASB).

Resurrect in new life. Help the client walk in new ways, blessing those who tempted him to form bitter roots, seeing such persons through the eyes of Christ, with honor, respect and unconditional love.

We call inner healing "prayer ministry" rather than "counseling" because it is a *ministry* more than a profession, and *prayer* is our most important tool. Insight and behavior change alone cannot transform us. Prayer against root sins makes behavior change effective and last forever!

What Happens After the Session: *Reconcile Broken Relationships*

What happens after the session? How will the client apply his healing? Will he need to change an attitude toward someone? Reconcile? Forgive? Apologize? Bless? Turn her heart toward her children/parents (which removes the curse of Mal 4:5-6)? Our healing is not for ourselves alone. This *R* is the ultimate goal of inner healing!

Is this helpful for everyone? Are there persons for whom this is contraindicated? Inner healing is indicated for most ongoing emotional or relational issues. It is contraindicated for issues that can resolve naturally without intervention or are purely organic in origin. Some issues are sometimes indicated and sometimes contraindicated. For instance: Grief can be resolved through processing emotion, but prolonged or delayed grief may indicate root issues. Burnout can be resolved through rest, but in some cases one may need to deal with roots that motivated the overworking so that burnout does not reoccur. Depression can be cured through inner healing if mild, or when severity has improved enough for the client to respond. Chemical imbalances may prevent inner healing from being effective in instances such as depression until medication restores one's ability to respond.

Addictions are sometimes cured through inner healing alone, but a twelve-step program and/or accountability partner or group is often needed as well. Inner healing is indicated only after we enable the client to avoid incorporating it into his denial system (for instance, blaming others: "My addiction is my parents' fault"). Chemical addicts need an extended period of sobriety before inner healing, lest chemicals in their bloodstream warp their judgment.

Psychoses are genetically based, but sometimes inner healing can resolve root issues that push fragile brain chemistry over the edge. This should be handled by seasoned inner healing counselors, with safeguards and with clients who have a track record of stability and are under the care of a psychiatrist.

THE ELIJAH HOUSE METHOD OF INNER HEALING AS EXPRESSED IN REAL LIFE

Rather than following one person's counseling sojourn, a close look at a few sessions with three clients will offer a more rounded view of inner healing.

Will's story: Relationships restored. "Will" tried to "fix" emotions by advising, setting things straight or blaming himself. Loved ones needed him to meet their hearts, not fix their problems—especially his daughter, who was riding the emotional roller coaster of her teen years. Not only was Will unable to give comfort, but he also couldn't receive it, except through pornography.

As a head pastor, Will felt that everyone's happiness depended on him. He recounted how an associate pastor split his church. He was terrified that people would think it was his fault, and his reputation would be ruined! He couldn't fix the situation, and worst of all, he couldn't fix himself.

When I asked what he felt, he replied, "Panicked, overwhelmed. The world was falling apart, and I was drowning in self-blame." I asked the Holy Spirit to remind him of a memory that felt similar. Will closed his eyes and listened. "When I was thirteen we lost the baseball championship by one run. I missed a fly ball over the fence. No one could have caught it, but I felt so guilty that I broke down and cried. I could tell that my Dad [the coach] wanted to offer comfort. It's the only time I remember him ever wanting to. It felt awkward, so I said, 'Go away.'"

I asked, "Did you mean it?" Will had never thought about that before. He listened to his heart and to the Lord. "No, I wanted him to pursue me. But I thought that if I admitted that, I would look weak."

"So what did you do with the hurt?"

"I decided not to share it or even think about it. I decided I didn't need any comfort." Will raised an eyebrow as a light went on. "And now I do the same thing with my daughter. When she loses a soccer match, something inside won't allow me to comfort her. I just walk away, and then wonder, 'Why did I walk away?' I'm just like Dad! And she reacts just like I did; she walks away from me."

Will asked the Lord to forgive him for judging his father and prayed to forgive Dad for neglecting to comfort him, not only that day on the baseball field, but many other times as well. He prayed to renounce inner vows to not be aware of or share his pain and to not need comfort. Tears began to flow as he felt God's soothing touch.

That night Will called his daughter and found her on the tearful side of her roller coaster. After bemoaning her teenage trials, she got a few words out between the sobs. "I miss you." Will's eyes began to water, and his voice cracked. "I miss you too. I know you're feeling lonely." She brightened as she thought, "This is my Dad?!" In the past, Will might have crooned, "You don't have to cry! I'll be home soon anyway." But for the first time, he neither had to "fix" her tears nor walk away. He just felt with her—without trying! The curse of Malachi 4:5-6 was lifting.

Inner healing took the force out of Will's pornography addiction. He had always been accountable, often dutifully sharing with his wife about temptations (even though it never helped). But the next time he shared, he felt her comfort! And because he was more in touch with feelings, from then on he was able to share his sexual needs more openly. Temptation immediately began to subside. In the five years since then, Will has fallen only once.

In his church and family, Will no longer has to perform to be loved. And he doesn't have to do God's job anymore; the world is securely in God's hands.

Daniel's story: Inner healing and deliverance. This is a composite of five men with eerily similar histories and the same type of demon. "Daniel" had difficulty hearing God and could not hear the hearts of his wife, his pastor or members of his church small group. Whenever they tried to speak gently into his life, he became defensive. I tried to explain how to hear God's still small voice, but I soon sensed that Daniel wasn't listening even though he looked attentive.

"Are you listening to me?"

"What? Uh . . . yes," Daniel replied.

I knew Daniel was lying. "What have I been talking about for the last few minutes?"

Daniel was speechless. "I, uh . . . I guess I wasn't listening." He laughed nervously. Although I knew the answer by a word of knowledge, I felt prompted to ask, "For the last few minutes have you been physically unable to hear?"

Daniel looked startled. "Yes!"

"How long has this been going on?"

"Since I was about eleven. Mom lectured me ad nauseam. If I showed even a hint of resentment, she would start all over again. At first I just shut her out by going inside myself. But I could still hear her, so somehow I turned down the volume. Eventually I began to experience moments of actual physical deafness."

Knowing the answer by a "word of knowledge" (1 Cor 12:8), I asked, "Have the times of deafness been getting longer?"

"Yes! I have felt afraid that they'll keep growing longer until I'm *permanently* deaf! Recently it lasted a few hours. It happens when anyone tries to speak into my life."

Again, knowing the answer, I asked, "Does it happen only when your wife is critical, or even when she shares in loving ways?"

"It used to happen only when she was angry, but now even when she compliments me!"

"Is she often critical?" (I sensed she was not.)

"No; not much."

I could tell that this had never occurred to Daniel. Such is the nature of self-justification. He was not only unaware that he had the most patient wife a man could wish for; but he had also actually been willing to sacrifice his hearing rather than divulge that he had a problem. Daniel shared at length about his mother's hurtful words. Active listening and comfort enabled him to pray to forgive her. He repented of a bitter root expectancy that loved ones would only criticize, and he renounced an inner vow to not listen to them. I cast away the demon, and the deafness never returned!

I suggested that Daniel call his wife. Daniel listened—really listened—as she tactfully but tearfully shared the pain of being treated like she wasn't worth being listened to. (His awakening conscience later prompted him to do the same for his pastor and friends.)

The next day I asked, "Do you see how this has kept you from hearing God? Ask the Lord." Daniel listened, and this time the answer came instantly. "When you shut out your earthly father and mother, you shut out your heavenly Father." Daniel asked God's forgiveness. He could now accept the wise counsel of loved ones. God had cured not only his physical deafness, but his spiritual deafness as well.

Layne's story: The resurrection side of healing. At a class on inner healing, Layne learned that repenting of a bitter root expectancy brings freedom not only to you, but to those you have judged. As students wrote in their journals, she felt convicted about lies she had believed about her dad. "He doesn't love us." "He doesn't care about his family." "He's mean." "He's stingy with his money." She had borrowed these from her mother, who had made sure her children knew who the culprit was in the predivorce war.

Layne realized that her mom wasn't altogether right. Dad was frugal, but not stingy; the family lived in a nice house and was well provided for. Dad wasn't a hugger, but he wasn't altogether unloving. Although law school crimped his time, he took his kids fishing, coached his son's baseball team, and helped with chores and homework. He was not as mean as Mom portrayed him, but he was demanding. "Why only one A on your report card?" he would ask. After the divorce (when Layne was fifteen), he became less involved for fear of Mom's unpredictable volatility and acid tongue. But he still regularly drove one and a half hours to take his children to lunch.

Bitter roots often edit the manuscripts of our lives, excising blessings from the page. Mom had convinced Layne that Dad's money was a controlling weapon, so Layne had vowed, "I won't put myself in debt to him." She tore up birthday checks (he kept sending them anyway).

Previous to the class, Layne had already relinquished that inner vow. Then she and her husband, Steve, had embarked on a business venture in which they had to trust God more than ever with finances. This had revealed a lie that God would not provide. She and Steve had asked the Lord to forgive them for projecting upon God their bitterness toward her father, and for the first time, they had begun to reap prosperity. Layne had also prayed to forgive her dad for demanding performance, and had repented of expecting the same demands from God.

But there was one step Layne hadn't yet taken. She confessed to her heavenly Father, "Forgive me for the lies I have believed about Dad. I don't know who he really is; please show me."

During the sixteen years of Layne's marriage, her father, who had moved to another state, had never visited, although she had visited him several times. His fatherly resolve had been worn down by a stormy second marriage and work at his new law firm, and—although it's no excuse—his children's attitudes. But when we surrender in prayer what we hold against others, changes occur in the spirit realm that can't be explained with words.

Less than a half hour after Layne arrived home that night, her father called and asked if he could visit. Two days later he was at her door. He gave a lingering hug and began to praise her: "I was always proud of you. You are a better parent than me. And if you ever wonder if you are successful, look at the faces of your sleeping children, and see if you have succeeded beyond most people."

Until then her dad had called only on occasions like Christmases and birthdays. From then on he visited often, and his new wife embraced the grandchildren as her own. He drew closer to Layne than her mother ever had. He became Steve and Layne's chief business advisor and even forgave a $2,000 debt she owed him. He encouraged her and frequently expressed his belief in her. And this "unaffectionate" man became liberal with hugs and kisses.

CONCLUSION

We follow the Spirit, not fomulas, because transformative power does not reside in the prayer, as if the words were a kind of magic. Rather, prayer petitions the God of forgiving love to come alongside and change a life, transforming us from inside out. Prayer aligns the believer to God's holy principles of sanctifying grace. Prayer delights the Father God of the prodigal—the God who comes running to greet us in joy when we humbly return home after wandering in barren lands. Prayer focuses the root issues, lighting up the dark sins, lies and judgments that have sabotaged us our whole life and allowing the Great Physician to excise the root rot—as spiritual cancer is replaced with truth and light and love everlasting. God alone enables us to live and walk, hope in him, for him and with him—there is no other like our God.

REFERENCES AND RECOMMENDED RESOURCES

Elijah House offers books on inner healing and the prophetic gift (inner healing is truly a prophetic ministry), as well as pamphlets, CDs, DVDs, MP3s, ebooks and other materials. Order at www.elijahhouse.org.

We conduct live and video schools on inner healing (for which students have occasionally received college or graduate level credits) and on the prophetic gift. Seminars are available on related subjects, and we offer workshops for graduates of the inner healing school.

One-on-one counseling is available onsite or through referrals to Elijah House–trained persons. Phone numbers can be obtained through our website or by calling Elijah House.

These products and services can also be obtained through Elijah Houses in other nations (consult our website).

3

Theophostic Prayer Ministry

Ed Smith

Theophostic Prayer Ministry emerged from the ashes of my burning out in the pastoral counseling practice that I had in the mid-nineties. At that time, I met weekly with a women's group of survivors of childhood sexual abuse. After several years of weekly therapy, each of the women had made connections between their traumatic past and their present behavior and had become less dysfunctional in their day-to-day lives. Nevertheless, their traumatic memories still carried emotional pain. I realized that I honestly did not know what else to do to help them.

I had come to realize that they were in emotional pain, not *because* they had been abused as children or that the memories themselves were producing the pain, but rather because of the *lie-based thinking*[1] that was harbored in the context of those abuse memories. Although each of the women intellectually knew the truth about their abuse, they remained in bondage to the continuing lie-based painful emotions associated with the abuse. I had mistakenly assumed that they would recover from emotional wounds simply by being given the truth. However, I eventually discovered that just because a person gains more knowledge simply does not guarantee any measure of emotional freedom. Just because these women intellectually knew that abuse was not their fault, that they were no longer being abused, or that they were not tainted, dirty and shameful because of what had happened to them, such knowledge did not free them from the feelings of

[1]This is a Theophostic term that refers to the core belief held in memory that produces negative emotion when triggered through present life situations.

shame, guilt, fear, panic and terror. The problem was that what they logically knew to be true was not consistent with what they experientially held to be true at the memory or core level.

They each logically knew the truth regarding their own abuse and were even able to give advice and encouragement to the other members, but when they themselves focused on their painful memories, they agonized as though they were little abused children all over again. I was at the point of giving up, having reached the end of my counseling rope. However, in this place I discovered this was where God is able to do his finest work.

How God Set Mary Free

Shortly after I came to the end of my counseling rope, I had an individual session with one of the survivors of sexual abuse (I will call her Mary). I asked her if we could try something different in her session that day. Instead of my offering insights, explanations or opinions, I suggested that, once we had identified the lie-based belief that was producing the emotional pain, we ask the Lord for his perspective and truth. She agreed. She had been wrestling with depression, panic disorder and phobias, and as a consequence, her marriage was struggling and her daily existence was in shambles. She focused on the pain within the memory of when she was abused. She curled into a fetal position, sobbing in pain. We identified the lie-based beliefs causing her shame and fear in the abuse memory. She believed that she was still in danger, that she was still dirty and shameful and that the abuse was somehow her fault. I then did something that had never occurred to me to do before: I asked Jesus to give his perspective and truth to Mary regarding what she believed.

I sat in my chair, not knowing what to expect. As I watched, Mary sat up, her countenance changed, and she said, "It's gone!" I immediately asked, "What is gone?" "I heard the Lord say that he was with me and that it was not my fault," she explained. "And I felt the fear and shame just leave, as though it had been lifted off of me!" I witnessed the Holy Spirit communicate his truth to her experientially (Jn 16:13).

I had Mary reexamine and feel through the memory. To both of our surprise, she was able to genuinely revisit her memory of abuse without feeling any of the painful emotions that overwhelmed her just minutes before. Since that session, Mary's depression and panic has lifted, her doctor has taken her off her medication, and her marriage has improved remarkably.

Mary's session occurred over a decade ago, but she still maintains that none of the previous pain in those specific memories has ever returned. When she revisits those traumatic memories she feels nothing but the peace of Christ. She experienced metamorphosis, the mind renewal that Paul described in Romans 12:2, and it has transformed her life.

What Does Theophostic Prayer Ministry Look Like?

TPM is not a list of steps to follow but is rather a process of prayer that provides some foundational guidelines. As I look at TPM principles today, I wonder why I didn't see them long before. These principles are not a new revelation—"there is nothing new under the sun" (Eccles 1:9)—I had simply overlooked that which had always been. The basic principles of TPM are based on simple biblical truths that are supported by neurological facts.

Please understand as you read this chapter that it is a very truncated description of the Theophostic Prayer Ministry process and is not intended to be applied based upon this brief overview. To attempt this ministry process without the full training may result in undesirable outcomes. Having said this, the basic process of this prayer model flows in this manner:

1. The facilitator helps the recipient to identify and focus on the presenting emotion.
2. The recipient begins to follow this emotion to its lie-based source.
3. The facilitator helps the recipient to identify any mental obstructions that may hinder the ministry process, such as the suppression of feelings, dissociation, self-distraction, internal imagery, demonic manifestation, sleepiness and fatigue, doubt, fear, anger, etc.
4. After following the emotion and working past any internal defensive barrier, the recipient should eventually land in an earlier memory and identify the lie-based core belief that is producing the pain.
5. The recipient will then offer this belief to the Lord for his truth and perspective.
6. If the person does not receive truth, the facilitator will help him or her to identify the reason for this.

7. When the recipient receives truth, *all* of the emotional pain that was associated with the belief will dissipate and be permanently replaced with the peace of Christ.
8. The facilitator will then have the person reexamine all of the memories that were visited to be sure that the previously exposed emotional pain is completely resolved and replaced with the peace of Christ.

WHAT ARE THE FOUNDATIONAL PRINCIPLES OF TPM?

What follows is a sampling of some of the basic TPM principles upon which this ministry approach is founded. The fuller training contains much more important information.

1. Our present situation is rarely the true cause of our ongoing emotional pain. Blaming what we feel on other people or our surroundings is easier than owning and being responsible for it ourselves. And yet, emotional pain in day-to-day life is seldom solely caused by what is happening in the present situation. Our circumstances stir up the painful emotions that are produced by core beliefs that we learned during earlier life experiences. We ask the ministry recipient to take responsibility for their own thinking and emotional status instead of shifting blame for their emotionally charged reactions.

2. Feelings are important indicators of our core beliefs. By design, pain acts as a warning system that indicates when something is wrong. As with physical pain, when our lie-based pain is triggered, we must learn to respond appropriately rather than look for ways to mask it or blame others. Our emotions indicate what we believe on an experiential level, regardless of whether the belief is based in truth or deception. If we experientially believe the truth that we are loved by God, we should feel loved by God. However, if we say "we are loved by God" but feel rejected, abandoned or unaccepted by God, then we experientially believe something else. If we truly believe that he will supply all our needs, we will feel secure and at peace no matter our financial status. However, if we experientially believe a lie, our emotional status will expose this reality. For this reason, we often say in TPM, "We feel whatever we believe." To deny what we feel is to refuse to expose our core belief and, thus, to keep us in its snare.

3. Only an encounter with the presence of Jesus, through the Holy Spirit, can free us from the lies we believe. People find freedom from the lie-based pain in their lives through personally encountering Christ and receiving truth from the One who is the Truth (Jn 16:13). And when God grants *new thinking,*[2] people come to "know the truth" and "come to their senses," and thereby "escape the snare of the devil" (2 Tim 2:25-26 NKJV). As the Holy Spirit changes our thinking, and we come to know the truth experientially, the raging swell of pain becomes a placid calm.

It is important to note that TPM is but one of many avenues through which a person can encounter the presence of Christ. Personal prayer, meditation on God's Word, teaching, spiritual counsel and instruction are also ways in which people can experience the Lord's presence. Apart from the presence of and inner work of Christ, we cannot live rightly. The truth is, much of what we identify as being spiritual in the Christian life is actually performance-based spirituality. So many of the "spiritual" things we do are really nothing more than any lost person could do if he just set his mind to doing it. True spirituality is a work of God—"Christ in you, the hope of glory" (Col 1:27).

4. A memory can hold two basic types of core beliefs—state-of-being and self-identity beliefs. A "state-of-being" belief defines my condition or the situation in which I believe I am (in danger, alone, trapped, going to die, etc.). A "self-identity" belief defines who or what I believe I am (worthless, powerless, bad, a defect, unlovable, etc.). Each of the two types of belief produces its own specific form of emotional expression. On the one hand, a state-of-being belief may produce irrational fears or phobias. State-of-being lies are often found at the root of panic disorders and posttraumatic stress. If being in an enclosed space, such as an elevator, triggers a core belief that I learned as a child when I was stuffed into a closet—such as "I cannot breathe," "I am trapped" or "I am going to die"—my panic and anxiety will likely overwhelm me.

A self-identity belief, on the other hand, may produce feelings of self-loathing, inferiority, worthlessness, rejection and so on. Lies such as "I am worthless," "I am a defect" and "I am unlovable" are all common.

5. There is a "dual mental process" in each of us that has a great bearing on the decisions we make moment by moment. Each of us possesses both conscious and unconscious thinking. Everything we believe was learned in

[2]The word for repentance found in 2 Tim 2:25 actually means to be granted a new way of thinking.

an earlier point in time. Much of this early learning is held in core belief at an unconscious level. By design, our minds interpret every new event using these previously acquired beliefs. This neurological process of association continually provides input as to how to respond to current situations. When a belief is accessed, it brings with it a corresponding emotion. And this emotion has great influence on the decisions we make moment to moment, both consciously and unconsciously. Whether or not we are willing to admit it, much of what we do is emotionally driven. We tend to either seek ways of self-medicating the stress, worry, anxiety, fears and depressions that we feel, or we act it out through blame-shifting onto the circumstance or onto those around us. And when making decisions that are motivated by lie-based pain, we rarely choose wisely.

6. People can hold two or more opposing beliefs at the same time. A person can logically know and quote the verse "My God shall supply all your need according to His riches in glory" (Phil 4:19 NKJV) while at the same time feeling totally stressed out over his finances. The reason for this is a condition described in the Bible as being "double-minded" (Jas 1:8). *Double-mindedness* is holding two or more opposing beliefs at the same time. If a person says they believe that God is the supplier of their needs, but lives in worry and anxiety, then he also experientially believes something contrary to this truth. Logical truth is made up of the facts and figures we have memorized along the way, but it is not necessarily our foundational experiential core belief. When our core belief and "facts and figures" are in conflict, we are in a double-minded state and are like a "wave of the sea, blown and tossed by the wind" (Jas 1:6).

7. Sinful behavior is often a vain attempt to manage our emotional pain. When our lie-based pain is triggered, choosing to act out sinfully is often less difficult than owning and addressing the reasons for why we are emotionally stirred up. When we feel depressed, dejected, stressed, fearful, alone or something else, we are more apt to eat when not hungry, please ourselves with immoral sexual activities, look for ways to entertain ourselves or find some other distraction, rather than rightly address the root of our emotional pain. So as we strive against sinning, we must also address the pain factor that often motivates our sinful responses. Otherwise, we may remain in an endless loop of trying to control our behavior but only achieving perpetual failure.

8. We are in emotional bondage due to two basic factors: belief and choice. Belief and choice are foundational to everything we do. Each of us has a reservoir of core beliefs that stands ready to interpret each and every new life experience. Sometimes we interpret the new situation based upon what we logically believe to be true. We make these kinds of decisions while driving a car, stopping and accelerating at the appropriate moment. These logical decisions tend to be free of any emotional influence. However, core beliefs that were learned through experience tend to be far more influential in decision making than the facts and figures we learn through study or instruction.

For example, a person might feel small, weak and powerless when his boss questions a decision he made concerning his work. He may logically know that the decision was a right one, but his feelings will not allow him to stand up and express himself, so he goes home and complains to his wife instead. These feelings of weakness and powerlessness are rooted in core belief. While life happens around us, our minds automatically and instantaneously search through our reservoir of experientially learned beliefs for interpretation. When our minds select the belief that best fits the situation, we automatically feel the emotion that corresponds with that particular belief. Some people try to override the initial flash of emotional pain by choosing to not act on it. We can choose to behave contrarily to the emotion we feel, but not without much internal conflict.

Everything that occurs in the ministry session will be determined by our freewill choices. No one and nothing, except our belief and choice, can keep us from experiencing the lasting freedom God desires for us. God is willing to give us truth, but he will not force us to remember memories, follow emotional pain or move forward in a ministry session. The recipient will feel, move forward, remember and so on when he or she willfully chooses to do so.

9. The written Word of God is the standard for validating what occurs in a ministry session. In all cases the message one receives during a ministry session must be held up to the Word of God in order to test its validity. Any "message" that a person may receive in a ministry session that is contrary to or an addition to what the Bible says is deemed false. Sometimes the truths people receive are actually reminders of scriptural truths they already "know." Other times they may have experiences that are not specifically modeled in the Scriptures but are not in conflict with what the Word of God says. God's Word is the standard.

10. Lie-based pain can only be removed as lies are replaced with truth, whereas the only remedy for sin-based pain is the cross of Jesus Christ. Theophostic Prayer does not seek to deal with the emotional pain that is the result of harbored sin. When we sin we *should* feel badly. All people are born into sin as a corporate consequence of Adam's sin: "Sin came into the world through one man, and death came through sin, and so death spread to all because all have sinned" (Rom 5:12 NRSV). God's Word convicts us of these wrongdoings through the Holy Spirit. Our right response is to confess, or agree with God (1 Jn 1:9), that what we have done is indeed sinful. God then may grant us repentance or literally a change of thinking, as seen in 2 Timothy 2:25, so we can turn toward God, submit to him and experience his indwelling power to live rightly.

11. Mind renewal is a lifelong process. Total release of all lie-based thinking is not possible within our earthly lifetime. As Christians, this ongoing process of sanctification, wherein the believer is set apart from the ways of the world for holiness, is accomplished through the indwelling Christ and with the submitted and willful cooperation of the believer. Mind renewal is a part of sanctification, occurring both through the accumulation of Bible knowledge and the replacement of lie-based core beliefs from the Holy Spirit's provision of personalized experiential truth for the believer.

Does TPM Have a Biblical Basis?

TPM is based upon the principles found in a multitude of Scriptures. These are outlined in the Theophostic Basic Training Seminar and the Theophostic Basic Seminar Manual (see references and recommended resources at the end of the chapter). A good example can been found in one of the Gospel stories, where we find the disciples are in a boat, straining at the oars, in the midst of a terrible storm. In fear, they finally call to Jesus, who is asleep in the stern of the boat. The differences in Jesus' and his disciples' perspectives can be seen clearly in the following Gospel account:

> A furious squall came up, and the waves broke over the boat, so that it was nearly swamped. Jesus was in the stern, sleeping on a cushion. The disciples woke him and said to him, "Teacher, don't you care if we drown?" He got up,

> rebuked the wind and said to the waves, "Quiet! Be still!" Then the wind died down and it was completely calm. He said to his disciples, "Why are you so afraid? Do you still have no faith?"

So how does God "show up" experientially and transform the client? The disciples panicked when the storm triggered their belief: "We are going to die." Had they understood (believed) who Jesus was, they could have been napping as well. Instead, they were seemingly controlled by the fear that these lie-based beliefs produced. Jesus' actions and response to the storm also revealed his belief system. He was at peace in the storm because he knew the truth. Upon awakening, Jesus spoke to the storm and calmed the sea. He followed this by speaking truth to his disciples and calming their fears. In fact, Jesus still asks these same questions of each of us as we find ourselves straining in the midst of the storm: "Why are you afraid?"

This is an important question in that it addresses the core of our belief. In a ministry session, I might ask the same type of question to a person who is in a painful memory: "Why do you feel what you are feeling?" I am not saying that we are wrong for feeling powerful emotions in the midst of a traumatic experience. Fear is a natural human response to danger, but it will cripple us if it remains indefinitely. Anger is appropriate in the moment of injustice (Eph 4:26), but inappropriate when it is left unattended to turn into resentment and bitterness (Eph 4:31). True shame and guilt are appropriate when we commit a sinful act, but if we continue to feel guilty after confessing the sin, it is no longer based upon the truth, and therefore no longer appropriate.

Furthermore, we overcome these distressing feelings not by just asserting our belief in God's truth alone, but by inviting and experiencing the presence of God in a close and intimate way. God in Christ coming near to us—and we coming near to him in obedience to his call—is what makes the difference. That Jesus was in the boat with the disciples—and not addressing them from the shore—was crucial to their experiencing peace amid the storm when Christ commanded it to be still.

Some people might ask, "Where is Theophostic Prayer mentioned in the Bible?" The truth is, you will not find the word *Theophostic* in the Bible. The name was created simply to describe this ministry process, using the Greek New Testament words *theos* (God) and *phos* (light). Theophostic Prayer is about God's Holy Spirit shining his light into the places of darkness in our minds and releasing us of the lies that have us held captive. God's doing this is very biblical.

TPM is not about counseling, healing memories, guiding or directing anything, but rather about mind renewal. Mind renewal occurs as the truth of God experientially replaces the falsehoods people believe. True mind renewal is always followed by life transformation that should then become evident in that area of a person's life. (Rom 12:2). A portion of mind renewal is accomplished as we grow in the "knowledge of Him" (Eph 1:17 NKJV). However, mind renewal is also accomplished as the Holy Spirit personally replaces our core belief, which is contaminated with falsehood, with his truth.

Does TPM View Human Beings Holistically?

TPM has the potential of impacting every area of the ministry recipient's life. Medical science has long acknowledged a strong mind-body relationship. For example, stress has long been listed as a leading cause of heart disease. And, as I have already stated, stress is usually a consequence of belief. We feel whatever we believe. If I am stressed then I believe something that is causing it. Many stresses are attributed to a person's current situations, such as loss of job, marital conflict, parenting issues, financial problems, relational issues and so on. However, even though these life issues are real and important, how they are interpreted and understood is still determined by what we believe at a core level. And our lie-based beliefs can create emotional reactions that are of no benefit to us and create problems with our health, mood, productivity, relationships and quality of life.

Does TPM Work with Couples?

The peace of Christ is necessary for us to have deeper, genuine, meaningful relationships with others and with God himself. Long before I developed TPM, I offered marital counseling to couples who were experiencing relational difficulties. Through cognitive restructuring I helped them somewhat to better communicate, resolve conflict and establish deeper levels of intimacy.

However, I discovered that a high percentage of the difficulty couples faced in marriage was not because they lacked relational skills, but because both held lie-based pain. Most couples seemed to get along fine until their lie-based pain was triggered, which would then cause them to act out against each other. I have witnessed many couples deepen their relationships simply by having their lie-based beliefs replaced with truth through an encounter with the Holy Spirit.

Have Any Researchers Tested TPM?

Fernando Garzon (2008) reports that people's relationship to God deepens as they find freedom from the lies they believe. Garzon assembled a team of mental health professionals and lay ministers to work through thirteen cases that tested each participant prior to, and following, the ten Theophostic Prayer Ministry sessions they were provided. The team used the Symptom Checklist 90R, the Spiritual Well-Being Scale, Brief Psychiatric Rating Scale and Dysfunctional Attitude Scale. The findings were very positive. All but one person participating in this research claimed to have had significant improvement both emotionally and socially. Eleven of the thirteen participants indicated that the prayer sessions had significantly improved their spiritual relationship with God.

These same positive findings were discovered by Tilley (2008) when she interviewed 2,818 individuals who had received at least one session of Theophostic Prayer. No screenings were made to determine whether the person's experience was positive or negative, but only that true Theophostic Prayer had been administered. Her findings showed that 94% of those who were surveyed reported that TPM had positively impacted their personal lives; 95% believed it deepened their relationship with God; and 84% reported complete resolution of all emotional pain in their hurtful memories in which they received ministry. Many of the ministry facilitators represented in this survey were probably not "experts" in using TPM. Nevertheless, whether the facilitators in this survey were seasoned veterans or novices, the fact that 2,818 people reported such high levels of satisfaction is noteworthy (Tilley, 2008).

Does TPM Work Best in Certain Kinds of Situations?

TPM does not attempt to fulfill what biblical counseling, pastoral care or general spiritual encouragements seek to accomplish. TPM is focused on only one thing: resolving lie-based pain rooted in core belief. When a person comes seeking help with communication skills, anger management, financial planning or principles in parenting, Theophostic Prayer is not the tool to use. However, if emotional pain accompanies any of these presenting concerns, TPM very well may be helpful in identifying the root cause and finding relief. However, finding freedom from the anxiety triggered by money issues will not help the person in balancing his checkbook. This is a life skill that will need to be addressed in a different setting.

TPM teaches that God has chosen not to violate our free will, and unless the person willfully chooses to take steps in the direction of truth, peace and freedom, no amount of prayer, coaching or advice will move them. Some other ministry approaches seek to identify personal vows and agreements made by the person during a painful life event and then lead them in prayers of renunciations. In these ministry models vows such as, "I will never let anyone hurt me again," "I will never be like her," "I will never allow myself to feel emotions again," "I will never let anyone close to me again" are confessed and "broken" through prayers of renunciation and the name of Jesus. This practice is not a part of Theophostic Prayer.

TPM understands that a vow is not the person's problem that needs to be renounced, but rather it is the person's solution of protection. The problem is the person's belief that holds the vow in place. For example, if, while in a session, Mary reports that she made a vow due to the trauma she endured as a child, a trained TPM facilitator would not advise renunciation of the vow, but rather encourage Mary to feel the emotions that are present. Those emotions will help uncover what she believed within the context of when the vow was made.

Until that belief is identified, owned and offered to Christ for his truth, the odds of Mary "releasing" the vow are slim to impossible since the vow is based upon her belief. However, once the lies that held the vow in place are replaced with truth, the vow loses its power or is no longer needed and will become meaningless.

TPM Is Not a Deliverance Ministry Focused on Casting Out Demons

In TPM the facilitator does not view the demon as an obstacle that has to be contended with, but rather evidence of a lie-based core belief. In TPM the person is not seen as a victim of the devil who needs to be rescued. What a demon can and cannot do is limited by the person's freewill choice and belief system. Demons cannot make a person sin or behave in any manner that the person does not willfully choose. Consequently, in a TPM session, when demonic activity is presented through an audible message, a visualization or any other form of manifestation, instead of addressing the demon the facilitator would encourage the person to connect with emotion that he feels and seek to identify the lie that is at its root. The reason for the demon's presence is rooted in that person's belief system. The person's emotion that is stirred becomes the bridge back to those beliefs. After following the emotion, identifying the beliefs and receiving Christ's perspective, the demons have no purpose, reason or right to stay. They have no choice but to flee. In fact, if the demonic activity actually helped to identify the person's belief so that he or she could offer it to Christ for renewal, then there was actually benefit in its being there. For this reason, demons are sometimes referred to as "lie detectors" by those using TPM.

A Final Case Study in Theophostic Prayer Ministry

Shari had come to talk with her pastor about the depression and anxiety she had been experiencing over the previous months. She was taking medication for her panic attacks, and it had helped some. However, subtle fears were present on a daily basis. Shari had tried to pray more, read her Bible and be faithful in attending the women's group at her church, but she was still struggling emotionally. She occasionally even entertained thoughts of suicide. Her pastor introduced Shari to the Theophostic Prayer Ministry approach.

After listening to the pastor, Shari agreed to allow him to administer the process. Within a few minutes, an enormous amount of pain began to surface, and Shari began to describe her memory of childhood pain. He prayed softly as she felt through the entire memory, feeling all of its fear and pain. He asked her to identify what she believed was causing her to feel what she was feeling. She reported that she believed she was going to die. She said things like, "I can't breathe! I'm suffocating" and "What happened was my fault."

In the midst of her immense emotional and physical pain, the pastor invited the Holy Spirit to reveal truth to her in the midst of her fear and panic. Suddenly everything changed. The pastor watched as a calming wave of peace washed over her. Shari immediately stopped expressing pain; her breathing relaxed, and her countenance changed from one of panic and anguish to one of complete peace and calm. She looked at the pastor with a smile of relief and sighed, "Jesus said that I am not there anymore and that I was not bad or shameful. It wasn't my fault." She then cried tears of relief and joy, and so did the pastor. He had never seen anyone move so quickly from such pain into such genuine peace. This pastor later told the friend who had introduced him to this ministry, "It was like I was standing on holy ground. It was indeed a very holy moment. God was in that place!"

REFERENCES AND RECOMMENDED RESOURCES

General information about Theophostic Prayer Ministry can be found at www.theophostic.com.

Garzon, F. (2008). *Pursuing peace: Case studies exploring the effectiveness of theophostic prayer.* Maitland, FL: Xulon.

International Association for Theophostic Ministry. (An international community of people using Theophostic Prayer Ministry.) Visit www.theophostic.org for more information.

Smith, E. (2007). *Basic seminar manual.* Campbellsville, KY: New Creation Publishing.

Smith, E. (2007). *Healing life's hurts through theophostic prayer.* Campbellsville, KY: New Creation Publishing.

Smith, E. (2007). *TPM basic training seminar* (DVD series). Campbellsville, KY: New Creation Publishing.

Tilley, K. (2008). *Current perceptions of the effectiveness of theophostic prayer ministry.* (Unpublished doctoral dissertation.) Southern California Seminary, San Diego.

4

Deliverance as Part of the Therapeutic Process

David W. Appleby

After over thirty years and more than one thousand cases, I have learned these truisms about deliverance as part of the therapeutic process:

- Demonization is much more common than most Christian professionals believe, but it is not so frequent that every problem can be ascribed to it.
- Salvation, by itself, does not expel any demons present, but it does change ownership and requires that any demons obey when confronted by the new owner (Christ).
- Demonic entities will lie, hide, confound and try to confuse anyone doing deliverance, but they are bound to respond truthfully when confronted in the name of Jesus Christ.
- Assessment is not so much a search for symptoms as it is a review of the client's life experience—and whether that experience may have exposed the client to demons.
- Assessment must always consider the overlapping possibility of sin, psychopathology and medical disease that may be at work in the problem and in aftercare.
- Deliverance should be considered when all other treatments have limited or no impact.

Let's consider how these various truths operate as Peter tells his story about his struggle with lust and sexual erotica.

Peter's Story

All of my adult life I have had a sense that, though I have been in church leadership and others have made positive comments about my family and my dedication to faith, inside I have been an ugly person. I have always believed that if anyone really knew the thoughts and the fears that I constantly struggled with, they would reject me. They would think I was really weird or a hypocrite or a madman.

Much of my mental energy went to fighting irrational desires—thinking that I might fall into sin and be discovered. If I saw a billboard for a "gentleman's club," I would wrestle in my thoughts for hours. I knew that I would never go there because it would be sinful. Yet the attraction and the need to fight the thoughts would sap my energy and focus. The same thing happened with the opportunity to view movies. Pornography did not hold an attraction to me because I know how disgusting it is. Yet I was attracted to erotic, tantalizing things, and again, it took me hours of resistance and fighting fantasies. Much of my time was wasted by the centrality and the power of these struggles.

Whenever I mentioned these struggles to other Christian men, they would say, "Welcome to the human race." I became frustrated and felt defeated because, though I had been a Christian for thirty-three years and had frequently taught about victory in Christ, I was plagued by these thoughts. I continually prayed for a new heart and a new mind. With the exception of a few periods of mission work or extreme overcommitment at work, the mental battles and fatigue were constant.

When I attended Dr. Appleby's seminar on deliverance (so I could help others!), I recognized that the characteristics of some of his clients were prevalent in my life. I asked him for a deliverance checkup, and he suggested we get together to see if there was a need for deliverance. When we met to pray about deliverance with my pastor, it became clear that I needed it. To be honest, I was relieved to hear that there was demonic influence in my patterns. Dr. Appleby's position of "Relax, it's just a demon" gave me both great comfort and hope. I had feared that it was just me, and that I had been incapable of changing my thought patterns no matter what I had tried over the past forty years.

After praying for wisdom and discernment, Dr. Appleby and my pastor led me through a series of declarations, renouncements and prayers. I had feared possible ugly manifestations or embarrassing behavior, but the conversation and the prayer were quiet. There were no manifestations other than some foul language that I willingly recounted when Dr. Appleby asked me the first thing that came into my head after asking the demon to show itself. As we prayed, I sensed a deep peace—a quietness that was unfamiliar. I left the deliverance not knowing if anything had really happened, but hopeful. Dr. Appleby simply said to wait to see if there was a difference in my life.

There most certainly has been a difference! The following are excerpts from my journal:

> *I went . . . to meet with Dave Appleby . . . today to see if I might need deliverance because of fighting secret urges all of my life, for as long as I can remember. Fighting being seduced by illicit things—much around sexuality—but mostly being drawn by curiosity, not a desire to actually participate. Having to fight fantasies about somebody trying to seduce me while I always successfully resisted.*
>
> *Dave [and my pastor] prayed and commanded any spirit associated with this stuff to name itself—I started laughing and the name "Jack" popped into my head with the thought, "You don't know Jack."*
>
> *Many of the thoughts and fears that I have struggled with over my whole adult life have centered on the thought that nobody really knows me. If they did they would find my thought life disgusting, hypocritical and just plain crazy. My inability to control these things, though I had held positions of Christian leadership and taught extensively about victory in Christ, would disqualify me from leadership, from really letting anybody know me and perhaps even from being a true believer. I certainly allowed the accuser of the brethren to cast doubt into my mind regarding my position in sonship with Christ.*
>
> *Because of these dark and embarrassing thoughts, I felt that nobody really knew me—and nobody knew Jack (in me). "Jack" is a nickname for Jacob, the supplanter. [Jack was also the name of the father of a girl who had seduced me into early sexual exploration before second grade. Reflecting on her behavior, I am fairly sure she had been sexually molested and that spiritual energy from*

her father, Jack, attached itself to me through her seduction and his presence on at least one occasion in our home when I was between five and seven years old.] After praying and renouncing and confessing and exposing all of this stuff, there is peace.

Inner truth. Consistency. Freedom. Jesus is amazing.

Sonship. Forgiveness.

Nothing to hide.

No fear of crashing and burning.

No fear of being alone because of being tormented by temptations and the need to resist them, or by accusations regarding my walk or character.

These accusations were the voice of the enemy telling me that Jesus couldn't possibly love a hypocritical, sin-consumed person who claimed to be a Christian.

Forty-five years of fighting comes to a close. The deep, dark, untellable secret is out, and over.

There was no manifestation to the exit of "Jack."

Dave says the evidence of deliverance is a changed life. He said to let him know how it goes from here on out. I'm tired. I'm relieved. I'm thankful. I'm at peace for the first time in decades.

For a number of years, I've prayed for a new heart and a new mind. I thought that I heard from the Lord that my heart was good, but I needed a new mind. I doubted my heart because of the constant struggles [and I doubted my ability to hear from the Lord because I thought my heart was wicked]. Now I have a new mind. Thank you Jesus!

Postscript. Since going through the deliverance, I have traveled and attended a professional conference in another city. The temptations weren't there. The struggles weren't there. The ambivalence of going away (and fearing being tormented) weren't there. I enjoyed the trip, my colleagues and the ability to rest in the Lord's presence. My mind was not only at peace, but more refreshed and relaxed and focused than it has been in years. My colleagues remarked at my youthful appearance, my relaxed nature and the "step up" in my professional presentation. Some had known me for years and had seen me present often. They commented that I had reached a new level of analytic and teaching ability.

I believe it is because my mind is free from being consumed, distracted and fatigued by demonic thoughts. Knowing that I am at peace with Jesus gave me a sense of confidence and peace that relieved the pressure of professional performance. I now am free to explore with creativity, focus and energy that had been invested in futile battle for decades. I can't wait to test drive this new mind! Thank you, Jesus!

In church, I have gotten prophetic words for the past four Sundays. I have worshiped more freely and with more emotion than I can ever recall. The curtain has been torn from top to bottom! I no longer have fears and doubts about Christ's love for me, despite sin and human shortcomings. I am experiencing sonship in a new way and mature Christianity at a new level. Life is good. God is great!

Author's note: Five years after the deliverance, I had lunch with this man and his wife. His comment was, "It is so good to have my head back" (Appleby, 2009, pp. 149-53). He is still doing well today.

Recognizing the Battle

What do you do if you are Peter? What do you do when you've been a Christian for years, been a pastor, church leader or simply a believer but are still being dominated by invisible forces that are more powerful than you are? What do you do when you've talked to ministers, counselors, psychologists and psychiatrists but have experienced no relief? I found myself in the deliverance ministry because of clients like Peter—good Christian people who, no matter how hard they tried, couldn't seem to get "unstuck." Their lives revolved around their pain, believed lies, false internal accusations and continuing torment.

As a pastor, counselor and graduate counseling professor (not to mention Christian), I thought that God should be able to intervene in the lives of his children as the Scriptures indicated—that he could and that we should be able to see significant life changes as a result of that intervention. Because the author of Hebrews said, "Let us then approach God's throne of grace with confidence, so that we may receive mercy and find grace to help us in our time of need" (Heb 4:16), I actually thought that they should be able to do that and receive help. But that wasn't happening. The client's prayer life was nonexistent, the Word of God was dust, and worship had become a spectator sport. The traditional spiritual disciplines of the church were exercises in futility. And I, for all my education and experience, realized that I had nothing to offer them besides the same old platitudes that both they and I had heard for years. I was embarrassed to repeat them.

It shouldn't be like this! I must be missing something! The only thing I hadn't looked at seriously was demonization. Without realizing it, I had become what C. S. Lewis called a "naturalist" and was engaging in "truncated thought." As he describes in his book *Miracles*:

> And since the Sixteenth Century, when Science was born, the minds of men have been increasingly engaged in those specialized inquiries for which truncated thought is the correct method. It is, therefore, not in the least astonishing that they should have forgotten the evidence for the supernatural. The only ingrained habit of truncated thought—what we call the scientific habit of mind—was indeed certain to lead to Naturalism, unless this tendency were continually corrected from some other source. But no other source was at hand, for during the same period men of science were becoming metaphysically and theologically uneducated. (Lewis, 1947, p. 43)

The unrelenting torment of my clients resulted in a thirty-year journey toward understanding the link between the psychological and the demonic.

But let's first define deliverance. *Deliverance* is the process whereby a demonic spirit's influence over an individual is broken and the freedom to choose is restored (Appleby, 2009). Deliverance does not make a person holy; it just removes the spiritual personalities that influence a person toward evil (Gal 5:13). The final product is an individual who is simply who they are, with all the bumps, bruises, wounds, and broken bones and hearts that go with living. If they have physiologically based issues (schizophrenia, chronic depression, etc.), these may also remain, unless God chooses to heal those disorders as well. Not every problem is demonic in the same way that not every problem is psychological or physiological. Like most factors in life, the boundaries tend to blur.

Deliverance is biblical. Of all the variety of spiritual interventions contained in this book, none of them are more clearly biblical than deliverance. It is hard to get around the fact that it was a large portion of Jesus' ministry (along with raising the dead and healing the sick). Deliverance was (and is) a power encounter that God chose to use to confirm that the kingdom of God had come. In addition, it is hard to argue against the fact that Jesus modeled this power encounter for the twelve apostles, and he expected and commanded both the apostles and his other disciples to do likewise (Mt 10:8; Mk 3:14-15; Lk 9:1-2; 10:17-20). The casting out of demons continued to occur among the followers of Jesus after his death and resurrection from the dead. It continued after the Day of Pentecost (Acts 8:5-8; 19:11-20) and all over the earth in this present day.

Deliverance is doing what Jesus did, what his disciples did and what we are supposed to do. Recall the opening story in our introduction. Deliverance is the gospel, the good news that Jesus took upon himself all the effects of our sin so that we would not have to bear those effects. Jesus died and rose from the grave so that we could be free. It is what Jesus said that he (and we, by extension, as his body) was called to do in Luke 4:18-19—namely, preaching good news to the poor, proclaiming freedom for the prisoners and recovery of sight for the blind, the release of the oppressed, and the year of God's favor.

Demons are evil spiritual entities who have personalities (Lk 8:27-30), have names such as Legion (Lk 8:30), use intelligent speech (Lk 4:33-34, 41; 8:28-30), and recognize the identity of Christ (Mk 1:23-24) and Paul (Acts 16:16-17). They exhibit emotions, trembling at their final judgment (Lk 8:28; Jas 2:19), rebel against God and appeal to Christ not to be thrown into the pit (Lk 8:32). They also had to obey both Christ and Christians when ordered to leave (Mk 1:27; Lk 10:17-20) (Appleby, 2009).

Defining demonization. *Demonization* is the proper term for what is commonly known as "demon possession," which is a confusing term. Different versions of the Bible sometimes refer to a person "being possessed by a demon." The Greek may be better translated as the person being "demonized." Possession implies ownership, and demons do not own the believer in that the believer is already the possession of Jesus Christ. Transfer of ownership occurs in the salvation experience. Instead of being "property owners," the New Testament views demons as squatters or invaders of territory that does not belong to them. Demonization could better be defined as "being under the influence or control of one or more demonic spirits" (Appleby, 2009, p. 52). This control can be minimal, or it can be major. It is best to view demonic involvement as being on a continuum that stretches from minimal to major involvement.

Demonization is one possible explanation for an individual's sense of having portions of their life beyond their control. Oftentimes the person is told "it's just you," or "it's just your flesh" and "you need to get your life together." Galatians 5:24 tells us that "Those who belong to Christ Jesus have crucified the sinful nature with its passions and desires." Sometimes the traditional spiritual disciplines such as prayer, meditation, fasting, worship and silence are recommended as a possible way of making this happen. Unfortunately, when none of these disciplines work we are at a loss as to what to do. After all, this remedy should have worked; we should be able to fix this problem. However, while the Scriptures tell us that we have the ability to crucify the flesh, there is nothing to suggest that demons can likewise be crucified. The spiritual disciplines will not free us from demonic involvement. Ephesians 6:12 tells us, "For our struggle is not against flesh and blood, but against the rulers, against the authorities, against the powers of this dark world and against the spiritual forces of evil in the heavenly realms."

Making accurate and discerning assessment. Mistaking the demonic for the flesh will result in endless frustration on the part of the individual, and an improper treatment strategy on the part of the counselor. Unless an accurate diagnosis takes place, successful treatment will be forever beyond reach. Deliverance is one tool given to the church to assist us in joining with Christ in his freedom-producing work.

Setting the captives free. Deliverance as practiced by Jesus, his disciples and us has as its purpose the removal of demonic influence for the purpose of setting the captive free so that he or she may serve God. It is also an indicator that the kingdom of God has indeed come, at least in part. Furthermore, it brings glory to God, as does healing. Consequently, deliverance is inappropriate for those who do not desire to become Christians or who are not Christians. Luke 11:24-26 says: "When an evil spirit comes out of a man, it goes through arid places seeking rest and does not find it. Then it says, 'I will return to the house I left.' When it arrives, it finds the house swept clean and put in order. Then it goes and takes seven other spirits more wicked than itself, and they go in and live there. And the final condition of that man is worse than the first" (NIV 1984). If a demonic spirit leaves a person who has no intention of having that space filled with the Holy Spirit, then he will be open to invasion by other, more wicked spirits. Thus, deliverance does not benefit anyone who is not a believer or would not be a believer.

Deliverance touches any aspect of a client's life that a demon can touch. We have seen in the Scriptures those suffering from what we in the twenty-first century would call physiologically based disorders "healed" when the demons left. We have seen Jesus and his disciples do deliverance that results in changes in both affect and behavior in their "clients." The Bible uses the word *healing* to reference freedom from physiological, psychological and spiritual maladies (Mt 17:18; Mk 5:15; Lk 8:35; 9:42; 11:14; Acts 8:7; 16:16-18). It is no different today. We regularly see people report healing of physical problems, as well as changes in cognition, affect and behavior. Why should it be otherwise?

Deliverance, as we practice it, views people holistically. Every system is connected to and influenced by all the others. Physical systems influence cognitive systems. They in turn influence and are influenced by affective and behavioral systems. Spiritual factors influence each as well. Client problems are a result of an interaction between these various systems. Demonic influences are just one more factor in an already complicated equation. Not everyone is demonized, and removing demonic spirits from those who are will not result in the solution to every problem, because deliverance is just one piece of the puzzle. We tell our clients that our goal is to see them become truly who they are. Most of what we are is the result of a combination of physiological, cognitive, affective, behavioral and spiritual factors.

When would deliverance be appropriately used with a client? A clinician friend of mine (and coeditor of this book) once commented that it would be almost impossible to develop a differential diagnosis for demonization because it can be caused by just about anything harmful in the life of the client (Ohlschlager, personal interview). In a sense he is correct, because demonization is not so much caused by a variety of factors, but by a client's reaction to these factors. Consequently, one person can experience a series of difficult life events and come through unscathed while another person can go through a set of identical circumstances and become overwhelmingly demonized. So, how can we determine if deliverance is a legitimate intervention? There are four main predictors.

Predictors of Demonization

Likely candidates. Persons plagued by repetitive destructive patterns across generations, those who find themselves being negatively defined by internal voices, and those who sense a destructive attachment to others with whom they have been emotionally or physically intimate are likely candidates for deliverance. We call these curses, ungodly oaths, and soul ties or hooks.

Curses. The Scriptures speak often of blessings and curses. While Christian mental health workers and even pastors are very comfortable with both the psychological and sociological explanations for cross-generational patterns of both positive and negative behaviors, the thought that spiritual dynamics could impact cross-generational patterns has been largely ignored, even though the Scriptures clearly attest to the reality of such dynamics. These generational patterns are called *curses.* Exodus 34:5-7 indicates that curses can afflict people and their offspring through to the third and fourth generation. These generational time bombs are activated as a result of God's judgment of disobedience and rebellion and can influence our physical, mental and spiritual well-being.

Oaths. Closely aligned with curses are oaths. Oaths are promises that are sometimes connected to a curse, as in, "I swear that I will do this, and if I don't . . ." (Gen 24:41; 1 Sam 14:24). Oaths were taken very seriously (Ex 20:7; Lev 19:12), and lying about an oath could result in death (Ezek 17:16, 18). Jesus bound himself with an oath in Matthew 26:63-64. Paul did so in 2 Corinthians 1:23 and Galatians 1:20. Even God bound himself by oath to keep his promises to Abraham, as seen in Hebrews 6:13-18. The power of these oaths, like curses, can span lifetimes, even generations. In all cases, an individual is voluntarily constrained by swearing an oath. "I will never allow myself to be put in a position to be hurt like that again." "There is no way that I will ever trust anybody again."

Soul ties. Other spiritual connections also develop between people. For lack of a better term, these are called "soul ties" or "hooks." These are demonically based sexual, emotional or spiritual attachments between one person and another or between a spirit and a person. Colossians 3:5 connects fornication, uncleanliness, inordinate affection, evil concupiscence and covetousness to idolatry (KJV). Scripture also suggests that the attachment that occurs during sexual intercourse is more than physical. It can be a positive connection such as the "one flesh" principle mentioned in Genesis 2:24, or a negative connection, as when the apostle Paul references the connection between young men and prostitutes (1 Cor 6:16).

Occult involvement. Involvement with the occult was a capital offense in Bible times; God hated it. Deuteronomy 18:10-11 says, "Let no one be found among you who sacrifices their son or daughter in the fire, who practices divination or sorcery, interprets omens, engages in witchcraft, or casts spells, or who is a medium or spiritist or who consults the dead." We often fail to take the occult seriously. This is one of the more challenging areas of deliverance because the client actively sought out demonic involvement. Many times demonic spirits will claim ownership because the client sought them out. Refer to Isaiah 8:19; Jeremiah 27:9; 29:8; Zechariah 10:2; Acts 16:16-18 for more information.

Traumatic experiences or victimization. Aside from the trauma of an initial assault, one's response to the assault is just as significant. Practices that result in a person's losing or surrendering control over their mind and body may result in demonic infestation. Such practices include drug and alcohol abuse; meditation or trance states; hypnotism; and situations that may cause tremendous fear or a sense of violation or trauma, such as rape or deep fear of rape, incest, molestation or abuse. With such a large portion of our population having been abused at some point in their lifetime, this is one of the most common open doors for demonization, particularly among women.

Long-term sin and disobedience to God's will. Any long-term disobedience to God's Word opens a person up to demonic involvement. This would particularly include sins where a person has made a decision to pursue a course of behavior that the individual knew was contrary to God's Word. Ephesians 4:26-27 tells us: "'In your anger do not sin': Do not let the sun go down while you are still angry, and do not give the devil a foothold." This verse refers to a situation in which a person chooses to sin and maintain that sin for a period of time. Long-term failure to yield to the Word of God may result in demonic involvement.

When God Steps In

During deliverance God shows up and radically encounters the client. As Christians we bring to the table the power of the name of our resurrected Lord and his delegated authority. If God doesn't show up, we might as well go home. While experience is valuable in that it gives us insight into the strategies of the enemy (2 Cor 10:10-11), no demon ever left because we think we know what we are doing or because we become emotionally or physically aggressive.

Each individual session is unique. God moves in ways that appear to match the needs of the client. The client finds that the demon will communicate with them when commanded to do so in the name of Jesus. Some spirits will speak to them in their minds, though for many the voice is quiet. Other times the client will have the necessary information spelled out for them in their mind's eye. Others yet will see pictures as some drama is being played out before them. Often the communication sounds like the client's own thoughts.

Sometimes the client will experience physical manifestations. They will experience sudden pain in different parts of their body: headaches or eye pain, pressure in their chests, or numbness on different portions of their bodies. Sometimes they will begin to shake or become violent, depending upon the level of demonization. Fortunately, these manifestations are rare, and I have never evidenced the horrific behavior (heads spinning, levitating, projectile vomiting) seen in many movies about deliverance.

Sometimes nothing visible happens; there are no visible manifestations. All the client becomes aware of is the small voice of the demonic spirit, an impression or a feeling that communicates to them what the demons have been commanded to communicate. As strange as this may sound, experiencing no significant manifestation often causes the client distress, in that they are expecting something spectacular to happen. A quiet and intense "counseling" session was not what they were expecting.

Sometimes the Lord shows up in unexpected supernatural ways in the work that the counselor is doing (e.g., the spiritual gifts—1 Cor 12). The counselor may have key unknown issues in the life of the client revealed, "knowing" things about which they have no knowledge. They may hear the words that the demons are saying, or be able to repeat what the Holy Spirit has just spoken to the client.

An additional factor that could also be described as "supernatural" in many respects has received comment from the many therapists who attend our sessions for the purpose of observation and/or training. They all note that within our normal session, we have reached a depth of discovery that they would rarely reach after more than a year of following standard counseling protocols.

All of these examples of God "showing up" and "transforming" the client encounter would be at best interesting were long term cognitive, affective and behavioral change not associated with the experience. Long-term anecdotal evidence would suggest that such a change does occur in a very high percentage of the clients with whom we work.

How God Steps In

The step-by-step process reflected in the following methodology appears to be sequential but may incorporate a series of differing feedback loops. In addition, and this is very strange for a counseling technique, it is important to recognize that little or no client information is necessary for this spiritual intervention to be successful. Since it is the Holy Spirit who is doing the intervention, he already knows all that can be known about the client. As therapists our job is not to "figure the client out," but to learn to listen to the direction of the Holy Spirit. Following is a brief summary of the standard model that we use in deliverance.

1. ***Brief assessment.*** When introduced to clients with whom we have had no contact prior to the session, we ask them to give us a five-minute summary of their presenting problem before we begin to work. God reveals what we need to know for the client to be free during the process. While training in counseling and psychology may be very helpful in understanding context, it is not necessary for the intervention to take place (consider the disciples!).
2. ***Prayer.*** In this prayer, we ask the Lord to forgive us our sins, give us whatever spiritual gifts we may need, protect us from whatever we may encounter in the deliverance and be allowed to join him in his ministry to our client.
3. ***Giving and receiving forgiveness.*** We address the issue of forgiveness, referencing Matthew 6:12-14, where Jesus tells us that if we don't forgive others he won't forgive us. We emphasize that forgiveness is not a feeling or emotion; it is a decision that becomes a fact.
4. ***Breaking curses, oaths and soul ties.*** In prayer, we break the power of generational curses, ungodly oaths, and ungodly attachments or soul ties. We also ask the client to renounce any occult demons or curses, family demons or curses, or assigned demons or curses. These are powers that dwell outside the client but who appear to empower the spirits who dwell within.
5. ***Determining demonic names.*** Command the ruling demon to give its name (Mk 5:9; Lk 8:30). We tell the client to tell us the first thing that comes into their mind following the command without filtering, discounting, trying to put it into a context, etc.

6. ***Confronting demonic tasks and associated lies.*** Command the ruling demon to tell us what it does. The Scripture records numerous times that a demonic spirit was a spirit "of" something. For example, in Hosea 4:12 and 5:4 are references to a spirit of prostitution. In Zechariah 13:2 it is a spirit of impurity. In Isaiah 19:14 it is a spirit of dizziness. Jeremiah 51:1 refers to the spirit of a destroyer. Sometimes their names are descriptive of the work they do (prostitution, destruction, etc.) and other times they are not (Bob, Frank, Sarah, Mary, etc.). Demonic spirits have specific tasks. We keep a record of both the demon's name and its task for the client. We do not question demons out of personal curiosity.
7. ***Confronting the demonic "chain of command."*** Demand the name of the demons that are attached to the ruling demon (both inside and outside the individual) and find out what they do. Demons tend to have a "chain of command" with the ruling spirit having multiple subordinates.
8. ***Facilitating client renunciation.*** Lead the client in a statement of renunciation of the demon in the name of Jesus.
9. ***Facilitating client command to leave.*** Lead the client as the client commands the demon to leave in the name of Jesus.
10. ***Facilitating a prayer of repentance.*** Lead the client in a prayer of repentance in which the client asks the Lord to forgive him/her for whatever he/she did to open the door to the demonic spirit.
11. ***Cast the demon out.*** Cast the demon out in the name of Jesus.
12. ***Do process over until all demons are gone.*** Go back and command the now-ruling demon to give us its name and task. Find who is attached to him. Do this process again and again until nothing responds to the command for a name.
13. ***Facilitate prayer for God's fullness.*** Pray that the Lord will fill this now-empty house (Lk 11:21-26).
14. ***Give clear instructions for aftercare.*** Review what the client can expect in the days ahead and what they can do to keep themselves demon-free (Jas 4:7).

Conclusion: A Gift to the Church

The ministry of deliverance is becoming increasingly well received by the Christian community as the powers of darkness seek the destruction of believers and the church.

Jethani (2012) writes:

> We have an enemy that is active and cunning. Rather than arguing about whether this enemy resides in a personal demonic presence or the corrosive power of the world's system, we should be asking God to help us see the terrible effects of this enemy among our people. Whatever the precise source, when we acknowledge that the excrement in our church is no less vile than in the surrounding community, it should humble us to see that we need a power beyond ourselves to overcome it. (p. 2)

The Spring 2012 issue of *Leadership Journal*, a publication of Christianity Today International, was given entirely to the topic of spiritual warfare. I believe that their willingness to address this topic represents a significant shift within our church culture. However, being driven by a need for personal freedom or freedom for our clients doesn't mean that we are entirely willing to surrender our desire to reframe spiritual warfare in general, or deliverance in particular, in ways that are compatible with our personal and clinical preferences. We want deliverance to be about something with which we are at least somewhat familiar, about lies rather than spiritual personages. We know how to handle cognitive distortions; we have a framework and a theology for that. We want to believe that we can counsel the client, find the distortion, retrain the client and see the client find freedom. We want truth to be the only thing that we need to see people set free (Jn 8:32), and we want freedom to come in a neat package that can be easily incorporated into church programs and Christian counseling centers. We don't want to either talk to or confront demonic spirits. The problem arises in that we know many people who know the truth of the gospel, who seek to walk in that truth, who do their best to resist the enemy, but who still find themselves in bondage.

Jesus and his disciples were aggressive in their taking the battle to the enemy. Jesus practiced the power encounter. He modeled it to his disciples and they, in turn, trained the church in the same way. The message was clear. There is a new Boss in town. The kingdom of God has come. The stronger man has come and taken ownership of the house and of all the strong man's possessions (Lk 11:21-22). We are taking back this territory because we are told to do so and because we can. The demons must submit to us. We have been given authority to trample on snakes and scorpions and to overcome all the power of the enemy; nothing can harm us (Lk 10:17-19).

In my work I deal with the lies that the enemy tells people every day. However, the lie is not the demon. It is the doorway through which the enemy enters. Both the lie and the demon need to be addressed in the deliverance process. If the counselor does not address the lie the door remains open for ongoing demonic attack. Addressing the lie and the demon together increases the likelihood of long-term freedom.

Some say that they prefer the method of deliverance Paul used, rather than the one found in the Gospels. They prefer what they call a "post-resurrection model": one that suggests that after the resurrection the enemy's power was lessened and freedom could come from standing in Christ and resisting the enemy. They point to Paul as a model. Yet it was Paul, and his "principalities and powers" language (Eph 6:12), who broadened the church's understanding of spiritual warfare beyond physical and psychological attacks on individuals to include attacks on churches and cultures as well (Twelftree, 2007).

Paul's apparent lack of interest in the subject of ministry is not because he considers the topic unimportant, but because of

> the epistolic and occasional nature of his writing . . . what he saw as the internal focus or use of the charismata. That is, in dealing with internal matters in his letters—not often touching on the church in relation to the outside world—it is not surprising that his references to exorcism should be cryptic to us, though perhaps clear to those who had experienced his ministry and were involved in a word-and-deed ministry in the world. (Twelftree, 2007, p. 77)

Paul describes the mark of an apostle in 2 Corinthians 12:12, namely signs, wonders and miracles. These acts, he says, he did among the church with great perseverance. Paul knew that Jesus conducted signs, wonders and miracles. It would be reasonable to assume that deliverance was part of that ministry, even as it was part of Jesus' ministry. Twelftree (2007) (pointing to Rom 15:19; 1 Cor 2:5; 4:20; 15:43) says that "Paul is probably saying not so much that his ministry was attested by signs and wonders, but that his ministry was conducted on the basis of, or strength of, the miracles (or Spirit)" (p. 66). Paul's ministry, like that of Jesus, rose out of the miraculous—out of the power of the Spirit. Just as Jesus' ministry was miracle based, so was Paul's. Jesus reported that he could only do what he saw his Father doing (Jn 5:19). Paul wanted to do the same thing. He wanted to do what he saw his Father doing. The same thing should be true for us.

What the Father was doing, both before and after the resurrection of Jesus, was bringing transformational life to his children. He is doing the same thing today. Deliverance is a Christian practice that has been a part of the church's ministry for two millennia. It can and is being incorporated into Christian counseling in ways that result in healing, in freedom and in new life and hope for clients that is expressed in truly life-changing ways. *Disclaimer: Licensed mental health professionals have been known to have their licenses removed for doing deliverance. Referral to a deliverance specialist is recommended.*

References and Recommended Resources

Appleby, D. (2009). *It's only a demon: A model of Christian deliverance.* Winona Lake, IN: BMH Books.

Bufford, R. K. (1988). *Counseling and the demonic.* Dallas: Word Publishing.

Dickason, C. F. (1989). *Demon possession and the Christian: A new perspective.* Wheaton, IL: Crossway.

Jethani, S. (2012, Spring). Winged Enemies. *Leadership Journal.* Retrieved from <www.christianitytoday.com/le/2012/spring/wingedenemies.html>.

Kraft, C. (1992). *Defeating dark angels.* Ann Arbor, MI: Servant Publications.

Lewis, C. S. (1947). *Miracles.* New York: Macmillan.

MacNutt, F. (1995). *Deliverance from evil spirits: A practical manual.* Tarrytown, NY: Chosen Books.

Murphy, E. (1992). *The handbook of spiritual warfare.* Nashville: Thomas Nelson.

Otis, G. (1997). *The twilight labyrinth: Why does spiritual darkness linger where it does?* Grand Rapids: Baker.

Prince, D. (1990). *Blessings and curses: You can choose.* Tarrytown, NY: Chosen Books.

Prince, D. (1998). *They shall expel demons: What you need to know about demons—your invisible enemy.* Tarrytown, NY: Chosen Books.

Spiritual Interventions, Inc. <www.spiritualinterventions.org>.

Twelftree, G. (2007). *In the name of Jesus: Exorcism among early Christians.* Grand Rapids: Baker Academic.

Unger, M. (1953). *Biblical demonology.* Wheaton, IL: Tyndale.

Unger, M. (1991). *What demons can do to saints.* Chicago: Moody Press.

5

Transformative Interventions in Biblical Counseling

Edward T. Welch

Biblical counseling strives to be ordinary. We aim for our theology and method to be shaped by Scripture, which should result in spectacular, attractive, penetrating and transformative counseling. How could it be otherwise if you counsel with Scripture? Yet our goal is still decidedly ordinary. By this we mean that we want our interventions to be accessible, so that any motivated and growing Christian could do them, and we want them to be transferable to everyday life, so that there is no divide between what we might say in a counseling office and what we would say to a friend over dinner. We see ourselves as applied theologians, as are all of us in the body of Christ.

Basic Principles

When we try to identify the guiding principles of biblical counseling, it means that we are identifying the most prominent theological propositions that animate our counseling, which is a very helpful exercise. Differences along the Christian counseling spectrum most likely can be reduced not just to our formal propositions but also to how we prioritize those propositions (Welch & Powlison, 1997a, 1997b). Here are my top three.

Everything is personal. "Personal" is crammed with meaning. It means that we are not citizens who live in a country in which there are thousands of fastidious laws and omnipresent prying eyes. It means that at the heart of the Christian faith is the God who reveals himself to us most fully in Jesus, and we—creatures who are like him—can understand, respond to, enjoy and be changed by him. Then he is moved by us and responds, and the cycle continues.

We have taken our cue, in part, from Herman Ridderbos's book *Paul: An Outline of His Theology* (1975), where he observed that Paul followed the traditional biblical pattern and went from indicative to imperative. That is, he first wrote about who Jesus is and what he has done, then he identified the implications of that truth for how we live. The Father takes the initiative; we respond, either for or against. We respond with joy, humility, worship, love, trust and appropriate fear, or with indifference, lukewarm hearts, rebellion and inappropriate fear. Life, at its very foundation, is about spiritual allegiances: personal responses to our Creator and Rescuer. George MacDonald, referencing G. K. Chesterton (1908), made the observation that those who enter a brothel are looking for God. Whether they are looking for him or running from him, MacDonald emphasized the personal, before-God nature of life. Life is lived *coram deo,* before the face of God.

People might respond to pain by running from him. A superficial and prescriptive "biblical" approach would say "Stop it" or "Be controlled by the Spirit rather than the flesh." In contrast, a personal approach might ask, "Whom do you love?"

From there, Scripture comes alive with possibilities. For example, a passage about idolatry from Isaiah 44:19-21 suddenly becomes an up-to-date analysis of addiction. It could be paraphrased like this:

> You worship a bottle [an image, a pill]. Beware, the object of your affection is a liar. It promises satisfaction, but it delivers emptiness (ashes)—any relationship with something inanimate will be empty. It promises life, yet it delivers death—when you commit your life to a dead god you become like your god. You forget that the living God made you and that you belong to him alone. Since you belong to him, he will not forget you. Even now he pursues you in love.

Biblical counseling would then highlight the knowledge of God. How can we turn from something we love and worship unless we can turn to something or someone better?

This is a sample of how biblical counseling applies "everything is personal before God." This principle also extends to the relationship between counselor and client. As God is personal, so are we. This means that counseling will be back and forth; both client and counselor moved and influenced.

When I first started counseling, my colleagues and I sat behind desks—big desks. Insightful students would occasionally ask why we did that, and our stock reply would be that we needed big desks so we could take notes, which was true but only in part. The desk also represented an implicit medical paradigm in biblical counseling that had ascendency in the early 1980s. That is, the counselor was the physician, the counselee the patient, and the counselor's job was to make an accurate diagnosis and write out the appropriate prescription. As we absorbed the personal and Jesus-centered nature of Scripture, the desks gradually made their way to a corner. Our method aligned with our more personal theology.

Scripture offers a comprehensive "psychology" and "psychotherapy." This is the principle for which biblical counseling is best known. But here is also where we think we are most ordinary. We expect Scripture to reveal the deepest understanding of people—how we are fashioned, why we are broken and how we can be refashioned. Therefore, we want Scripture to invade everything we do, which includes every academic discipline. There are some things we do and there are some disciplines to which Scripture speaks more fully than others. For example, Scripture speaks more about murder than it does exercise, and it speaks more about our understanding of what motivates people than it does microbiology and geology, but the Creator has claims on everything and his words give true and deeper meaning to all things.

What does Scripture say about modern problems such as Asperger's, bipolar disorder and eating disorders, all of which can be quite complicated and are not obviously addressed in Scripture? The study of human nature compels us to humility. Yet even when the person in front of us is enigmatic, we know that we have the Spirit, and as we pray for wisdom from the Spirit, we receive wisdom. Included in this wisdom are the insights of church history, the larger body of Christ and the world around us.

Scripture and secular observations. This emphasis on Scripture has contributed, in part, to the perception that biblical counselors are obscurantists who avoid secular observations. More accurately, however, we are led by the principle that God speaks to everything, and our instincts are to relentlessly mine Scripture. As a result, our writings tend to be heavier on Scripture than on secular research, though these ratios can be influenced by the topic. For example, mania might drive us to secular literature sooner than anger. Yet even with mania, which is not specifically identified in Scripture, we still want Scripture to hold court. In this case that hegemony could mean that we are *embodied* souls. Mania challenges us to unpack the embodied nature of our existence, which we do through Internet research, memoirs, technical studies about mania and friends who struggle with it.

From there, we go back and forth: knowing the person, searching how Scripture speaks to that person's experience. Meanwhile, one of Scripture's nuggets is that mania cannot morally incapacitate us, though it can make wise living very difficult. For example, when we cannot imagine negative consequences, which is characteristic of mania, we might be more prone to pursue risky and foolish paths. Also, mania is quite confident. It is happy to talk but less inclined to listen. After all, why listen when you have superhuman insight? The path of wisdom demands an unusually mature faith in these conditions. I'll say more on this in the next section.

Comprehensive, not exhaustive. We do not believe that Scripture gives exhaustive theory and method for all the problems of life. Such a system is not possible and, if it were, it certainly would not be biblical. An exhaustive and fully detailed system would leave us smug in our own understanding. Prayer and faith would be a mere formality, a giving thanks for all the knowledge we have received rather than a cry for help.

Our distinctive is not that we avoid secular insights. Our distinctive is that we persevere in bringing Scripture's oversight into our counseling theory and practice.

Our struggles are with sin and suffering. Since Scripture says so much, we are always looking for ways to simplify, which Scripture itself does with summaries such as "love God and love your neighbor." One way to simplify our problems is to see them in two larger categories: sin and suffering.

> Look on my affliction and my distress
> and take away all my sins. (Ps 25:18)

Sin is "any want of conformity unto, or transgression of, the law of God" (Westminster Shorter Catechism, Q.14). To put it more personally, sin is when we opt for our own kingdom rather than live in our Father's, or it is when we dishonor our Father and live for our own desires, and we can find it with only a cursory survey of our own hearts.

Suffering includes the sins of others against us, the deleterious effects of weaknesses in the body and brain, and the afflictions we can experience at Satan's hand.

As with sin, every day will impose the brand of suffering on every human being. Note that weaknesses of the body and brain are included in suffering. Biblical counseling has had an agenda to understand the body and its various afflictions since its inception (Emlet, 2002; Welch, 1991, 1998). Here it is again: we are spiritual (souls), and we are embodied.

Consider mania once more. One common accompaniment to mania is extramarital sex. A useful implication of a theology of embodied souls is that violations of God's commands are matters of the heart. The body cannot make us sin. The body can make life miserable, but it is never the locus of sin. "The spirit is willing, but the body is weak" (Mt 26:41 NIV 1984). At their worst, souls sin and bodies suffer. This means that adultery is not simply the mania talking. A person who belongs to Jesus, and is therefore committed to sexual boundaries, will not be sexually reckless while manic. To excuse sinful behavior as a chemical imbalance is to render us subhuman.

Yet biblical counseling does acknowledge that our physical bodies can certainly complicate our lives. They can bless us with health or curse us with mental confusion and unprovoked emotions. Such brain differences do not relieve us from the human tasks of growing in wisdom, faith and obedience, but they certainly encourage patience among those who want to love and help. In mania, we assume that the brain is temporarily "weak," and we suspect that this particular weakness includes a strong dose of chemical courage that makes someone less able to process social cues. In other words, if a person's morality was controlled by the opinions of others instead of the fear of the Lord—"I won't be adulterous because I will get in trouble with my wife"—then adultery will be a natural consequence of mania.

The challenge with this principle—that our struggles are with sin and suffering—comes when we move from theory to practice. It is not easy to know when to talk about suffering and when to talk about sin.

Scripture itself resists predictable ministry approaches. Sometimes it leads with sin, other times with suffering. Sometimes God focuses on sin when we might expect him to stress mitigating circumstances, such as a harsh wilderness (e.g., Num 14:11). Sometimes he identifies the difficult circumstances even though his people live in blatant idolatry (e.g., Jer 23).

Sometimes he asks us to keep both suffering and sin in mind (e.g., Heb 12:1).

The Good, the Hard and the Bad

Given the Scripture's resistance to predictable ministry approaches, counselors make judgments that cannot always be determined in advance. As a general rule, biblical counseling follows these priorities: first see the good in the person, then the hard and then the bad.

With the *good* we are following the apostle Paul's pattern: "I always thank my God for you because of his grace given you in Christ Jesus" (1 Cor 1:4). This was the first thing he said to a group that was not doing well. Next, we are especially attentive to suffering (the *hard*). Our primary goal is not to uncover sin but to know Christ, and we can get to Jesus from any starting point. Then, when we talk about sin—the *bad*—we have already seen the bad in ourselves and we know that the bad can become a redemptive good. Sinning, of course, is not good, but being able to see sin and forgiveness are gifts from the Spirit, and those are very good.

Compassion Above All Else

While priorities can quickly change, compassion is the sine qua non of counseling. God's fullest self-revelation in the Old Testament was when he proclaimed to Moses, "The Lord, the Lord, the compassionate and gracious God" (Ex 34:6). This was while the people were worshiping other gods and pining away for Egypt. It is not the only thing God says to his people, but it is the first thing, and that makes it the priority in biblical counseling.

My Story

Everyone has a story behind his or her counseling or therapeutic practice (Moriarty & Collins, 2010; Worthington, 2010), and these stories are essential if we are to have profitable discussion across the Christian counseling spectrum. Our personal stories place our interests and emphases in a context. With that in mind, here are a few relevant pieces of my own story.

I always had people interests, so I decided to major in psychology in college with tentative plans to become a psychologist. Psychology, however, did not satisfy those interests. Its questions were engaging but its answers lacking. As a result, I found myself interested in the "hard science" side of psychology, where clinical relevance was sketchy but observations were reliable. I considered a move toward medicine, though I was concerned that it would be too mechanistic for my tastes. One month before I graduated from college, I converted to Christianity and everything changed. I decided to postpone graduate school plans and matriculate in a seminary in order to learn how Scripture could infuse whatever I did.

Exposure to and embrace of biblical counseling. While in seminary I read Jay Adams's *Competent to Counsel* (1970) and then had the opportunity to observe counseling at the Christian Counseling and Educational Foundation. My people interests were reignited. Christian counseling was a fledgling movement in those days, so what I read and saw seemed radical and new. I didn't anticipate that Scripture could speak with such depth into the details of everyday life.

After seminary and then graduate work in psychology, I accepted a counseling and teaching position at CCEF, which is where I am now. When I came to CCEF there were two related movements that had their impetus from Jay Adams's seminal book. One was the National Association of Nouthetic Counseling (NANC), which aimed to stay within the boundaries of Jay's teaching. The other was CCEF, which never identified itself as Nouthetic but steered a more moderate course under the leadership of Jay's early partner, John Bettler. The work at CCEF soon became known as biblical counseling with a small *b*, as a way to say that we did not own the domain name.

When I came to CCEF there were only a few books that represented its position, but there was a maturing educational program, and two of the three principles mentioned here were well established: Scripture speaks to everything, and our struggle is with sin and suffering. The other—everything is personal—which we now consider to be primary, took a few years to emerge out of our understanding of biblical theology. Its basic idea was simple: all Scripture is about Jesus (Lk 24:27).

Jesus-centered theology. Scripture contains laws, songs, poems, laments, lists, stories and prophecies, and all those genres ultimately are about Jesus, the Alpha and Omega of life. That was the start. Then desks went into corners, we became less predictable in counseling because everything about Jesus is not what we would expect, we encouraged our students to enjoy counselees, and our counseling looked more and more like everyday life rather than a professional consultation. After more than thirty years of counseling and teaching biblical counseling, my enthusiasm for the systematic application of Scripture to life continues to grow.

Biblical Counseling in Action

Biblical counseling doesn't have specific steps. As in most human relationships, we can script our initial greetings and not much else. We do, however, have a goal. We want to offer the wisdom and encouragement that comes from the gospel of Jesus, and we have a basic map for how to get there. We want to hear about the places where the person feels stuck or hurt. We want to engage and respond personally to what we hear and, together, discover more details of Scripture's retelling of the person's story.

Accessing Scripture. The challenge is to identify biblical themes that are suited for this retelling with the client. A concordance will only take us so far, and without promising means of accessing Scripture we have little incentive to search it. This, I suspect, is an area for important discussion among Christians who do counseling and therapy.

One strategy is to identify themes within the account of creation, the fall and the exodus from Egypt. Scripture builds on these three events. In creation we learn that everything is referenced to the Lord. He made all things so all things belong to him. The world is personal. It always points us to the Creator, our final reference point.

In the fall, sin opened our eyes to our nakedness before other people and blinded us to our nakedness before God. But when God shows up in the garden, we discover that our human-to-human nakedness points to our much more troubling before-God nakedness. One is embarrassing, the other is lethal. In response, the Lord begins the long process of redemption.

The third category, which includes the exodus from Egypt and the wilderness wandering, is rich with counseling material on both suffering and sin. Much biblical thought on suffering borrows the wilderness theme: there are hardships and dangers galore; these hardships become the occasion for all kinds of temptations; God is with us in the wilderness; Jesus won the battle with temptations; and the Spirit will empower us in our battle.

The horizontal reveals the vertical. A theme is introduced in Numbers 14 in which the people are grumbling and complaining against Moses and Aaron and threaten to go back to Egypt. There is no mention of the

Lord. As far as the people can tell, their quarrel is with their human leaders. Moses, however, reminds the people of the true explanation of their behavior: "Do not rebel against the Lord" (Num 14:9; cf. Num 5:6). This is followed by the Lord's even more scathing assessment in Numbers 14:11: "How long will these people treat me with contempt?"

This theme is by no means a cornerstone of biblical counseling, but it is useful and illustrates one way of accessing Scripture. As such, consider some of its applications. From this theme, complaining has become a common test case in our counseling classes. We come back to the topic because we can find it in ourselves, we can easily excuse it, we are often blind to the before-God core of it, and Scripture's penetrating gaze reveals things that we could never have discovered on our own yet make perfect sense when we can finally see.

When we grouse about the long line in the mall or the hidden cell phone charges, we are not complaining against the Lord, as far as we know. Yet we experience the world as fundamentally personal. Little do we realize that we are holding God in contempt, saying, "What have you done for me recently?" We are, implicitly, exalting our desires and saying that God should be the servant of our desires.

The horizontal reveals the vertical: our daily lives—our thoughts, actions, relationship, work or leisure—reveal our relationship with Jesus Christ. The horizontal (our relationships with people) reveals the vertical (our relationship with the Lord). If we want to examine our spiritual growth, we should ignore what propositions we believe. We might even gloss over the status of our spiritual disciplines, at least at first. We simply watch the way we live.

"The horizontal reveals the vertical" also has a more positive expression. Contentment in difficult circumstances points to our satisfaction in the Father. Jesus gives other illustrations of this connection. He points out that some people will reveal godliness in their lives and they might not even know it (cf. Mt 10:40; 25:37-40). In such situations, counselors have the privilege and obligation to identify this stealth glory.

There are things we can see with the naked eye. We can see kindness and mercy, bitterness and retaliation. Secular psychology observes this and much else. But all those things that are seen with the naked eye are only seen in part. They need revelation so they can be interpreted by what is unseen. Only Scripture, applied by the Spirit, allows us to see life in three dimensions in which we see ourselves, our relationships with other people, and our relationship that animates everything else—our relationship with the Creator and Redeemer.

Case Studies

Any mini intervention worth its salt has first intervened in the counselor's life and is still intervening. That is the story of my uneasy relationship with the wilderness principle of how the horizontal reveals the vertical. It works for me. It reveals me. It orients. It directs. It has been used by the Spirit to change me.

The theme applied to the counselor. For example, I don't tend to be an ostensibly bad person. If you followed me around on a normal day, you would not find seething anger, slanderous remarks or a stash of porn. I am, for the most part, nice. I am not proud of that, but that's the way it is. My wife is nice too. She is a more sanctified version of nice than I am. But every once in a while she says something to which I take offense. In response, I get quiet, turn away and wait for her to see the error of her ways.

Then this particular principle comes rushing in: What have you [my wife and the Lord] done for me recently? I review the scenario and consider my own heart. I am silent and turned away. I am punishing my wife.

Lord, have mercy. "Sheri, please forgive me."

But I am not done. The horizontal reveals the vertical. I know what my turning away says about my relationship with my wife. What does it say about my relationship with the triune God?

It says that I am a good guy who needs less grace than most people. Being nice, I can judge those who are not as nice. I prefer to be God rather than give judgments to him. I am indifferent to how God relentlessly pursues me. He is turned toward me, even when I turn away from others. I hold his grace and mercy to me in contempt. And the list could go on.

I acknowledged my wrong to my wife, which is a good thing, but most anyone who takes marriage seriously could do that. In itself it is good but not transformative. It becomes life-changing as I recognize that my actions toward my wife have been actions of contempt toward the Lord—my life is about me and my personal kingdom. I can then seek forgiveness for the sin beneath the sin, and set off to be amazed at the ways of God with his people. All true change must travel through the person of Jesus.

A useful theme that was not useful. A forty-year-old married mother of three, who worked in the church nursery, came for counseling/mediation because of conflict with a coworker. She was furious because the coworker asked her to retrieve one of the children and give the child to a waiting parent.

"The nursery rules are clear. That is the doorkeeper's responsibility!" Her coworker was in the midst of changing a dirty diaper. The horizontal reveals the vertical. What we see in a relationship with a coworker will reveal the relationship with the Lord.

Here is dialogue from our fifth session together:

"I was wondering if you might use rules as a way to keep your distance from relationships. Love can be messy, and sometimes we trust in rules as a way to avoid that messiness."

"Yes, I do that." Her response was immediate and matter-of-fact.

"Then here is something even more important than what happened in the nursery: If you use nursery protocol as a way to distance yourself from people, you can use God's laws as a way to distance yourself from God. The deal you have brokered with God is that you do the right thing and he leaves you alone."

She nodded, as if I was stating the obvious. I had articulated her true religion. Insight can lead to transformation, but only if there is a willing heart. In this case, insight was meaningless. She was committed to her religion. There was nothing else to do. The coworker—though mystified at first by her coworker's response to what was apparently an egregious sin—did apologize, the woman returned to the nursery, relationships became more formal and other coworkers walked on eggshells, which is exactly what the counselee wanted. The world had been put back on its axis. Rules were clear, the law of love with all of its unpredictable corollaries was packed away, her deistic god was conveniently distant and busy with other matters, and she was content to live with that fragile and false peace.

A theme used to bear fruit. A thirty-five-year-old single man had been in and out of psychiatric hospitals since high school. Paranoid schizophrenia, bipolar, schizo-affective and borderline personality disorder were a few of his diagnoses. The presenting problem was that he came to a church small group in a suspicious frame of mind and quickly began accusing group members of slander and telling the group leader that he was not even a Christian.

The group responded masterfully. They tried to affirm their love for him and clarify their motives. These comments, of course, only inflamed him, but the group persisted in humility and patience.

Here is dialogue from our first meeting after I heard his story about being in the group:

"Yikes, you must be feeling accused right and left. One accusation. Then another. Sure, you experience accusations from other people, but that is no big deal compared to the accusations you feel before the Lord. Those accusations are the real issue, are they not?"

"Man, no matter what I do I always feel condemned." He was talking about his relationship with the Lord. His sense that other people accused him was simply an echo of how he never felt okay before the Lord. From there we could unpack the cross and its implications. While we were enemies, Christ died for us. When we are faithless, he remains faithful. We are cleansed by his blood, not by our attempts to try harder. The hardest thing to do in the Christian life is simply to believe what God says.

Without any direction from me, he asked forgiveness of the group and asked them to pray that he would discern satanic accusations and rest in the righteousness that comes from faith. In one sense his behavior in the small group was the schizophrenia talking. But he intuitively knew that "weakness" is never an excuse for sinful behavior, so he confessed his actions to the group and they forgave him with joy, and they used it as a time to confess their own sins.

Then we settled into ordinary yet supernatural conversations about how God's forgiveness and love have no human analogy. They are truly holy. We took turns applying passages in Hebrews about our High Priest who sat down because there was nothing left to do. The final, perfect and pleasing sacrifice had already been made. This client still can be taken off guard by what he believes are the subliminal accusations of others, but he can quickly be pointed to the deeper matter of his relationship with God through Jesus. For someone living with some of the most difficult diagnoses in mental health, such insight is truly transformational.

The Breadth of Biblical Counseling

It is precarious to pick one principle and a few case studies to demonstrate biblical counseling in action because there are dozens of identifiable methods we use, and we find that these methods apply to the broad scope of human problems.

We think of biblical counseling as a regular feature of everyday life. It extends to work, leisure, relationships, goals and daily hardships. We are working to show its application to the DSM categories of modern psychiatry (CCEF, 2011). And we are eager to bring the themes of Scripture to the new problems that seem to emerge in each decade, from the Dissociative Identity Disorder (Welch, 1995) in the 1980s to the gaming addictions of today.

This is not to say that biblical counseling has secretly been curing the world's psychological and psychiatric problems. We cannot promise anything beyond what Scripture promises. For example, Scripture offers no guarantee that the various means of grace will cure schizophrenia, mania or attention deficit disorder. In other words, Scripture does not promise that following Christ will relieve the hardships of life. Instead, it may often intensify hardships. We do believe, however, that the application of Scripture to the problems of life can lead to sanctifying fruitfulness, a growing faith, a clear conscience, peace, a renewed sense of belonging, hope and love.

Future Directions

Biblical counseling is a work in progress. In this decade we are especially interested in having our method catch up to our theory. Our classes, books and articles tend to be theologically rich, but our case studies can sound wooden and one-dimensional. As such, we want to illustrate the more personal and relational features of biblical counseling as well as its creative and improvisational character.

We also hope to correct biblical counseling's public relations problem. Specifically, we find that the broader field of Christian counseling identifies us as fundamentalists, perceived as primarily and aggressively antipsychology. In response, we hope to communicate that nuances of integration will always be important, but from our perspective, biblical anthropology and methods of accessing Scripture are where we could have more useful conversations. Most Christians agree on the basics of the integration issue: we must be careful in the way we use secular data. We believe that the focus on integration has marginalized other critical discussions.

Meanwhile, we want to become more ordinary, which is a loaded word. It includes simple but not simplistic, obvious and intuitive but never what we would expect, and accessible but with endless depth. It is worthy of pages of explanation but able to be summarized in a sentence, such as Christ and him crucified.

"Ordinary" can be done by friends over coffee, but is accompanied by a research and development agenda that will last as long as human beings experience sin and suffering. In this sense, biblical counseling aspires to be ordinary, though we know that goal will always be just barely out of reach because our models can see God dimly, not in the brightness of his glory, and can only approximate Scripture and never capture it fully.

References and Recommended Resources

CCEF is the primary locus for research and development in biblical counseling. CCEF.org provides weekly postings of blogs, short articles and videos. The site also includes longer articles from and information about the *Journal of Biblical Counseling*, and it identifies recent books by the primary contributors, which include Michael Emlet, Tim Lane, David Powlison, Winston Smith, Paul Tripp and Ed Welch.

Adams, J. (1970). *Competent to counsel.* Grand Rapids: Zondervan.

CCEF. (2011). *2011 annual conference.* Retrieved from <ccef.org>.

Chesterton, G. K. (1908). The cockneys and all their jokes. *All things considered.* London: Sheed and Ward.

Collins, G. (2010). Foreword. In G. Moriarty & G. Collins (Eds.), *Integrating faith and psychology: Twelve psychologists tell their stories* (pp. 9-15). Downers Grove, IL: IVP Academic.

Emlet, M. (2002). Understanding the influences on the human heart. *The Journal of Biblical Counseling, 20*(2).

Ridderbos, P. (1975). *Paul: An outline of his theology.* Grand Rapids: Eerdmans.

Vos, G. (1975). *Biblical theology.* Carlisle: PA: Banner of Truth.

Welch, E. (1991). *Counselor's guide to the brain and its disorders.* Grand Rapids: Zondervan.

Welch, E. (1995). Biblical insight in multiple personality disorder. *The Journal of Biblical Counseling, 14*(1).

Welch, E. (1998). *Blame it on the brain?* Phillipsburg, NJ: P & R Publishing.

Welch, E., & Powlison, D. (1997a). Every common bush afire with God: The Scripture's constitutive role for counseling. *Journal of Psychology and Christianity, 16*(4).

Welch, E., & Powlison, D. (1997b). Response to Hurley and Berry. *Journal of Psychology and Christianity, 16*(4).

Worthington, E. (2010). *Coming to peace with psychology.* Downers Grove, IL: IVP Academic.

Part Two

TRANSFORMATIVE PARADIGMS FOR CHURCH OR CLINIC

6

Spiritually Oriented Cognitive Behavioral Therapy

A Christian Approach to Transforming People by the Way of Christ

Siang-Yang Tan

Spiritually oriented cognitive behavioral therapy (SO-CBT) is a significant part of religious and spiritual therapies, or R/S therapies, that are also described as religiously accommodative treatments when they have a narrower focus on more specific religious approaches to treatment; for example, conservative Christian or Muslim therapies (see Worthington, Hook, Davis & McDaniel, 2011). In this chapter, I will describe a biblical, Christian approach to SO-CBT (see Tan, 2007, 2011a; Tan & Johnson, 2005; see also Tan, 2013) that can be used to help transform people by the way of Christ.

Christian SO-CBT is only one specific example of many religious and spiritual treatments and interventions that are now available for integrating religion and spirituality in psychotherapy, including cognitive behavioral therapy or CBT (e.g., see Aten, McMinn & Worthington, 2011; McMinn & Campbell, 2007; Pargament, 2007; Plante, 2009; Richards & Bergin, 2000, 2005; Sperry & Shafranske, 2005; Tan, 1996, 2007, 2011a, 2013; Tan & Johnson, 2005; Worthington, Hook, Davis & McDaniel, 2011). Plante (2009), for example, recently described the following thirteen spiritual practices or tools for enhancing psychological health that can be used in SO-CBT, and more specifically Christian SO-CBT: prayer; meditation; meaning, purpose and calling in life; bibliotherapy; attending community services and rituals;

volunteerism and charity; ethical values and behavior; forgiveness, gratitude and kindness; social justice; learning from spiritual models; acceptance of self and others (even with faults); being part of something larger than oneself; and appreciating the sacredness of life. A brief review of CBT and SO-CBT will now be provided before describing a more specific biblical, Christian approach to SO-CBT.

CBT and SO-CBT

CBT in general, or secular CBT, has been defined as "a more purposeful attempt to preserve the demonstrated efficiencies of behavior modification within a less doctrinaire context and to incorporate the cognitive activities of the client in the efforts to produce therapeutic change" (Kendall & Hollon, 1979, p. 1). CBT therefore emphasizes that problem thinking and problem behavior underlie problem feelings such as anxiety, anger and depression. It aims at changing problem feelings by modifying problem thinking and behavior. Cognitive techniques in CBT include cognitive restructuring of maladaptive, dysfunctional, irrational or distorted thinking; imagery techniques; and coping self-talk. Behavioral techniques in CBT include relaxation training, exposure treatments, assertiveness or social skills training, activity scheduling, contingency management, and modeling. CBT has received substantial empirical support for its efficacy with a wide range of psychological disorders (see Butler, Chapman, Forman & Beck, 2006; see also Tan, 2011a).

More recently, contemporary CBT has expanded to include the third wave of behavior therapy (the first wave being traditional behavior therapy and the second wave being traditional CBT) that consists mainly of relatively contextualistic treatment approaches emphasizing mindfulness (i.e., focusing attention on one's immediate experience in the present moment) and acceptance (i.e., with an open, receptive and curious mindset, without judgment or censure) (Hayes, Luoma, Bond, Masuda & Lillis, 2006). The major mindfulness and acceptance-based approaches to CBT (see Roemer & Orsillo, 2009; Shapiro & Carlson, 2009) include Acceptance and Commitment Therapy or ACT (Hayes, Strosahl & Wilson, 2012), Mindfulness-Based Cognitive Therapy or MBCT (Segal, Williams & Teasdale, 2002), and Dialectical Behavior Therapy or DBT (Linehan, 1993). They have some spiritual foundations in Zen Buddhism but can also be consistent with other contemplative spiritual and religious traditions such as Roman

Catholic or Eastern Orthodox. Empirical evidence for their efficacy or effectiveness has grown significantly in recent years (see Shapiro & Carlson, 2009; Tan, 2011b). While they have some spiritual roots, they are not explicitly religious or spiritual therapies and therefore are not usually included in reviews of such therapies (Tan, 2013).

SO-CBT is another recent development in contemporary CBT. It includes more broad-based, nonsectarian, spiritual approaches to CBT as well as more narrowly focused, specific religiously accommodative CBT approaches, including Christian, Muslim, Jewish, Taoist and Buddhist versions (Tan, in press). Religiously accommodative SO-CBT usually includes the use of specific spiritual interventions with religious clients, such as sacred scriptures or writings in cognitive restructuring of dysfunctional thinking, religious imagery for anxiety management, and prayer and scripture reading in session or as homework to help clients cope better with emotional difficulties such as depression, anxiety and anger.

The empirical evidence for the efficacy of SO-CBT approaches has also recently increased. Hook et al. (2010) reviewed twenty-four controlled outcome studies or randomized clinical trials for only mental health problems, for empirically supported spiritual and religious therapies, including SO-CBT. Eighteen of the twenty-four studies focused on SO-CBT. The results showed that Christian accommodative cognitive therapy or CBT for depression and twelve-step facilitation for alcoholism were efficacious, and Muslim CBT for depression as well as anxiety were efficacious when combined with medication. The following religious and spiritual therapies were deemed possibly efficacious: Christian devotional meditation for anxiety, Christian accommodative group treatment for unforgiveness, spiritual group treatment for unforgiveness, Christian accommodative group CBT for marital discord, Christian lay counseling for general psychological problems, spiritual group therapy for eating disorders when combined with existing inpatient treatment, and Buddhist accommodative cognitive therapy for anger in a prison setting.

In a more recent and larger meta-analytic review of outcome studies on religious and spiritual therapies, using fifty-one samples from a total of forty-six separate studies involving 3,290 clients, Worthington et al. (2011) concluded that religious and spiritual therapies were generally more effective than no treatment, and also did better than alternate psychotherapies on both psychological and spiritual outcomes. Twenty-four samples from twenty-one separate studies in this meta-analytic review specifically focused on SO-CBT. There is therefore increasing empirical support for the efficacy of SO-CBT, but more and better controlled outcome research is still needed.

CHRISTIAN SO-CBT

A biblical, Christian approach to SO-CBT, as described by Tan (1987), will:

1. Emphasize the primacy of agape love (1 Cor. 13) and the need to develop a warm, empathic, and genuine relationship with the client.
2. Deal more adequately with the past, especially unresolved developmental issues or childhood traumas, and will use inner healing or healing of memories judiciously and appropriately.
3. Pay special attention to the meaning of spiritual, experiential and even mystical aspects of life and faith, according to God's wisdom as revealed in Scriptures and by the Holy Spirit's teaching ministry (John 14:26), and will not overemphasize the rational, thinking dimension, although biblical, propositional truth will still be given its rightful place of importance. The possibility of demonic involvement in some cases will also be seriously considered and appropriately dealt with.
4. Focus on how problems in thought and behavior may often (*not* always, because of other factors, e.g., organic or biological) underlie problem feelings (Rom. 12:1, 2; Phil. 4:8; Eph. 4:22-24), and will use biblical truth (John 8:32), not relativistic values, to conduct cognitive restructuring and behavioral change interventions.
5. Emphasize the Holy Spirit's ministry in bringing about inner healing as well as cognitive, behavioral, and emotional change. It will use prayer and affirmation of God's Word in facilitating dependence on the Lord to produce deep and lasting personality change, and will be cautious not to inadvertently encourage sinful self-sufficiency (cf. Phil. 4:13).
6. Pay more attention to larger contextual factors like familial, societal, religious, and cultural influences, and hence will utilize appropriate community resources in therapeutic intervention, including the church as a body of believers and "fellow priests" to one another (1 Cor. 12; 1 Pet. 2:5, 9).
7. Use only those techniques that are consistent with biblical truth and not simplistically use whatever techniques work. It will reaffirm Scriptural perspectives on suffering, including the possibility of the

"blessings of mental anguish", with the ultimate goal of counseling being holiness or Christ-likeness (Rom. 8:29), not necessarily temporal happiness. However, such a goal will include being more open to receiving God's love and grace, and growing thereby to be more Christ-like, and overcoming mental anguish due to unbiblical, erroneous beliefs (i.e., misbeliefs).

8. Utilize rigorous outcome research methodology before making definitive statements about the superiority of cognitive-behavior therapy. (pp. 108-9)

This Christian SO-CBT is a Christ-centered, biblically based and Spirit-filled approach to therapy. It includes explicit integration where appropriate, with full informed consent from the client (usually a Christian). Explicit integration of Christian faith and therapy involves "a more overt approach that directly and systematically deals with spiritual and religious issues in therapy, and uses spiritual resources like prayer, Scripture or sacred texts, referrals to church or other religious groups or lay counselors, and other religious practices" (Tan, 1996, p. 368).

I have previously provided a more detailed description of this biblical Christian approach to SO-CBT (Tan, 2007; see also Tan & Johnson, 2005). I will now briefly summarize its major characteristics, focusing particularly on its use of prayer and inner healing prayer and Scripture.

Assessment. The first session with a client is usually a two-hour intake interview in which I engage in history taking, problem listing and goal setting with a client in a warm, genuine and empathic way. I also ask the client about his or her religious/spiritual background and denomination if any, and whether the client is interested in the explicit use of spiritual resources such as prayer and Scripture in therapy and in open discussion of spiritual and religious issues. If the client indicates interest in and provides informed consent for a Christian SO-CBT approach to be used in therapy, then we proceed to do so. If not, I will use more standard CBT and implicit integration that is more covert, and not explicit integration (see Tan, 1996, 2007). Appropriate personality and psychological assessment or testing is also conducted at this intake session. Christian SO-CBT does not mean that prayer and Scripture or other spiritual disciplines such as confession and forgiveness (see Tan, 2011a, pp. 357-62) are used in every therapy session. Standard CBT interventions are also employed, with prayer and Scripture used only when appropriate.

Prayer, including inner healing prayer for past painful memories (Tan, 2003; see also Garzon & Burkett, 2002), and Scripture should be ethically and sensitively used with clients who have given their informed consent. Such spiritual and religious Christian interventions should not be used with more severely disturbed or psychotic clients who are experiencing acute, florid symptoms that need to be controlled first by antipsychotic or other appropriate medications. The use of prayer and Scripture is also not appropriate for Christian clients who are experiencing active rebellion or intense anger at God and who are not interested in using such religious resources at the present time. The Christian SO-CBT therapist needs to prayerfully exercise patience and proper timing in employing spiritual and religious resources such as prayer and Scripture and other spiritual disciplines in therapy, even with Christian clients.

Intervention. While there are many interventions that can be used in Christian SO-CBT, including both standard CBT techniques (see Tan, 2011a, pp. 217-35, 257-70) as well as more specific Christian spiritual resources, this section will focus on two major Christian SO-CBT interventions: prayer (including inner healing prayer) and the use of Scripture (see Tan, 2007, pp. 103-9).

Prayer. Prayer can be described as communication or communion with God that includes both verbal and silent versions (e.g., Benner, 2010). Prayer can therefore include various types or forms such as contemplative prayer (quiet, meditative prayer), intercessory prayer (praying for oneself and others), inner healing prayer and listening prayer, as well as different dimensions or aspects (e.g., confession, thanksgiving, praise or worship of God, forgiveness, petition for oneself, and intercession for others). Prayer can be used, when appropriate, at different times, such as before, during, or after the therapy session, at the beginning or at the end of the therapy session, or at any time during the therapy session. Prayer can be offered aloud with the client in an explicit way, or silently with the client, or implicitly and silently within the therapist without involving the client (see Tan, 2011a, pp. 344-52). Prayer (and confession) is a powerful and effective means of healing according to Scripture (Jas 5:16).

For some clients who are still struggling with painful, even traumatic memories from the past (e.g., physical, sexual or emotional abuse, abandonment, rejection, harsh criticism, neglect, or deprivation), a specific form of prayer called inner healing prayer or healing of memories may be particularly helpful and relevant. Garzon and Burkett (2002) have described healing of memories (or inner healing prayer) as "a form of prayer designed to facilitate the client's ability to process affectively painful memories through vividly recalling these memories and asking for the presence of Christ (or God) to minister in the midst of this pain" (p. 42).

I have developed the following seven-step model for inner healing prayer, first described in 1992 (see Tan, 2003, pp. 20-21):

1. Begin with prayer for protection from evil, and ask for the power and healing ministry of the Holy Spirit to take control of the session.
2. Guide the client into a relaxed state by using brief relaxation strategies (e.g., slow, deep breathing, calming self-talk, pleasant imagery, prayer, and Bible imagery).
3. Guide the client to vividly recall in imagery a painful past event or traumatic experience, and to deeply feel the pain, hurt, anger, fear, or other emotions associated with the painful memory.
4. Prayerfully ask the Lord, by the power of the Holy Spirit, to come and minister to the client His comfort, love and healing grace (even gentle rebuke where necessary) in whatever way He knows will be helpful and healing to the client. It may be Jesus' imagery or other healing imagery, music (song/hymn), specific Scriptures, a sense of His presence or warmth, or some other manifestation of the Spirit's working. Usually, no specific guided imagery or visualization is directly given at this point (unlike some other approaches to inner healing prayer). The emphasis here is to be open, receptive and accepting toward what the Lord wants to do, and therefore to be more contemplative in prayer before Him.
5. Wait quietly upon the Lord to minister to the client with His healing grace and truth. Guide and speak only if necessary and led by the Holy Spirit. In order to track with the client and what he or she is experiencing, periodically ask the client: "What's happening? What are you feeling or experiencing now?"
6. Close in prayer (usually both the therapist and client will pray).
7. Debrief and discuss the inner healing prayer experience with the client. If appropriate, assign homework—inner healing prayer that the client can engage in, during his or her own prayer times at home. (Tan, 2007, p. 104)

Hypothetical case example of inner healing prayer. The following is a hypothetical case example of an inner healing session conducted with a woman client named Jane, later on in therapy. Jane was experiencing a distant relationship with God, partly because she had a father who was not emotionally close to her. She was also having some symptoms of mild depression and fatigue.

Therapist: As we discussed in our last session, and you have read about the seven steps of inner healing prayer, do you feel ready today to begin this prayer intervention focusing on the painful memory of your emotionally distant father?

Client: Yes, I'm ready.

Therapist: Before we begin, let us remember that this is prayer and not a technique per se. Let us be open and receptive to what the Lord wants to do today, with no specific demands or expectations on our part, okay?

Client: Okay.

Therapist: Good. I will begin with the first step. Please close your eyes and be in a receptive, prayerful mode as I pray: "Dear Lord, we pray that you will protect us from evil, and come in the presence and power of the Holy Spirit, and minister to Jane your healing grace and truth for the painful memory she has. Thank you for your love and presence with us. In Jesus' name we pray. Amen." Now keep your eyes closed and continue in a prayerful mode as I move on to the second step.

Client: Okay.

Therapist: Now, Jane, I would like you to use the relaxation techniques that you learned a couple of sessions ago, to help you relax as deeply and as comfortably as possible. [The therapist guides Jane in the use of slow, deep breathing and calming self-talk—e.g., "Just relax . . . take it easy . . . letting go of all tension . . . from the top of your head all the way down to your toes . . . relax more and more deeply . . ."—and pleasant imagery—e.g., lying on the beach on a beautiful sunny day.] How are you feeling now?

Client: I'm feeling very relaxed.

Therapist: Good. Now I would like you to switch the focus of your attention to something that is not as pleasant. I would like you to go back in your imagination and see yourself as a young girl in elementary school, and picture your father at home sitting in his chair and reading the newspapers, and not paying attention to you. Can you relive that scene in your imagination? Is it clear?

Client: Yes, I can see it as if it's happening again. It's actually quite painful [with some tears in her eyes].

Therapist: Okay. I would like you to continue to see that scene clearly and to experience your feelings as fully as possible.

Client: I can feel the painful emotions [with some more tears].

Therapist: I know this is hard for you, but continue to experience these painful feelings.

Client: Okay.

Therapist: Also, please tell me aloud while keeping your eyes closed, Jane . . . what are you experiencing now, how are you feeling and what's happening?

Client: I'm feeling lonely . . . and deeply hurt . . . that my father is still hiding behind his newspapers and not noticing me although I try to get his attention . . . I wonder if he really loves me. I feel alone and ignored [with tears].

Therapist: [After some time has passed] Jane, continue with that painful scene in imagery. At this point, I would like to pause and pray for the Lord to come and minister to you, by the power and presence of the Holy Spirit, and to touch you with his healing grace and truth, okay?

Client: Okay.

Therapist: "Dear Lord, I pray that you will now come by the power of the Holy Spirit, to walk with Jane into this painful memory, and lovingly minister your healing grace and truth to her in whatever way is needed, according to your will. Thank you, in Jesus' name. Amen." Now Jane, just wait . . . and be in a receptive, open prayerful mode allowing the Lord to minister to you.

Client: Okay.

Therapist: [After a few moments have passed] Jane, please tell me now what's going on. What are you experiencing or feeling?

Client: [With some tears but a smile on her face] I actually sense the presence of Jesus with me, although I can't see his face clearly. He is having lunch with me, spreading out a blanket with a picnic basket . . . and he eats a leisurely lunch with me, giving me his full and loving attention . . . and he tells me that I am very precious to him. [With some tears] I really feel close to him . . . with warmth and joy and . . . deep peace. I feel that I can experience God more now as a loving and present heavenly Father or Parent.

Therapist: Good. Just continue to let the Lord minister to you.

Client: Okay.

Therapist: [After some moments have passed] Can you tell me now what's happening, what you are feeling or experiencing?

Client: Yes . . . I continue to experience the presence of Jesus. He is gently telling me to let go any resentment I may have toward my father, and to forgive him . . . at least he works hard to provide for my material needs. I can also see more clearly now that this is the way my father expresses his love for me . . . and I actually feel more gratitude and some warmth toward him now, as I . . . forgive him. I also ask God to forgive me of any resentment or wrong attitudes . . . toward my father all these years. I feel more released and at peace.

Therapist: That's beautiful, Jane. Anything else before we close in prayer?

Client: No.

Therapist: Okay. Let's close in prayer. Would you like to start?

Client: Okay. "Dear Lord, thank you so much for this deeply touching and healing time with you. Please continue to heal me and make me whole so that I can know you more deeply and serve you better. Thank you in Jesus' name."

Therapist: "Dear Lord, we thank you for your healing grace and loving truth that you allowed Jane to experience today. Continue your healing work in her life, and be with us as we go on with the therapy sessions here. In Jesus' name. Amen." Jane, just before you go, do you have any comments or questions about this experience in inner healing prayer that you've just had? Let's debrief and discuss it now.

Client: It was a deeply healing experience for me, thank you. Could I use these steps of inner healing prayer on my own, in my daily quiet time with the Lord?

Therapist: Yes, that's a good idea. Are you okay with doing this as a "homework assignment"?

Client: Yes, and thank you again!

Therapist: You're welcome, Jane. Take care and God bless! See you again next week.

(Adapted from Tan, 2007, pp. 105-7)

Inner healing prayer of course does not always proceed so smoothly, and it is not a panacea for all kinds of problems. However, it can be a very helpful Christian prayer intervention in Christian SO-CBT, to facilitate deeper levels of emotional processing as well as cognitive restructuring. Its emphasis on a more contemplative and receptive prayer mode is consistent with recent mindfulness and acceptance-based approaches to contemporary CBT (see Tan, 2011b). However, controlled outcome research specifically evaluating the efficacy of inner healing prayer for particular problems is currently lacking and needed (see Garzon & Burkett, 2002).

Scripture. Another major intervention in Christian SO-CBT—especially in cognitive restructuring of unbiblical, distorted and dysfunctional thinking—is the use of Scripture as God's inspired Word (Jn 8:32; 2 Tim 3:16). In standard CBT, cognitive restructuring of dysfunctional or distorted thinking usually involves asking the following crucial questions: "On what basis do you say this? Where is the evidence for your view or conclusion?"; "Is there another way of looking at this?"; "What if this view or conclusion is true? What does it mean to you?" In Christian SO-CBT, the following are other key questions that can be used in conducting cognitive restructuring of unbiblical, dysfunctional thinking: "What does God have to say about this?"; "What do you think the Bible has to say about this?"; "What does your faith tradition or church or denomination have to say about this?" These questions are a central part of using Scripture in Christian cognitive restructuring (see Tan, 2007, p. 108).

The Bible or Scripture can be used in Christian SO-CBT for the following purposes: to comfort, clarify (guide), correct (cognitively restructure), change character, cleanse, convict (convert) and cure (heal) (see Ps 119:9, 11, 97-100, 105; Jn 8:32; 15:3; Rom 10:17; 2 Tim 3:16; Heb 4:12; 1 Pet 1:2-3; 2:2). More specifically, Scripture can be used in various ways in Christian SO-CBT: "indirectly by alluding to biblical truth or directly by generally referring to teachings or examples in the Bible or specifically citing biblical texts by chapter and verse; by reading, meditating, memorizing, hearing, or studying Scripture or assigning it for reading, study, memorization, or meditation in between therapy sessions" (Tan, 2007, p. 108).

Scripture should be carefully and sensitively used in an ethical way in Christian SO-CBT, with proper biblical interpretation, because the misuse or abuse of Scripture in therapy can lead to harmful effects on clients. Monroe (2008) provides the following questions for use by Christian therapists to help them clarify why they may want to use Scripture with clients: "Why do I want to have them read this text? What do I hope to accomplish through it (e.g., to be provoked, taught, comforted, connected to something greater than self, to change one's focal point, etc.)? What barriers might hinder this goal? How might they misinterpret my intervention?" (p. 56).

Hypothetical case example of the use of Scripture. The following is a hypothetical case example of the use of Scripture in helping Jane to cognitively restructure or change her distorted and unbiblical way of thinking about anger:

Client: I feel badly whenever I experience even mild anger at my father. I tend to block the anger out because I believe that it is wrong or sinful for me as a Christian to get angry at all. But the anger doesn't really go away, and I feel more fatigued and depressed eventually.

Therapist: Let's take a closer look at your specific thought or belief that anger is always wrong. On what basis do you believe it is true? What do you think the Bible has to say about this?

Client: I remember there are verses commanding us to put away anger and wrath. I feel guilty whenever I feel anger.

Therapist: Okay, would you like to look at the Bible more closely and see what it actually says or teaches about anger?

Client: Oh, yes!

Therapist: Can you think of any other Bible verses or passages that are relevant to our discussion?

Client: Not really. Hmmm . . . I do recall Jesus throwing out the moneychangers in the temple. So maybe there is a type of anger like when God gets angry or Jesus gets angry, and it's not sinful . . . but I still feel that when I get angry, it's not okay, because I'm not God.

Therapist: So, you already see that at the very least, when Jesus or God gets angry, it is not wrong, so there is a type of anger that may not be sinful. Some call this righteous indignation. Can you think of other Bible verses or passages that may teach this more directly?

Client: Come to think of it, didn't Paul say something like, "Be angry but do not sin"?

Therapist: That's a good text you recalled. Ephesians 4:26. Would you like to read it?

Client: Sure [reads from the Bible the therapist hands over to her].

Therapist: What do you think Ephesians 4:26 means?

Client: Well, at least it says we can be angry but must not sin in our anger.

Therapist: It sounds like you are seeing now that anger is not always sinful.

(Adapted from Tan, 2007, pp. 108-9)

A biblical, Christian approach to SO-CBT that includes the use of prayer and inner healing prayer, and Scripture when appropriate, can be a powerful and effective way of helping people be transformed by the way of Christ, especially when God steps in through such interventions. His healing presence and truth can be directly experienced by clients who are open and receptive to the Holy Spirit's ministry and the power of Scripture as God's inspired and eternal Word. While the empirical evidence supporting the efficacy of Christian versions of SO-CBT has grown in recent years, more and better controlled outcome research is still needed. A biblical, Christian approach to SO-CBT as described in this chapter is a major example of helping clients in a Christ-centered, biblically based and Spirit-filled way. It should be conducted in a professionally competent, ethically responsible and clinically sensitive way, in dependence on the Holy Spirit and with the client's full informed consent (see Tan, 2011a, p. 340).

References and Recommended Resources

Aten, J. D., McMinn, M. R., & Worthington, E. L., Jr. (Eds.). (2011). *Spiritually oriented interventions for counseling and psychotherapy.* Washington, DC: American Psychological Association.

Benner, D. G. (2010). *Opening to God: Lectio divina and life as prayer.* Downers Grove, IL: InterVarsity Press.

Butler, A. C., Chapman, J. E., Forman, E. M., & Beck, A. T. (2006). The empirical status of cognitive-behavioral therapy: A review of meta-analyses. *Clinical Psychology Review, 26,* 17-31.

Garzon, F., & Burkett, L. (2002). Healing of memories: Models, research, future directions. *Journal of Psychology and Christianity, 21,* 42-49.

Hayes, S. C., Luoma, J. B., Bond, F. W., Masuda, A. L., & Lillis, J. (2006). Acceptance and Commitment Therapy: Model, processes, and outcomes. *Behaviour Research and Therapy, 44,* 1-25.

Hayes, S. C., Strosahl, K. D., & Wilson, K. G. (2012). *Acceptance and Commitment Therapy: The practice and process of mindful change* (2nd ed.). New York: Guilford.

Hook, J. N., Worthington, E. L., Jr., David, D. E., Jennings, D. J., II, Gartner, A. L., & Hook, N. (2010). Empirically supported religious and spiritual therapies. *Journal of Clinical Psychology, 66,* 46-72.

Kendall, P. C., & Hollon, S. D. (Eds.). (1979). *Cognitive-behavioral interventions: Theory, research, and procedures.* New York: Academic Press.

Linehan, M. M. (1993). *Cognitive-behavioral treatment of borderline personality disorder.* New York: Guilford.

McMinn, M. R., & Campbell, C. D. (2007). *Integrative psychotherapy: Toward a comprehensive Christian approach.* Downers Grove, IL: IVP Academic.

Monroe, P. G. (2008). Guidelines for the effective use of the Bible in counseling. *Edification: Journal of the Society for Christian Psychology,* 2(2), 53-61.

Pargament, K. I. (2007). *Spiritually integrated psychotherapy: Understanding and addressing the sacred.* New York: Guilford.

Plante, T. G. (2009). *Spiritual practices in psychotherapy: Thirteen tools for enhancing psychological health.* New York: Guilford.

Richards, P. S., & Bergin, A. E. (2005). *A spiritual strategy for counseling and psychotherapy* (2nd ed.). Washington, DC: American Psychological Association.

Richards, P. S., & Bergin, A. E. (Eds.). (2000). *Handbook of psychotherapy and religious diversity.* Washington, DC: American Psychological Association.

Roemer, L., & Orsillo, S. M. (2009). *Mindfulness- and acceptance-based behavioral therapies in practice.* New York: Guilford.

Segal, Z. V., Williams, J. M. G., & Teasdale, J. D. (2002). *Mindfulness-based cognitive therapy for depression: A new approach for preventing relapse.* New York: Guilford.

Shapiro, S. L., & Carlson, L. E. (2009). *The art and science of mindfulness: Integrating mindfulness into psychology and the helping professions.* Washington, DC: American Psychological Association.

Sperry, L., & Shafranske, E. P. (Eds.). (2005). *Spiritually oriented psychotherapy.* Washington, DC: American Psychological Association.

Tan, S.-Y. (1987). Cognitive-behavior therapy: A biblical approach and critique. *Journal of Psychology and Theology, 15,* 103-12.

Tan, S.-Y. (1996). Religion in clinical practice: Implicit and explicit integration. In E. P. Shafranske (Ed.), *Religion and the clinical practice of psychology* (pp. 365-87). Washington, DC: American Psychological Association.

Tan, S.-Y. (2003). Inner healing prayer. *Christian Counseling Today, 11*(4), 20-22.

Tan, S.-Y. (2007). Use of prayer and Scripture in cognitive-behavioral therapy. *Journal of Psychology and Christianity, 26*, 101-11.

Tan, S.-Y. (2011a). *Counseling and psychotherapy: A Christian perspective.* Grand Rapids: Baker Academic.

Tan, S.-Y. (2011b). Mindfulness and acceptance-based cognitive behavioral therapies: Empirical evidence and clinical applications from a Christian perspective. *Journal of Psychology and Christianity, 30*, 243-49.

Tan, S.-Y. (2013). Addressing religion and spirituality from a cognitive behavioral perspective. In K. I. Pargament, A. Mahoney & E. P. Shafranske (Eds.), *APA handbooks in psychology: Vol. 2. APA handbook of psychology, religion, and spirituality*. Washington, DC: American Psychological Association.

Tan, S.-Y., & Johnson, W. B. (2005). Spiritually oriented cognitive-behavioral therapy. In L. Sperry & E. P. Shafranske (Eds.), *Spiritually oriented psychotherapy* (pp. 77-103). Washington, DC: American Psychological Association.

Worthington, E. L., Jr., Hook, J. N., Davis, D. E., & McDaniel, M. A. (2011). Religion and spirituality. In J. C. Norcross (Ed.), *Psychotherapy relationships that work* (2nd ed., pp. 402-19). New York: Oxford University Press.

7

Christian Holism

Offering the Holy Spirit the Tools of Our Trade

Charles L. Zeiders, Douglas Schoeninger,
Herman Riffel, Robin Caccese
& Julie Wegryn

Introduction: Toward Christian Holism

Psychologists can measure normalcy, define madness, develop therapeutic paradigms and list the nuances of human nature with utmost precision. We have biofeedback, psychometrics, psychoanalysis, cognitive therapy, positive psychology, behavior modification and a host of deeply promising projects in the research and development pipeline. To be sure, our discipline has advanced accurate understanding of the soul's essential properties and has scientifically harnessed this knowledge to clinically mitigate the deep agony of the human mind. But, despite our advances and genuine effectiveness, our discipline remains incomplete. Theoretically, scientifically and therapeutically, we fall short of the fuller effectuality that awaits us. We need Christ.

It is through the Christian revelation that psychology will find its maturity. In our incorporation of the divine breakthrough recorded in the New Testament, our theories will become more accurate, because we will develop them in the light of truth. Our therapies will become more powerful, because we will submit them to the Source of power. Our knowledge of human nature—as good but fallen, redeemed through Jesus, loved by a powerful, active, triune God—will have tremendous impact on our disciplinary pursuits. Because God created humanity, all psychological science implicitly situates research data in relation to the Creator. Because the sovereign God heals, we can submit our therapeutic interventions to his sovereignty and enjoy a therapy the nature of which is saturated by grace. Cognitive or dynamic interventions can become so imbued with divinity that the clinician's technique and the patient's receptivity uncannily unfold toward health. For psychology there are blessings afoot. And these blessings stem from our recognition that the "clinical Christ"—the activity of the God of the Christian revelation throughout the realms of our discipline—desires to redeem, relate to, heal, love and empower us. The clinical Christ seeks to bring us individually and corporately into a level of exuberant wholeness that is ultimately endless and utterly wonderful. The clinical Christ is the Lord of the transformative psychology of *Christian Holism*. This chapter explores different aspects of the clinical Christ, Christian Holism and their implications.

A group of colleagues and I have spent years experiencing the clinical Christ in our practice of Christian Holism. From our spiritual/clinical experience, we felt an obligation to develop a theology of psychotherapy. Under the auspices of the Institute for Christian Counseling and Therapy, we formed the Think Tank for Christian Holism. The Think Tank consisted of three licensed psychologists, a minister and pastoral therapist, and an author and publisher of religious books—all practicing Christians and veterans of psychological and spiritual practice. From our efforts emerged the tenets of Christian Holism.

Tenets of Christian Holism for Psychotherapeutic Practice

Central tenet. The central tenet of Christian Holism for psychotherapeutic treatment is that the Holy Spirit is fully present in the clinical situation, with and within the therapist and the client(s), and is actively engaged in the treatment process.

The Holy Spirit is completely present to the clinician and the client. The Holy Spirit is omnipresent, present everywhere and in every time of the client's life, without losing any particularity, and the Holy Spirit is omniscient, present to and discerning all realities, objective and subjective. The Holy Spirit works within and through the clinician and heals the client because the Holy Spirit honors the clinician and loves the client. The Holy Spirit works within the divine relatedness of the Holy Trinity, behaving toward the clinician and the client in an ongoing, person-loving way. The blessing of the Spirit's presence and activity unfolds both immediately and over time. The Holy Spirit is the prime mover of the healing process. The Holy Spirit acts with perfect and complete clinical competence, because the Holy Spirit is God's competence present with us.

The central tenet is the most import idea that governs our therapy. The Spirit is in the midst of treatment and is therapeutically active. We know this because God loves us (Jn 3:16). Naturally God wants us to do well—to find salvation, joy and health. Thus, he sent Jesus. Jesus wants the good things that the Father wants for us (Jn 8:28), so he sent the Spirit (Jn 14:18). When clinicians and clients pray, the Spirit will gladly become present to them clinically. The Spirit of truth counsels the counseling; then the benefits of the all-powerful, all-knowing, all-loving God become manifest in the midst of the clinical enterprise.

God is present everywhere. Christian Holism emphasizes this profundity. In this approach, the Holy Spirit is believed to be especially present when invited by clinician and client to advance treatment in the name of Jesus Christ. The Spirit is ontologically present and helpful in the clinical situation. This is foundational.

Tenets proceeding from the central tenet.

1. *Christian Holism is centered in Jesus Christ.* The entire process of psychotherapy is explicitly under the lordship of Jesus Christ. Treatment is conducted in his name.

Christian Holism is centered in Jesus Christ because "Christ is Lord of the cosmos and of history" (Catechism of the Catholic Church, 1994, p. 191). Since Christ is Lord of all things, therapy is authentically ordered when our therapeutic service is under Christ's dominion. Clinically, we find that Christ enjoys helping patients, because he cares for them so much. Jesus of Nazareth brought good news to the afflicted, liberty to captives, sight to the blind and freedom to the oppressed, and he proclaimed God's favor (Lk 4:18-19). Made Lord of treatment, Jesus continues to do these kind things by sending his Spirit to those treated.

2. *Christian Holism concerns itself with placing psychological theories and interventions at the disposal of the Holy Spirit.* Rather than ask, "How do I intellectually integrate my training in social science with Christian doc-

trine?" the practitioner of Christian Holism asks, "How does the Holy Spirit want to use my training to help this client?" In Christian Holism, placing social science at the disposal of the living God is the paramount concern that trumps problems of theoretical integration.

Accomplishing scholarship that integrates psychological theories with Christian theology is important, but the mission of Christian Holism calls for asking God to quicken therapeutic skills and theories to bless those called to our offices. If our secular orientations are cognitive behavioral, Jungian or otherwise, we ask God to bless those skills and theories in a way that makes the truth in them useful in the course of God's healing action. While religious faith cannot substitute for clinical skill, neither can clinical skill find wholeness or manifest its deeper therapeutic value without being graced by the God who wants to bless our clients utterly.

Christian Holism is more concerned with service to Christ and integration into Christ, rather than with integration of secular psychological knowledge with Christian faith and doctrine. The concept or goal of integration can be a head trip. For example, an integration question is, "How can I marry cognitive behaviorism to Christianity?" One can do that, but this is not the essential focus of Christian Holism. Rather, centering in the lordship of Jesus, one might ask, "How does God wish to use my cognitive behavioral expertise for his healing purposes now?" You could just as easily ask, "How does God want to use my muscle testing? How does God want to use my understanding of analytical psychology? How does God want to use my rich theological training for his purposes now?" So while Christian Holism is concerned with integration of secular and revealed knowledge, what we are more concerned with is putting the things developed in the secular world, or even in other religious systems, under Jesus' lordship for his use.

3. *Christian Holism views the Hebrew and Christian Scriptures, the Old and New Testaments, as inspired by the Holy Spirit and as a valid source of inspiration and guidance for psychotherapeutic treatment.* Therefore, Scripture is useful to guide case formulations and interventions. While Scripture reveals truth, interpretations are, of course, colored by human imperfection. Hence, when utilizing Scripture to guide treatment, the clinician must exercise theological humility. Read in humility, under the Spirit's guidance, Scripture assists the psychological enterprise by shedding light on how God improves the health of patients. In Christian Holism,

Scripture is used to help reveal God's healing movements, as led by the Holy Spirit. Scripture is an anointed resource, a rich, unique medium for God's guidance and personal address of the client and therapist.

"Sacred scripture must be read and interpreted in the light of the same Spirit by whom it was written" (Catechism of the Catholic Church, 1994, pp. 37-38). In terms of Christian Holism, this means that Scripture is most therapeutic when the Spirit is invited to inspire textual meaning in light of the Spirit's healing ministry to the client. Further, while Scripture has both collective and individual significance, the Spirit arranges these meanings in the minds of both client and clinician in ways that offer hope and promote health. Because Scripture reveals truth about God and man, Scripture is revered. However, Christian Holism carefully avoids idolizing Scripture, reserving worship only for the God who inspires revelation and healing through the faith's documents.

Read in humility, under the Spirit's guidance, Scripture assists the psychological enterprise by shedding light on how God improves the lot of man and offers guidance for the specific persons in treatment. In my experience of using Scripture in treatment, I find a creative dialectic between Scripture and psychological theory. Reading Scripture through the lens of social science and reading social science through the lens of Scripture opens up treatment options and understandings.

4. Christian Holism views creeds and catechisms similarly to the way it views Scripture. Christian Holism thinks of creeds and catechisms as powerful statements of core beliefs and core convictions, which help to position the intellect in such a way that the entire person may develop openness to the presence and healing reality of God. In Christian Holism, creeds and catechisms are not end points but points of opening toward the God of healing and to the dimensions of God's presence to us as Father, Son and Holy Spirit.

Christian Holism appreciates that creeds and catechisms preserve central ideas about the Christian faith and reality. When the Holy Spirit makes them instruments of healing—such as by positioning the discouraged intellect to conceptualize God's love and anticipate healing grace—creeds and catechisms become therapeutically practical. Christian Holism also appreciates that Christians and others will hold varying conceptions of Christianity and reality in good faith. While deeply respecting the creeds, Christian Holism holds that people are loved by God—not due to creedal affiliations, but because people are made in the *imago Dei* and God simply loves people. The therapeutic purpose of creeds is to open clients to God's healing love and to create an open place in the mind that can be inhabited by the felt experience of the Trinity.

For me, Christian Holism adheres to the essential Christian doctrines embodied in the creeds. I am referring to the Nicene Creed and the Apostles' Creed. I know that historically the church was aware of the need to have a bottom line, or core beliefs. It is great to have the freedom of the Holy Spirit, which our earlier tenets discuss, but there is also a bottom line and that is doctrine, core belief. The Apostles' Creed is regarded as the formulation of the essential convictions of the Christian faith. The Nicene Creed asserts the truth and integrity of the Trinity. For me these things are not up for grabs. We worship a triune God, three in one. We can have other things as peripherals, but this statement is bedrock belief. I conduct my therapy with these conceptual tools in mind.

5. *Christian Holism is ecumenical.* There are two reasons for this.

    1. All Christian churches (or ecclesial communions) have valuable practices that can enter, or be availed, in the therapy situation to allow the Holy Spirit healing opportunities. Clinical ecumenism allows the healing goodness inherent in the gifts of the different ecclesial communions to enter therapy at the Spirit's pleasure, according to the client's healing need.

    2. Since the church is one body containing multiple and often competing units of organizational authority, the human, organized church is dissociated. Psychotherapeutic ecumenism honors the essential unity of the church and works to heal the dissociation of the human, organized church within the clinical microcosm.

Catholic and Orthodox churches, for example, impart the Spirit's grace through sacraments. Evangelical churches do this through emphasis on revealed truth and ethical responsibility, Quakers through contemplative listening, Pentecostals through charismatic experience and so on. Clinical ecumenism allows the healing goodness inherent in the gifts of each of the churches to enter therapy at the Spirit's pleasure. Clinical ecumenism opens treatment to the universe of spiritual gifts contained within the entire body of Christ. By acknowledging that the Spirit-given gifts of competing communities complement each other and belong together, the small clinical situation contributes to healing dissociation within the larger church situation.

To concretize the diverse and valuable giftedness worked out in the various communions, we could go on to talk about the healing value of the sacraments in Catholicism and Orthodoxy, the emphasis on revealed truth and ethical responsibility in evangelical Christianity, the importance of listening to God in Quakerism, and the efficacy of charismatic experience among Pentecostal denominations. Such a discussion deserves its own think tank.

6. Christian Holism distinguishes itself as a psychological perspective in its conviction that men and women are made in the image of God—not only like God in nature and attributes, but made for relationship with God. It views images of humanity depicted in neuropsychology, psychoanalysis, cognitive behaviorism, phenomenological schools and others as useful but incomplete constructs of the human being. Drawing on Scripture and theology, Christian Holism sees in the essential created human imago a freedom to love, choose, create and reason within the joy of an essential, lively, ebullient relation with God, self, others and creation. Christian Holism finds that "made in the image of God" implies a kinship between man and God and calls for the imitation of God as God is embodied in Jesus Christ.

> Since [people are] made in God's Image every human being is worthy of honor and respect; [people are] neither to be murdered (Gen. 9:16) nor cursed (Jas. 3:9). "Image" includes such characteristics as "righteousness and holiness" (Eph. 4:24) and "knowledge" (Col. 3:10). Believers are to be "conformed to the likeness" of Christ (Rom. 8:29) and will someday be "like him" (1 Jn. 3:2). [People are] the climax of God's creative activity, and God has "crowned [human beings] with glory and honor" . . . (Ps. 8:5-8). (Barker's NIV text note, 1985, p. 7)

Christian Holism appreciates that the reality of human nature lies within the image of God (the *imago Dei*) in people. Within the image, we find the reality of the individual person: an entity like God, precious to God, worthy of honor—a creature to be well-treated and intrinsically lovable. Christian Holism acknowledges that the full glory of the person's humanity reflects the divinity of Christ.

Clinically, this means we draw upon models of human nature found in the various psychological schools and use them in service to the Spirit's work to repair and restore the true psychological substance of patients—that is, the image of God in clients. But our therapy squarely faces the fact that final restoration of true human nature necessarily takes place as the result of God's supernatural, redemptive action alone—a restoration that is far beyond the reach of crude therapeutic technique or well-meaning theological or psychological babbling. In the end, therapist and client enjoy the truth that our deepest humanity is restored by God acting graciously.

In this particular tenet, I am saying that we have a unique view of human nature that distinguishes itself from the other psychological doctrines: Christian Holism's view of human nature is distinct from the reductive neuron doctrine of neuropsychology; we distinguish ourselves from the image of man as a talking beast or the aware animal of psychoanalysis; we go far beyond Cognitive Therapy and Rational-Emotive Therapy's image of man as a creature evolving into an ideal thinker, and far beyond the radical behaviorists who see us as nothing more than a series of responses to stimuli. Our perspective of man is the *imago Dei*—the likeness of the human creature to God.

7. The whole meaning of imago, at the root of everything, is homecoming. In other words, the whole pursuit of human life has to do with reconciliation, with God, with self, with those in the human community. We are meant to be in union with God, with others, within ourselves, with our generations, with nature. The goal of life is union, or actually reunion. This is the beginning and ending, the whole thrust and meaning of healing. Wholeness grows from engagement of God and others and the natural world. And one's growing wholeness contributes to calling forth the wholeness of others, which develops as authentic response.

Clients are brought home to themselves and rightly related to all things, because "the grace of God has triumphed in them" (McBrien, 1994, p. 1105). When the Spirit transforms people into themselves, the outcome is vast harmonization with all things that exist. This harmonization, this homecoming, is "a process, to be completed when the Kingdom of God is fully realized at the end of history" (McBrien, 1994, p. 1106). Treatment offers itself as a small part of this large process, becoming a vessel through which the Spirit pours his harmonizing grace, rightly ordering the patient's relationship with self, God, others, history and creation. Through this grace the client—after being blessed to face the problems of human pain—is exited from disorder and brought home to all good things. This homecoming is Spirit-driven, dynamic and ongoing.

8. Christian Holism offers a specific view of psychological treatment and healing. It submits treatment to the divine's intention for complete redemption of people, to reverse the damaging impact of the fall, to end levels and sources of separation from God, and to conclude alienation from the *imago Dei*. This is done by placing social science under the lordship of Jesus Christ. Under Christ's dominion, treatment relies on natural therapeutic processes and supernatural grace to accomplish these healings. Christian Holism finds that natural therapeutic processes are available through psychotherapy and the application of medicines. Christian Holism finds that the benefits of natural therapeutic processes unfold over time. Christian Holism also appreciates the reality of supernatural grace. Supernatural grace comes directly to the beloved as the result of God's sovereign activity on the beloved's behalf. The benefits of supernatural grace can be instantaneous.

The purpose of treatment includes but exceeds the mitigation of clinical syndromes and character pathology. With God's help, treatment becomes a part of the unfolding of God's profoundly healing purpose for the client. This involves remission of personal and inherited sins through the work and person of Jesus Christ, restoration of communion with God, and restoration of harmonious communion with self and others. Christian Holism annexes social science into the kingdom of God, and the Holy Spirit is asked to enter the clinical situation. Then either of two forms of healing may occur: (1) healing through evident natural means, or (2) healing through evident supernatural means.

It may please God, for example, to allow people to get well through good things in the created order, like antidepressants or cognitive restructuring. Or it may please God to heal a mood disorder immediately, directly and supernaturally. Because Christian Holism finds the Holy Spirit to be clinically present and supremely competent, it finds natural therapeutic processes and supernatural healing both to contain equal measures of God's grace.

9. Christian Holism employs both "secular" (psychological and relational-ethical) and "sacred" (spiritual-biblical) interventions to participate in the Holy Spirit's ministry to the client. Christian Holism employs tools such as psychodynamic insight, cognitive restructuring, dream work and other interventions along with healing of memories, forgiveness, confession and other spiritually based therapies.

Simply put, it is the experience of practitioners of Christian Holism that God utilizes both secular and sacred therapies to achieve wholeness in patients. For this reason, the resources of social science are viewed as holy, and the accouterments of faith are seen as therapeutic.

10. Christian Holism is practiced by a therapist who provides sanctuary in which the client's healing process can unfold. The therapist does this by attending to his or her own psychospiritual issues, withholding judgment in humility, borrowing the Holy Spirit's therapeutic love of the client and honing psychotherapeutic expertise, all as a fellow traveler, a brother or sister in the body of Jesus, in the body of God.

The therapist's intention is to offer the client a safe clinical environment in which to heal—a sanctuary. In this sanctuary, the therapist further does not hide behind professional vanity. Understanding himself or herself to be in need of grace, the therapist provides service to the client in humility. To the extent possible, the therapist will have such good will for the client that he or she will embody the Spirit's love for the client. This is understood to be a charism to be well guarded against inappropriateness—but essential to the healing process. Further, practitioners of Christian Holism develop clinical expertise, recognizing that the Spirit enhances naturally obtained clinical skills by supernaturally empowering them in service to the therapy of brother and sister patients.

Christian Holism: A Case Example

Christian Holism activates treatment in such a way as to drive a more complete psychotherapy. The agreement between therapist and patient to join faith in the ocean of clinical grace opens the patient to enjoy the benefits of the medical model while experiencing the third person as the driver of therapeutic process. In the following case example, Christian Holism was the organizing clinical doctrine and was explicitly welcomed by the patient through his informed consent.

> In an inpatient facility, the attending physician referred a schizoaffective man to me. Throughout his life his disease had tormented him and tempted him to despair. For years, this sixty-two year old Irish Catholic man had suffered both from the symptoms of manic depression as well as lapses into the delusions and hallucinations that characterize paranoid schizophrenia. Despite the fact that his psychiatrist had sensibly medicated him on antipsychotic medication, he feared relapsing again. His fear was not unrealistic. In the last five years, he had suffered relapses of mood and psychotic symptoms that left him frightened and in need of an overhauled regimen of antipsychotic medication. Two years before we began our work, he had gradually begun to reclaim his religious faith. Daily he read the catechism and weekly he attended

mass. He was also faithful in his prayers. In therapy, he confided to me that, while he found the renewed practice of his faith comforting, he still feared his mental illness and had difficulty conceptualizing where God was in the midst of his affliction. Then he reported the following dream:

> *On a dark night, I walk through dimly lit streets. A cat-like creature stalks me in the darkness. I feel it gaining ground. The creature closes in on me. I am very nervous. Then I see a fence. A little, narrow entrance way is the only means through the fence. As I get closer, the night watchman undoes a security barrier to the entrance. I slip through the tiny gate. Then the night watchman closes up the entrance just before the cat-like creature catches up with me. Feeling safe from the creature, I relax and look about the protected, fenced-in compound. I realize that this facility is a power company's power plant.*

We conducted the dream interpretation collaboratively, treating the dream allegorically and following his associations to find their meaning. The cat-like creature represented the devil, described by St. Peter as a "lion looking for someone to devour" (1 Pet. 5:8). This man had been tempted to lose faith and despair that God would protect him in the face of his recurrent mental illness. The cat-like creature represented the devouring quality of the bedeviling despair. The narrow gate, however, represented his escape from losing hope. Since this man had resumed his Christian practice, he had entered through the narrow way into the kingdom of God. Since Jesus watches over his flock, we recognized Christ as the night watchman, welcoming this man into the protection of the kingdom of God. Because the dream concluded in a power plant, the man realized that he was under the protection of God's kingdom, a kingdom that generates tremendous protective power on his behalf. For him, the most important point of the dream concerned the revelation that God protected him from despair in the midst of his recurrent illness, despite the fact that his illness remained a thorn in his flesh.

Six weeks after this dream, our interpretation was put to the test. The man's symptoms returned, and he was hospitalized in a psychiatric ward for some time. I felt concerned about him, but upon his return from the hospital, he in fact did not succumb to the faith-destructive belief that Our Lord had abandoned him. The Holy Spirit had arranged his dream and its meaning for him. The deep meaning inherent in his dream's symbols, offered him understanding, allegorically designed for him by the Holy Spirit, to ward off despair that would make him interpret his recurrent mental illness as God's abandonment. "To the contrary," he told me as we resumed our sessions,

"God has been protecting me in the midst of this disease." As a practitioner of Christian Holism, I would have been satisfied at this statement. After all, my patient experienced the Holy Spirit's management of therapy so that he received an astonishing dream that warded off a spiritually lethal collapse of faith. But God's pursuit of this man's rejuvenation persisted. Just days after his discharge from the psychotic unit, he dreamt again.

> *I am aware of a Presence. I look and see Jesus. At first, I am afraid. Then I feel his love for me. It is enormous and strong. Jesus' love for me affirms me so completely that I love him back deeply. Jesus leaves me, but the experience of his love is indelible. Something in me has changed.*

This dream did change him. While the first dream promised protection from despair, this dream left him with an unshakable understanding of his importance to Our Lord. Even weeks following this dream, the man felt deeply moved by his new identity—a beloved man of Christ. Together, these two dreams shifted him from the temptation to interpret his psychiatric situation as God's abandonment, to the realization, not only of God's protection and acceptance, but most importantly of his beloved status, his specialness to Jesus. A third dream in this series came shortly.

> *I enter a boxing ring. I wear boxing gear and am ready to fight. I hear my father yell, "Fight for Ireland and the faith." When I wake up, I feel determined.*

This final dream was important. Exploring the symbols, we agreed that his father's voice represented God the Father's encouragement for the man to spiritually fight for the liberation of human spiritual ground occupied by forces of darkness. By continuing in his acts of devotion, this man participates in the fight that ultimately liberates God's creation from the forces of darkness—a fight that will also liberate him from his own illness, either in this life or the next. A beautiful point is that the dream dignifies the man with the status of a spiritual fighter. The dream provides him with an identity of a Christian soldier, rather than as a mentally ill man. This dream-given identity as an earthly fighter for the kingdom of God preserved him (and me) from the temptation to lose his real identity to his illness. The dream prevented us from falsely basing his identity on his Schizoaffective disorder, as many survivors of mental disorders do. At this writing, he practices Christianity with dignity and aggressive faithfulness. He rightly believes that, despite the mystery of his suffering, he is under God's protection, deeply loved by Jesus, and has been commissioned to fight the good fight through his devotions. Importantly, he identifies himself as a Christian soldier, rather than as a Schizoaffective. (Zeiders, 2001, pp. 61-64; used with permission)

Of special note is that both client and clinician experienced the therapeutic process to be saturated by the third person of the Holy Trinity; this is in keeping with the central tenet of Christian Holism. For a detailed discussion of this case that exposes the material to other tenets of Christian Holism, see Zeiders et al., 2011.

CONCLUSION

As an approach to mental health treatment, Christian Holism comprises several important tenets. Among these foundational principles is the central tenet: the assertion that the Holy Spirit is fully present and active in the clinical situation. Other important tenets of Christian Holism are as follows:

- Treatment is conducted under the lordship of Jesus Christ.
- Psychological theories and interventions are annexed into the kingdom of God by placing them at the disposal of the Holy Spirit.
- Under the Spirit's guidance, Scripture inspires and guides psychotherapeutic practice.
- Creeds and catechisms open clinicians and clients to the healing reality of God.
- Ecumenical in outlook and practice, treatment welcomes and loves all the healing gifts contained within Christendom.
- Conceptualized in terms of the image of God (*imago Dei*), essential human nature implies a freedom to love, choose, create and reason within the joy of a lively ebullient relation with God, self, others and creation.
- Treatment participates in the reunion of the person with all good things, including God, self, others and creation.
- Natural healing processes and miraculous healing are recognized as having equal measures of God's grace; both are excellent and equally welcome in the healing process.
- Christian Holism finds that, under grace, social science is holy and faith is therapeutic.
- Practitioners of this therapy view themselves as fellow travelers with clients and humbly participate in God's healing love for the client.

These tenets are not meant to be exhaustive or unchangeable. Rather, they are meant to guide the use of this transpersonal psychological theory and practice in the context of the Christian clinical situation. As the Holy Spirit continues to unfold God's plan, the tenets of Christian Holism will expand and change. This must necessarily happen because the tenets of Christian Holism are subject to the love and pleasure of a living God.

References and Recommended Resources

Barker, K. (Ed.). (1985). *The NIV study bible*. Grand Rapids: Zondervan.

Fabricant, S., & Schoeninger, D. (1987). Evaluating methods and theories of healing. *The Journal of Christian Healing*, 9(1), 35-41.

McBrien, R. (1994). *Catholicism*. New York: HarperCollins.

United States Catholic Conference. (1994). *Catechism of the Catholic church*. New York: Doubleday.

Zeiders, C. (2001). Dreams and Christian holism. *Journal of Christian Healing*, 22(3-4), 58-71.

Zeiders, C. (2004). *The clinical Christ: Scientific and spiritual reflections on the transformative psychology called Christian holism*. Birdsboro, PA: Julian's House.

Zeiders, C., Schoeninger, D., Riffel, H., Caccese, R., & Wegryn, J. (2001). Tenets of Christian holism for psychotherapeutic treatment. *The Journal of Christian Healing*, 22(3-4), 5-41.

Zeiders, C., Sperry, L., Paul, G., & DeMar, J. (2011). A multi-disciplinary discussion of the God-inspired dreams of an institutionalized Roman Catholic schizoaffective patient. *Journal of Christian Healing*, 27(1), 16-28. Retrieved from <http://www.actheals.org/Pearl/JCH.html>.

Permissions

Special thanks is offered to the Institute for Christian Healing (formerly the Institute for Christian Counseling and Therapy), to the *Journal of Christian Healing*, and to Julian's House for permission to redact and reprint the main body of this material from:

Zeiders, C. (2004). *The clinical Christ: Scientific and spiritual reflections on the transformative psychology called Christian holism*. Birdsboro, PA: Julian's House.

Zeiders, C., Schoeninger, D., Riffel, H., Caccese, R., & Wegryn, J. (2001). Tenets of Christian holism for psychotherapeutic treatment. *The Journal of Christian Healing*, 22(3-4), 5-41.

8

Contemplative Focused Prayer in Christian Counseling

J. Mark Shadoan

Unfortunately, much Christian counseling neglects prayer interventions since researching such an experiential behavior is difficult. This chapter will discuss Contemplative Focused Prayer's (CFP) effect on the client's spiritual and clinical goals and on the counseling process. Is CFP a practical intervention that Christian counseling can use efficiently, compatibly and responsibly in healing a client's clinical problem(s)? The chapter will discuss CFP's background, research and integration into counseling, as well as a case example.

Background of Contemplative Focused Prayer

Initial research on CFP came in the 1970s via its secularization as a relaxation technique. Herbert Benson (1975), a Harvard cardiologist, considered the potential of meditation to enhance cardiovascular health. Benson found a simple focusing technique common to many religions that could serve as a relaxation technique. This research proved Benson's hypothesis that as the mind can produce stress and impair bodily functions, it could also create relaxation and heal the body. This connected the mind and body, thus challenging the conventional view that they were separate functions. Benson's subjects had significant improvement in lowering hypertension, plus improvement in overall mental and physical health.

Many subjects asked if they could do the relaxation response as a form of prayer. Benson kept separate data on these subjects and nonprayer subjects. He found the prayer subjects more disciplined with the practice and having greater physical gains. Incorporating one's faith to the relaxation response gave it a booster effect. Benson called this effect the Faith Factor, which he wrote about in *Beyond the Relaxation Response* (1984).

Historical Context of Contemplative Prayer

Contemplation and solitude were distinct features of discipleship through the early centuries of Christianity. In the third century, several men forsook conventional life to live in the North African desert. There they practiced contemplation and solitude. They wrote and preached about their experiences and became known as the Desert Fathers (Merton, 1950). Classic Christian writers, most notably Brother Lawrence (1982), have described their experiences with contemplative prayer. Brother Lawrence was a cook in a medieval monastery and a soldier convert who sought to abide in Christ regardless of the routine tasks he had to perform—"to do all as unto the Lord." The Christian world, then and now, noted his book and example.

By the Reformation many early Protestants, such as Luther, were contemplatives. The Spanish Catholic leaders imprisoned contemplatives who protested the corruption of their church. Seminaries began to promote an academic and less experiential approach to knowing God. Protestants eventually discarded contemplation, it being "too" Catholic a practice. Meanwhile Catholic leaders censored the practice, since its advocates challenged institutional corruption. Hence, contemplation became an arcane and marginalized practice.

Father Thomas Merton (2003), a convert to Catholicism, rejuvenated contemplation during the mid-twentieth century. This spurred on a contemplative movement in the Catholic church, which quickly spilled into the evangelical church. Counselors, pastors and authors such as Beth Moore, Rick Warren, John Ortberg, Charles Stanley, Chuck Swindoll, Richard Foster and Frank Meier all advocated the use of contemplative prayer. Nevertheless, one can also find evangelicals proclaiming it as Godless, a disguised Eastern practice, a focus on self, and other misconceptions discrediting contemplation. Caught in the minor similarities of transcendental meditation to contemplative prayer, these dissenters do not discuss contemplation as a means to "abide in Christ" or to "be silent before God." They neglected that a relationship with God is a spiritual experience beyond our human faculties. They ignored that God and believer desire a reciprocal connection.

Often verbal prayers are about our agendas and expectations of God versus honest requests for God to do his will. Contemplation is a two-way connection with God. It is working on God's side of prayer: the side God uses when we are quiet, still, receptive and alone. These are not natural states for many Christians when they verbally pray. Contemplation in order to hear God requires that we quiet both heart and mind in order to be able to listen clearly with our inner ear.

What Is Contemplation?

To examine what CFP is, let us consider how it is different from similar forms of prayer. Eastern meditation practices focus on attaining a certain state of consciousness, self-awareness or inner wisdom. The primary goal is finding self, not God. Whether self-knowledge, self-purification or self-wisdom is the goal, it is still focused on the self and does not truly transcend the self to any genuine God-consciousness. Or it confuses God-consciousness with the self-exaltation that is often fostered in self-absorbing practices.

The goal of CFP is encountering God inwardly, which simultaneously causes self-confrontation and a dying of the willful self. The foundation of CFP is the personal/transformative/sanctifying relationship with God. Learning to experience God is not contradictory to the Bible. James 4:8 tells us, "Come near to God and he will come near to you." CFP enlists the exterior efforts of devotion and fellowship in tandem with the interior experiences of contemplative reflection, listening to God and the enjoyment of a peace that passes understanding.

Awareness of God's presence. CFP's focus is on developing awareness of God's presence, not on changing negative behavior. Counselors and clients need to avoid making behavior change the prime focus or motive in CFP, which counseling can imply. Again, the problem is that such a focus is on self, not God. CFP surfaces and bypasses the client's defenses. Personal change becomes a therapeutic byproduct of a deeper spiritual intimacy with God. This is promoted by the sanctification process of counseling, and motivated by the exhortation of the counselor.

Developing the mind of Christ. CFP is a practical and disciplined means of developing the mind of Christ. This occurs through silence before God.

One increasingly enjoys the contemplative experience via tapping into the love of God that he expresses to the soul. The client learns to discipline one's internal processes that impose on the person's time with God. CFP helps one to focus and live in the present with God. The present is where we find him and discover what he has to share, teach or correct within us. Contemplation is an appropriation of God's presence into our day-to-day living. A clinical definition of contemplation is a disciplined appropriation and enjoyment of God's Spirit within us, which sanctifies and grounds our identity, purpose and meaning in Christ as a unique channel for expressing his love.

Overcoming anxiety. Existentially, contemplation confronts the client with a death of self-anxiety. This is a resistant fear of the willful self to release control to God, even if that means personal despair and spiritual alienation. The mere act of contemplation requires a surrender of time. The discipline of silence and waiting on God confronts one's empirically driven, quick-fix mentality. The humility of the process requires a surrendering of expectations of God, others and self.

Procedurally, CFP is a means to quiet the mind, ready the spirit, relax the body and prepare for the deeper, more experiential contemplative state. CFP requires picking a focus of a sacred word, phrase or image that has significance to the client. The client learns to focus and thus settle his or her mind, spirit and body first into a relaxed state. This will precede an eventual state of contemplation that suspends time and brings an awareness of the inner peace and love of Christ. A detailed explanation will follow.

How Does Contemplative Focused Prayer Work?

As one becomes aware of God through CFP, a fine-tuning of this awareness develops with practice. One learns to attend to yearnings of the Spirit throughout the day. CFP in its broadest form is what St. Paul described as praying unceasingly (1 Thess 5:17 KJV). It is the ongoing connection and comfort of his love that bypasses the personal wounds of our lives that question or inhibit spiritual peace.

Research indicates that religious coping methods such as prayer may buffer, moderate or deter stressful reactions (McCullough & Larson, 1998; Pargament & Brant, 1998). People who pray frequently suffer less psychologically or physically after a major stressor (McCullough & Larson, 1998). Richards and Bergin (1997) wrote that contemplation could have strong generalizability to a range of clinical problems and settings. Contemplative prayer is found to be a workable adjunct to Christian counseling (Finney, 1985; Shadoan, 2006; Treichel, 1992). Since contemplation is done outside of one's sessions, it incorporates prayer into counseling and diminishes the ethical and clinical apprehensions some raise about the in-session use of verbal prayer.

How CFP works in the counseling process.

Stages of contemplation. Foster (1992) discusses three stages of contemplation. The first is recollection, being the quieting of the mind and readying it for the second stage, which is peacefulness and mental receptivity to God. The third stage is spiritual ecstasy, which is a work God does within the person.

Stages of therapeutic change. First, there is success in learning to manage one's contemplative focus, and a growing desire to experience God. Second, spiritual and/or behavioral changes occur, perhaps subtly and at times dramatically. Clients report new behaviors, insights and emotional peace and strength in situations where they had behaved differently. Some "lapse" into old inadequate behaviors, or any of the barriers separating them from God in the past. Dormant, well-ingrained barriers or memories of the subconscious can emerge. In this manner, contemplation is working therapeutically to purge and heal them. Third, one becomes progressively aware of God during the day in the presence of one's thoughts, behaviors or emotions.

The therapist's role. During counseling, the client should discuss whatever insight or experience that surfaced from one's CFP time. The therapist helps the client explore and make therapeutic sense of this material. The therapist encourages the client to stay with his or her CFP process. If the client is overanxious or finds "mental chatter" too difficult to manage, then the therapist and client collaboratively work at an adaption of CFP. Research (Shadoan, 2006) notes that some clients need to focus on an image from Scripture, such as Jesus walking on water. Others prefer to say a verse softly. Moreover, some might need to stop focusing and pray out distracting concerns, and then resume their CFP. The therapist's job is to help the client from becoming discouraged and to experiment with different ways of contemplation to find what works most effectively.

The counselor acts as coach and exhorter. Often clients partially grasp the effects of their prayer time. An open-ended interview helps process their experiences. With Socratic questioning, and avoidance of providing immediate interpretations, the therapist helps the client gain clarity of a healing process. Thus, clients form a narrative, which connects their reflections into a cogent understanding of CFP's effects.

Steps to doing CFP.

Step 1: Preparation.

1. Find a quiet place and sit comfortably with the head bowed or leaned back, and eyes shut.
2. Verbally present oneself to God: "Lord, I am here to experience your presence. I am learning to seek you without expectations, except to know you deeper. Help me to focus on you, and I thank you for this time now."
3. Confess sin or ask God to help with any barrier to this prayer time.
4. Set a timer for prayer time. Avoid checking time.
5. Initially, to get relaxed, pay attention to one's breathing, slowing it down or practicing deep breathing.

Step 2: Sacred focusing. Choose a sacred focus such as a sacred word, object or image that will help anchor a wandering mind. The goal is not to "empty the mind," but redirect attention back to the sacred focus. A sacred word should be one or two syllables: "Jesus," "Father" or any sacred word that helps remind one of the prayer's purpose. Repeat the word in a whisper. A sacred image is a mental image that reminds one of Jesus. A sacred or symbolic object could be a picture in one's Bible, a cross, a burning candle or even a picturesque view.

Step 3: Redirect mental activity. Keep attention to the sacred focus. Let wandering thoughts pass through the mind, which is what they will do unless one tries to stop them. Simply redirect attention back to the sacred focus. Note distractions in the mind. Such thoughts are often the unconscious "mental chatter" one has throughout the day. This can be material to discuss in therapy.

Step 4: Rest. Repeat the sacred focus and keep redirecting back to it if the mind drifts. Eventually one will feel a relaxed state. Begin with a minute or more and add time each day for one week. Work up to ten to twenty minutes. It is recommended to do no more than twenty minutes, twice a day.

Step 5: Mental activity to avoid. Avoid reflection, analysis or self-criticism during CFP. Let these thoughts pass and redirect attention to the sacred focus. Do not try to understand any experience, simply allow it to occur.

Step 6: Reentry. When prayer ends, allow time to reenter a normal state of mind. Arise slowly, stretch and walk about.

Step 7: Reflection. Reflect, possibly journal insights or reactions of the experience. Note experiences that can be material for counseling sessions.

IMPLICATIONS FOR PRACTICE

As Merton (1969) writes, contemplation is not super spirituality. He discusses that novice contemplatives have initial difficulty with nondirected prayer. Silence seems disheartening, even distressing. What the novice learns is that God's intimate language is silence. With practice, the novice experiences the peace of contemplation.

Nineteen Christian adults in Christian counseling were trained in CFP. After four weeks, they were interviewed about their experiences. The following benefits were summarized from their exit interviews (Shadoan, 2006).

Spiritual benefits

1. Learning to become silent before God,
2. Learning to recognize and disengage the mental distractions from God's peace and guidance throughout the day or during prayer,
3. Developing an active attention to God's inner presence,
4. Deepening their spiritual life through experiencing greater intimacy with God in prayer that carried over through the day,
5. Learning to listen to God and follow his will by developing the practice of surrender to God,
6. Developing an increased spiritual self-discipline in prayer,
7. Recognizing God's influence in them and his presence around them in their daily activities, especially when confronted by troubling circumstances or inner conflicts,
8. Improving personal focus during prayer,
9. Learning to initiate spiritual rest in prayer, and

10. Deepening their love for God and the experience of God's love and acceptance by learning how to ready their body, mind and soul for contemplative prayer.

Psychological benefits

1. Diminished distressing emotions and improved emotional control,
2. Improved self-concept and self-worth,
3. Improved self-monitoring and self-knowledge,
4. Improved interpersonal functioning,
5. Increased self-confidence and assertiveness in social situations and pursuing personal goals,
6. Increased personal insights and problem-solving skills,
7. Increased skill in relaxation and stress-management ability, and
8. Improved mental focus and task performance.

From this and other research (Finney, 1985; Treichel, 1992), CFP is shown as a promising and advantageous practice, both clinically and spiritually. It did not distract or detract from the clinical process; if anything, it sped up and improved the counseling process, according to subjects (Shadoan, 2006). It was easy to learn and compatible with treatment.

Clinical Considerations

Like any other intervention, CFP is appropriate in some situations and less so in others. Problems of living may be readily addressed, especially if the client tends to be spiritually inclined. Other clients, especially those suffering from psychoses, may be opening the door to an unhealthy place by giving themselves to contemplative prayer in that the godly imagination is often called into play. It is for this reason that proper assessment is important.

After a clinical/spiritual history and assessment are done, and treatment goals and diagnosis are made, a discussion of incorporating CFP can occur. The counselor provides a rationale for CFP, explains how it works and how it complements client goals, and describes informed consent details, clinical aspects of CFP and research efficacy. In a mutual discussion about its use, a client can say no to CFP, ask any questions or state any reservations, all without the counselor trying to impose one's clinical or religious ideas. Foremost, counselors should reflect on personal prayer beliefs and practices, especially discussing any discomfort praying with clients or advocating the use of prayer with a client.

Indicators for incorporating CFP are:

1. Is spiritual growth a goal for counseling?
2. Are clinical or spiritual issues involving prayer and religion hampering the counseling process?
3. Has a supportive, collaborative counseling relationship formed that permits a mutual discussion of prayer orientation?
4. Has a brief spiritual history been taken by the counselor with the client?

Contraindications for incorporating CFP include:

1. When prayer is not a part of the client's lifestyle, or not part of the therapist's belief system, especially if one does not believe in CFP;
2. The client is psychotic, delusional, has grandiose spiritual beliefs or is substance abusing;
3. The client does not express an interest in spiritual practices or prayer; or
4. CFP does not align with the treatment goals.

Koenig (2002) adds these reasons to avoid prayer, which can apply to CFP.

1. The client believes one's problems are God's punishment;
2. The questions create discomfort or agitation; or
3. Problematic spiritual issues, experiences or concerns are surfaced.

Spiritual assessment. Counselors should assess what a client knows about prayer, especially CFP, and how comfortable a client is with this prayer form and prayer in general. Consider and explore the feelings clients have about God, prayer and CFP. Be sensitive to past wounds by religious authorities and peers causing deep hurts and resentments toward God. The counselor needs to explore these experiences before any discussion of CFP can be considered.

Ethically and clinically, a brief spiritual history should be part of an initial assessment. Koenig (2002) states this is necessary to help the clinician become familiar with the person's religious beliefs, to help with treatment planning, to understand how faith operates in coping with (or in creating) problems, and to identify and address spiritual needs.

Taking a history has implicit purposes:

1. The client's spirituality is recognized and shown respect.
2. It illuminates motivations supporting clinical and religious behavior.
3. It provides data on the client's support system and resources within the community.
4. It informs the client that the counselor is willing to discuss spirituality in the future.

Questions are client, not dogma, centered. There are four basic areas to cover according to Koenig.

1. Does the client use religion or spirituality to help cope with problems, or is it a source of stress, and if so, how?
2. Is the client a member of a supportive spiritual community?
3. Does the client have any troubling spiritual questions or concerns?
4. Does the client have any spiritual beliefs that might influence psychological care, positive or negative?

Since Koenig's questions deal with general spirituality, the following questions were designed for understanding the client's quality of prayer life. This includes some clarity in their frequency of prayer, comfort level and satisfaction with prayer. Clients who find prayers very unrewarding, difficult and infrequently practiced might be poor candidates for CFP. Instead, helping them with obstacles to verbal prayer would make more clinical and spiritual sense as a preceding goal to CFP.

1. How would the client describe their prayer practices? How close do they feel to God in prayer?
2. What frustrations do they experience with prayer?
3. How comforting do they find prayer?
4. Do they find prayer a one-way or two-way communication with God?

Rationale for the incorporation of CFP.

1. CFP provides a simple method for experiencing God's love.
2. CFP works by helping the client learn to be silent before God.

3. CFP is a means to learn how to "abide in Christ" (Jn 15:4-11) and experience spiritual growth.
4. The following verses provide a scriptural rationale: Ps 46:10; 54:6; Mt 16:24; 28:20; Lk 12:21; Jn 3:3; 14:16-21, 23; 15:4-11; Acts 17:28; Rom 8:16; 14; 17; 1 Cor 12:7; 2 Cor 13:5; Phil 4:1-7.
5. The research shows effectiveness in reducing anxiety, improving spiritual well-being (Shadoan, 2006; Levin & Chatters, 1998; Finney, 1985) and reducing depression (Shadoan, 2006; Propst, 1996). It is an important ingredient in psychological change (Blanton, 2003) and has been effective with problems of substance abuse recovery, reducing risky behaviors and increasing self-esteem, and in reducing anxiety, anger and depression (Larson et al., 1997).
6. CFP has a long history back to the early Christian church as a means to growing closer with God.
7. There are no known risks to doing CFP. However, distressing memories, thoughts or images can surface in a "purging" effect that can cause discomfort. If this occurs, the client should stop CFP and discuss this with their counselor. If the client needs to stop CFP, this is understood.
8. It is important to recognize and observe barriers to God's influence in one's life, and to recognize God's voice and direction.

Advise the client that a "dry period" can be expected, in which nothing seems to be happening or CFP is boring. The client may wonder, is anything going to happen? Anyone is going to find this at some point. This period increases clients' awareness of the need for Christ in their lives. Encourage them to persist in CFP.

Distressing memories or discouraging thoughts or beliefs can occur as a sense of purging these memories out or becoming aware of them in one's conscious spiritual life; thus a resolution process can begin. Stop prayer if distress continues, and talk about this in therapy. Use verbal prayer and ask God for his assistance.

Case Illustration

Fritz, age fifty-one, a professionally trained counselor and pastor, now partially retired from disability, wanted to learn contemplative focused prayer as a supplement to his personal counseling and for reducing stress. Fritz suffers from a rare illness, systemic mastocytosis. Physical or psychosocial triggers can cause an overabundance of mast cells and histamine that dump into the blood system, which can cause dangerous vascular failure. The dangerous symptoms begin as a loss of consciousness and dropping blood pressure, and result in emergency care to provide injections to restrict the mast and histamine surge. Mast cells exist in the immune system to counter parasitic or allergic entities. Avoidance of stress, injections to control the condition, anti-anxiety medication and psychotherapy are the treatment regimen.

Ironically, the illness also causes anxiety and panic attacks, the very triggering agents that set off this deadly ailment. The illness has no cure. Fritz has had multiple emergency visits to save his life. Since participating in a study that examined the effectiveness of CFP with Christian counseling (Shadoan, 2006), Fritz has not been to the emergency room. His last emergency room visit was the week before learning CFP in July of 2005. Fritz exists with the ailment. However, he is now on low doses of medications.

Fritz participated in a group training session on the use of CFP. The session included a video disk and manual on how to do CFP. Due to his condition, Fritz began CFP minimally for forty-five minutes daily. He now has two or more sessions for sixty or ninety minutes. Although his time far exceeds the recommended amount, given his extreme need for stress reduction the normal amount seemed too little to be helpful. Over the years, he has found two or more extended sessions helpful in meeting his medical needs. He is aware of his stress reactions and will practice the technique immediately. Thus, he can have six or eight times of CFP in a day. The result is he stops the rising anxiety he feels and prevents a triggering effect of the stress. Initially, he used the cross as a sacred focus. The cross image acted much like a screen-saver image in his mind: swirling, flashing forward, and rising and lowering in his view, which is typical and suggests the stress and turmoil of one's mental state. CFP helps us step into our minds to observe this effect. By two weeks, Fritz was comfortable practicing CFP for forty-five minutes a day. The cross image began to slow down and become static as he was able to anchor his focus to the image.

Due to his medical condition, he had to retire as a pastor in his forties. The condition, which he has had since young adulthood, worsened with time, as even moderate stress became a triggering factor. This loss of work left him empty and angry. He lived in an attitude of self-pity, which he did not recognize. As he practiced CFP, he discovered that the anger left him within a month. It was not a point of counseling intervention. It was something he kept on a slow burn in his mind. With the sense of love from God he received from CFP, the anger went away. This realization struck him while having his exit interview for the CFP study.

Fritz does some men's counseling for a Christain practice. He advocates the use of CFP to these men, and in his church. He is quick to make the point that CFP is not just a "technique" to be added to counseling models or interventions. CFP is more than a technique or tool. It is a direct reciprocal line between God and believer. It does more than provide behavioral change, which he considers just a Band-Aid. It goes deeper into the soul and heart of the person by connecting one with the Holy Spirit. Over time, he realized another change in his life. A fellow Christian confronted him about his self-pity, which was due to his illness and its effects on his life. Fritz became very offended and angry, but through the years, he has found that the self-pity was indeed there. With CFP, it has dissipated.

As with the relaxation response, CFP has an initial effect of lowering blood pressure and releasing endorphins that counter stress. Moreover, CFP is more than relaxation. It provides an experience of God's presence in our quietude. His love is experienced without any effort on our part but being still before him. Fritz's experiences with this complete love have provided him personal acceptance of his limitations and illness. He became mentally and spiritually free to discover a new ministry to men. His anxiety reactions are almost gone, so he can do activities that provide fulfillment and meaning. Instead of being a retired pastor, he is now a part-time assistant pastor. His anger and resentment were washed away in God's love that provided Fritz an acceptance of his disability—a love that provides the experience of God's acceptance of him, which in turn provides him that peace that passes understanding, and the self-love and acceptance that is realized through the practice of CFP.

Fritz's spiritual growth and well-being were goals of counseling. He has a personal and active relationship with Christ, grounded in a traditional theology. His self-pity, anger toward others and anxiety provided major blocks to his relationship with God. Through CFP, he experienced God's love directly. It bypassed his cognitive and emotional blocks and connected with his soul. God loved Fritz even though Fritz had his doubts and his issues with God.

Fritz was informed of the initial difficulty of learning to be still and quiet. However, research showed by starting with just one minute initially, and then adding a minute to each subsequent session, by two weeks the client will be doing the prayer effectively (Shadoan, 2006). *The Handbook for Incorporating Contemplative Prayer in Christian Counseling* (Shadoan, 2007) provides an assessment and teaching protocol for helping the client, handouts and a manual that will assist them to learn contemplative prayer. Encouraging the clients to keep a prayer log is also helpful for session discussions.

Many clients wonder if it is helping them. Asking the client clarifying questions of their experiences helps to gel what is occurring. It obviously helps if the counselor has practiced CFP on some basis. This will help them assist the client and provides their own understanding of the experience. After a couple of weeks, the client usually is experiencing some progress with CFP. If they are doing well with it, ask questions about their experiences. Often the client needs to form a narrative of their experience, which questions will help them develop. Having this narrative gives them detailed awareness of their experiences. New insights will often surface as the interview progresses.

References and Recommended Resources

Benson, H. (1975). *The relaxation response.* New York: Avon.

Benson, H. (1984). *Beyond the relaxation response.* New York: Avon.

Blanton, P. G. (2003). Creating narratives from meditations: A model for marital therapy. *Marriage and Family: A Christian Journal, 6*(1), 45-55.

Brother Lawrence. (1982). *The practice of the presence of God.* Springdale, PA: Whitaker House.

Finney, J. R., & Malony, H. N. (1985). An empirical study of contemplative prayer as an adjunct to psychotherapy. *Journal of Psychology and Theology, 13,* 284-90.

Foster, R. J. (1992). *Prayer: Finding the heart's true home.* San Francisco: HarperSanFrancisco.

Koenig, H. (1999). *The healing power of faith: Science explores medicine's last frontier.* New York: Simon & Schuster.

Koenig, H. (2002). *Spirituality in patient care.* Radnor, PA: Templeton.

Larson, D. B., Swyers, J. P., & McCullough, M. E. (1997). *Scientific research on spirituality and health: A consensus report.* Radner, PA: Templeton.

Levin, J. S., & Chatters, L. M. (1998). Research on religion and mental health: An overview of empirical findings and theoretical issues. In. H. Koenig (Ed.), *The Handbook of religion and mental health* (pp. 32-52). London: Academic Press.

McCullough, M. E., & Larson, D. R. (1998). Future directions in research. In H. Koenig (Ed.), *The handbook of religion and mental health* (pp. 98-112). London: Academic Press.

Merton, T. (1950). *What is contemplation*? Springfield, IL: Templegate.

Merton, T. (1969). *Contemplative prayer*. New York. Bantam/Doubleday.

Merton, T. (2003). *The inner experience: Notes on contemplation*. San Francisco: HarperSanFrancisco.

Pargament, K. I., & Brant, C. R. (1998). Religion and coping. In. H. Koenig (Ed.), *The handbook of religion and mental health* (pp. 112-20). London: Academic Press.

Propst, L. R. (1996). Cognitive-therapy and the religious person. In E. P. Shafranske (Ed.), *Religion and the clinical practice of psychology* (pp. 291-407). Washington, DC: American Psychological Association.

Richards, P. S., & Bergin, A. E. (1997). *A spiritual strategy for counseling and psychotherapy*. Washington, DC: American Psychological Association.

Shadoan, J. M. (2006). *The effectiveness of contemplative focused prayer in psychotherapy: A multiple case study*. Doctoral dissertation, Argosy University at Sarasota, FL.

Shadoan, J. M. (2007). *Therapy in solitude: A manual for incorporating contemplative focused prayer in Christian counseling* (self-published ebook and emanual). Raleigh, NC: Lulu Press. <http://contemplativefocusedprayer.com/resources.html>.

Treichel, M. J. (1992). *Contemplative prayer in pastoral counseling*. Doctoral dissertation, Columbia Pacific University. Dissertation Abstracts order number LD02511.

9

God Is Present

The Concept of Christian Counseling at IGNIS, the German Association for Christian Psychology

Werner May

The fundamental consideration and the aim of IGNIS, the German Association for Christian Psychology—to introduce the Christian faith, the biblical truths, the gospel of Jesus Christ, the presence of God into psychology—created conditions that gave rise to a new psychology, Christian psychology.

A statement by the German theologian Dietrich Bonhoeffer (1975) was our frequent companion at the beginning:

> The place where the question regarding the reality of God and that regarding the reality of the world receive an answer simultaneously is known by only one name: Jesus Christ.
>
> In this name God and the world are encompassed. All things have their being in Him (Col. 1:16). From now on, it is not possible to speak accurately about God and the world without speaking of Jesus Christ. All definitions of reality which ignore Him are abstractions. (p. 207)

It was on this understanding of reality that a Christian psychology and also Christian counseling were to be founded.

At the beginning of our construction of a Christian psychology from 1986 on, we worked through the classical charismatic and evangelical Christian counseling—for example, concepts from the Inner Healing Movement (including John and Paula Sandford, 1982 et al.) or the Nouthetic Counseling of Jay Adams (Adams, 1986 et al.) both theoretically and practically. As a further influencing factor, the initiators of IGNIS had in principle been through the entire palette of secular psychotherapeutic training of the day (psychoanalysis, behavioral therapy, body-oriented therapies and humanistic approaches such as Gestalt Therapy or client-centered therapy after Rogers), but were fascinated by God's working and the statements of the Bible as well as by the multiplicity of Christian counseling movements. The working of the Holy Spirit is part of our understanding of counseling, just as prayer and biblical concepts such as forgiveness play a role. In other words, the counseling dialogue is not only an interaction between the counselor and the counselee, but is a three-way exchange: God is present.

A biblical view of humans and the world forms the foundation of Christian counseling (Coe & Hall, 2010; Johnson, 2007). Jesus Christ becomes the Lord of psychology (Johnson, 1997). Admittedly—as any scientific approach should admit—we were more or less unconsciously looking through the lenses of our own socialization. Our theological lenses focused above all on the healing dimension of the Christian faith and charismatic experiences with the Holy Spirit. This led to an approach to the gospel and the Bible differing from, for example, a soteriological approach. This original approach will still have an influence, even if one later turns to further themes of dogmatics, practical theology or exegesis.

Efficacy Factors in Christian Counseling

Besides the six well-known nonspecific efficacy factors of psychotherapy (after Pfeifer, 1991)—a supportive, trusting therapeutic relationship; finding rational causes as explanations for the difficulties of the counselee; outlining new ways of tackling these difficulties; strengthening the expectation of help; leading into experiences of success; and the emotional involvement of the counselor—we rely on seven specific efficacy factors: God's sovereign acting in love; knowledge of and insight into truth; freely made decisions and willful turning to life and love; faith, as the capacity to hope with firm confidence and not to doubt what one cannot see (Heb 11:1); daring to enter loving relationships; forgiveness and reconciliation; and responsible learning processes with "faithfulness in the small things" (Mt 25:14-30).

In these seven specific efficacy factors of Christian counseling, the six nonspecific efficacy factors mentioned previously are in principle already incorporated. They are, in our view, an interesting discovery in therapy research, as they can be summarized with three very familiar biblical terms: faith, love and hope.

The seven phases of a counseling dialogue. These efficacy factors must be given room to act in the therapeutic dialogue. To this purpose, IGNIS has developed a seven-phase concept that we have been using now for more than twenty years in our three-year training in Christian counseling, and which we have been able to pass on in many church seminars (see A. May, 2004).

This seven-phase concept is subordinate to the leading of the Holy Spirit. The dialogue structure has the aim of maintaining orientation among the many layers of a complex of problems. The seven-phase model was originally developed for the purpose of training. In a concrete counseling session, only one of the phases may take place, or the order may be changed. The structure is not a "straitjacket," but rather a silver thread that constantly reminds us of the fellowship with God in the dialogue situation.

This being led by the Holy Spirit is not only an unconscious process to which one entrusts oneself in prayer, but it can also be sought consciously. Inner perceptions and intuitive thoughts have their source, in the sense of a causal attribution (Heckhausen, 1980), externally and stably, in God's speaking, because God is a person who has revealed himself as one who speaks ("My sheep listen to my voice" in Jn 10:27), who is close to me in the Holy Spirit and who has promised me, in his love, his help. Why should he not speak?

Here we need a "humility in erring" in opening ourselves to a learning process that is open for feedback and correction and sensitive to misuse and, at the same time, the courage to trust, whatever our own imperfections may be.

Phase 1: Preparation. For planned dialogue sessions, it is important to us that a dialogue already begins before the counselee enters the room. A certain time for inner preparation should open the "spiritual space" in advance. The first need in this preparation is that the counselor consciously places herself in her relationship with God (i.e., lays down before God all that has been occupying her thoughts at that time, whether this be another counseling session or other activities and encounters, and reflects on whether anything stands between her and God that requires cleansing).

Second, the counselor will reflect on her relationship with the counselee. (For a first session, for example, the counselor may ask: What information is available? What feelings do I have about the counselee? In further sessions: What was the topic of the last session? Which notes did I make? How does our relationship look? Where should I alter my behavior? What feelings have arisen in me? How do I evaluate cognitively and emotionally the process so far?) She wishes to avoid a meeting with the counselee that, instead of being direct and open, is conditioned by a preconception.

Third, the counselor looks ahead to the imminent session (What point have we reached in our process? What topic is set for today? Do I have to ask about agreements made in our last session? Is there anything I still have to prepare?).

Finally, the counselor prays for faith for this person and trusts in God's guidance of the dialogue, consciously placing his own expectations in God's hands, asking for his help and requesting concrete impulses.

Phase 2: Meeting. Prepared by the clarification of his relationship with God and with the counselee and encouraged by prayer, the counselor is ready to begin the actual session with the counselee, in the phase called "meeting." Here there are two focal points: building a relationship and gaining insight into the counselee's set of problems.

With his intrinsically open attitude toward relationships, the counselor tries to allow trust to grow. Two messages—"You are loved, regardless of what you do or do not do!" and "You have a right to be!"—establish a basis for the other person to open himself and, together, we ask which process of change is appropriate. It is a matter of wishing to understand and not of presenting quick solutions.

The important point is, therefore, to enter into trustful contact with the counselee, to "pick him up" at the point where he stands, and to communicate to him that the Christian counselor is genuinely interested in how he feels and what his problem is. The aim is to work through this complex of problems by, for example, posing questions, focusing as much as possible on concrete situations.

Phase 3: Quietness before God. To be able to bring some order into the usually copious information from the phase of meeting, a time of quietness before God is helpful. Not only the Christian counselor, but also the counselee, reflect on what has been said and heard and seek clarity regarding the next step or steps. In this stage, the aim is to listen to God and to ask *him* for solutions and answers, or at least to sort what has been heard and to compose thoughts about the further course of the session. Here it will become clear that both persons stand before God on the same level of dependence. Both are—despite differences in tasks, experience and competence—dependent on God's help. Regardless of how much the counselee is suffering, it is essential not to fail to communicate to him that he still has available resources, and that his faith, above all, is a resource.

Phase 4: Teaching dialogue. After the phase of quietness before God, there follows an exchange concerning the thoughts and feelings that have become clear to the counselee and the counselor, and concerning impulses that they feel to have been given by God.

From this exchange, a so-called teaching dialogue can develop if the counselor recognizes a gap in knowledge and understanding on the part of the counselee that leads the latter to a dubious interpretation of his situation or to a problematic decision or hinders him in making progress. In this teaching dialogue, solutions or steps and knowledge needed in preparing for a solution are worked out with the help of the Bible.

While retaining complete clarity regarding the teaching matter presented, the counselor will at the same time respect the freedom of the individual and avoid applying manipulative pressure to the counselee regarding how he should understand these thoughts or act on them in his concrete situation. He helps the counselee to understand better his reactions to what has been heard in a better way and to react with honesty. This is what gives this phase its dialogue character.

To accompany the inner processes of the counselee, the counselor orients himself on the principle of leading and following. He takes care to lead by his teaching in such a way that he is always in contact with his vis-à-vis. This means, for example, that he does not pass on the biblical impulses in a tempo or manner that overwhelms or repels the counselee or causes him to detach himself internally. For the aim is that the other should be able to go along with this teaching, should be able and willing to follow the guidelines as his personal situation, constitution and state of faith permit. The counselee must always be aware that he has to, and is entitled to, make his own decision, even if this contradicts the suggestion made by the counselor.

The aim is to use questions to encourage the counselee to express what is happening inside him. Nonverbal and verbal answers help in becoming aware of the feelings, reactions and realizations in the heart of the counselee. In this way the counselee should be encouraged to discover the decision that is to be made, of his own accord and at this moment, regarding himself and his situation. It is about the decision that is possible for him at this time.

Christian counseling is thus both directive and nondirective.

Phase 5: Prayer. The counselee can be open, inexperienced or closed regarding personal prayer. He decides whether to bring before God or not what has been gathered from the dialogue.

If it has become clear that the counselee is ready for a decision and what this decision is, he will usually express this decision aloud before God in prayer. It can also initially happen that in prayer only questions are expressed, hindrances named or requests made that hidden factors be uncovered or that clear thoughts for a decision be given.

When a counselee formulates clearly before another person what he has realized and resolved, it becomes more real and binding for him. When he formulates it before God, he acknowledges at the same time that, in making this decision, his trust is not in his own strength but in God's grace, in which he is called and equipped to good works.

Sometimes this prayer of decision is followed by a further phase of prayer in which the Holy Spirit works through his gifts (prayer-counseling): the Holy Spirit uncovers, touches healingly and lovingly, and grants new insights (see Zeiders, 2010).

Phase 6: Integration. After prayer, the Christian counseling dialogue still is not over. It is now important to integrate what has been experienced into the world of the counselee. It may also be important to ask how the counselee evaluates the dialogue so far. What, in his opinion, could happen because of the decision just made?

Above all, it is necessary to work out what this dialogue means for the daily life of the counselee, for tomorrow and the days after. "Homework" may be agreed upon (i.e., concrete commitments regarding what the counselee wishes to do in the time until the next meeting). These commitments have to be in keeping with the capacities of the counselee.

Paul Watzlawik (1991) cites an Italian proverb in this context: "Between talking and doing there lies the sea" (p. 104). It seems difficult for us human beings to turn theoretical insights into practice.

Phase 7: Assessment. In the phase of assessment, after the counselee has left, the counselor makes summarizing notes and, above all, prays and lays the exchange in God's hands. This does not consist only of intercession for the counselee. Any weaknesses in the counselor's actions in the dialogue just finished, or his concern for the counselee, can also be brought before God.

Our structure for a Christian counseling dialogue will now be illustrated in two case reports. They also show that the phases cannot always be followed in a fixed order. As already said, they are nothing more than a guideline for cooperation with God through the Holy Spirit.

Case 1. The first example of Christian counseling will show the whole dialogue, according to the seven phases outlined above (see Hartmann, 1998, pp. 23-25).

Preparation. In the preparation, I had sought God in prayer and prepared internally for the dialogue with Mr. S. This woke in me faith in the presence of God in the imminent dialogue. He has a plan and instruction for this person too; he knows him and his problem.

Meeting. Mr. S. has a severe problem with self-esteem; he has difficulties accepting himself. His opening statement, the very first sentence he speaks coming through the door, is: "Oh dear, when I just look at myself!" During a dialogue about his family, he looks back on his parents fondly. He even speaks of a "golden childhood." One would have supposed that there was never a situation that he found in any way oppressive or destructive. When I ask about concrete situations, in which he experienced rejection, he remembers a teacher he had in PE for seven years. This gym teacher often made Mr. S. hang from the rings in sport lessons. Because he was somewhat corpulent, he hung there and was unable to perform the given task. It frequently happened that the gym teacher then made fun of him in front of the whole class and said: "Hey, just look at this, this limp sack!" One can imagine what this meant for a young person to be humiliated like this repeatedly over seven years.

After giving this account, Mr. S. says: "If I were to meet this teacher again on the street today . . ." (here he moves his hands as if wringing out a towel). But, because he has been a Christian for some time already, he immediately adds: "I know, I know, forgiveness, but I do not forgive him!"

Quietness before God. The situation seems lost irrecoverably. Mr. S. knows that he really should forgive, but right at the start he refuses to do this. In a silent call to God for help, I recognize that we should find out in dialogue what minimal decision Mr. S. is prepared to make today.

Teaching dialogue. In the teaching dialogue, the aim is to lead Mr. S. closer to the possibility of forgiving, a possibility to which he has reacted with such vehement rejection. What steps of trust toward God can he make today? Mr. S. comes up to this decision: I would like to reach the point of being able to forgive.

Prayer. I lead Mr. S. toward making a firm statement of this readiness in prayer before God. This prayer is roughly as follows: "Lord Jesus, I confess my anger to you and the refusal in my heart. I cannot forgive this teacher now, but I wish to reach the point of being able to forgive. Thank you that you are helping me in this."

Integration. I make it clear to Mr. S. that, with this minimal decision, he has given God room to continue working on him and to lead him to the decisive point at which it really comes down to forgiving. The homework is of a general nature—namely, not to forget the topic of forgiveness.

Assessment. After the dialogue, I commit this person to God in prayer with the expectation that God will continue to work on him and will take him seriously regarding the decision made today. I pray that God will lead him to further points of decision and that he will arrive at genuine forgiveness.

Later: Two weeks later, at the next session, Mr. S. says that he has noticed during the past few weeks that, every time he thought about this teacher and imagined how he would meet the teacher on the street and what he would do to him, a feeling of "power" arose in him and that forgiveness would have meant the loss of this power. In the further course of the dialogue, it becomes clear to him that these thoughts about what he would do to this teacher are a source of power that he considers acceptable to Jesus. But when I ask him what Jesus is to him, Mr. S. finds himself in a dilemma. Suddenly he understands that, on the one hand, there is Jesus, offering himself as a source of strength, and on the other hand, the source of wrath and revenge from which he is drawing strength.

It becomes clear to us that it was a matter of which source of strength he wishes to choose. After some inner battling, he is ready to decide for Jesus as his source of life. But this also means forgiving the teacher and along with that, giving up his access to that "cistern" (self-made source of life) that he has as a root of unforgiveness.

Case 2. Our second example of Christian counseling shows the inner dynamic of a teaching dialogue (W. May, unpublished).

The couple M., married for almost twenty years, with four children, had been coming once a month for individual or joint counseling sessions for half a year. Peter, an engineer, was a very rational person. His wife, Inge, a teacher, had repeatedly suffered depressive phases over more than twenty years with a strong self-esteem problem. One of the consequences of the long history of the illness was a bogging-down of the communication paths between the partners.

The main topic in the previous session had been a return to work on Inge's part, which she repeatedly wished to break off because she felt the position was beyond her abilities.

Before and after the Christmas period, I received calls for help from both sides. In response, a session together was scheduled. Peter came alone, however, as Inge was too tired. Peter was afraid that she could again fall into the depths of a depression.

In our session, Peter expressed the wish that the past with Inge should never catch up with him again. He wished for himself "no longer such thin ice," but that he should be capable of carrying loads. I told him that overcoming the past is made possible above all by forgiving. His reaction showed that, although he had been a committed Christian since his youth, he had an inadequate concept of the process of forgiving. With that, the topic for a teaching dialogue was provided: forgiving others.

I showed him with the help of Romans 12:19-20 what the essence of forgiving is. "Do not take revenge, my dear friends, but leave room for God's wrath, for it is written: 'It is mine to avenge; I will repay,' says the Lord. On the contrary: 'If your enemy is hungry, feed him; if he is thirsty, give him something to drink. In doing this, you will heap burning coals on his head.'"

Forgiving does not mean quickly saying "think nothing of it." It means refraining from revenge, including all forms of subtle, indirect revenge. This refraining is possible if we know that God does not forget or look away from wrongs but, at the same time, would happily forgive the other. Peter was very glad that I explained to him that forgiving was no superficial process—on the model of this "glossing over"—but that the guilt of the other must be identified concretely, and he does not have to see anything through rose-tinted glasses. This was new to Peter and gave him hope. What would it concretely mean for his life?

I asked him to describe a situation in which forgiveness was appropriate. He recounted how Inge had often humiliated him in front of the children and thus destroyed his authority and given him a feeling of helplessness. On the basis of this situation, we worked out precisely what his accusations toward Inge were. As I explained to Peter how he could formulate them in prayer, declare his refraining from revenge and then express forgiveness, I noticed a hesitation. I therefore bored a little deeper: "Are there any more questions on this topic? Resistance to concrete steps? Doubts regarding the necessity? Incomprehensible feelings?"

He said that something was holding him back—perhaps his injured pride. So we spoke about this "something," his injured pride. The initial aim of the teaching dialogue had to be postponed, as this new topic had taken on higher priority. It would not have made sense to motivate him "by hook or by crook" to forgive, today and at once, as the "best" decision. For if he reached this decision only automatically, perhaps out of pious ambition or on the basis of prejudices against God (fear of punishment or hope of reward for being good) or for my sake, it would not really have been his free decision. For Peter, the next important step was to admit his injured pride.

LEVELS OF THERAPEUTIC KNOWLEDGE

To use the seven-phase model of counseling or other concepts you learn in a counseling training in a helpful way, it is important that counselors receive training on different specific levels.

A first reason to enter training is, in many cases, the experience that, in everyday life or in counseling at church, quite concrete questions are asked to which one has no answer: "How should we behave when our child wets himself three times a day?" "How can I master my fear of examinations?"

Such "how" questions are plentiful. They are about how changes can happen. To answer them, one needs a so-called knowledge of transformation—a model for an inner process of forgiveness or a reconstruction of cognitive behavioral modification within the framework of a biblical view of man and the world (W. May, 2004).

Alongside, we have other questions of interest—the "why" questions: "Why do I have such fear of examinations?" "Why do we constantly argue in our marriage?"

All answers to these "why" questions can be grouped together under the term *knowledge of explanation* (also known as *knowledge of conditions* or *knowledge of disorders*). This knowledge appears vitally important in offering a counselee help, not simply on the basis of common sense and one's own life experience, but of competence.

During training itself, however, one discovers very quickly that the material presented relates not only to methods of transforming and possible explanations of disorders, but also has much to do with the counselor himself as a person. Because, besides the obviously interesting questions about how and why, there are other scientific areas of which a counselor likewise requires knowledge if he or she is to act responsibly: the knowledge of relationships, of one's self and one's calling.

Under knowledge of relationships, we understand a basic knowledge of human relationships, how they arise, what forms they take, what dangers they are exposed to, and what constitutes normal or pathological communication.

Everything a person does happens within relationships; what use would all knowledge and skills be if one could not pass it on? Furthermore, relationship problems, particularly related to communicative behavior, are often in the "background," leading to "foreground" disorder. Christian counseling, because of its biblical understanding of man, especially works on a relational, relationship-orientated basis.

Counselors additionally require self-knowledge. They must have learned to perceive themselves, their strengths and weaknesses, their self-assessment and their self-images, important life experiences, pivotal events and formative reactions in their own life histories.

If I wish to help someone else, my involvement should relate to their questions and to their experience of the problems, not to my own reactions on an emotional level. Without a training in self-awareness, there is a danger that I as the counselor react myself with transference or projection. In order to avoid being an example of "the blind leading the blind," it is important to know one's own weaknesses and mistakes and, particularly, the extent of one's personal reaction to specific disorders.

Not least, a counselor requires knowledge of her calling. This includes the knowledge that every Christian is called into the fellowship and intimacy of the Holy Spirit. Besides this general calling, it is necessary to find out the special tasks given by God, to consider, test and confirm what one's own purpose and divine calling is. One can believe, in specific counseling challenges too, that God equips and carries those he has called.

While knowledge of transformation and explanation take up a considerable part of the training, and while this is the area in which the largest measurable growth in knowledge is occurring, the more important basis for therapeutic/counseling work bearing a long-term blessing is being built on the three other areas: knowledge of relationships, one's self and calling. Ministering to people does not begin with technical competence (*Sachkompetenz*), but has its main resource in personal and social competence (*Personkompetenz*).

Change of Perspectives

The five levels of knowledge lead us to another important aspect of Christian counseling. Not only in the counselor's training but also in the understanding of our counselees, the personal levels are the most important. We shall not fall victim to a fundamental intention of psychology: to explain the reality of the human being in laws, with the aim of being able to control human life through therapy, counseling and pedagogy.

In opposition to this basically technical, repair-oriented approach, we should use all our knowledge as "knowledge of detection" (*Findewissen*). Knowledge of detection instead of knowledge of repairing in Christian psychology means: the emotional/mental area is not causal, but personal and thus creative! This is one of the main tenets of Christian psychology. The emotional/mental area is therefore not subject to causal laws as is the material area. We can at best make statements about probability, which say little about the concrete individual case. Ultimately, psychology cannot do what it originally set out to do, which is make causal statements about concrete persons. One caveat, however, would be that the more the personal disintegrates and the material gains in influence, the more laws of behavior can be applied (e.g., the development of addiction).

Knowledge of Detection Has Several Functions

- It increases understanding of the other person and thus allows a more intensive relationship, which in turn influences the course of the counseling.
- It prepares the "ground of knowledge" so that I, along with the other person, can discover the unique path to healing, which, from the perspective of Christian psychology, will also happen with the help of the Holy Spirit.
- All models and theories, including those in the area of knowledge of disorders and transformation, must first of all take a step back, far enough to let the particularity of the individual case become 100 percent visible. The individual case has priority!

Therefore, we want to help our counselees to be equipped and strengthened as a people to go with God through the peaks and troughs of their daily lives. Counseling is a relationship within time limits, intended to promote the ability to live in the everyday relationships and tasks of the counselee's real environment with our ever-present God.

References and Recommended Resources

Adams, J. (1986). *Competent to counsel: Introduction to nouthetic counseling.* Grand Rapids: Zondervan.

Bonhoeffer, D. (1975). *Ethik* (8th ed.). München: Chr. Kaiser.

Coe, J. H., & Hall, T. W. (2010). *Psychology in the Spirit: Contours of a transformational psychology.* Downers Grove, IL: IVP Academic.

Halder, K. (2011a). *Die Grundlagen Christlicher Psychologie. Ein Lehrbuch. Band 1: Zum Wirklichkeitsverständnis der Psychologie.* Kitzingen: IGNIS-Edition.

Halder, K. (2011b). *Die Grundlagen Christlicher Psychologie. Ein Lehrbuch. Band 2: Zum Wirklichkeitsverständnis der Christlichen Psychologie.* Kitzingen: IGNIS-Edition.

Hartmann, W-D. (1998). *Das Seelsorgegespräch—Sieben Phasen, die Gott Raum geben.* Kitzingen: IGNIS-Edition.

Heckhausen, H. (1980). *Motivation und Handeln. Lehrbuch der Motivationspsychologie.* Berlin: Springer.

Johnson, E. (1997). Christ the lord of psychology. *Journal of Psychology and Theology,* 25(1), 11-27.

Johnson, E. (2007). *Foundations for soul care: A Christian psychology proposal.* Downers Grove, IL: IVP Academic.

May, A. (2002a). *Der Mensch als bedürftige Person—Störung und Heilung.* Kitzingen: IGNIS Fernkurs.

May, A. (2002b). *Der Mensch als bedürftige Person—Psychotherapeutische und seelsorgerliche Konzepte.* Kitzingen: IGNIS Fernkurs.

May, A. (2004). *Der Mensch in Beziehung zu Gott. Teil 3: Grundzüge Christlicher Therapie bei IGNIS.* Kitzingen: IGNIS-Fernkurs.

May, W. (2004). *Schluss mit schlechten Gewohnheiten.* Kitzingen: IGNIS-Edition.

May, W. (2012). Christian psychology around the world. *The EMCAPP Journal,* 1. Retrieved from <www.emcapp.eu>.

Pfeifer, S. (Ed.). (1991). *Seelsorge und Psychotherapie—Chancen und Grenzen der Integration.* Moers: Brendow.

Sandford, J., & Sandford, P. (1982). *The transformation of the inner man.* Springfield, MO: Victory House.

Watzlawic, P. (1991). *Die Möglichkeit des Andersseins.* Bern: Hans Huber.

Zeiders, C. (2010). *The clinical Christ: Scientific and spiritual reflections on the transformative psychology called Christian holism.* Retrieved from <www.drzeiders.com/the-clinical-christ>.

10

Transformation Through Christian Emotion-Focused Therapy

Lydia C. W. Kim-van Daalen
& Eric L. Johnson

We love because he first loved us.

1 John 4:19

The Power and Importance of Emotional Experience

Despite the fact that emotions can be unsettling, overwhelming and distorted, many in the Christian tradition have argued for the necessity of affective experience in the Christian faith (Elliott, 2006). This chapter offers a rationale for a Christian model of emotion-focused therapy and a preliminary outline for its practice. The relation of reason and affect is admittedly puzzling and has led to a history of continual disagreements in Christianity. Ever since the ancient Greeks, reason has usually been placed above the emotions in the Western intellectual tradition (Campos, Dacher & Parker, 2008). This has resulted in many models of soul care, both secular and Christian, that put their emphasis on beliefs and rationality—more recently termed *cognition*—in the process of change. Truth is foundational to the Christian faith. Yet an overemphasis there can lead to the neglect of other important aspects of Christian transformation, like the emotions. As we will see, the significance of emotions to human well-being is evident, first and foremost, in God's Word. Secular psychology research and personal experience suggest the same.

Before we examine these sources, a definition of emotion would be in order. We understand emotion to be an aspect of the human soul that results from a complex set of interactions among psychological, sociocultural and neural-hormonal biological systems, and has the following features: Emotion (1) is meaningful; (2) is mediated by previously stored experiences and socialization; (3) is bivalent (e.g., positive [e.g., happiness]/negative [e.g., anger/anxiety/sadness]; pleasure/displeasure) (4) varies in terms of arousal level; (5) is based on a certain cognitive construal and in turn generates cognitive processes such as emotionally relevant appraisals; (6) activates widespread physiological adjustments to the arousing conditions; and (7) motivates action that is often (though not always) expressive and goal directed (Bandura, 1998; Kleinginna Jr. & Kleinginna, 1981).

Scriptural evidence. God created emotions, and Christian Scripture provides abundant examples of the importance of emotions for the Christian life. Many means of spiritual transformation have a strong emotional component. The worship of God, for example, would seem to be an intensely emotional affair (Pss 145–150). Emotional experience would seem to be essential to the fruit of the Spirit (Gal 5:22-23), including love, joy and peace. The experience of God's love, in particular, can be deeply emotional, moving believers to worship (Ps 115:1) and to love others (1 Jn 4:8). Furthermore, the Christian community offers opportunity for many emotional experiences (Rom 12:9-15; 1 Cor 12:25-27; 1 Thess 2:19-20; 2 Jn 1:12). Finally, many forms of scriptural discourse would seem intended to evoke emotional experience and movement toward God, including vivid stories, word pictures, provocative language, songs, parables and so on.

One also finds in Scripture many examples of the intentional expression of emotion (Ex 3:7; Lam; Joel 1:14; Lk 18:7). The Psalms especially record believers expressing all kinds of emotions to God—for example, praise and joy, as well as doubt, anger and fear—richly modeling the honest expression of one's heart. In some instances people cry out spontaneously from the bottom of their hearts (Ex 2:23; Judg 2:18; Rom 8:23); in others the emotions are expressed in carefully crafted form—for example, the songs and poems in the Psalms and Lamentations. We see in such examples earnest dialogue with God. Even though believers know that God already knows what is in their hearts (Ps 44:21; 139:23; Lk 16:15), they often tell him what is there. We might surmise that emotion expression in prayer has additional benefits, like revealing to the one praying what is going on internally and creating an open heart into which God's truth can be poured. This too is illustrated in the

Psalms, where the psalmist often opens up honestly to God and is blessed by remembering God's past deliverances and compassion (e.g., Ps 77).

Research evidence. Secular psychology research has also validated the benefits of emotional experience and expression. After first emphasizing behavior, and then cognition, the importance of affect has become widely recognized in modern psychology (Fosha, Siegel & Solomon, 2009). This emphasis to affect has found its way into psychotherapeutic practice in the form of what have been termed the *experiential* or *emotion-focused therapies*. Research on these therapies has confirmed the importance of emotional experience to healthy human functioning; high levels of experiencing—described as a combination of emotional engagement and cognitive reflection, or mentalization, have been found to be associated with positive therapeutic outcomes. Greenberg and others have studied these changes and formulated the most influential model based on this information called simply Emotion-Focused Therapy (EFT) (Greenberg et al., 1996; Johnson, 1996; Greenberg, 2002, 2010a, 2010b). This model is now considered an empirically validated form of therapy for depression (Greenberg & Watson, 1998; Watson, Gordon, Stermac, Kalogerakos & Steckley, 2003; Goldman, Greenberg & Angus, 2006), as well as marital distress (Johnson & Greenberg, 1985; Baucom, Shoham, Mueser, Daiuto & Stickle, 1998; Honarparvaran, Tabrizy, Navabinejad & Shafiabady, 2010). Preliminary studies have also shown that secular EFT is potentially effective in the treatment of trauma, interpersonal problems (Greenberg, Warwar & Malcom, 2008), and eating disorders and anxiety disorders (Greenberg, 2010b).

At the core of this type of therapy is the conviction that only when emotion schemes are accessed is therapeutic change possible (Greenberg et al., 1996). Emotion schemes are complex mental structures composed of cognitive, affective, motivational and relational elements. Therapists help counselees access dysfunctional emotion schemes in order to modify their components, enabling counselees to obtain new meaning and a new understanding of the self in relation to the world (Greenberg et al.). The therapeutic relationship is essential in the process of change and so is the active experiencing of clients. EFT therapists facilitate and support their counselees' emotional processing and suggest interventions in session that promote the fullest, deepest experience and expression.

Anecdotal evidence. Finally, the lives of God's people also reveal the importance of emotional experience and expression for change. Many Christians can testify that they had known mentally for a long time that God loved them, yet were plagued with feelings of unworthiness and unloveableness. Not until they experienced God's love in some way, be it in a sermon, a song or in counseling, did it become a transforming reality in their lives.

Our own journey and our counseling with others leads us to believe that truth and cognitive insight are foundational to God's soul-healing agenda, but we have seen people benefit the most from God's Word when it was appropriated in a context of a deepening exploration of their hearts and emotions.

Why Are Some Christians Skeptical of the Emotions?

If emotions are so important, why have many Christians been so suspicious of them? We can only give a cursory response (for a fuller response, see Elliott, 2006; Roberts, 2007). First, some Christians are reacting to a self-oriented, subjectivity-driven culture, knowing that God is the center of the universe, not the individual and his or her subjective feelings and desires. Second, young children are characterized by a lack of emotion regulation, and one of the marks of maturity is the ability to regulate one's emotions, so strong emotions seem to be immature. Related to this, troubled adults are often too easily moved by their emotions and impulses, and express them inappropriately. Third, many emotions seem to be intrinsically sinful—for example, lust, bitterness, jealousy and envy. All these facts have given emotion experience and expression perennially a bad reputation.

As a result, many contemporary Christians have rightly recognized that Christian emotion maturation first involves God pulling believers out of themselves and an ultimate concern with their feelings and desires, and centering and grounding their souls upon God and his Word. The problem arises when this *first* stage in emotion maturation is made the *whole* Christian approach to the emotions. As one increases in God-centeredness and groundedness in the objective truths of Scripture, the *second* stage of emotional maturation involves inward deepening (Kierkegaard, 1990): learning how to listen to, manage and work with one's heart, and experiencing and expressing one's emotions *in Christ,* in ways that promote authenticity, emotion regulation, impulse control, the overcoming of sinful emotion patterns and the healing of emotional dysfunction. Because God created humans as emotional and cognitive beings, Christians who remain in stage one will have warped and truncated souls, with the less-than-perfect parts of their souls pushed out of awareness. This hinders their growth, makes them rigid in their ethics and relationships, and often leaves them "stuck" in falseness and empty performance.

A Proposed Model of Christian Emotion-Focused Therapy (CEFT)

The Trinity is of the greatest importance to CEFT (Johnson, 2007). Christian emotional transformation is ultimately dependent upon believers having been united to the life, death and resurrection of Jesus Christ through faith, so that they are once and forever identified by the Father with his Son. This reality declared true by the Father grants believers the right to open up their souls, lives and stories to increasing saturation with the love, forgiveness, perfect righteousness and suffering of Christ by means of the Holy Spirit. When counselees open their hearts to God, the Spirit works in their thoughts, emotions, desires, action tendencies and relational structures. The Spirit further uses counselors to facilitate this process as they connect emotionally with the client and image of God through love and challenge. We turn next to consider what a CEFT session might look like.

Before the session. It is helpful if counselors prayerfully open their heart to the Spirit's guidance, knowing that he is able to bring about change (Ps 33:13-22; Is 26:3-9; 30:18). Their own negative emotions or distracting thoughts can be brought to God so they can be fully present to God and the counselee in faith, love and hope.

During the session. Several stages can be distinguished.

Stage 1: Discover. In stage 1, counselors discover the nature of the counselee's emotion struggle. First, counselor and counselee pray together to ask for the Spirit's guidance in their interaction. Second, the counselee considers what issue to work on in session, possibly with input from the counselor. Third, the counselee is invited to share details about the issue, so that they have a common understanding of the problem. The final step of this phase is the discovering of the core negative emotions related to the issue.

Stage 2: Uncover. In stage 2, the counselor aims to create a "space" for counselees to uncover—that is, to experience and explore—their negative emotions. The purpose is to uncover themes, memories and attitudes associated with a particular negative emotion they are experiencing or would like to explore. The counselor can use several techniques. These can range from suggesting counselees describe a recent event in which the negative emotion was felt while the counselor gently probes for details to promote the most vivid experience possible; helping counselees to stay with a certain feeling that they then try to describe in various ways; offering a metaphor that aptly labels the feeling; encouraging role-playing of an emotion-causing event; or focusing on bodily feelings to try to understand their meaning.

In uncovering, the counselor accepts whatever comes, regardless of its ethical value. Some Christians may question this stance, but it is necessary if counselees are to learn how to trust their created emotion system and perceive the truth being communicated by it for the greater good of getting healing from their negative, and sometimes sinful, emotions. One can only begin to address those emotions (whether legitimate or sinful) *after one has consciously acknowledged their existence.* Some Christians tragically neglect exploring their inner dynamics out of an understandable but misguided fear of offending God (and perhaps some perfectionism). However, God already knows what's in people's hearts; whatever sin emerges into consciousness has already been atoned for by Christ on the cross; believers are already perfect in Christ; and God desires to free their souls from remaining sin. The counselor is essential here to communicate God's redemptive agenda through an empathic, loving, exploring and challenging orientation that helps counselees manage their anxiety while going deeper in the experience and expression of their emotions, so they can understand better what their emotions mean.

Stage 3: Recover. The goal of stage 3 is to recover one's emotions. Perhaps this stage could be termed *redemptive recovery,* because it promotes the believer's experiential identification with Christ's redemption, particularly his death and resurrection. In the first phase of this stage—the cross phase—negative emotions are experienced in light of Christ's death on the cross. In the second—the resurrection phase—counselees learn to experience their union with Christ's resurrection and transition smoothly into a more positive emotion state. Thus, they are being "raised from the dead" of their negative emotions. This involves differentiating the quality of one's negative emotions as legitimate or sinful (and sometimes they are both).

Legitimate negative emotional experience is that which is appropriate, according to God's view of things, like sadness at the loss of a friend or anger at injustice, or guilt after committing a sin. Moreover, because God created our emotion system, there is usually some core goodness identifiable in every emotional experience. In the cross phase, when a legitimate negative emotion is identified, the counselee should be encouraged to experience it as fully as possible and, ideally, to express it verbally, and then to surrender it to the Lord. This should be followed by the resurrection phase, in which the counselee receives a positive emotion that modifies or replaces the negative emotion through some Christian consideration (e.g., a felt recognition of God's love). This owning of the legitimate emotion affirms and strengthens the believer's created self and its emotion equipment that are in this process being experientially redeemed.

By contrast, because of human fallenness, some emotions (or aspects of an emotion) are sinful. In such cases, in the cross phase, the counselee is to take responsibility for sin, seek to experience contrition (Lk 18:13), confess/express it to God (1 Jn 1:9)—in effect taking the sinful emotion (along with its guilt) to the cross and crucifying it, as it were, with Christ (Rom 8:13; Col 3:5)—and then repent, that is, "turn" from it psychologically. In the resurrection phase, with reference to sin, the goal is to experience a gospel-driven "emotion shift" that results from a felt sense of forgiveness.

Regarding the cross phase, surrender (of the good in negative emotions) and confession (of the sinfulness) both involve taking ownership for one's emotional experience. Whether legitimate or sinful, believers are to take their emotions to God in Christ and, whether surrendering it or repenting of it, identify them consciously with his work on their behalf, releasing them to God and in the process strengthening their new/created self and weakening their old self (Eph 4:22-24; Col 3:10). When dealing with emotions about having been sinned against (e.g., through neglect or emotional, physical or sexual abuse), the multifaceted developmental goal for the counselee is to experience legitimate emotions—like anger toward the perpetrator, grief over what has happened and the associated anxiety—as steps to eventual experiences of God's love, comfort and compassion with reference to the mistreatment, making possible substantial redemptive recovery. Some sin on the part of the survivor (e.g., hatred of the perpetrator) is not surprising, since we are all sinners. However, it is essential that the focus begin with the experience of being sinned against, since only after those feelings start to be substantially resolved will the survivor be able to take appropriate responsibility for his or her own remaining sin and eventually forgive the perpetrator. This entire process may take many months or even years.

The resurrection phase should be experienced as a relatively smooth (not abrupt) emotional modification of the cross phase resulting from the experiential appropriation of the truths of the gospel: a "being raised from the dead" of one's negative emotions. Figure 10.2 illustrates what takes place during stage 3.

Evaluation of the negative emotion	Phase 1: Bring negative emotion to the cross: if legitimate, identify with Christ's suffering and surrender to Christ; if sinful, confess and repent in light of the cross	Phase 2: Receive new emotion through Christ's resurrection: a sense of God's love, forgiveness, strength for a difficult situation, contentment

Figure 10.1. Recovery stage

Stage 4: Cover. Stage 4 is the "cover" or extension stage. The goal here is to help counselees take the newly received and experienced truths further into their hearts and lives, so that more of their lives will be "covered" and permeated experientially with their union with Christ. The counselor and counselee will need to collaborate on ways to consolidate, deepen and elaborate the new emotional experiences in daily life, through discussion or specific courses of action. For example, homework may be assigned, like meditating on certain parts of Scripture, watching a particular movie, listening to music, doing Scripturally guided imagery or journaling, practicing new behaviors with others, and so on. These plans serve to strengthen and further instill the truths experienced in session. The session can itself be closed with a prayer.

After the session. The counselor ideally should take some time to reflect on what has happened, opening up again to the guidance of the Spirit. He or she may sense new direction for the next meeting, be moved to intercessory prayer for the counselee, become aware of personal sin that can be addressed or a mistake that was made that can be learned from, and so on. Finally, the counselor can take notes on what happened during the session and record any subsequent insights.

BEFORE THE SESSION
- Counselor spiritual preparation

DURING THE SESSION

Stage 1: Discover
- Prayer
- Choose problematic issue
- Provide details
- Discover salient emotion

Stage 2: Uncover
- Experiencing and exploration of the emotion in order to uncover the root

Stage 3: Recover
- Phase 1: Experiencing the cross: Bringing one's negative emotions to the cross
- Phase 2: Experiencing the resurrection: Being raised from the dead into a new emotional state

Stage 4: Cover
- Reflection
- Course of action
- Prayer

AFTER THE SESSION
- Counselor closure

Figure 10.2. The process of Christian emotion-focused therapy

Some Christian Emotion-Focused Strategies

Specific emotion-focused interventions may be called for in each phase. We will highlight a few here in more detail. Empathy-based and relational interventions are always valuable (especially in the beginning stage of the session), in order to build the therapeutic alliance and create a safe, sacred space for counselees to explore confusing, painful or sinful dynamics. Such interventions include the full and genuine presence of the counselor as an ambassador of Christ, affirmation, empathic attunement, a collaborative stance based on fundamental counselor-counselee equality as brothers or sisters in the Lord and so on. The secular versions of these qualities are considered common factors in all therapy, but they are especially important in emotion-focused therapy, because of the shame and anxiety counselees typically associate with negative emotion and because empathy is especially conducive to the promotion of emotional reflection and experience.

Different kinds of problems can be addressed with a variety of Christian emotion-focused interventions. For example, those struggling with a problem that seems overwhelming can imagine Jesus holding the felt problem in his hands (Ps 31:15; 55:22). A counselee with anxiety might picture (and feel) herself casting the anxiety on to Jesus (1 Pet 5:7), perhaps picturing the anxiety as a black rock, at first located in the body wherever the anxiety is felt. Some interventions can help counselees experience God as their ultimate caregiver. For instance, counselees might imagine themselves being carried by angels (Ps 91:12) or held in the arms of God (Deut 33:27; Is 40:11). Meditating on these biblical pictures may help people open their hearts to God, their ever-present, ultimate Therapist, in whatever troubling situation they face throughout the week.

The counselor may also suggest interventions that help bring to light the internal dynamics of the counselee—for example, the empty-chair or two-chair techniques, long used in secular emotion-focused therapy (Greenberg, 2010a). The empty-chair technique involves having counselees speak to someone in their past or present about whom they may have unresolved negative emotions. The two-chair technique can guide the counselee to examine and understand conflicting aspects of the self. However, as we will see below, these experiential techniques can be used in distinctly Christian ways.

As suggested above, a primary goal of Christian emotion-focused therapy is the experiential application of the gospel and the believer's union with Christ in his death and resurrection to modify the counselee's emotional responses to particular problems. Thus, in the case of emotional problems that are the result of traumatic events, the emotion memories of the events can be suffused with new emotions flowing from a fresh construal of the event in light of the believer's union with Christ. For example, counselees could be invited to vividly recall the details of a hurtful event, activating the associated negative emotions, and then imagine Christ entering into that setting angry at the injustice done to them (Rom 14:11-12; Eph 5:6; Col 3:6), then sending away the felt shame and fear that it produced, and then counselees could finish with the realization that God is "for them," and nothing can separate them from his love (Rom 8:31-39), resulting in a modifying of their painful emotion memories.[1] One can also use the one-chair technique about someone in the counselee's past, and ask the counselee to consider and say aloud what Jesus might say to the offending party or to the counselee.

When there appear to be internally confusing or opposing aspects of the

[1]It should be pointed out that working with trauma survivors requires specialized training and should not be attempted without such training.

self, these can be enacted using the two-chair technique, where the aspects take turns speaking to each other, or dialogue with Christ, so that the oppositional aspects undergo redemptive transformation. After teaching counselees about their "old self" (Rom 6:6; Eph 4:22; Col 3:9) and their "new self" (Eph 4:24; Col 3:10), counselors can use the two-chair technique to facilitate a lively conversation between them, with the counselee sitting in one chair and giving voice to the feelings and attitudes of the old self, and then moving to the other chair to verbalize the feelings and attitudes of the new self, while being coached to allow the new self to assert itself over against the old self on the basis of union with Christ (Johnson, 2007).

Another strategy could involve a guided-imagery experiment in which counselees visualize their sinful attitudes/old self being crucified and buried, or taken off as dirty clothes, and replaced by the new self who has been raised to newness of life. Those who struggle with excessive shame and guilt may picture themselves in meditation being carefully created by God (Ps 139:13-18), being seated with Jesus in glory (Col 3:1-4), or being first washed by the blood of Christ (Heb 9:14; Rev 7:14) and then dressed by Jesus in gloriously bright, white robes (Is 61:10; Rev 7:15). Such biblically guided interventions help people develop their ability to relate their thoughts, emotions and lives to Christ at all times, so that God's truth, presence and redemption can be experienced amid one's daily concerns.

A Case Illustration of CEFT

Jill is a single woman living with her parents. In her past she experienced physical and mental abuse by a relative. In addition, she currently suffers from several medical issues, some of which may be more psychosomatic in nature. Jill has struggled with panic attacks and also attempted suicide twice five years ago. The presenting issues for Jill were generalized anxiety disorder, frequent negative self-talk, and difficulty trusting that God is good and would provide for her in her health, relationships and job.

In the eighth session, the counselor attempted to explore her emotions (the discover stage). At first, Jill had trouble connecting with her real feelings and trusting the safety of the counseling process. She reported afterward that the counselor's empathic responses helped her sense more of God's love for her and lower her defenses, which enabled her to move a little deeper into experiential exploration of her issues.

Trust in God was chosen as the topic to work on during this session.

In the uncover stage, feelings associated with trusting God were explored, resulting in Jill's admission of fear, her belief that God was not really on her side, and her tendency to figure things out by herself and, thus, act without dependence on God. She was able to connect these aspects with her frequent high levels of anxiety and periodic feelings of sadness.

Entering the recovery stage, Jill admitted that she knew with her head that she could trust God and that he was a safe haven to her, but her emotions and her consequent way of living contradicted this knowledge. The counselor shared a relevant Bible verse, and Jill confirmed that God was indeed to be trusted. Jill was brought through the cross and resurrection phases using a distinctly Christian guided meditation designed for believers experiencing anxiety. This guided meditation began with some simple breathing and relaxation exercises to calm her down, using a distinctly Christian script. During this meditation she was encouraged to imagine Christ in a way that would provide her with a sense of safety (she was given a list of suggestive biblical metaphors—e.g., Christ as her shelter, protected under God's wings, or come up with one of her own). She was then invited to think about something that provoked her anxiety, to acknowledge and express the negative feelings she was experiencing, and to then open up her soul to God.

Jill said that she knew that God knew what was in her heart and loved her in spite of her fear and that she could express this all to him with freedom. She also confessed what she called her sin of unbelief at the core of the fear. After surrendering her anxiety to Christ, Jill was then encouraged to focus on God's view of her in Christ and actively consent to the resultant positive feeling, during the resurrection phase of the meditation. She said she felt acceptance. Enough time was given so that she could allow this emotion to settle deeply into her spirit.

In the cover stage, we discussed the effects of our time together. Jill said she felt deeply relaxed upon focusing on the metaphoric image of Christ, and she reported experiencing a profound emotional shift later in the session when she surrendered her anxiety to God. We discussed how she could practice this on her own during her devotions in the coming week when she was feeling anxious. She was also encouraged to recall the metaphoric image she used at the beginning, during moments throughout the day when she had difficulty trusting or was experiencing episodes of anxiety. In the weeks to follow she reported that these exercises frequently helped her when she struggled with anxiety. She also came to have a much stronger sense that God was on her side, and she reported a gradual lessening of her anxiety.

CONTRAINDICATIONS

Before finishing we should acknowledge that CEFT may not be best for everyone. According to Greenberg, emotion suppression therapies, like cognitive therapy, may be more helpful for those who have serious difficulties controlling their emotions (for example, in panic or impulse disorders), providing them with effective short-term coping skills. Also uncovering affect may not be helpful for those who score 50 or lower on the Global Assessment of Functioning (GAF) Scale (McCullough et al., 2003)—evidenced by having no friends; severe difficulties in day-to-day functioning; an inability to manage affect well enough to control addictions or aggressive impulses; and a more fundamental instability or fragmentation in one's sense of self and others—since the uncovering of their feelings would likely lead to too much distress, impairing their emotional functioning even more. Low motivation, severe stressors and a lack of psychological-mindedness may also be indications that CEFT is an inappropriate intervention.

CONCLUSION

Most Christians, however, will likely benefit from CEFT. As mentioned, secular EFT has convincing empirical support. Moreover, 75 percent of the disorders found in the DSM-IV-TR consist of problems with emotions or emotion regulation (Werner & Gross, 2010), suggesting the value of emotion interventions. It is now widely acknowledged that emotional processing is key to acquiring self-insight, increasing motivation to change and receiving deeper healing. CEFT promotes many of the same kinds of outcomes that secular EFT seeks—the exploration, processing and resolution of problematic emotions and the experience of new, healthier emotions—but it does so by means of Christ's redemption applied by the Holy Spirit, and it leads to an increasingly Christ-centered, rather than human-centered life. It is hoped that future research will document the efficacy of a Christian version of EFT. Learning to be emotionally alive and open to the transformation of one's emotions in Christ would seem to be important for anyone who desires to grow psychologically and spiritually in Christ.

References and Recommended Resources

Allender, D. B., & Longman, T. (1999). *The cry of the soul: How our emotions reveal our deepest questions about God.* Colorado Springs: NavPress.

Bandura, A. (1998). *Self-efficacy: The exercise of control.* New York: Freeman.

Baucom, D. H., Shoham, V., Mueser, K. T., Daiuto, A. D., & Stickle, T. (1998). Empirically supported couple and family interventions for marital distress and adult mental health problems. *Journal of Consulting and Clinical Psychology, 66,* 53-88.

Borgman, B. S. (2009). *Feelings and faith: Cultivating godly emotions in the Christian life.* Wheaton, IL: Crossway.

Campos, B., Dacher, K., & Parker, M. P. (2008). Emotion. In C. D. Spielberger (Ed.), *Encyclopedia of applied psychology* (pp. 713-22). Amsterdam: Elsevier.

Elliott, M. A. (2006). *Faithful feelings: Rethinking emotion in the New Testament.* Grand Rapids: Kregel.

Fosha, D., Siegel, D. J., & Solomon, M. (2009). Introduction. In D. J. Diana Fosha & M. Solomon (Eds.), *The healing power of emotion: Affective neurosceince, development, and clinical practice* (pp. vii-xiii). New York: W. W. Norton & Company.

Goldman, R., Greenberg, L. S., & Angus, L. (2006). The effects of adding emotion-focused interventions to the therapeutic relationship in the treatment of depression. *Psychotherapy Research, 16,* 537-49.

Greenberg, L. S. (2002). *Emotion-focused therapy: Coaching clients to work through their feelings.* Washington, DC: American Psychological Association.

Greenberg, L. S. (2010a). *Emotion-focused therapy.* Washington, DC: American Psychological Association.

Greenberg, L. S. (2010b). Emotion-focused therapy: A clinical synthesis. *Focus, 8,* 32-42.

Greenberg, L. S., & Paivio, S. C. (2003). *Working with emotions in psychotherapy.* New York: Guilford.

Greenberg, L. S., Rice, L. N., & Elliott, R. (1996). *Facilitating emotional change: The moment-by-moment process.* New York: Guilford.

Greenberg, L. S., & Safran, J. D. (1987). *Emotion in psychotherapy: Affect, cognition, and the process of change.* New York: Guilford.

Greenberg, L. S., Warwar, S. H., & Malcom, W. M. (2008). Differential effects of emotion focused therapy and psychoeducation in facilitating forgiveness and letting go of emotional injuries. *Journal of Counseling Psychology, 55,* 185-96.

Greenberg, L. S., & Watson, J. (1998). Experiential therapy of depression: Differential effects of client-centered relationship conditions and process experiential interventions. *Psychotherapy Research, 8,* 210-24.

Greenberg, L. S., & Watson, J. C. (2005). *Emotion-focused therapy for depression.* Washington, DC: American Psychological Association.

Honarparvaran, N., Tabrizy, M., Navabinejad, S., & Shafiabady, A. (2010). The efficacy of emotionally focused couple therapy (EFT-C) training with regard to reducing sexual dissatisfaction among couples. *European Journal of Scientific Research, 43*(4), 538-45.

Johnson, E. L. (2007). *Foundations for soul care: A Christian psychology proposal.* Downers Grove, IL: InterVarsity Press.

Johnson, S. M. (1996). *The practice of emotionally focused marital therapy: Creating connection.* New York: Brunner/Mazel.

Johnson, S. M., & Greenberg, L. S. (1985). Emotionally focused marital therapy: An outcome study. *Journal of Marital and Family Therapy, 11,* 313-17.

Kierkegaard, S. (1990). *For self-examination. Judge for yourselves!* (H.V. Hong & E. H. Hong, Trans.). Princeton, NJ: Princeton University Press. (*For self-examination* originally published 1851; *Judge for yourselves!* originally published 1875).

Kleinginna, P. R., Jr., & Kleinginna, A. M. (1981). A categorized list of emotion definitions, with suggestions for a consensual definition. *Emotion and Motivation, 5*(4), 345-79.

McCullough, L., Kuhn, N., Andrews, S., Kaplan, A., Wolf, J., & Hurley, C. L. (2003). *Treating affect phobia: A manual for short-term dynamic psychotherapy.* New York: Guilford.

Owen, J. (1852). The grace and duty of being spiritually minded. In J. Owen & W. H. Goold (Ed.), *The works of John Owen* (Vol. 7). New York: Robert Carter & Brothers.

Paivio, S., & Nieuwenhuis, J. (2001). Efficacy of emotion focused therapy for adult survivors of child abuse: A preliminary study. *Journal of Traumatic Stress, 14,* 115-33.

Pennebaker, J. W. (1990). *Opening up: The healing power of expressing emotions.* New York: Guilford.

Roberts, R. C. (2003). *Emotions: An essay in aid of moral psychology.* Cambridge, UK: Cambridge University Press.

Roberts, R. C. (2007). *Spiritual emotions: A psychology of Christian virtues.* Grand Rapids: Eerdmans.

Tallon, A. (2008). Christianity. In J. Corrigan (Ed.), *The Oxford handbook of religion and emotion* (pp. 111-24). New York: Oxford University Press.

Watson, J. C., Gordon, L. B., Stermac, L., Kalogerakos, F., & Steckley, P. (2003). Comparing the effectiveness of process-experiential with cognitive-behavioral psychotherapy in the treatment of depression. *Journal of Consulting and Clinical Psychology, 71,* 773-81.

Werner, K., & Gross, J.J. (2010). Emotion regulation and psychopathology: A conceptual framework. In A. Kring & D. Sloan (Eds.), *Emotion regulation and psychopathology: A transdiagnostic approach to etiology and treatment* (pp. 13-37). New York: Guilford Press.

11

Facilitating and Building On the God Encounter in Formational Counseling

Terry Wardle

It has been twenty years since I stopped on the sidewalk that led to the lockdown facility standing in front of me. I couldn't hold back the fear and sadness raging inside for one more moment. I cried uncontrollably. I believed that it was the end of life as I knew it, a death of most everything I held near to my heart.

Something had gone terribly wrong, and for months I continued a rapid descent into the darkness of depression and agoraphobia. By all appearances, everything about my life was good and successful. In the years preceding I had advanced in my professional life: pastor, author, seminary professor and administrator, conference speaker. I had achieved many of my goals and even exceeded some expectations. Yet at what I thought was the pinnacle of my ministry journey, the fall downward began, accelerating the further I went.

For months I worked to hide what was happening. The Christian community does not always have a generous attitude toward emotional brokenness. I did everything I knew to find relief, but to no avail. Ultimately the time had come for a more aggressive approach, and so, with nowhere else to turn and all hope yet unborn now dead, I had only a few steps to take into the psychiatric hospital. What I did not know at the time was that it was my first steps into a new ministry that would eventually lead to the development of a paradigm of care called *formational counseling.*

I spent a month in the psychiatric hospital, followed by two weeks in a residential aftercare facility. It was a Christian program that worked to integrate biblical principles into its counseling and therapeutic protocols. The caregivers were good people, deeply committed to the Lord, and genuinely helpful at many levels. My time there did help me move from virtual emotional immobility to being able to at least limp along. The battle with depression and anxiety was far from over, but I was somewhat better.

Anyone who has struggled with chronic emotional pain is grateful for "better." If anyone has ever battled fear, anxiety, compulsive behaviors, obsessive thinking or other debilitating emotional storms 24/7, "better" is a welcome gift. Early on I fought extreme anxiety virtually every minute of the day. To have someone help relieve that pain for even an hour or two a day was a priceless gift. "Better" was for me, and for many others in similar struggles, almost more than I could hope for. When the caregivers serving in this psychiatric hospital helped me get "better," I was, and in large part still am, deeply grateful.

While broken people are often grateful for "better," in the end they want more. I know I did. And what the Lord wants for them and for all broken people is nothing less than transformation. *That level of change only happens when broken people encounter the Lord Jesus Christ personally, and yes, experientially* (emphasis from the editors).

Born out of my own journey through the dark night, formational counseling is an approach that integrates three modalities of care and formation: spiritual direction, pastoral counseling and inner healing prayer, all aimed at positioning broken people for transforming encounters with Jesus Christ. Caregivers using formational counseling are equipped to apply the essential components of each of these disciplines as part of their ministries to broken men and women. They are equipped with the appropriate protocols, skills, understandings and perspectives of each discipline.

Formational counseling also incorporates important aspects of many traditional therapeutic models used today, such as Rational Emotive Behavior Therapy, Person Centered, Gestalt, Existential, Behavior Modification and Cognitive Behavioral Therapy. Importantly, formational counseling recognizes and includes the primary physiological, neurobiological, emotional and spiritual aspects of affect regulation, attachment and early childhood trauma. Current neurobiological and developmental research verifies the need to assess and integrate understanding of past physiological and emotional responses with unprocessed feelings left over from experience.

Yet central and essential to all of these modalities of care is one overriding concern: facilitating an encounter with the Lord that brings to the care receiver a level of transformation and deep change that skills, concepts and perspectives alone can never do.

Defining Formational Counseling

Broadly defined, formational counseling is a ministry of the Holy Spirit, moving through the Christian caregiver, bringing the healing presence of Jesus Christ into the place of pain and deep brokenness. Looking at each of the various parts of this definition will help lay an adequate foundation for the later discussion of formational counseling. And most certainly, the starting point begins with understanding that the ministry of the Holy Spirit is essential to effectiveness in formational counseling.

A ministry of the Holy Spirit. Caregivers who desire to minister to broken people through the protocols of formational counseling must embrace an animated pneumatology. Sadly, more than a few Christians have little more than a conceptual understanding of the ministry of the Holy Spirit. While able to articulate a theology of the Spirit, not all are familiar or even comfortable with the existential dimensions of the third member of the Trinity. Tozer once referred to the Holy Spirit as the "Forgotten One," and building upon that notion, Francis Chan (2009) recently wrote a helpful book on the same topic. Chan rightly emphasizes that Christians must not marginalize the Holy Spirit either in life or in Christian service. Nowhere is this admonition more essential than when ministering to broken people.

Formational counseling is completely dependent upon the Holy Spirit. Caregivers do not pull formational counseling from their caregiving tool belts as a set of skills to be appropriately applied. Instead it is the Holy Spirit who pulls the formational counselor out of *his* tool belt, using them to position broken people for transforming encounters with the Lord.

The Christian caregiver. This then brings us to the second aspect of formational counseling: the caregiver. The Holy Spirit does move through the Christian caregiver, and as such, the spirituality and level of maturity of the caregiver do matter in the process. Formational counseling demands that the caregiver be on his or her own journey of healing, allowing their own wounds to become a source of healing to others.

The formational counselor needs to be equipped to effectively position broken people for God encounters. Levels of understanding and efficiency in the protocols of formational counseling are certainly necessary. Knowing the foundational principles of spiritual direction, pastoral counseling and inner healing prayer are essential. Over and above all of this stands the Christian concept of incarnational ministry, central to the life and ministry of Christ.

Embracing incarnational ministry. Saying yes to incarnational ministry means establishing an empathic connection with the broken men and women they serve. What Jesus did for us, the formational counselor must do for the broken. We must identify with the person in order to position them for healing encounters with the Lord. It is clear that it is not the protocol of care that most impacts the healing journey of the broken but the nature of the therapeutic relationship that exists between caregiver and care receiver (Siegel, 2001).

The formational counselor must be willing and able to connect empathically with the care receiver. Through eye contact, body language, facial expression, tone of voice and attentiveness, the formational counselor must be present to the broken person and able to resonate with what they are feeling (Hook & Ohlschlager, 2002; Siegel, 2001). The formational counselor must do that in such a way that the care receiver senses that connection and willingly and appropriately entrusts himself/herself to the formational counselor's care.

Empathic connections matter. The ability to tune into the internal struggles of another not only builds trust, but it also provides a light to the path of change needed in the life of the wounded and hurting person. Empathy is the foundation of growth and change and must not be ignored when helping people encounter Christ for transformation (Perry, 2010). Transformation is a relationship-dependent experience, and in the case of formational counseling, it is a threefold connection: the care receiver, the caregiver and the presence of the Holy Spirit.

Encountering Christ. Hurting, wounded people need more than concepts, steps, principles and perspectives. While all are important, the transformational dynamic of formational counseling rests on the God encounter.

More than all else, people need to experience the presence and power of Jesus moving upon the wounded and hurting places deep within their lives.

Enlightenment-based education has resulted, in far too many cases, in an information-driven approach to problem solving. The fundamental assumption of this approach is that the journey toward change is along the path of reason, and if we can change the way one thinks we can then see the person change. Unfortunately, history will tell us that not all problems can be addressed by reason alone. There needs to be, in many cases, an experiential encounter that actually serves to bring a deep life-changing transformation that words alone cannot accomplish.

Integrating neurobiology. The science of neurobiology continues to provide new and incredible insights into the way the brain is developed and shaped. Foundational to positioning people for a God encounter is the notion that the brain is in part wired, and as such rewired, through emotion-laden experiences. In *Searching for Memory,* Daniel Schacter (1996), behavioral scientist from Harvard, writes about a concept of memory that is foundational to the God encounter essential to formational counseling. Building in part from the work of Endul Tulving, Schacter identifies three basic types of memory: procedural memory, semantic memory and episodic memory.

Procedural memory. Procedural memory comprises those activities that we are able to do automatically. While initially one would have had to think about what a certain "procedure" involved, a time comes when a person is able to remember how to function in it without consciously thinking. It becomes part of a larger category of memory called instinctive memory. Take writing, for example. When someone first endeavored to engage in writing, he or she had to think about all the steps necessary. They tried to remember the correct way to hold a pencil, make the shapes of the alphabet, move a hand across the paper from left to right and so forth. But in time all that "procedure" was remembered in such a way that they were able to do it without consciously considering all the steps.

Semantic memory. Semantic memory essentially involves remembering concepts, words, facts, data and other bits of knowledge. When someone remembers the story of Jesus at the Mount of Transfiguration, they are using semantic memory. If asked to recite the Gettysburg Address, they would need to access semantic memory. Semantic memory is important to life and enables people to recall the many pieces of information that have been stored in the brain, for use when needed.

Episodic memory. Episodic memory is essentially what is involved when we remember an event that occurred in our lives. I easily remember something that happened at least fifty years ago in my grandmother's kitchen. I had gone into her house late one afternoon after basketball practice. As I entered the kitchen, my grandmother was making sugar cookies. The smell was wonderful. I saw the cookies on the table and asked Grandma if I could have one. She smiled and moved to the table to choose one for me.

Grandma reached over and took one of those large, sugar-coated cookies from the table and handed it to me. It was warm in my hand. I took it to my lips, and as I did the aroma was fresh, and sweet, full of the scent of vanilla and sugar. I took a bite of the cookie, and it was soft and seemed to melt in my mouth. I remember feeling happy in that moment. Grandma's sugar cookies were good, and I wanted to eat some more.

Notice all the ingredients of this memory. First, it engaged all five senses. I heard, saw, smelled, touched and tasted in that one encounter. The episode also elicited feelings of happiness. I engaged in a series of actions, and I derived some meaningful conclusions from it all, including that Grandma's sugar cookies were good for me to eat. Episodic memories are powerful because in remembering, a person reexperiences senses, feelings, images, actions and meaning. Broken people are most often wounded by traumatic events that form episodic memories, but in this case overwhelmingly negative ones. It is very difficult to eliminate the effects of a negative episodic memory upon senses, feelings, images, actions and meaning through procedural or semantic memory alone. It is not that they are unimportant to the process. They are simply not powerful enough to free a person from unprocessed emotional upheaval caused by a traumatic episode of the past.

> Emotional experience is not processed through language and logic; as the right hemisphere speaks a language of images, sensations, impressions, and urges toward action, therapeutic discourse must be conducted in a language that the right hemisphere speaks. Therapies dealing with disorders that are fundamentally emotional in nature need to be able to reliably access sensory, motoric, and somatic experiences to engage them in a dyadic process of affect regulation and eventual transformation. This re-

> quires the bottom-up processing approach of experiential therapies rather than a top-down approach of most cognitive and insight focused therapies. (Fosha, 2003, p. 229)

To release unprocessed emotions of the past and heal traumatic memories, people need more than information. They need to encounter Christ, allowing Jesus to enter the episodic memory of the past. When that happens, the images, senses, feelings, actions and meanings of the negative past are faced, reexperienced, processed, released and then overpowered by a new episode with Jesus.

Into the place of pain and brokenness. Henri Nouwen (1977) believed that behind the brokenness and pain that people experience are stories begging to be heard. "It is no exaggeration to say that the suffering we most frequently encounter in ministry is a suffering of memories. They are wounding memories that ask for healing" (p. 21). Jesus is willing to enter these pain-filled stories and bring deep levels of healing and freedom to hurting and broken people.

In *Healing Care, Healing Prayer,* I wrote about a cause-and-effect relationship between wounds and responses. It is illustrated in figure 11.1.

Life Situation
Dysfunctional Behavior
Emotional Upheaval
False Belief
Wound

Figure 11.1. Relationship between wounds and responses

When people are *wounded* in life, be it caused by a traumatic event or less stressful experience, it does far more than cause initial pain. It often negatively impacts what they believe about themselves, their world and even God. Those *false beliefs*, in turn, create powerful and unpleasant feelings that chronically stir within, bringing significant discomfort to their lives. That *emotional upheaval* is dissettling, and over time not always consciously linked to the internal false beliefs. But the discomfort is significant and as a result, people engage in a wide variety of *dysfunctional behaviors* designed to kill the emotional pain. Those dysfunctional, sinful responses to the internal feelings are acted out in the *life situation* of their daily lives.

Caregivers equipped in formational counseling are educated in various protocols of care that position people to encounter Christ at each level of the structure. As noted earlier, this process is highly relational and aimed at episodic engagements with Christ that ultimately bring deep change and transformation to the care receiver. This process is best illustrated by integrating a case study into this discussion (Wardle, 2001, pp. 132-42).

Seeing Connie

Connie had set up an appointment and specifically asked that my wife, Cheryl, be there for the session. I had reviewed all the background information provided through her life script, so her choice to meet with my wife and I seemed more than appropriate. She was the wife of a local pastor serving a small yet growing charismatic fellowship. They had been married for five years and were in many ways enjoying favor both in the community and within their congregation. However, there was growing tension within her marriage, and it was hard pretending that all was well when the stress was so great at home.

In the initial session Connie shared that she and Dave were experiencing tensions in their relationship. She also mentioned that they had been to marriage counseling, yet saw little improvement in the situation as a result. A friend, knowing both the nature of the problems they faced and the power of inner healing, suggested that she see us for formational prayer.

Trauma impacting sexual intimacy. After the usual introductory comments and opening prayer, Cheryl and I encouraged Connie to share the reasons for her coming. On many levels Connie and Dave had a solid Christian marriage. They deeply loved the Lord and dearly loved each other. But in one area of the relationship there was ongoing tension and disappointment: sexual intimacy. Since their first night together, sex was a source of disagreement and at times heated arguments. Initially, from Connie's perspective, Dave wanted sexual intimacy far more than she was willing to engage. For a long time she pointed to Dave as the one with the problem, and wanted him to just back off. However, after countless discussions, Connie was willing to admit that she was actually resistant to sexual intimacy. Assuring us that it was not about loving Dave, she said that she struggled with physical intimacy and would get tense and upset whenever Dave approached the issue, regardless of how gentle he might try to be at the time.

Connie told us that she had employed various methods to keep Dave at a distance with respect to this issue. Any reasonable excuse was given, as well as various avoidance behaviors. However, in time she would be aware of his desire to connect and Connie would either suffer through the moment or simply say no to Dave. His disappointment and unhappiness were equally hard for Connie to face, only adding to her already shameful feelings about this part of their marriage.

Talking about feelings was not easy for Connie, but it held the key to deeper issues related to her sexual difficulties. Eventually she shared a combination of emotions regarding her relationship with Dave. On the one hand, there was relief whenever he would back away. Somehow she felt safer and better about herself whenever they did not engage in sexual activity. On the other hand, she felt sadness over the level of disappointment Dave had, as well as more than a little personal disappointment that her sexual issues were getting in the way of what she hoped for in their relationship.

The harder issue for Connie was talking about the feelings that would arise whenever Dave would approach her sexually. Convinced that feelings tell us a great deal about what we believe about our world, our God and ourselves, I pressed on to help Connie articulate what was obviously very painful for her. Without going into details unnecessary for our discussion, I can share that Connie talked about fear, shame and guilt more than any other emotions when it came to sexual advances by Dave.

The Holy Spirit enabled us to take the journey to a deeper level, as he revealed serious distortions that fueled the emotional upheaval in Connie's life. Pointedly, yet sensitively, I asked her to share what she believed to be true of herself with reference to her sexual relationship with Dave. In time Connie talked to Cheryl and me about believing she was dirty and sinful to be engaged sexually, and that she always felt worthless after the two of them were intimate.

Disclosing the rape incident. At one point, with a combination of courage and great hesitation, Connie spoke of what she had told no one before, not even Dave. Connie shared that she had not been allowed to date until she was sixteen years old, restrictions placed upon her by loving parents who wanted to protect her as much as possible. Sadly, they were not able to shield her from another's ugly sin, for on her very first date she was raped. Connie had gone out with a friend of her older sister, and his aggressive behavior caused Connie to experience sexuality in a way God never intended. Full of fear, rage and shame, she told her sister about what happened. While sympathetic, she demanded that Connie say nothing, which only made things worse for her. Pain unexpressed leads to despair and depression as little else can.

This event caused Connie indescribable pain, which she chose to address in a most unfortunate way: she became sexually promiscuous for several years. By moving in and out of short-term relationships that were sexually oriented, she was seeking a level of acceptance from others that she was unable to offer herself. Every time she engaged in relationships of this type, she came away feeling used, unworthy and covered with guilt and shame.

Understanding different layers of pain. I share this story to illustrate the identifiable structures of formational counseling. It is not my intention at this point to describe the process of healing prayer, but instead to talk about the five different layers of pain and wounding that must be addressed along the path to well-being. Connie's story provides a narrative that follows the structures of healing. By recognizing the pattern, the caregiver will be able to apply the same structure when helping the hurting people who will turn to her for help.

Fifth layer: Life situations. The caregiver should think of addressing the structures of healing as the process of peeling an onion. At the outer layer is the individual's *life situation,* the context where the person experiences his or her pain and difficulty. For Connie, the life situation was her sexual relationship with Dave. It was there that she experienced deep pain and heartache.

Fourth layer: Dysfunctional behavior. The layer beneath the life situation is that of the *dysfunctional behavior* the individual is embracing. In Connie's story, the dysfunctional behavior was the unhealthy way she responded to her husband's desire for sexual intimacy. Connie had confessed to initially projecting the problem onto Dave, complaining that he had unreasonable expectations. She also employed various avoidance behaviors, as well as rigidly refusing Dave's advances repeatedly. Her response was not healthy, and while appearing to offer short-term relief, it was planting the seed for long-term heartache in their relationship. Admittedly she was hurting deeply, and there was an explanation for her behavior. Be that as it may, her response was not healthy and had to be seen for what it truly was: dysfunctional.

Third layer: Emotional upheaval. Why did Connie embrace a level of dysfunctional behavior? Because she was experiencing *emotional upheaval* in the life situation she faced with Dave. Sexual intimacy brought bad feelings to the surface for Connie. She experienced fear, shame, guilt and anger whenever she was required to be sexual with her husband. Those feelings were powerful and painful. She tried to kill the pain the best way she knew, whether that was by blaming Dave for being oversexed, or finding ways to avoid the moment. Most important here is the fact that her behavior was driven by something much deeper: emotional upheaval. It is not enough to address the reaction she was having to sexual intimacy without recognizing the emotions that drove her actions. To do so could lead to solutions that would be barely effective in the short-term and useless over time.

Second layer: False beliefs. Feelings are linked to the thoughts that we have about ourselves and the people in our world. Connie felt upheaval when Dave approached her sexually because of what she believed about herself and about the meaning of sexual relations. Past experiences had shaped several powerful *false beliefs* that Connie had grown to accept as absolute truth. She believed that she was damaged goods as a result of the rape she had experienced years earlier. She also believed that to give herself to Dave in that way meant that she was easy and worthless. These thoughts had taken shape years earlier and were still very much alive at the core of her being. They were in no way based upon the truth of who she was in Christ, yet she subconsciously embraced these distortions whenever Dave approached her. The false belief that she was permanently defective created great emotional pain.

First or inner layer: Deep unresolved wounds. By now it is possible to see what shaped the distortions Connie had regarding sexual activity. She had been deeply *wounded,* first by rape and later by repeated affairs outside the bonds of marriage. These wounds were significant and filled with pain. Having never dealt with the matter in counseling, Connie suffered a great deal of grief and heartache. These wounds were compromising her well-being as she related to her husband in a very important aspect of their relationship. Broken people, like Connie, must open themselves to the healing touch of the Lord at the deepest level of their lives. There they can experience the power of the Holy Spirit's presence that brings hope and healing where heartache once reigned supreme.

Unaddressed wounds create a great deal of deep pain in a person's life. They also often give shape to *false beliefs* relative to the way people view themselves, others and God. These lies give birth to a significant amount of *emotional upheaval* that is debilitating and distracting for a broken person. In an effort to control or kill that pain, hurting people adopt various *dysfunctional behaviors,* which are then employed within a particular *life situation.* This pattern can be identified in most all of the stories that broken people will bring.

Operation of a cause-and-effect process. I want to reemphasize that there is a cause-and-effect relationship going on in people's psychospiritual issues. To treat the outer layers without identifying and ministering to the deeper issues will not lead to long-term healing and transformation. If all a caregiver does, for example, is address a dysfunctional behavior and help a person say no to that behavior, they are not addressing that which drives the problem in the first place. The issues that are beneath the behavior must be touched by the power of the Holy Spirit.

THE PATH TO TRANSFORMATION

The goal of formational counseling is to position people for a transforming encounter with Christ in the places of their deepest pain and greatest dysfunction. Through the ministry of the Holy Spirit a significant change will take place in this pattern. The wound becomes a place where the person has met the Lord and experienced his empowering grace. The lies are replaced by the truth of who they are in Christ Jesus, which brings a significant amount of comfort and peace even in the midst of life's difficulties and trials. This peace then enables them to experience empowered living, which is lived out within the individual's life situation. The illustration of that would be as follows.

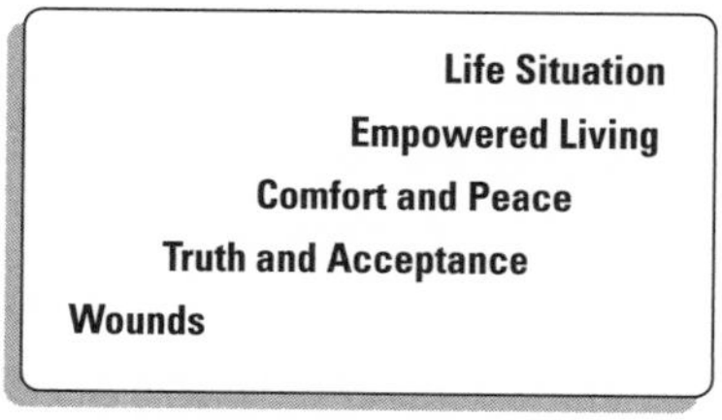

Life Situation
Empowered Living
Comfort and Peace
Truth and Acceptance
Wounds

Figure 11.2. Empowered living

A person is able to choose an entirely new path—a healing path ordained by God—in response to the wounds that have occurred in his or her life. This change takes place because of the encounter he or she had with the Holy Spirit. The wounds, instead of leading to a destructive series of cause-and-effect reactions, become a place of strength and healing, which then births an entirely new way of responding to the hurt and pain. This healing is deep and it is lasting, all because *it is the Lord who does it through the formational counselor.*

This process with Connie, as with all that took place, required time and patience. It was also critical that the Holy Spirit was present and free to move at all times. The Spirit enabled Connie to hear and accept the truth. The Lord spoke of his deep affection for her, as well as the truth that she was his beloved child, gifted, holy, totally forgiven and free in him. He also reinforced the message of his cleansing, which established Connie as both pure and worthy in his sight. To say the least, this encounter with the Spirit of truth was transformational for Connie. His words were spoken into the depth of her soul, powerful enough to silence the distortions that she had held for so long. The truth then brought Connie to an entirely new place emotionally.

Previously Connie had fought to forget all about the wounds that she had received those years before. Unfortunately, the pain was powerful and the voices very loud and debilitating. But Connie was able to hear a new word in the very place where lies had once kept their evil vigil. Truth opened the door to God's comfort and peace, and the storm that raged inside was stilled by the presence of Jesus. Connie actually pictured in her mind a stream of love cleansing her of all the past and empowering her to move on to an entirely new place in life. This reality birthed feelings entirely different from those she previously knew. There was joy, a sense of worth and freedom, each replacing negative feelings that had harassed Connie for a long time.

Fruit of the God Encounter

Connie's encounter with the Holy Spirit had done more than touch the wounds of the past. It empowered her to move out in life with a newfound strength and grace. She was able to talk to Dave about what happened. Connie knew she could do it with the help of the Lord. Certainly there was a reasonable level of nervousness, and more than a few unknowns. But Connie felt secure in the hand of the One who did know all about her tomorrows. Backed by prayer, Connie was able to tell Dave what had long remained a secret. Her confidence helped him respond with grace and tenderness, a sure sign that Jesus was right in the middle of this entire situation, as he so often is for the people he loves.

Formational counseling is a Holy Spirit–empowered ministry, flowing through empathically immersed caregivers who skillfully position people to encounter the living Christ in the memories of traumatic events, so that people can be set free from resulting destructive false beliefs, emotional upheaval and dysfunctional behaviors. Integrating the disciplines of spiritual direction, pastoral counseling and inner healing prayer, formational counselors find themselves present to episodic engagements between the Lord and people desperate for his transforming touch. These connections—between Christ, the people in need and the formational caregiver—often birth a worshipful response reminiscent of those found in Scripture: "Encountering Jesus is amazing!"

References and Recommended Resources

Christian caregivers from the United States and dozens of other nations have been trained in a series of basic and advanced seminars that integrate the principles of formational counseling with episodic engagements with the Lord. These seminars, sponsored by Healing Care Ministries, are held several times a year at The Institute of Formational Counseling at Ashland Theological Seminary in Ashland, Ohio. Information about these seminars and other resources of formational counseling are available at www.healingcare.org.

Individuals who want to be academically equipped in formational counseling can do so at Ashland Theological Seminary. Courses in formational counseling are offered at the master's level, and the seminary has a doctoral program with a concentration in formational counseling. In addition, the seminary offers a certificate program in formational prayer through The Institute of Formational Counseling. Information about these and other seminary programs can be found at www.seminary.ashland.edu.

Chan, F. (2009). *The forgotten God: Reversing our tragic neglect of the Holy Spirit.* Colorado Springs: David C. Cook.

Fosha, D. (2003). Diadic regulation and experiential work with emotion and relatedness in trauma and disorganized attachment. In M. Solomon & D. Siegel (Eds.), *Healing trauma* (pp. 221-81). New York: W. W. Norton.

Hook, J. P., & Ohlschlager, G. (2002). The empathic Christian counselor: Skilled helpers influencing client action. In T. Clinton & G. Ohlschlager (Eds.), *Competent Christian counseling: Foundations and practice of compassionate soul care* (pp. 203-22). Colorado Springs: WaterBrook Press.

Nouwen, H. (1977). *The living reminder: Service and prayer in memory of Jesus Christ.* San Francisco: HarperSanFrancisco.

Perry, M. S. (2010). *Born for love: Why empathy is essential and endangered.* New York: William Morrow.

Schacter, D. L. (1996). *Searching for memory: The brain, the mind, and the past.* New York: Basic Books.

Siegel, D. (2001). *The mindful therapist: The clinician's guide to mindsight and neural integration.* New York: W. W. Norton.

Siegel, D. (2010). *Mindsight: The new science of personal transformation.* New York: Bantam.

Wardle, T. (2001). *Healing care, healing prayer: Helping the broken find wholeness in Christ.* Abilene, TX: Leafwood.

Wardle, T. (2007). *Strong winds, crashing waves: Meeting Jesus in the memories of traumatic events.* Abilene, TX: Leafwood.

12

The Healing Cycle

A Transformational Model for Group Work

Jan Paul Hook & Joshua N. Hook

There has been a long history of using small groups to promote healing and transformation in people's lives. In the field of psychology, evidence has accumulated supporting the effectiveness of group interventions for helping to promote emotional health and well-being (Yalom & Leszcz, 2005). Furthermore, researchers are beginning to discuss how to incorporate religion and spirituality (R/S) into group work (Cornish & Wade, 2010), and some research studies have examined group interventions that have been adapted to incorporate a Christian worldview (e.g., Combs, Bufford, Campbell & Halter, 2000; Rye & Pargament, 2002).

In general, research investigating interventions that have been adapted to incorporate clients' R/S beliefs and values have had positive results. Clients in R/S interventions usually outperform clients in control groups, and have equivalent psychological outcomes (e.g., depression, anxiety, etc.) as clients in similar secular interventions (Hook et al., 2010). Furthermore, clients in R/S interventions often show greater improvements in spiritual outcomes (e.g., spiritual well-being, closeness to God) than clients in similar secular interventions (Worthington, Hook, Davis & McDaniel, 2011).

There are several reasons why it might be helpful to incorporate Christian approaches into group interventions. First, for Christian clients, incorporating Christian approaches provides concrete evidence that the intervention is consistent with their R/S beliefs and values, which is often preferred by clients who are highly religious. Accommodating client preferences modestly enhances outcomes and decreases premature termination (Swift, Callahan & Vollmer, 2011). Second, incorporating Christian approaches may provide clients with a wide array of metaphors, imagery and tools that may help improve the effectiveness of the intervention. For example, prayer can be used as a tool to help with the forgiveness process (Rye, 2005). Third (and perhaps most pertinent for the present chapter), incorporating Christian approaches into group interventions invites the person of Jesus Christ and the Holy Spirit into the process of transformational change.

The Healing Cycle is a transformational model for group work that is interpersonal in nature and is consistent with a Christian worldview (Hook & Hook, 2010). This model has been used in psychotherapeutic group contexts for individuals with serious psychological problems, as well as in process groups run by lay leaders in church ministries, such as support groups, recovery groups and even Bible studies. Thus, it is a model that is flexible and widely applicable to a number of group settings and formats.

I (JPH) began to use the Healing Cycle in my psychotherapeutic work with men who struggle with sexual addiction. I found that in this population, group work provided additional therapeutic opportunities and more positive outcomes than in my individual work with this population (Hook, Hook & Hines, 2008). In addition to using the Healing Cycle in a psychotherapeutic group context, I have also used it in my work in church ministries supervising group leaders who are running support groups in ministries, such as marital restoration and divorce recovery. The Healing Cycle could also be applicable for Bible study leaders, to help them encourage group members to go beyond the content of their study and into deeper application, sharing and connection. In these settings, group leaders often have difficulties helping group members to share deeply about their problems and struggles. Also, group leaders often have difficulties facilitating interpersonal interaction in their groups. The Healing Cycle is a model that addresses both of these difficulties.

In this chapter, we first describe the steps of the Healing Cycle. Second, we provide a scriptural basis for this group intervention. Third, we describe four foundational elements of the intervention important for group leaders. Fourth, in terms of application we describe situations that are well-suited for this group intervention, as well as situations that are contraindicated for this intervention. Fifth, we provide a case study that illustrates use of this intervention.

STEPS OF THE HEALING CYCLE

There are six steps of the Healing Cycle (see figure 12.1): grace, safety, vulnerability, truth, ownership and confession (Hook & Hook, 2010). Each step leads to the next. The final step of confession facilitates further experiences of grace, and the cycle continues.

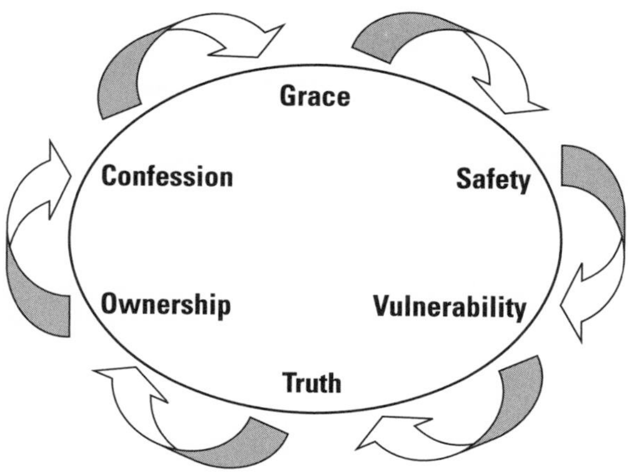

Figure 12.1. The healing cycle (Hook & Hook, 2010)

The experience of grace. Grace is foundational to the Christian faith and comes from God, who grants us unmerited kindness and favor. Group members often bring to a group very few interactions of experienced grace. Instead, group members bring experiences of judgment and criticism resulting in feelings of guilt and shame. Group leaders can help group members begin to work in group by acknowledging their own stories of brokenness and grace, and offering grace through their interactions with group members (e.g., being "for" the group members, showing kindness and caring through words and gestures, giving space and time to work, offering forgiveness for failures, etc.).

Feelings of safety. It is difficult to share in an environment that feels unsafe. In a group context, group members who feel unsafe will likely not share, and if they do share, the content will likely stay on a surface level. Thus, it is important for the group leader to take proactive steps to promote safety in the group. One important step to create safety is to develop group boundaries or commitments that all group members agree to. Boundaries we enforce in our groups include confidentiality, no judgments/criticism, no advice, do your own work, it's okay to pass, do not dominate and maintain consistent attendance. Group leaders must also work to stop boundary violations when they occur in group.

Vulnerability in sharing. For group members to experience emotional healing, growth and transformation, they must be able to share vulnerably about their problems and struggles in the group. There are several strategies group leaders can implement in order to help group members share vulnerably, including modeling purposeful self-disclosure, using active listening skills (and helping other group members to listen well), validating group members when they share and helping group members link with and connect to a group member's sharing. Linking is especially important to encourage vulnerability. Group members bring to group the fear of being alone in their pain. The ability to link one person's experience with another ensures that no one is alone in their brokenness.

Discovering truth about oneself and one's situation. In most group settings, an important goal is to gain insight or truth about one's problems. Often as a result of working in group and listening to the work of others, group members will begin to discover new truths about themselves. Also, especially in a context of grace and safety, group members will be able to hear truth, whether it is from a teaching, from a book or Bible study, or feedback about themselves from the group leader and (more importantly) other group members. The manner in which truth is shared is important. Group leaders must learn how to give feedback in the context of love, and coach group members how to do this as well. Truth that is given in an unloving manner will not be well received. Truth is necessary in order for change to happen, and most leaders agree that truth is what group members need most. For too many group leaders, however, speaking truth is the starting point. Without the foundation of grace and safety, truth will likely not be received well no matter how brilliantly it is presented. Instead truth will likely be experienced as criticism or judgment, and group members will feel unsafe. When this happens, group members will shut down, become superficial or leave the group. It is imperative that the cycle begins with and is grounded in grace. Only with the foundation of grace and safety can truth be shared and received.

Taking ownership for one's truth. Ownership involves taking responsibility for one's situation and acknowledging one's contribution to both the cause and maintenance of one's problems. Ownership is one of the most difficult steps of the Healing Cycle, but it is important for change to take place. Group members cannot change what they do not own. There are several techniques that are helpful for encouraging group members to stop making excuses and take ownership of their problems. For example, group members often make up stories about their problems that may or may not be accurate. Group leaders can help group members note that their perceptions of situations may not always reflect reality, and may actually be contributing to the maintenance of their problems. Group leaders can also help group members own their own problems by working with the projections of group members. When group members make a judgment about another group member, often these judgments reveal some hidden truth about the person making the judgment.

Confession. Confession gives voice to the truth that is owned and puts it into relationship. Confession to God is an important step of healing and growth, but we have also found that confession to others in a group context is extremely powerful and necessary. Confession in group is powerful because it makes guilt and forgiveness concrete (Kettunen, 2002). True confession also often involves not only admitting one's wrongs but also a commitment to change one's behavior. A group can be a great place to make a commitment to change because group members can hold each other accountable for confessions and commitments made in group.

After a confession is made, group leaders and members can respond to the confessor with grace and support. In a well-functioning group, this support is received and the confessor has a powerful experience of grace. And the cycle continues. The experience of grace leads to increased feelings of safety. Feelings of safety allow group members to share with more vulnerability. Sharing vulnerably, again, allows truth to be discovered and received. Truth that is discovered and received allows group members to take ownership of their truth. Truth that is owned is able to be confessed in group, and the confessor can make a commitment to change. A group member who honestly confesses receives support from the group, which gives the group member another and deeper experience of grace, and healing happens.

Scriptural Basis

There is ample scriptural support for the idea of using small groups for the purpose of transformative emotional and spiritual growth. To begin with, it is important to acknowledge that God is the author of change. So often group members think they need to change by themselves. We believe that no one heals alone. The apostle Peter wrote that it is God's "divine power" that is at work to create change and that through him one can "escape the corruption in the world caused by evil desires" (2 Pet 1:3-4). However, people need others as well in order to heal. In my (JPH) work with men who struggle with sexual addiction, I ask the question, "Have you brought your struggle to God?" The response I get is usually, "Yes, often. Many times I have prayed for release and healing." Then I ask, "Whom else have you shared your struggle with?" The response I often get is, "No one. You are the first person."

We believe one of the reasons there is little healing is because others have not been invited into the healing process. God uses people to do his work, and we are "stewards of God's grace" (1 Pet 4:10). Jesus modeled this kind of work. He spent the majority of his time teaching and fellowshiping with a small group of disciples. The early church spent a large amount of time in small groups (Acts 2:42). Jesus taught that where two or three are gathered, he is among them (Mt 18:20). Paul wrote to the church in Thessalonica that they should continue to encourage and build one another up (1 Thess 5:11). The writer to the Hebrews encouraged readers to continue to meet together in small groups, encouraging one another toward love and good deeds (Heb 10:24-25).

There is also scriptural support for each step of the Healing Cycle. Grace is foundational to Christian spirituality: we are "saved by grace" (Eph 2:8). Through grace God heals us and enables us to "stand" in relationship with him (Ps 40:2; Rom 5:2). Spiritual growth involves learning to "grow" in grace (2 Pet 3:18). Furthermore, as we grow in our own understanding of grace, we are better able to comfort and lead others into their own experience of grace (2 Cor 1:3-5). Our ability to extend grace then leads to safety, as there is no fear in love, but perfect love drives out fear (1 Jn 4:18). To ensure safety, group members are encouraged to do their own work rather than judge others (Mt 7:1, 3-5). Safety leads to vulnerability, which allows group members to put out their burdens so that those burdens can be carried (Gal 6:2). Sharing vulnerably leads to increased receptivity to truth. Jesus taught that when his followers understood truth, it would set them free (Jn 8:32). Paul taught that truth should be communicated in the context of love and grace (Eph 4:15). Receptivity to truth leads to ownership of one's truth, which is necessary to make changes. Consider the example of David, who took ownership of his sin with Bathsheba when confronted with truth from the prophet Nathan (2 Sam 12:13; Ps 32:5). Truth that is owned is able to be confessed to both God and community. God promises forgiveness if we confess our sins to him (1 Jn 1:9). Furthermore, God connects confession in community with healing (Jas 5:16). Finally, confession in a group leads to deeper experiences of grace.

FOUNDATIONAL ELEMENTS

The Healing Cycle is interpersonal in nature, and thus incorporates principles from interpersonal group therapy, which arose from the work of Irvin Yalom (Yalom & Leszcz, 2005). In his work, Yalom has identified several therapeutic factors that facilitate growth and change in groups, including universality, altruism, instillation of hope, imparting information, corrective recapitulation of primary family experience, development of socializing techniques, imitative behavior, cohesiveness, existential factors, catharsis, interpersonal learning and self-understanding. Research has shown that cohesiveness, or feelings of trust and belonging experienced by group members, is the most important therapeutic factor for transformation and growth (Yalom & Leszcz, 2005).

In addition to Yalom's therapeutic factors, there are four other foundational elements that we encourage group leaders to stress when implementing the Healing Cycle.

Commit to work on oneself. Group leaders should continue to work on themselves, especially in the areas of understanding their own stories of brokenness and grace. Offering an experience of grace is fundamental to jump-starting transformation and growth in the Healing Cycle. This experience of grace is not often something that can be taught like an academic subject, but it is "caught." Indeed, we have noted several individuals in our lives who, through our interactions and relationships with them, seem to really "get" grace. Often these individuals have done significant work on their own experiences of brokenness and have experienced grace. If group leaders have not been able to experience grace for their hurts and areas of brokenness, it is unlikely they will be able to create a group environment that fosters experiences of grace for group members. Like Jesus said to Simon the Pharisee, when the "sinful" woman demonstrated the ability to love well, "Whoever has been forgiven little loves little" (Lk 7:47). In order for group leaders to extend grace well, they need to own their own experience of grace.

Use oneself through purposeful self-disclosure. Self-disclosure is a controversial issue (Hanson, 2005), but when implementing the Healing Cycle, group leaders should use their clinical judgment and incorporate purposeful self-disclosure. The important rule we use when deciding whether or not to self-disclose is that self-disclosure should be used for the good of the group as a whole rather than to meet the needs of the group leader. For example, it might be helpful for group leaders to model vulnerable sharing or how to give loving feedback. However, it would not be helpful for group leaders to work on their own issues during the group session. Group leaders should have their own group (or therapist) for this purpose. We also note that group leaders should prioritize inviting sharing and feedback from group members over disclosing their own thoughts, feelings and reactions.

Focus on facilitating interpersonal interaction among group members. Often (especially in beginning groups) group members will direct their sharing toward the group leader, and there will be little interaction between group members. Group leaders should explicitly set up norms that encourage interpersonal interaction between group members. For example, if a group member wants to share, we invite that group member to pick a person that he or she wants to be in relationship with while sharing. Once a group member has shared, we invite the other group member to give his or her feedback and reaction. Furthermore, group leaders should explicitly create links between group members. After a group member has shared, we often ask whether any other group member can relate to what was shared. This allows group members to form connections with each other and realize that they are not alone in their pain and struggles.

Invite the person of Jesus Christ and the Holy Spirit into the group process. We trust the promise of Jesus that wherever two or three are gathered, he is there (Mt 18:20). We believe that spiritual and emotional health are closely intertwined and that God is an integral part of the process of healing and transformation.

Application and Implementation

The Healing Cycle is a flexible model for group work, and thus is applicable for a wide variety of settings. It can be used in psychotherapeutic groups for various kinds of psychological problems. It can be used in settings where all group members share the same type of problem (e.g., addiction) or in settings where group members present with different types of problems. The Healing Cycle can also be used in church group settings such as support groups, recovery groups and even Bible studies. This model has potential for use in any type of group that desires increased levels of connection and sharing.

Despite its flexibility, there are some situations where the Healing Cycle would likely not be the best model for group work. First, the Healing Cycle uses terms and concepts that are explicitly Christian, and this should be discussed during the informed consent process. Adopting a group intervention to R/S is trickier than adopting an individual intervention because group members may differ in their R/S beliefs and values, and all group members must accept the R/S elements present in the intervention. Group members who do not wish to have Christian elements incorporated with the group work may not benefit from this model.

Second, the Healing Cycle is predicated on consistent interpersonal interaction between group members, thus it may need to be modified for group members who struggle with interpersonal interaction (e.g., group members who are psychotic or struggle with a personality disorder or intense social anxiety).

Third, it is necessary for group members to follow set boundaries and guidelines (e.g., confidentiality) to ensure the safety of the group. Group members who are unable or unwilling to adhere to these boundaries are unlikely to benefit from this type of group and may actually sabotage the work of other group members.

Case Study

The following case study is adapted and expanded from Hook and Hook (2010). We have changed the names to ensure anonymity. The case study follows the experience of Sam, who is a member of my (JPH) group for men who struggle with sexual addiction. There are currently eight members in the group. The group is open, meaning that new members can join at any time (although there is a limit of ten members in the group). The group is also open-ended, meaning that group members may stay and work as long as is necessary; however, there is a minimum six-month commitment. The group meets weekly and is co-led by myself and another therapist. I have made it a priority to continue to explore my own stories of brokenness and grace, and to meet regularly with my own small group to discuss these issues. In this way, I hope to be able to create a group context that offers group members an environment characterized by grace.

Sam is new to the group. He is married, but has struggled with acting out by having a series of extramarital affairs. Tom is a seasoned group member who has experienced months of sobriety. In one session, Tom shared that he had acted out this past week by having a sexual liaison with another man. Sam jumped in and called Tom a pervert and asked how he could do such a thing, especially after months of sobriety. At that point, I spoke up, interrupted the group process, and reminded Sam (as well as the rest of the group) about the boundary of not judging other group members but doing his own work (maintaining safety). Sam was responsive to this challenge and admitted that he too had acted out this past week, although it was in a different way than Tom.

Reinforcing boundary violations when they occur is an important aspect of creating and maintaining safety in the group. When Sam made his judgment, I reinforced the boundary that group is the place to do one's own work, to look at the "plank" in one's own eye before pointing out the "speck" in another's eye (Mt 7:1-5). I asked Sam to look at where his judgment was coming from. Creating and maintaining boundaries ensures safety.

In another group session, Sam shared that he had acted out sexually by masturbating during the previous week. Sam reported feeling angry at himself and scared of being judged, similar to how he had judged Tom previously. At this point, I asked the group if anyone could relate to Sam (linking). When Joe said yes, I invited him to share his connection with Sam. Joe said that although he did not act out last week, he has a similar experience when he does act out. He too gets angry and scared of judgments. In this way Sam felt connected to Joe and less alone in his self-disclosure. He then became even more vulnerable and was able to share more about his story, talking about his anger and going deeper, acknowledging his feelings of fear and sadness toward himself about acting out. I validated his feelings and commented about the courage he had to jump in and share. Linking provided continued safety for Sam, freeing him to be more vulnerable. It was also important for me to continue to extend grace by validating and encouraging Sam.

During his sharing, Sam said that he was sad about his acting out, but he did so with a smile on his face. I gave feedback (truth) by saying, "I hear you saying you were sad when you acted out, but as you said it, you were smiling. Can you say what that smile is about?" Sam responded by saying that he felt uncomfortable or vulnerable because he has never really shared his sadness before. He did not know how to share sadness or how that feeling would be received. I encouraged him to share the feeling again, but without the smile. As Sam worked on his sadness, he became more congruent and clear in his communication. He also experienced the freedom of speaking his truth in the context of love. Again, I invited linking and feedback. I asked if any group members could relate and how they felt about Sam speaking his truth. Others connected and shared how courageous Sam was. Their responses extended grace and kept the group safe.

During a subsequent session, Sam accused another member, Joe, about being a "wimp" because Joe was afraid to confront a colleague about a work conflict. Naturally, Joe got defensive. Joe got angry and reacted. I stopped the conflict and invited Sam to reflect on his judgment, to look at the "plank" in his own eye. I asked, "Are you willing to take a look at what you just said? What is that about for you?" I further added, "You called him a wimp for not confronting. Who are you afraid to confront? Where in your life are you a wimp?"

Sam was initially reluctant, but he eventually acknowledged that he was afraid to confront his wife and was really angry at himself. Instead of owning his anger, it came out as a projection. As Sam took ownership of his projection, Joe, who had originally been judged, then dropped his defensive posture and did some work around his fear of confronting his colleague. There was a "speck" in Joe's eye, but he wasn't about to look at that speck when Sam confronted him. But as Sam explored and took ownership of the "plank" in his own eye, Joe relaxed his defensive posture and was open to explore his own speck.

I invited Sam, who made the initial judgment, to confess his judgment to Joe. Sam explained that his judgment was really about himself, and he apologized. The confession was received by Joe and reconciliation occurred between the two. This led to greater connection and intimacy. Commitments were made by both men to support each other in their work to face their fears of challenging others. This process of confession was healing for both parties and resulted in a further experience of grace.

In summary, Sam entered the group having acted out by having multiple extramarital affairs. He needed grace. Initial grace came from the leader, who extended grace to Sam based on his own experiences with brokenness and grace. In order for Sam to feel comfortable sharing, he needed the group to be safe. He broke a boundary of no judgments, and he was confronted by the group leader. Reinforcing boundaries provided a structure of safety that helped allow Sam to share vulnerably. He was able to share his struggle with acting out. His vulnerability was reinforced through listening, validating and linking. Sam was not alone in his pain. As a result of his sharing, Sam was able to discover and receive truth about himself. Sam was able to discover additional truth about himself by owning his projections and judgments. Sam was then able to confess his judgment and experience grace and reconciliation in the group.

The Healing Cycle allowed Sam to experience increased connection and intimacy with the other men in the group, which was a new experience for him. As the group continued to be safe, Sam was able to do further work, enabling him to experience grace from the leader and other group members, and ultimately the grace of God. The more Sam experienced grace and truth about himself, the more he began to meet his needs in healthy, godly ways, and the less he needed to act out sexually through his addiction.

Conclusion

The Healing Cycle is a model for group work that is designed to help group members experience transformation and emotional and spiritual growth. The foundation of the Healing Cycle is an experience of grace—especially grace that flows from the heart of God. The structure of the Healing Cycle is safety. With this foundation and structure in place, group members are able to share vulnerably, own the truth about themselves, confess their truth to God and group members, and experience lasting change.

References and Recommended Resources

Combs, C. W., Bufford, R. K., Campbell, C. D., & Halter, L. L. (2000). Effects of cognitive-behavioral marriage enrichment: A controlled study. *Marriage and Family: A Christian Journal, 3*, 99-111.

Cornish, M. A., & Wade, N. G. (2010). Spirituality and religion in group counseling: A literature review with practice guidelines. *Professional Psychology: Research and Practice, 41,* 398-404.

Hanson, J. (2005). Should your lips be zipped? How therapist self-disclosure and non-disclosure affects clients. *Counseling and Psychotherapy Research, 5,* 96-104.

Hook, J. N., Hook, J. P., & Hines, S. (2008). Reach out or act out: Long-term group therapy for sexual addiction. *Sexual Addiction and Compulsivity, 15,* 217-32.

Hook, J. N., Worthington, E. L., Jr., Davis, D. E., Gartner, A. L., Jennings, D. J., II., & Hook, J. P. (2010). Empirically supported religious and spiritual therapies. *Journal of Clinical Psychology, 66,* 46-72.

Hook, J. P., & Hook, J. N. (2010). The healing cycle: A Christian model for group therapy. *Journal of Psychology and Christianity, 29,* 308-16.

Kettunen, P. (2002). The function of confession: A study based on experiences. *Pastoral Psychology, 51,* 13-25.

Rutan, S. J., Stone, N. W., & Shay, J. (2007). *Psychodynamic group psychotherapy* (4th ed.). New York: Guilford.

Rye, M. S. (2005). The religious path toward forgiveness. *Mental Health, Religion, & Culture, 8,* 205-15.

Rye, M. S., & Pargament, K. I. (2002). Forgiveness and romantic relationships in college: Can it heal the wounded heart? *Journal of Clinical Psychology, 58,* 419-41.

Swift, J. K., Callahan, J. L., & Vollmer, B. M. (2011). Preferences. *Journal of Clinical Psychology, 67,* 155-65.

Worthington, E. L., Jr., Hook, J. N., Davis, D. E., & McDaniel, M. A. (2011). Religion and spirituality. *Journal of Clinical Psychology: In Session, 67,* 204-14.

Yalom, I. D., & Leszcz, M. (2005). *The theory and practice of group psychotherapy* (5th ed.). New York: Basic Books.

13

How God Comes Near and Transforms Us Through Forgiveness

Everett L. Worthington Jr., Aubrey L. Gartner, David J. Jennings II, Chelsea L. Greer & Yin Lin

Forgiveness and love are the two foundational truths of Christianity. Every human is created in God's image and through common grace can forgive. But every human needs forgiveness because all people are fallen. And also because people are fallen, unforgiveness rears up like a vicious beast amid the most well-meaning people even in overtly Christian settings.

In the present chapter, we describe an established treatment theory and protocol for people who are experiencing difficulties forgiving another person. The REACH Forgiveness model is a spiritual and psychological intervention that is grounded in biblical theology. Evidence for its effectiveness has been established by clinical science in investigations across many laboratories. Its use has been widespread in lay counseling, counseling by congregational pastors, pastoral counseling, couple counselors, family counselors, group psychoeducators, marriage enrichment specialists and individual psychotherapists.

Personal Testimony of the Originator of the REACH Forgiveness Model

Who doesn't need forgiveness? I (Everett) certainly do. After I became a Christian, someone challenged me one day to try an experiment: to try to live for a full day without sinning in thought, word or deed. Predictably, I failed the test. Repeatedly. At the end of my informal experiment (no doubt significant at the $p < .0000001$ level), I concluded that I was a confirmed sinner, unable through my own effort to eliminate sin. I needed forgiveness from God.

I needed to forgive others too. This was dramatically made evident in a seemingly trivial matter. I was a counseling psychology doctoral student at the University of Missouri–Columbia (UMC). UMC had programs in both counseling and clinical psychology. In one class, Behavior Modification, I had a clinical psychology professor who was, I believed, prejudiced against counseling students. So I coded the number of times he looked at, talked to and asked questions of students each class period. Adding each category, calculating the means and standard deviations, and (I blush to admit) calculating *t*-tests, I found that he was prejudiced. Not surprisingly, I earned a B in the course.

I carried a grudge against him for over ten years. One night, evangelist Joy Dawson invited the audience to imagine being in the room with a person against whom they held a grudge. "What would happen if Jesus walked in?" she asked. My petty expectations that Jesus would comfort me were dashed. I imagined Jesus comforting him. I saw the vileness of my own sin of unforgiveness. I forgave. I experienced the lightness and freedom that comes through the forgiveness of God and through forgiving others.

Forgiveness attracted me. I needed forgiveness—from God and from others—and I needed to grant it to people who needed it. As a psychotherapist, I found that I could actually help others give it to and receive it from each other, and sometimes to receive it from God. That led me to develop the five steps to REACH forgiveness. I have worked with graduate students and professional colleagues around the world to develop the method into one that you can use easily and effectively. We have used it as lay counselor–led programs in local churches as far away as the Philippines and in many settings in churches and Christian colleges. Let our current research group at VCU give you an overview of the method as it might be used by Christians.

Biblical Theological Basis of the REACH Forgiveness Intervention

To forgive is human (McCullough, Sandage & Worthington, 1997). Forgiveness is part of common grace—like love, reason and communication.

As Augustine argued, it isn't an act itself that is Christian, but it is the motive and the use of the act that make it Christian. Forgiveness between married partners could be granted and experienced through one's own strength, with the aim of strengthening the marriage. Or, forgiveness could be granted and experienced under the leading of God to provide the foundation for one's own worship or as a doorway to invite a wayward spouse back into the marriage and also back into God's kingdom.

What's the motive in the act? Importantly, then, any method of teaching people to forgive, even one derived from Scripture—while vitally important—is vain if one forgives for the wrong reasons. For instance, if a partner wants to forgive only as a cease-fire until a divorce is arranged, forgiveness is not sanctified. Or, if a partner seeks forgiveness for wrongdoing yet does so to manipulate the spouse and continues to take advantage, forgiveness is worse than none.

Does God always want people to show forgiveness? God always desires for people to love. Yet love can be shown as compassionate yielding or as tough, justice-demanding pressure. I believe that God wants Christians to practice forgiveness daily. In Jesus' disciples prayer, he said, "For if you forgive other people when they sin against you, your heavenly Father will also forgive you. But if you do not forgive others their sins, your Father will not forgive your sins" (Mt 6:14-15). We note several things from that passage.

1. For followers of Jesus, divine forgiveness of some sins is contingent on our interpersonal forgiveness of sins against us.
2. The sins being talked about are not one's state of sin—that is, Jesus was not talking about justification. First, this is a prayer to the disciples—presumably those who already were allied to Jesus. Second, if this were justification, it would contradict the main message of Christianity—that justification is up to God, not to human behavior. If all we had to do was forgive all of the sins against us to be justified, salvation would be up to us.
3. We have the power to forgive and we are accountable for attempting to do so.
4. It is unclear whether the forgiveness required of people is to be "complete." The Bible never mentions "complete" forgiveness.

5. The type of forgiveness that the prayer implies is decisional forgiveness rather than emotional forgiveness (Worthington, 2003). Emotions are not completely under volitional control. Therefore, emotional forgiveness is not completely subject to a person's will. Decisional forgiveness has emotions associated with it, but mostly decisional forgiveness is an act of the will. Thus, it can be turned toward God more easily than can emotional forgiveness. Of course, God wants people to be both decisionally and emotionally forgiving, but it is the decisional forgiveness that God requires.

God initiates; people respond. We forgive because God first forgave us. Yet, our motive should not be based on a quid pro quo—a kind of, "I've been forgiven, so I'm duty bound to forgive even though I don't feel like it." Instead, we forgive as a grateful response to receiving God's gift of forgiveness of our sin (i.e., justification). We are to forgive as an act of love. We are to display mercy. We are to be altruistic, which comes from a sense of accurate empathy toward a needy person and not through self-interest.

But people who are not Christians have not received justification. Should they too forgive? Can they expect divine help in forgiving? Many theological debates are imbedded in these questions.

Biblical theology of forgiveness. Worthington (2003) outlines a biblical theology of forgiveness. He asserts that God's heart was constantly turned toward forgiveness and restoration of a wayward humanity—which is evident in Genesis. An early passage of God's forgiveness and justice (Ex 34:6-7) emphasizes God's love and mercy, but it clearly does not forget justice. However, as Scriptures on forgiveness developed chronologically (see Ex 20:5-6; Num 14:17-18; Deut 24:16; Neh 9:17; Ps 86:5, 15; 103:8-10; 130:3-4; 145:8-9; Jer 31:34; Dan 9:9; Joel 2:13; Jonah 4:2; Mic 7:18-19), mercy was emphasized more than was justice.

Forgiveness without repentance. Worthington (2003) argued that Scripture mandated that humans forgive unilaterally. Namely, there is not a convincing biblical justification for waiting until an offender has repented prior to granting forgiveness (see Worthington, 2003). (The passage in Lk 17:3, "if they repent, forgive them," is not definitive. It does not say what to do if the offender does not repent. The biblical case is that Christians are also to forgive him.)

Forgiveness and unforgiveness. Importantly, Worthington (2003) also argued that not all offenses and injustices result in *unforgiveness*. Unforgiveness develops out of a delayed grudge-holding that fuels resentment, bitterness, hatred, anger, aggression and fear. Many ways of dealing with injustice are consistent with Christianity. Thus, forgiveness is not always *necessary* when one is offended. Alternatives include relinquishing the matter to God, forbearing, accepting and moving on, or seeking justice. Forgiveness is needed once; unforgiveness is ensconced.

Can Christians forgive better than other people? Worthington (2003) also addressed this question. It may be better stated as, "Can a person forgive better if he or she were Christian than if he or she were not Christian? What is the difference (if any) that being a Christian makes?" While recognizing that to forgive is human, Worthington (2003) argues that Christians might indeed practice forgiveness better than many others.

Foundational Elements of Intervention from a Bio-Psycho-Social-Spiritual Framework

The key to the psychology of decisional forgiveness is its differentiation from emotional forgiveness. In Worthington's (2003) five steps to the REACH forgiveness psychoeducational model, participants are led through exercises to help them make a decision to forgive. Most of the time is used to work through steps to replace negative unforgiving emotions with positive emotions (emotional forgiveness). The emotional replacement hypothesis suggested by Worthington has accumulated much supportive scientific evidence (see Worthington, 2006).

Proper structures for forgiveness. In the Christian version of the five steps, an analogy is used to motivate the intervention. The participants are told that using the five steps is like using wooden forms to shape concrete in building a load-bearing pillar to support a ceiling. The REACH steps are like the wooden forms. They shape the concrete. The concrete is likened to the Holy Spirit forming permanent change in one's heart. The concrete, not the wooden forms, is the basis of the pillar. Yet the forms are structures that God uses to bring about forgiveness. Other structures might be ecclesiastical structures, like worship, confession, praise, participation in sacraments of baptism or the Lord's Supper, prayers of request (McMinn et al., 2008), and prayers of intercession by another.

In fact, within the intervention, Worthington (2003, 2009, 2012) uses prayers, private experiential interpretation of Scripture (using an adapted *lectio divina* method), religious imagery, prayer for the one who harmed the participant, and other ecclesiastical methods to help the participant replace negative unforgiving emotions with positive other-oriented emotions.

Responding to the murder of mother. Worthington (2003) reports anecdotally how he dealt with the murder of his mother in 1995. Apparently a youth in search of treasure, thinking that his mother was away from home, bludgeoned her with a crowbar when she discovered the youth. While thinking systematically through the REACH model, Worthington suddenly recalled an earlier time of rage over the murder in which he pointed to a baseball bat and said, "I wish whoever killed Mama were here. I'd beat his brains out."

That emotional memory led him to ask, *Whose heart is darker here—the heart of this young man who has little ego control, or my own, a forty-eight-year-old Christian who had counseled others and written books on how to forgive?* Worthington was convicted that his own heart was darker. Yet he was confident that through Jesus' substitutionary death, he could be forgiven. *Who am I,* he thought, *to hold a grudge against this young man if I can be forgiven?*

He humbled himself and came before God seeking forgiveness; God set him free of hatred and resentment. God had broken in and transformed his life. He is quick to admit, though, that his rapid forgiveness of the young man is from grace and mercy, not from his own character. Recall the grudge he held for ten years against his Behavior Modification teacher.

REACH Forgiveness Step by Step

Description of the five steps to REACH forgiveness. REACH is best taught in psychoeducational groups. After defining forgiveness, people talk about the hurt and then decide to forgive as much of it as possible. Then they seek to increase their emotional forgiveness. The five steps to REACH emotional forgiveness are as follows:

R = Recall the hurt without blaming or self-pity;

E = Empathize with the person who hurt you (includes sympathy, compassion and love);

A = Altruistic gift of forgiveness is granted;

C = Commit to the emotional forgiveness you have experienced; and

H = Hold on to forgiveness when you doubt you have forgiven.

The step-by-step REACH forgiveness method is laid out in Worthington (2003, 2006, 2009) and also described in a variety of other sources (e.g., Lampton, Oliver, Worthington & Berry, 2005; Worthington, Mazzeo & Canter, 2005). Free, downloadable and modifiable leader and participant manuals for the psychoeducational groups are available for twenty hours of group intervention for both secular and Christian settings (Worthington, 2012). And for Christian-oriented psychoeducational groups, "best-six hour" manuals for leader and participants are available.

Clinical Assessment

In most counseling, forgiveness is not the presenting problem. Rather, unforgiveness is more likely to emerge as a problem over the course of counseling. Unforgiveness results from unhealed interpersonal wounds in a person's past or present life. At other times, forgiveness can be on the surface. For example, in couple or family therapy, partners or family members may have hurt each other many times and might present with a poor relationship that is characterized by conflict, communication problems, intimacy problems and forgiveness problems.

Clients who are Christian might experience guilt and self-condemnation due to their inability to forgive. Many feel such guilt because Jesus, in teaching his disciples, said, "For if you forgive other people when they sin against you, your heavenly Father will also forgive you. But if you do not forgive others their sins, your Father will not forgive your sins" (Mt 6:14-15). For Christians, some might (mis)understand this to mean that holding unforgiveness could result in their loss of an eternal relationship with God. Others, however, will interpret this in a much more limited sense, that at the final judgment of believers, their own judgment of another person will be held against them. Either way, though, for a person who believes that forgiving is a religious obligation, a persistent failure to forgive is guilt-producing.

We suggest that there are three levels of clinical assessment.

Level one assessment. The first level of clinical assessment is screening. Screening can be as simple as asking people whether they believe that lack of forgiveness plays a central role in their problems. This can alert the counselor to address forgiveness. Screening for forgiveness might be undertaken only if a counselor finds that the client has anger or hostility, relationship problems, or interpersonal stress-related problems. It can be as simple as a quick follow-up question. If the verbal probe suggests that the client struggles to forgive an event, the clinician can use two single-item instruments to quantify the degree of decisional and emotional forgiveness (DFS & EFS; on a scale from 0 = *no forgiveness* to 4 = *complete forgiveness*). These items can provide a quickly assessed baseline used throughout counseling to track the client's forgiveness.

Level two assessment. If forgiveness does become a major focus of counseling, the counselor might want to conduct a level two assessment of whether forgiveness of a particular transgression is needed. Level two assessment can use questionnaires such as the Transgression Related Interpersonal Motivations Inventory (TRIM; McCullough et al., 1998). If the person is attempting to become a more forgiving person, rather than forgive a particular relationship or transgression, the Trait Forgivingness Scales (TFS; Berry et al., 2005) might be administered as a baseline. If forgiveness of self is a concern, the Heartland Forgiveness Scale might prove useful (HFS; Thompson et al., 2005).

Level three assessment. It is important to consider an additional type of assessment. Level three assessment occurs during counseling and is intended to direct the client's attention to a topic that is therapeutically relevant. The psychotherapist might administer brief forgiveness instruments during the session to measure the client's changing levels of forgiveness and unforgiveness. Level three assessments can be compared to the baseline level two assessments to demonstrate change and increased forgiveness as therapy progresses.

Clinical Intervention and Applications

The REACH forgiveness model has been tested many times. Wade, Worthington and Meyer (2005) reviewed forty-two empirical studies up to 2004—several of which were studies of the REACH model. Since then, it has been used in a variety of educational and clinical settings. Clinically, this model can be used as an adjunct to counseling. For example, instead of taking time in counseling, the counselor can ask the client to attend a weekly forgiveness group designed to teach and promote forgiveness.

The REACH model has been used with Christian college students (Lampton et al., 2005; Stratton et al., 2008), romantically jilted college Christian women (Rye & Pargament, 2002) and divorced individuals who are Christians (Rye et al., 2005). The REACH model has also been used in other countries. For example, it was adapted for use in churches in the Philippines (Worthington et al., 2010). DiBlasio and Benda (2008) used decision-based forgiveness with Christian and secular couples. The REACH forgiveness model has been used with secular marriage enrichment (Burchard et al., 2003; Ripley & Worthington, 2002; Worthington et al., 2005) and secular parenting enrichment (Kiefer et al., 2010).

Indications and Contraindications for a Forgiveness Intervention

Indications. Just because the counselor detects unforgiveness does not mean it must be dealt with in counseling. Any person will, at times, be unforgiving and will also manifest other sins. The counselor is neither responsible for nor able to deliver the client wholly without blemish, spotless and clean. Rather, the counselor works with the client to achieve the client's goals.

Any counselor will face limitations in working with a client, which often depend on the clinical setting. For example, in an overloaded secular counseling agency with a waiting list of troubled clients, a student trainee might not have the luxury of working with a client on promoting Christian growth toward a healthier life of prayer and worship. By contrast, within a conservative church counseling center, a Christian counselor might not agree to work with an unmarried couple to improve their cohabitation relationship—even though the same counselor might work with similar clients in a student training clinic at a secular university.

Indications that a forgiveness intervention is needed include the following. First, unforgiveness is a presenting problem or becomes a focal issue during counseling. Second, forgiveness is necessary to progress toward other valued counseling goals. Third, the counselor observes that unforgiveness is harming the client.

Contraindications. Some transgressions have not developed into unforgiveness. They might yield to direct treatment that is less time-consuming than a forgiveness intervention. For example, a couple might come to counseling after heated arguments. The counselor might determine that the couple's problem is not unforgiveness as much as it is poor conflict resolution.

Clients may also enter therapy for particular problems that they do not believe should be forgiven. If a person does not believe in forgiveness for a particular problem, the counselor should not force it on the client. Let's take three common examples. First, some people believe that forgiveness of heinous crimes, like murder, is impossible in practice. They might assert that only the murder victim has a right to forgive the murderer, and because the murder victim is no longer alive, forgiveness by the client is wrong. Second, some Christians believe that an offender must repent before being forgiven, and without repentance, the client won't forgive. Third, people might confuse forgiveness and reconciliation, believing that if one forgives, the relationship must be restored.

This can be harmful. It conflates forgiveness (which occurs within a person's skin) with reconciliation (which concerns rebuilding trust in a relationship in which trust has been damaged). While the counselor might consider all three of these lines of reasoning to be misconceptions by the client, the counselor should realize that some theologies or philosophies make such arguments in good faith. For example, Jewish theology often argues that murder is unforgivable. Also, some Christians argue that repentance is needed prior to forgiveness. Even Christian theologians at times suggest that forgiveness implies that reconciliation is a necessary consequence.

The counselor is not a theologian and should not engage clients in theological argument. Even though a Christian counselor may find it useful to discuss a point of theology, theological discussions can divert therapeutic attention from the client's presenting issues. Even if the counselor can convince the client that he or she is wrong, such as in one of the lines of reasoning described above, the theological debate may alienate the client. It can also cause the client to terminate therapy prematurely.

No issue is too difficult to forgive. However, some issues are harder to forgive than others and may require more time. Some problems have been found to take sixty or more hours of counseling (e.g., incest survivors) to forgive the perpetrators. Thus, although no issue may in principle be too difficult to forgive, it might not be worth the time for some clients. Decisions to engage in a forgiveness intervention need to be made within the overall treatment program and need to make a justifiable contribution to the client's well-being.

Case Studies

In a variety of publications, case studies have been presented using the REACH forgiveness model. Worthington and DiBlasio (1990) describe a couple who had not made progress in couple therapy. The couple seemed stuck in their unforgiveness. They had been taught communication skills, conflict resolution skills and experiencing intimacy with each other using Worthington's Hope-Focused Couple Approach (Worthington, 2005; for a review, see Jakubowski, Milne, Brunner & Miller, 2004).

Yet the partners kept coming back to many of their old wounds. The couple therapist, DiBlasio, suggested to the couple that because of the power of past hurts in the marriage, they needed to work on forgiveness. DiBlasio then suggested that each one spend the week thinking of all the ways he or she had *wronged* the other partner. He had the couple take turns confessing their wrongs as they held hands and faced each other. The couple deeply confessed their wrongdoing and forgave each other.

Worthington, Mazzeo and Canter (2005) describe a case in which an early married couple worked through a psychoeducational nine-hour treatment manual with a "marriage consultant" to promote forgiveness. (The treatment manual—Forgiveness and Reconciliation through Experiencing Empathy, or "FREE," for couples—is available for free download: Worthington, 2012.) The intervention taught people to REACH forgiveness and to move across a bridge to reconciliation (see Worthington, 2003, 2006).

For a case of forgiveness in individual psychotherapy, including verbatim transcripts involving sixty-three client-psychotherapist interchanges, we can get a flavor of how the conversations between psychotherapist and client might unfold (see Worthington, 2006). Clara (a pseudonym) began talking in psychotherapy about her inability to forgive her father for his alcoholism and all the heartache it had caused her and her family. This became the focus of psychotherapy for at least two full sessions. In the following excerpt, the psychotherapist (abbreviated T in these excerpts) begins to intervene with client Clara (Cl).

Clara expressed difficulty in controlling her negative ruminations that led to "raging" toward her father's memory. She discussed her difficulty forgiving her father.

Cl-24: So, I want to forgive him. But I've wanted to forgive for years, and I can't make myself. Every time I try to forgive, I get angry all over again within a day or two.

T-24: What would it mean if you forgave him? What would be different about your life?

After discussing the benefits she presumes she would experience—mostly in terms of positive moods and freedom from self-condemnation over not forgiving—the client and therapist moved toward a working definition of forgiving.

T-26: You said that you had tried to forgive him many times. How did you try to forgive?

Cl-27: You know, I just said I forgave him.

T-27: Hummm?

Cl-28: What do you mean, "Hummm?"

T-28: Just putting together what you were saying—you'd just say you forgave him and then suddenly feel completely free of hate and anger.

Cl-29: [Laughs] Yeah, I guess it doesn't make sense now that I think of it. It sounds a little unrealistic that I ought to feel so free of the hate just because I said I forgave him.

T-29: I think it is important to decide you want to forgive. So you are on the right track. I also think it is important that you get rid of your hatred and anger toward your dad. That is a part of forgiving. But maybe those two parts of forgiving are not joined at the hip. (Worthington, 2006, excerpts from p. 163)

The psychotherapist uses whatever techniques and methods he can to help the client self-discover motivations (benefits) to try to focus therapy on forgiveness, to mobilize her efforts to try to forgive, to change her thinking and to develop a different understanding of forgiveness—as involving decisional and emotional forgiveness (without necessarily using those terms with the client). Once the definition is accepted, the therapist can work with the client to move through the five steps to REACH forgiveness.

CONCLUSION

In the present chapter, we have defined two types of forgiveness and shown that forgiveness is intimately linked with Christianity in people's lives. The research on forgiveness is voluminous, and much of it can be applied to people who wish to attend psychotherapy that deals with forgiveness. The findings are useful in terms of designing assessments at levels one and three, as well as for the few people where forgiveness becomes the major issue of psychotherapy (for which level two assessment is appropriate).

We have one recommendation of paramount importance for clinicians: if your client wants to experience more forgiveness, he or she must spend more time thinking about forgiving. There is a reliable dose-and-response relationship between the amount of time people spend trying to forgive and the amount of forgiveness that they experience (Wade et al., 2005). The forgiveness rate is about one-tenth of a standard deviation improvement per hour of concentrated intervention. To put this in perspective, over six months of weekly psychotherapy, a typical client is likely to gain about 0.8 to 1.0 standard deviations. Thus, the amount of change in forgiveness is substantial, but is slow going—requiring about ten hours of intensive psychotherapy to gain one standard deviation in forgiveness. Almost no psychotherapy has the luxury to focus on forgiveness for ten hours. Typically in psychotherapy, forgiveness is not the major focus. Therefore, a psychotherapist might spend two or three hours, over the course of twelve to fifteen hours of psychotherapy, specifically focusing on forgiveness.

The crucial questions for the clinical science of forgiveness, the psychotherapist, pastor or lay helper who has limited time to work with a client are the same: Which specific interventions are necessary for change? Which are both necessary and sufficient for change? And which are the most powerful at inducing the most change in the least amount of time?

Key questions for the Christian are: How can we invite God's active intervention into a person's life without manipulation, invasiveness or imposition? How can we get out of the way, help the client deal directly with God and let God transform the person through forgiveness?

References and Recommended Resources

Essential Readings

Worthington, E. L., Jr. (2003). *Forgiving and reconciling: Bridges to wholeness and hope.* Downers Grove, IL: InterVarsity Press.

Worthington, E. L., Jr. (2006). *Forgiveness and reconciliation: Theory and application.* New York: Brunner-Routledge.

Worthington, E. L., Jr. (2009). *A just forgiveness: Responsible healing without excusing injustice.* Downers Grove, IL: InterVarsity Press.

Websites

Ripley, J. S. (<www.hopecouples.com> or <www.mmatecenter.com>). Resources for Hope-Focused Couple Counseling, including downloadable resources, readings, reports of research, demonstration DVDs and a training curriculum for certification as a Hope-Focused Couple Counselor.

Worthington, E. L., Jr. (<www.people.vcu.edu/~eworth>) Free, downloadable manuals.

Training DVD

Worthington, E. L., Jr. (R.E.A.C.H. Forgiveness; DVD of psychoeducational group training at Southwestern Baptist University, Bolivar, MO, February 2010; a six-hour group edited to two hours of training on two one-hour DVDs; available from the first author for $5).

References

Berry, J. W., Worthington, E. L., Jr., O'Connor, L., Parrott, L., III, & Wade, N. G. (2005). Forgiveness, vengeful rumination, and affective traits. *Journal of Personality, 73,* 1-43.

Burchard, G. A., Yarhouse, M. A., Kilian, M. K., Worthington, E. L., Jr., Berry, J. W., & Canter, D. E. (2003). A study of two marital enrichment programs and couples' quality of life. *Journal of Psychology and Theology, 31,* 240-52.

DiBlasio, F. A., & Benda, B. B. (2008). Forgiveness intervention with married couples: Two empirical analyses. *Journal of Psychology and Christianity, 27,* 150-58.

Greene, J. D., Sommerville, R. B., Nystrom, L. E., Darley, J. M., & Cohen, J. D. (2001). An fMRI investigation of emotional engagement in moral judgment. *Science, 293,* 2105-8.

Jakubowski, S. F., Milne, E. P., Brunner, H., & Miller, R. B. (2004). A review of empirically supported marital enrichment programs. *Family Relations, 53,* 528-36.

Kiefer, R. P., Worthington, E. L., Jr., Myers, B., Kliewer, W. L., Berry, J. W., Davis, D. E., Miller, A. J., Van Tongeren, D. R., Hunter, J. L., & Kilgour, J., Jr. (in press). Training parents in forgiveness and reconciliation. *American Journal of Family Therapy.*

Lampton, C., Oliver, G. J., Worthington, E. L., Jr., Berry, J. W. (2005). Helping Christian college students become more forgiving: An intervention study to promote forgiveness as part of a program to shape Christian character. *Journal of Psychology and Theology, 33*(4), 278-90.

McCullough, M. E., Rachal, K. C., Sandage, S. J., Worthington, E. L., Jr., Brown, S. W., & Hight, T. L. (1998). Interpersonal forgiveness in close relationships II: Theoretical elaboration and measurement. *Journal of Personality and Social Psychology, 75,* 1586-1603.

McCullough, M. E., Sandage, S. J., & Worthington, E. L., Jr. (1997). *To forgive is human: How to put your past in the past.* Downers Grove, IL: InterVarsity Press.

McMinn, M. R., Fervida, H., Louwerse, K. A., Pop, J. L., Thompson, R. D., Trihub, B. L., & McLeod-Harrison, S. (2008). Forgiveness and prayer. *Journal of Psychology and Christianity, 27,* 101-9.

Ripley, J. S., & Worthington, E. L., Jr. (2002). Comparison of hope-focused communication and empathy-based forgiveness group interventions to promote marital enrichment. *Journal of Counseling and Development, 80,* 452-63.

Rye, M. S., & Pargament, K. I. (2002). Forgiveness and romantic relationship in college: Can it heal the wounded heart? *Journal of Clinical Psychology, 58,* 419-41.

Rye, M. S., Pargament, K. I., Pan, W., Yingling, D. W., Shogren, K. A., & Ito, M. (2005). Can group interventions facilitate forgiveness of an ex-spouse? A randomized clinical trial. *Journal of Consulting and Clinical Psychology, 73,* 880-92.

Stratton, S. P., Dean, J. B., Nonneman, A. J., Bode, R. A., & Worthington, E. L., Jr. (2008). Forgiveness interventions as spiritual development strategies: Comparing forgiveness workshop training, expressive writing about forgiveness, and retested controls. *Journal of Psychology and Christianity, 27,* 347-57.

Thompson, L. Y., Snyder, C. R., Hoffman, L., Michael, S. T., Rasmussen, H. N., Billings, L. S., Heinze, L., Neufeld, J. E., Shorey, H. S., Roberts, J. C., & Roberts, D. E. (2005). Dispositional forgiveness of self, others, and situations. *Journal of Personality, 73,* 319-59.

Wade, N. G., Worthington, E. L., Jr., & Meyer, J. (2005). But do they really work? Meta-analysis of group interventions to promote forgiveness. In Everett L. Worthington, Jr. (Ed.), *Handbook of forgiveness* (pp. 423-40). New York: Brunner-Routledge.

Worthington, E. L., Jr. (2003). *Forgiving and reconciling: Bridges to wholeness and hope.* Downers Grove, IL: InterVarsity Press.

Worthington, E. L., Jr. (2005). *Hope-focused marriage counseling: A guide to brief therapy* (Rev. ed. with a new introduction). Downers Grove, IL: InterVarsity Press.

Worthington, E. L., Jr. (2006). *Forgiveness and reconciliation: Theory and application.* New York: Brunner-Routledge.

Worthington, E. L., Jr. (2009). *A just forgiveness: Responsible healing without excusing injustice.* Downers Grove, IL: InterVarsity Press.

Worthington, E. L., Jr. (2012, August). Forgiveness Intervention Manuals. *Virginia Commonwealth University Department of Psychology Faculty Page.* Retrieved from <http://www.people.vcu.edu/~eworth/>.

Worthington, E. L., Jr., & DiBlasio, F. A. (1990). Promoting mutual forgiveness within the fractured relationship. *Psychotherapy, 27,* 219-23.

Worthington, E. L., Jr., Hunter, J. L., Sharp, C. B., Hook, J. N., Van Tongeren, D. R., Davis, D. E., Miller, A. J., Gingrich, F. C., Sandage, S. J., Lao, E., Bubod, L., & Monforte-Milton, M. M. (2010). A psychoeducational intervention to promote forgiveness in Christians in the Philippines. *Journal of Mental Health Counseling, 32*, 82-103.

Worthington, E. L., Jr., Mazzeo, S. E., & Canter, D. E. (2005). Forgiveness-promoting approach: Helping clients REACH forgiveness through using a longer model that teaches reconciliation. In Len Sperry and Edward P. Shafranske (Eds.), *Spiritually-oriented psychotherapy* (pp. 235-57). Washington, DC: American Psychological Association.

14

Praying the Scriptures Within Cognitive/Behavioral/ Systems Therapy

George Ohlschlager

Life is not measured by the number of breaths we take,
but by those moments that take our breath away.

Plaque on the wall of AACC kitchen

When you judge people,
you have no time to love them.

Mother Teresa

Then Jesus went about all the cities and villages,
teaching in their synagogues, preaching the gospel of the Kingdom,
and healing every sickness and every disease among the people. . . .
And when He had called His twelve disciples, . . . He gave them
power over unclean spirits, to cast them out, and to heal
all kinds of sickness and all kinds of disease.

Matthew 9:35; 10:1 (NKJV)

After I spent four years doing intensive community mental health practice as a clinical social worker in small-town and rural Iowa, I moved back to Humboldt County in Northern California to join a friend to launch The Redwood Family Institute in 1988. It was there, as a Christian counselor and California LCSW, that I began to develop a Christ-centered approach to change by praying client-chosen and image-rich Bible verses with my clients to enhance inner healing and godly intimacy.

I learned about inner healing ministry from my friend and practice partner Peter Mosgofian, an LMFT and Vineyard pastor who had long practiced charismatic inner healing in both his pastoral and psychotherapeutic roles. Inner healing prayer—which is highlighted in numerous chapters of this book—is an explicit form of interventional Christian prayer aimed at helping clients "who have unresolved painful memories of their past that may involve deprivation or neglect, abandonment, rejection, harsh treatment or criticism, physical or sexual abuse, and trauma" (Tan, 2011, p. 345).

When learning this practice, I was also struck by the similarities of inner healing prayer to the process of guided visualization, a cognitive therapy technique often used in relaxation and anxiety reduction (see chapter by Tan in this book, 2013, 2011, 1992; and chapter by McDonald and Johnston in this book, 2013). In Christian counseling throughout the 1990s and into the new century, there was controversy around whether to impose a guiding visualization by the therapist, or to let the client choose a preferred image, or to let the Holy Spirit bring it to the client as God saw fit. All these approaches were being done by Christian therapists all over the country, with fairly persuasive rationales being offered for each one (see Seamands, 1985; Payne, 1991; Flynn & Gregg, 1993; Smith, 2002/2005).

Developing a Transformative Spiritual/Clinical Process

Psychotherapy outcomes research during this time was revealing the great influence of both client factors and the therapeutic alliance between therapist and client (see Lambert, 1986). Believing also in the revelatory power of the Bible, I began to stitch together a client-centered counseling process that honored all three of these important variables for change. I started to encourage clients to choose their favorite Bible verses—Scripture that we would pray aloud together both to serve as an invitation for God's healing presence to appear, and to increase client investment in and responsibility for the therapy. Not only did God come alive in the scriptural text, but clients also nearly always had a favorite verse—something we believed by faith that God would bring to the client's mind in this therapeutic context (see Tan, 2007).

A transformative process model for Christian counseling—what is now full and robust (see chap. 22 on integrative model)—was developing in nascent form in my work with clients during this Northern

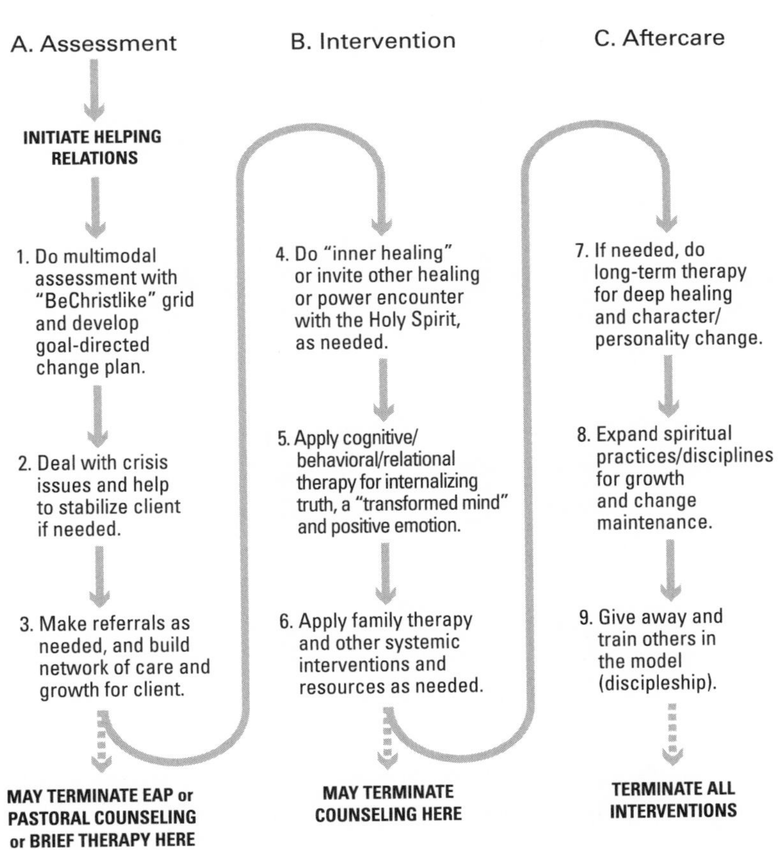
A Transformative Spiritual/Clinical Intervention Model
For Comprehensive Change, Growth and Discipleship
A. Assessment
B. Intervention
C. Aftercare
INITIATE HELPING RELATIONS
1. Do multimodal assessment with "BeChristlike" grid and develop goal-directed change plan.
2. Deal with crisis issues and help to stabilize client if needed.
3. Make referrals as needed, and build network of care and growth for client.
MAY TERMINATE EAP or PASTORAL COUNSELING or BRIEF THERAPY HERE
4. Do "inner healing" or invite other healing or power encounter with the Holy Spirit, as needed.
5. Apply cognitive/behavioral/relational therapy for internalizing truth, a "transformed mind" and positive emotion.
6. Apply family therapy and other systemic interventions and resources as needed.
MAY TERMINATE COUNSELING HERE
7. If needed, do long-term therapy for deep healing and character/personality change.
8. Expand spiritual practices/disciplines for growth and change maintenance.
9. Give away and train others in the model (discipleship).
TERMINATE ALL INTERVENTIONS

Figure 14.1. A model for transformative spiritual/clinical intervention

California sojourn.[1] Three stages of change and growth—assessment, intervention and aftercare—were acknowledged and followed. Three steps of distinctive practice were done or reviewed in each stage, for a total of nine possible steps from beginning to end. This integrative inner healing/cognitive behavioral/social systems counseling model is comprehensive, eclectic and holistic, and honors both the biblical text and the person-in-environment (P-I-E) structure that has been the root intervention in clinical social work for over thirty years now.

ASSESSMENT PHASE

After doing dozens of hybrid applications of "Scripture praying" in the late 1980s and early 1990s, I began working clinically with a middle-aged woman who had recently been divorced, and was referred to us after hospitalization for major depression and a fairly serious suicide attempt. She presented as being depressed in mood, lonely, despondent and full of anger. She often came to sessions in a prickly and surly mood, just daring me (and everyone else she encountered) to fulfill her worst expectation of criticism and rejection. Her negative self-talk was chronic and full of self-loathing—she hated herself as much as she hated her abusive family and ex-husband.

This was clearly a case where psychiatric intervention (which she was receiving) and cognitive behavioral therapy were needed to calm her chaotic emotions and challenge her toxic self-talk to replace it with the truths of Christ (see BeChristLike grid in chapter 12 for assessment, and change process in chapter 15 of Clinton and Ohlschlager, 2002). However, it quickly became clear that these therapies alone, though helpful, would not be enough. She was still struggling with suicidal thinking and was upset she had not died in her first attempt. She needed the transforming touch of her Maker, a healing touch by her heavenly Father and parent-lover from on high (I believe that "inner healing"—however God is invited to come alive—is largely a loving reparenting work of his broken children by God the Father, working through the Holy Spirit, enabled by the shed blood of Christ, who atoned for all of our sins).

[1] I want to thank the Rev. David Stenner, at that time the pastor of the Fortuna Episcopal Church in Fortuna, California, for his loving care of me and my family, and for spiritual mentoring in my life in the ways of Christ during my years in Northern California.

Transformative Spiritual Intervention

Choosing Christ as the caring shepherd. In the intervention phase—focusing initially on inner healing and reconciliation with God—I encouraged the client to choose a favorite Scripture, which we then prayed together as an invitation for God to show up and mightily perform his loving wonders. My client, though a confessing Christian, had not been in her Bible for a long time, and admitted to being very angry with God. While married, she had prayed fervently for God to change her husband and save her marriage—and in her judgment, he did not.

Most importantly, she wanted to return to God—she admitted her great need of him, as well as her great ambivalence about approaching him. At the core of her soul, she was convinced that God was extremely angry with her and loathed her as much as or more than she did herself. This was a terrible psychospiritual dilemma—a dilemma that she had consistently failed to resolve in her own strength. She clearly needed God's help to break the impasse, but was unable to get past her anger and hesitation toward God to do so.

Seeking consent, first and foremost. After about four or five sessions together, and after our working alliance had developed some trust and strength, I asked if there was any part of the Scriptures that she remembered enjoying. Without hesitation she stated, "Oh, yes, I've always loved the Twenty-Third Psalm."

"Ah, yes," I responded, "the Shepherd's Psalm."

"Yes, it's probably my favorite verse in the whole Bible . . . at least the favorite one I can remember." Her responsiveness emboldened me to stay on this path.

I then queried as gently and softly as I could, "What if we prayed that Psalm together, asking God to come alive in the verse and the imagery? Asking him—as it states in verse 3—to 'restore your soul' unto him?"

Her eyes flared in surprise, and her face squinted up in a big frown as she folded her arms across her chest and pulled herself away from me and back into the chair. She said nothing but her body language was clearly screaming, "No way!" It was the first event that seriously threatened to rupture our therapeutic alliance.

I continued smiling at her and said nothing, letting the request take hold as I prayed silently to God for an opening. And it came within moments (which is somewhat unusual, as the process of gaining client commitment and consent for this procedure can often unfold over one or two sessions).

Slowly she softened her posture and, after a couple minutes of increasingly uneasy silence in which she realized how serious I was in seeking this spiritual path, she asked, "And if I want to quit at any time . . . What if I say 'Stop!' will you do so?"

"Absolutely!" I retorted. Then, in a paradoxical move, I decided to assert to her my complete commitment to her safety by going the second mile of protecting her boundaries. "In fact, if I sense anything amiss, I'll ask you if everything is okay . . . and I may stop this myself whether or not *you* give me a clear signal."

She smiled at this, visibly relaxed in her chair, and verbally and in her body language consented to go forward with me in an exercise that proved to be life-changing for both of us. We then talked for a few minutes about basic ground rules and what to do depending on various contingencies like fear or the presence of distressing images. We discussed how to see and hear spiritually by tuning into our "mind's eye" and "inner ear"—training our inner, spiritual senses to become receptive to the voice and presence of God. At this point I made it clear to her that God is a living Person with a will of his own, that he is sovereign and cannot be directed or contained like some magical jack-in-the-box. We would not be doing "guided imagery" as such, but instead would invite and allow God to come alive in his way and time, according to the images contained in the Scripture.

Beginning prayer together. When she was ready, we both closed our eyes and she followed along as I began to pray out loud, yet intoning very softly the text of Psalm 23.

"The Lord is my shepherd, I shall not want . . . He makes me lie down in green pastures; He leads me beside still waters . . ."

"Yes, I see him!" she exclaimed as she broke into and interrupted the rhythm of the moment. "He's in a green field next to a quiet lake."

"What is he doing?" I asked, aware that my face was starting to flush, and I felt a change in the spiritual-emotional climate in the room. I could only conclude at that moment that the Holy Spirit was very present and ushering us both into heavenly places. I was getting excited and did not want to miss or be tardy when God came alive in my consulting room.

"He is smiling at me," she exclaimed in genuine surprise, "and he is holding out his hand to me, wanting me to come and take hold of him. Uh, oh . . . I can't believe this . . ." Her voice trailed off to a whisper. She then sobbed a huge, grieving, exhaling sob, and surrendered herself to holy ministrations that were no longer invisible to her. The moment was supernatural, affecting us both, and completely charged the room with a transforming electricity from on high.

"He restores my soul," I continued, barely whispering, "and leads me in the paths of righteousness for His name's sake."

"Oh, yes! Now he is very near to me . . . smiling at me . . . Wow! With eyes full of love for me . . ." She broke out again in huge sobs, and didn't stop. She was looking upward, as if staring into his face with a combination of fear and surprise and rapture.

"O Lord," she said, trembling in body and voice, and speaking toward the ceiling. "Are you sure you want to take hold of me? I'm so dirty . . . so unworthy . . . so angry . . ." She was sobbing in great, heaving exhalations of breath and sin.

Unmerited love poured out. I must admit that, by then, I was crying as well—but mine were tears of joy and amazement at what I was seeing take place right in front of me. The God of all comfort was coming alive, pouring out his love and changing the life of this broken woman who had surely known much more rejection and pain than love and joy in her life.

"O Lord . . . thank you, Thank You, THANK YOU!" she cried out. She was, by now, totally unaware of my presence, transported to a transformational place beyond these earthly bounds. Heaven had broken into my office, and I was so close, so delighted and honored to be participating in this. The living God had surely broken into our mundane world at that moment, and time and space seemed to take on highly elastic properties. Although I had experienced his presence before in counseling, this was of a different order, of knowing the presence and power of God deeply, carried along at a level of supernatural awareness that I had never known before in my counseling work.

Soon she was wailing in grief and surprise and joy, and mumbling things I couldn't quite understand. I continued to cry as well, overwhelmed by the rapture of the moment. The presence of God's Spirit in the room was so palpable, so unmistakable, penetrating to the depths of our souls.

"Shall I go on?" I finally asked, not quite sure what to do next and praying that God be in complete control.

"Yes, yes, please," she insisted. "There is so much more to do . . ." she trailed off, as if listening to another voice. This transformation—from frightened, faithless, angry and resistant to being open, receptive and hungry for more—was miraculous enough. What amazed me so was that a lifetime of rejection, abuse, lies and misbelief were melting away in the space of just one incredible session.

"Yea, though I walk through the valley of the shadow of death, I will fear no evil; For You are with me; Your rod and Your staff, they comfort me."

"Oh, Lord, that was you with me when I was dying on my bed, wasn't it? You were there with me even when I was killing myself!" She was completely incredulous. Her head was tilted upward and her tear-streaked face was contorted in a look of surprise and wonder. It was clear that she was stunned by the love of God being poured out onto her—love beyond measure instead of the condemnation and abandonment that she had so long predicted and expected. She was fully exposed to and embraced by the God of love, and for the first time in a very long time, she was humbled and receptive to it.

Heaven comes alive in the consulting room. Again, she was no longer talking to me, but conversing directly with God. And he was fully present with her, surrounding her completely with his healing and transforming love. As she told me later, God held her in an experiential embrace that was so loving and intimate. He held her in his arms and told her that he was there—that he never had left her in the past nor would he ever leave her in the future. He took her to a place of complete and utter brokenness—and was showering her with a love that gave no place for denial or resistance.

She broke out into huge sobs once again and believed in this deep transforming and healing love for the first time in her life. She later described the experience as one of "being born again again." She began to thank God for saving her life, for rescuing her from her suicidal delusion and for being present with her in life-changing love at that moment.

Love facilitating forgiveness. She cried out for forgiveness, so aware in his presence of how sinful she was. And instead of condemnation and judgment, she described how God blessed her with forgiveness and held her all the more tightly in his loving arms. She was being cleansed in the midst of her sin and brokenness, but instead of feeling hopeless and suicidal, she was feeling her God surrounding her with his love like never before. When our time was done, she was still caught up in this amazing encounter with God, so she spent the next hour in our quiet client room before she went home. I had a permanent grin that propelled me through the last session of the day. I drove home in wonder and amazement at how powerfully God had shown up, and at the impact he had had on both of our lives.

Lessons learned as a therapist and ethicist. God's appearance in this session was so powerful and unmistakable, tangible like never before or after this session. I have long concluded that the client was likely at great risk to attempt suicide again, and I believe that God became so powerfully alive because that suicidal risk was so powerful. Great risk seems to engender great responsiveness and a powerful presence of our ever-loving God.

In all this work, the sovereignty of God was so evident in the way he always appeared according to the need of the client at that moment, for even though I sought and hoped for God to show up again as he did then, it never again happened at that level of depth. God seems to consistently match his level of appearance to the need of the moment—it always happened in a way to meet client need at a special turning point in their lives. Clients who connected deeply with God, who received his loving-kindness so overwhelmingly, were often changed forever as the Holy Spirit came alive and rendered deep transformative change. Surprisingly, client needs seems to be more relevant than client faith, for God shows up even when they expect the worst from God or nothing at all.

As a clinical ethicist, I have heard that it was inappropriate for therapists to love their clients deeply, especially if that love was prone to be experienced erotically. God, however, made it clear to me that his agape love is the most powerful healing force in the universe—how could I refuse to transfer that love toward clients, especially when consent was given? Though secular powers would dismiss and delegitimize even that kind of love, if the client consents to it and the therapist is open to it, God then delights in delivering it to anyone in need. There truly is no legitimate law against that kind of healing love. Understanding and participating in this kind of love—the love of God for all those who would receive it—fundamentally altered the way I practiced psychotherapy from that day until I retired from full-time clinical and mediation practice in 1999.

Keys to Beginning the Process

Since the early "common factors" and meta-analytic research at the time was revealing client factors as one of the most significant influences in therapy outcomes (Lambert, 1986; Wampold, 2001), and since the level of client resistance often determined whether or not they were even slightly open to godly intervention, early on I decided to let clients determine the best route to connecting to God via client-chosen biblical imagery. I applied a three-phased step-down process that was linked to the degree of openness (or not) of the client to such intervention:

1. When clients were most open to God, we both yielded to the Holy Spirit, asking for and believing by faith that God the Holy Spirit would implant in us the needed imagery or word from the Scriptures that he wanted the client to know at that moment in his or her life. While some inner healing practices insisted on one particular way as the only truly Christian intervention, I found that the degree of client openness versus resistance by the client best determined whether or not this approach was doable.
2. When clients were cut-off from God but had some history with him and the Bible, I would ask them to scan their memories for a favorite verse or image of Jesus that they remembered fondly. I then would use that, as in the case above, as the organizing image or verse for reconnection with the God who was ready to do miraculous interior work.
3. When clients were cut-off from God and had no or a limited Christian history, but when they were open to godly intervention and gave consent for it, I would often suggest a simple metaphor that was strong on client safety and imagery from the Scriptures—such as Psalm 23; Jeremiah 29:11-14; Matthew 11:28-30; or Colossians 3:12-17.

Cognitive/Behavioral/Relational Therapy

After this life-changing session, my work with this client concentrated on forgiveness and mind change via cognitive behavioral therapy. She reported in a subsequent session—and counseling with her was so easy and fruitful from that session forward—that God had made possible by his transforming presence what was utterly impossible for her to do in her own strength. She realized then that the Christian life—that sanctification and maturity—was something that only God and not she herself could produce. This revelation was life changing as it freed her from the chronic failure that is built into a performance-based Christian life.

Throwing off a crushing load via forgiveness. Over the next several sessions God enabled her to forgive her ex-husband and her abusive family, and to set her free of the poisonous legacy that her history had forged upon her. God transported her Bible focus onto Matthew 11, guiding her into throwing off the crushing poison of anger and fear, and entering the rest that God promises to all those who come honestly unto him. She willingly "put on the yoke of Christ" and learned how light and freeing such yoke was—a yoke of truth-being-accepted-in-love. She admitted, without any prodding, how light and easy was the yoke of Christ compared to carrying the yoke of sin and death for so long.

Doing spiritual cognitive behavioral therapy. For the next three months of mostly weekly sessions, we worked in a Christian spiritual mode of cognitive behavioral therapy. She quickly learned how to identify and refute the lies she believed and to replace with God's truth the many lies she had come to believe in her years of darkness (see Thurman, 1991; Tan, 2011, and chapter in this book; Vernick, 2000, and chapter in this book). For example, connected to the work above, she renounced the lie that a godly yoke was heavy and restricting—lies that the enemy and the world had reinforced for a good portion of her life.

Truth, a transformed mind and new emotions. God also freed her of the automatic habituation to self-hatred and self-loathing that had dominated her thinking and emotional life. There were four lies embedded in her mind that were most tenacious and treacherous for her:

- "You are junk, and your life is not worth living or saving."
- "God is angry with you, and does not care whether you live or die."
- "Family and friends have abandoned you, and you are all alone."
- "There is no hope—you might as well die and be done with it."

The strength and toxicity of these lies were revealed in her suicide attempt—actions that nearly killed her. However, when taken out of the darkness and analyzed in the light of God's truth, it made sense to her why she was driven to the brink of death. The cognitive triad of depression—worthless, helpless and hopeless judgments that are applied to oneself and to God—also became evident as we noted these lies and discovered how often she ruminated and dwelt upon them. It quickly became clear to her how much of her thought and affective life was dominated by these lies and their many variants.

Successfully battling the enemy. We then recalled the story of Jesus in the wilderness, being tempted by the devil, and used that story as a powerful model for counteraction in her own life. For each lie, we developed a resounding scriptural truth that she would pronounce openly and against the lies of the enemy when they came upon her. She recounted Psalm 23 and our time with God in this session whenever the enemy lied about God and asserted that God had not truly "restored her soul" and did not love her with his great and life-changing love.

Moreover, when the enemy attempted to show how hopeless she was, she would shoot back with a personalized form of Romans 15:13—"Now may the *God of hope* fill me with all joy and peace in believing, *that I may abound in hope by the power of the Holy Spirit*" (NKJV). And when the enemy attempted to discourage her by reminding her how alone and lonely she was, she recalled how God had moved her to forgive her family and how reconciliation with some family members had already begun.

Mind you, it was not that she didn't have occasional trouble with those toxic thoughts after this life-changing session, but it was the session and its powerful fruit that she often called to mind—and often verbalized out loud—whenever she became aware that her old dead tapes were starting to play that poison all over again. She also learned to use the deadly thoughts of the enemy as a cue to stop what she was doing and remind herself of God's goodness and revival in her heart. These were powerful processes that strengthened in her what God had done and defeated the enemy whenever he attempted to ensnare her all over again (and the enemy often works overtime to reensnare a Christian who has been set free to live in God's abundant ways).

AFTERCARE PHASE

The aftercare phase concentrated not on long-term counseling, but on anchoring her in the two spiritual disciplines that are usually at the core of most discipline work with revived Christians—prayer and Bible study. All the other disciplines tend to rest upon these two legs for evangelical believers—anchoring and strengthening prayer and Bible study allows one to pursue and live maturely in any other discipline one might choose to learn and use in one's life.

In her case, she combined prayer and the Bible by relearning the valued role of *lectio divina,* or listening to God and praying the Scriptures as a pathway to Christian peace and maturity. She left the Catholic church when she became a Christian as a young adult, but decided to rejoin a charismatic Catholic church in our community after our work together. She also became deeply involved with a group using *lectio divina,* and with the Cursillo community in Humboldt County. Cursillo was a unique ecumenical and renewal community that held a nearly equal number of Protestants and Catholics, many of whom experienced Cursillo as a reawakened spiritual event in their lives.

Lectio divina is an ancient art of combining silence with contemplative prayer, practiced at one time by all Christians. As a person focuses and slowly prays the Scriptures, God enables his Word to become a means of union with him. This practice has been kept alive over the centuries in the Catholic monastic tradition and is one of the precious treasures of Benedictine monastics and oblates. Among the Benedictines, liturgy was tied to daily labor, and time was set aside for *lectio divina* to discover in daily life an underlying spiritual rhythm. Within this rhythm, contemplatives discover an increasing ability to offer more of themselves and their relationships to God the Father, and to accept the embrace that God is continuously extending to us through the person of Jesus Christ.

When we read the Scriptures we learn to be able to listen for the still, small voice of God (1 Kgs 19:12; Ps 46:10)—which is God's voice touching our hearts. This quiet listening, or "atunement" to the presence of God in the Scriptures, becomes the seed of an ever-strengthening relationship. In *lectio divina* we learn to heed the command to listen and turn to the Scriptures, knowing that we must "hear" the softly speaking voice of God. In order to hear God, to really know his presence experientially, we must learn to love silence and become adept at quieting the mind. The practice of *lectio divina*, then, requires that we first quiet down in order to hear God's word to us. Listening in silence is a reverential listening in a spirit of both humility and awe (see Dysinger, 1990).

Conclusion

There is nothing quite like surrendering to the living God and allowing him to use you to bring life and love to another. To become a participant, a cocreator of new life in the heart of a seeking person, is one of the great privileges of the

Christian life, of Christian counseling in particular. Tim Clinton and Pat Springle (2012) reveal the truth of the gospel in their new book, *Breakthrough:* "The human heart longs for attachment, and that's what God offers in the gospel of Christ. The message is simple: We are wonderfully made, tragically fallen, deeply loved, completely forgiven, and warmly accepted in Christ."

Therefore, professional Christian counselors should refute the lie that any spiritual practices—that inviting God in Christ to show up and bring miraculous change in psychotherapy—is illegitimate and to be avoided. Although some secularists would assert that any and all such spiritual practices are not proper for mental health professionals, this assertion fails to respect both the cardinal clinical doctrine of client self-determination and the religious liberties that are part of our constitutional rights as citizens of the United States (see appendix chapter by this author).

Competent adult clients and their therapist are free to invite God into and define legitimate spiritual goals in professional clinical relationships—and to do so without any interference by the state. Moreover, when the empirical foundations of Christian counseling are becoming so well established (Hook et al., 2010; Worthington et al., 2009), it is absurd to believe or argue that God has no right to participate in the process.

God is truly a love force to be reckoned with, and when needy clients are brought face-to-face with the God of the Bible, healing and change can and do happen in both mundane and miraculous ways. I am all for letting God be God, without the state interfering in any way in these holy relations.

References and Recommended Resources

Clinton, T. E., & Ohlschlager, G. (2002). *Competent Christian counseling: Foundations and practice of compassionate soul care.* Colorado Springs: WaterBrook.

Clinton, T. E., & Springle, P. (2012). *Breakthrough: When to give in, how to push back.* Brentwood, TN: Worthy Publishing.

Fr. Luke Dysinger, O.S.B., (1990). Accepting the embrace of God: The ancient art of LECTIO DIVINA. *Valyermo Benedictine, 1*(1).

Flynn, M., & Gregg, D. (1993). *Inner healing.* Downers Grove, IL: InterVarsity Press.

Hook, J. N., Worthington, E. L., Jr., Davis, D. E., Jennings, D. J., Jr., Gartur, A. L., and Hook, J. P. (2010). Empirically supported religious and spiritual therapies. *Journal of Clinical Psychology, 66*(1), 46-72.

Karls, J. M., & O'Keefe, M. (2008). *Person-in-environment system manual* (2nd ed.). Washington, DC: NASW Press.

Lambert, M. J. (1986). Implications of psychotherapy outcomes research for eclectic psychotherapy. In J. C. Norcross (Ed.), *Handbook of eclectic psychotherapy*. New York: Brunner/Mazel.

Lazarus, A. (1981). *The practice of multi-modal therapy.* New York: Springer.

Pargament, K., & Krumrei, E. (2009). Clinical assessment of client's spirituality. In J. Aten & M. Leach (Eds.), *Spirituality and the therapeutic process: A comprehensive resource from intake to termination.* Washington, DC: American Psychological Association.

Payne, L. (1991). *Restoring the Christian soul: Overcoming barriers to completion in Christ through healing prayer.* Grand Rapids: Baker Academic.

Seamands, D. A. (1985). *Healing of memories.* Wheaton, IL: Victor Books. (Republished as *Redeeming the Past.* Wheaton, IL: Victor Books, 2002).

Smith, E. (2002/2005). *Healing life's hurts through theophostic prayer.* Campbellsville, KY: New Creation.

Tan, S.-Y. (1992). The Holy Spirit and counseling ministries. *Christian Journal of Psychology and Counseling, 7*(3), 8-11.

Tan, S.-Y. (2007). The use of prayer and scripture in cognitive behavioral therapy. *Journal of Psychology and Christianity, 26*(2), 101-11.

Tan, S.-Y. (2011). *Counseling and psychotherapy: A Christian perspective.* Grand Rapids: Baker Academic.

Thurman, C. (1991). *The lies we believe.* Nashville: Thomas Nelson.

Vernick, L. (2000). *The truth principle: A life changing model for spiritual growth and renewal.* Colorado Springs: WaterBrook.

Wampold, B. E. (2001). *The great psychotherapy debate: Models, methods, and findings.* Mahwah, NJ: Erlbaum.

Worthington, E. L., Jr., Hook, J. N., Davis, D., & Ripley, J. S. (2009). Empirically supported Christian treatments for counseling. *Christian Counseling Today, 16*(3), 35-36.

Part Three

TRANSFORMATIVE INTERVENTIONS FOR CLINICAL PRACTICE

15

Christ-Centered Visualization and EMDR in Healing Trauma

Arlys Norcross McDonald
& Paula Johnston

Trauma is defined as "a startling experience that has a lasting effect on mental life; a shock." One may experience it or observe it. It overwhelms one's senses and ability to cope.

When psychotherapists talk about trauma, they are generally referring to events that would be upsetting to nearly everyone and that involve a reaction of fear, helplessness and/or terror. Determining trauma is relative. What is traumatic for one person is not necessarily traumatic for another. Traumatic events can overwhelm our ability to cope and can result in intense fear, extreme feelings of helplessness and a crushing loss of control.

Symptoms and Process

The symptoms of posttraumatic stress disorder—PTSD—span two classes of simultaneous and diametrically opposed behaviors. In one type, the traumatized person cannot get away from their trauma: they are forced to relive the original event through intrusive symptoms such as flashbacks, nightmares, panic attacks and obsessive thoughts. In the other, they can't get near it: they are compelled to insulate themselves from reminders of the trauma through avoidance symptoms such as social isolation, emotional numbing and substance abuse. Trauma victims also have physiological reactions, such as insomnia, hypervigilance and the tendency to be easily startled by any reminder of the event, such as a particular sound, smell or touch (Shapiro & Forrest, 2004, pp. 13-14).

Some survivors of trauma recover with no professional intervention. Some block out the trauma, either fully or partially, then "function," but fail to become all that God intended. Many develop PTSD, with the following behavioral symptoms: intense fear, horror, helplessness, flashbacks, disorganized or agitated behavior, numbing or denial of feelings, avoidance of stimuli associated with the trauma, nightmares, persistent increased arousal or anxiety, and so on (see DSM-V for a more complete description of PTSD).

The initial reaction to trauma is shock or denial, often followed by anger as the target of the cause of the trauma is sought. God is often blamed, or at least his love and goodness are questioned. Bargaining follows as an attempt to control the uncontrollable. When the bargaining does not change the reality, depression descends like a very dark oppressive blanket of shame, guilt and total helplessness, with a quiet desperation. Self-pity, suicidal thoughts, self-defeating behaviors and grief over what will never be would be typical at this stage. Finally, the goal of trauma therapy—acceptance—is pursued, along with the belief that healing and a good life are still possible.

Physiological Reactions to Trauma

Physical reactions to trauma occur in both our bodies and our brains. Neuropsychological responses occur that result in right-brain overstimulation and minimized left-brain functioning (Lansing, Amen, Hanks & Rudy, 2005; Francati, Vermetten & Bremner, 2007). Extended exposure to trauma creates multiple abnormalities in the brain. Trauma influences:

- The hippocampus, which is association with motivation and emotion.
- The amygdala, which moderates feelings, expressions, emotional memory and the recognition of emotion in others. Long-term trauma can result in heightened arousal, anxiety and hypervigilance as seen in PTSD.
- Movement, learning and executive functions (decision making, troubleshooting, managing new or difficult situations, and dealing with habits and temptations).
- The heart, lungs, sweat glands, kidneys, digestion and reproductive organs; a part of the brain that is also associated with decision making,

emotional response modulation, and rational cognitive and emotional function. Overstimulation due to trauma creates emotional numbing, denial, disorganization and inability to problem solve.

- Both cortisol and CRH (a corticotrophin releasing hormone) levels, which are heightened. Failure of these systems influences the immune system, increasing the risk for illness, inflammatory responses and even autoimmune diseases (Selye, 1976; Glaser et al., 1987).

Trauma, especially long-term trauma, powerfully impacts cognition, affect and behavior (not to mention our physical being).

EMDR Defined

Eye Movement Desensitization and Reprocessing (EMDR) is a successful method for treating trauma that rapidly and effectively releases anxiety, disturbing emotions and negative thoughts associated with trauma. "It is a complex and powerful method of psychotherapy that integrates many of the most successful elements of a wide range of therapeutic approaches. In addition, it uses eye movements or other forms of rhythmical stimulation, such as hand taps or tones, in a way that seems to assist the brain's information processing system to proceed at a rapid rate" (Shapiro & Forrest, 2004, pp. 4-5). Further, "EMDR includes elements of mindfulness, somatic awareness, exposure, and cognitive therapies" (R. Shapiro, 2010, pp. 93-94). Shapiro (2001) has also stated:

> One of the simplest ways of describing EMDR's effect is to say that the target event has remained unprocessed because the immediate bio-chemical responses to the trauma have left it isolated in neurobiological stasis. When the client does EMDR, active information processing is initiated to attend to the present stimulus. This processing mechanism is physiologically configured to take the information to an adaptive resolution. (p. 323)

EMDR was developed by Francine Shapiro in 1989, when she "noticed that the upsetting emotions accompanying disturbing thoughts disappeared as her eyes moved rapidly back and forth" (Shapiro & Forrest, 2004, p. 270). EMDR permits neural processing by low frequency stimulation of the brain, thus modifying memories in a safe environment (Rasolkhani-Kalhorn & Harper, 2006). After EMDR, brain scans found increased activity in both the anterior cingulated gyrus and the left prefrontal cortex in patients, which is responsible for discriminating between imagined and real fears (Levin, Lazrove & van der Kolk, 1999; Oh & Choi, 2007). Therefore, the objective evidence of brain scans shows the effectiveness of EMDR in reprocessing traumatic events effectively. Robin Shapiro (2010) has also said of EMDR:

> EMDR is a therapy for the entire spectrum of trauma. With well-attached, affect-tolerant clients, you can often completely clear one-event traumas in a few sessions. What does clearing mean? It means that clients can hold a traumatic event in mind while experiencing no symptoms of PTSD: no negative cognitions, no old, bad sensations, no flashbacks, and later, no bad dreams. Of course, the more pervasive the trauma . . . the more sessions you need. You can use EMDR to transform . . . relational traumas and attachment deficits that create so many personality, attachment, and secondary dissociation disorders. And tied with ego state therapies, you can use it to clear the catastrophic attachment and pervasive trauma of tertiary dissociation. (p. 93)

Christ-centered visualization. Visualization is a therapeutic technique used as a way of fostering healing and changing perceptions that are destructive distortions and lies. The process of visualizing a traumatic event, combined with EMDR, enables survivors to release fear and anxiety associated with the event. Spiritual truths that are visualized can bring healing and comfort that words alone cannot. For example: visualizing the Lord's presence as described in Hebrews 13:5-6 (Amplified) can eliminate overwhelming feelings of aloneness and abandonment: "For He (God) himself has said, I will not in any way fail you, nor give you up, nor leave you without support. I will not, I will not, I will not in any degree leave you helpless nor forsake nor let you down (relax my hold on you)! Assuredly not!"

Current research on the efficacy of visualization and EMDR. Current research and brain scans help us understand the power and value of visualization versus talk therapy or cognitive behavioral therapy. Visual pictures are processed by the right frontal lobe of the brain, which is where traumatic memories are stored. Visualization has been utilized by coaches for years, because it activates the same brain regions as if it were the actual situation (Lang, 1979; Murphy et al., 2008).

Two of the research psychiatrists who have focused on trauma and brain functioning, Drs. Bessel van der Kolk and Daniel Amen, have both demonstrated the efficacy of EMDR combined with visualization, documenting case studies of clients with PTSD who were treated with EMDR and displayed "marked normalization" of brain activity (Amen, 1998, p. 183). Van der Kolk also conducted neuroimaging after cognitive behavioral therapy without EMDR and demonstrated its failure to create significant brain activity changes (Van der Kolk, 2002).

Melding together God's love and his truth. We know of the necessity of God's love and the presence of the Holy Spirit when we have received God's forgiveness and salvation. We know that he is the truth that leads to healing and that he uses everything for our ultimate good. While we desire to leave the past behind, our bodies and brains prevent that. This method corrects that and allows the return of normal functioning and moving on to the present. Hope for the future is essential (Ps 42:11 LB; Jer 29:11). The biblical truths of forgiving a perpetrator and self are central tenets. Revenge must be left to the Lord (Rom 12:17-19).

When using EMDR and Christ-centered visualization, there are three important spiritual components for both the client and counselor: (1) pray for truth and wisdom; (2) listen for God's answers; and (3) follow the Lord's healing direction. No one hears God perfectly, so the Bible must be our ultimate standard of truth. Prayer must be a part of the continuing process. Truth will be revealed to the client as the treatment continues. Let them lead the way; they will set their own pace.

EMDR poses no spiritual challenges. On the contrary, EMDR can be used by trained therapists, through the power and direction of the Holy Spirit. Godly visualization is a powerful tool that can release anxiety from trauma. It gives peace about truth, and creates hope and direction in the client's own unique recovery process.

Treating Other Clinical Symptoms

EMDR can be used for a variety of other symptoms in addition to trauma and PTSD. Robin Shapiro includes

> distressing physical sensations, eating disorders, phantom and chronic pain (Wilson & Tinker, 2005), beliefs about the self (Knipe, 2005), anxiety disorders, and depression (Manfield, 1998) . . . familial and cultural introjects, traumatic couples issues, anxiety disorders, some forms of depression, obsessive-compulsive personality disorder, medical trauma, and multiple chemical sensitivities (R. Shapiro, 2005, 2009a, 2009b). . . . Children are the best subjects for EMDR. They process more quickly than adults. In the time

> an adult would be just getting started, a child will say "Done" and mean it. Some boys like it because they don't have to talk too much. . . . Boys often like the technology. (R. Shapiro, 2010, pp. 96-97)

EMDR is especially useful for clients who have limited resources: those with little time, money or social support.

Evaluating the Truth of Memories

EMDR using visualization may be the safest method of evaluating the truth of traumatic memories (McDonald, 1995). Clients retain full consciousness and control at all times, unlike drugs or hypnosis, creating less opportunity for suggestibility by leading questions from the therapist. Guided visualization can create false memories, especially for young children and suggestible clients (McDonald, 1995; Loftus, Doyle & Dysert, 2008; Bruck et al., 2010). It is important for counselors to encourage clients to sort out facts from fears and fantasies. Visualizations may be accurate, but they may also be partially false, based on the client's perceptions at the time, rather than the reality of the situation. Visualizations can also reveal fears or fantasies, similar to dreams, and thus are not strong enough evidence to convict the accused.

Possible Contraindications

Validating childhood memories that are partially or fully blocked from consciousness. Some have questioned if EMDR and visualization elicit accurate childhood memories. To date, there has not been sufficient research to validate the truth of memories. Because *perceptions* of trauma create the disturbance, information is only as accurate as the individual's discernment. Anxiety can originate from fears rather than from actual incidents. Therefore memories may be a combination of fears and events and are not to be taken as literal or accurate without validation. There has been no evidence that EMDR implants false memories. In fact, there is no therapeutic method that is less suggestive, since all of the initial information and the ongoing connections come from the client (McDonald, 1995).

EMDR therapists are also trained to focus on potential dangers of unexpected flashbacks or overload. It is a powerful tool that creates connections between current anxiety and childhood or adult trauma, and should be conducted only by trained therapists.

Robin Shapiro voices her concern about fragile EMDR clients, because this powerful technique often takes minutes to break through decades of emotional defense and dissociation. "If you want your most distressed clients to stay alive, intact, and in therapy, you will help them titrate the re-experiencing of affect and cognitions that went with years of horrible abuse. Don't try to do EMDR without formal training. It's so powerful you can hurt people with it, if you don't know what you're doing" (R. Shapiro, 2010, p. 98). Counselors must practice "closing down" the emotions of a trauma if the work is not complete by the end of the session. This is a critical process addressed in the EMDR training.

Clients who have a pending court testimony. Some have equated EMDR to hypnosis, as an altered state of consciousness, which would be inadmissible in court. However, EEG and brain scan research demonstrates normal brain waves during EMDR, and thus it is admissible in court (Shapiro & Forrest, 2004). However, it is often advisable to delay EMDR until court proceedings are completed, because the lack of anxiety and reaction to a trauma may decrease the believability of a testimony.

The Process of Applying EMDR and Visualization

Complete a thorough history and assessment. See the uniqueness of each person in these areas: their pretrauma personality/pathology; the age of onset and termination of trauma; developmental issues; frequency and severity of abuse; the personality of perpetrator; the relationship between perpetrator and survivor; the nontrauma history; and their personality and defenses. An important component of early therapy is creating an imaginary "safe place," which is a visual picture of a beautiful garden-like setting, which is for the Lord and the individual only. This is extremely important for comfort whenever the feelings become overwhelming. This is also helpful in assessing an individual's relationship with the Lord in terms of their feelings of trust, closeness, obedience and availability. It often reveals feelings that may contradict their theological knowledge. Visualizing the Lord's love and presence at all times is often the rudder that allows survival in the difficult and painful memories. (It's worth noting again here that EMDR requires extensive training and should not be tried by someone who has not been properly trained.)

Preplan the therapeutic interventions for this unique individual. Teach self-soothing and self-care. When trauma occurs, many individuals have difficulty eating, sleeping, exercising and functioning. Even when the trauma has occurred years prior, some remain in this overwhelmed state. A guided visualization of caring for a traumatized child often exposes the areas where self-care and self-soothing need to occur. Assessing the client's ego strength and previous method of surviving difficult situations will reveal the degree and kinds of support that have been successful.

Freezing or numbing is a common reaction to trauma. It seems to be God's method of enabling us to cope with the overwhelming nature of a trauma, until someone arrives to assist us. However, we are not meant to remain in that state. Dissociation occurs when the numbness or splitting from the feelings is not resolved.

Trauma survivors who have dissociated describe the trauma from a distance, as if they are watching it occur to someone else. This is especially common for children who do not reveal the trauma, but keep it a secret, often because of threats from the perpetrator. As a client visualizes their "safe place" with Jesus, they may be encouraged to prayerfully ask the Lord to reveal to them pictures of the split-off or dissociated parts, such as a hurting, angry, terrified or controlling child. They may also have split-off adult parts. Understanding these splits, their interrelationships and their relationship to the Lord provides a clearer road map to the extent and type of therapy required. "Safety, readiness, and dissociation assessment are mandatory. . . . The fastest way to find undiagnosed DID (dissociative identity disorder) is to do EMDR without screening" (R. Shapiro, 2010).

It is important to evaluate available methods for release of feelings (terror, anger, denial, guilt, shame, sadness, grief, helplessness, hopelessness, etc.). Understanding the client's comfort with various feelings often provides a direction for therapy. If a client is unable to access certain feelings, it may be helpful for them to picture themselves with that feeling in the safe place with the Lord.

Plan the method of providing safety during therapy. Develop a support system, with family or friends, who are informed about the possible needs during therapy. Visualizing and feeling the Lord's continual presence provides the core support whenever possible. If abuse has occurred from a father or father figure, this may be difficult or impossible. Introducing and experiencing both visualization and EMDR enable the client to give informed consent, as well as to have clear expectations.

Assess the advantages of hospitalization, day treatment and weekly sessions. Trauma therapy is often emotional "surgery," and minimal functioning may be the result during the intense portion of the therapy. Because of this, the McDonald Therapy Center has developed an intensive day-treatment program, which is often the easiest method for a client to deal with trauma. Hospitals rarely deal with trauma because of the current requirements by most insurance that only permits stabilization followed by out-patient therapy. Weekly therapy becomes overwhelmingly painful for many clients when the pain isn't resolved and they must remain in the pain until the next session. The day treatment has been the most successful and least traumatic for clients.

Decrease PTSD symptoms through EMDR and visualization. Trauma treatment without EMDR is like surgery without the anesthetic. All of the feelings associated with a trauma are reactivated during therapy but are quickly reduced through EMDR. Trauma processing includes "selecting the picture that represents the target, identifying the negative cognition, developing a positive cognition, rating the validity of cognition, naming the emotion, estimating the subjective units of disturbance, and identifying body sensations" (R. Shapiro, 2010, p. 95). This brings together the image, cognitions, emotions and body sensations.

The result is that 84 to 90% of the clients with trauma associated with rape, natural disasters, loss of a child, catastrophic illness or other trauma have recovered from PTSD in three sessions. Other psychological methods addressing trauma achieved a 55% success rate in seven to fifteen sessions (Shapiro & Forrest, 2004).

It is essential to isolate and work on only one trauma at a time, until anxiety is resolved. This may require EMDR for each separate aspect of the trauma. Visualize Jesus as the Comforter during the trauma, but do not attempt to change reality. Spiritual truths that are visualized often bring healing and comfort that words alone cannot. For example: visualizing the Lord's presence as described in Hebrews 13:5-6 (Amplified) can eliminate overwhelming feelings of aloneness and abandonment. As a client pictures the truth and reality of God's presence, these things replace the pictures of the trauma.

The goal is the release of feelings, without overwhelming the client. This involves visualizing Jesus with each of the feeling parts, and his acceptance and direction for healing. It is important to visualize Jesus cleansing the shame and guilt, which is so frequently a debilitating result of trauma, especially abuse in any form. Journaling of feelings, including writing a letter that will not be sent to the perpetrator, is usually helpful. Encourage appropriate expression of anger, moving from helplessness and victimization. Utilize EMDR and visualization for any anxiety regarding the expression of feelings, identifying the cause of the fear. This may be related to a previous trauma, when a client was abused or threatened for expressing a specific feeling, such as anger or sadness.

Allow the necessary time for the grieving and healing process, picturing the Lord as our Shepherd walking through the valley with us. Find the necessary steps for integration, visualizing each split and the healing the Lord intends for this part. Fill the emptiness left when trauma is removed. Christian media, as well as fellowship, are very helpful.

Identify the cognitive distortions, replacing them with biblical truth. This is a more extended process, as one pictures the Lord renewing the mind with specific Bible verses contradicting the lies that resulted from the trauma. Retell the trauma story, and the "meaning" it has in the present. Using EMDR and visualization, the client pictures the traumatic memory and is then able to completely endorse the positive belief: for example, "It's over," "I'm safe now," "I'm blameless," "I'm lovable."

Fear and anxiety resulting from trauma are often held in our body, either at the place where the trauma occurred, if it was physical, or wherever tension is held. A mental scanning of one's body searches for any area of discomfort or pain, continuing to use EMDR and visualizing the Lord's healing of that particular area.

Most clients need to resolve the question of "Where was God when this happened?" and their bitterness at his "failure to intervene or stop the trauma." This must be the client's resolution in line with their theology, not the counselor's. *The Shack* (Young, 2007) is an excellent narrative revealing the many spiritual concerns occurring after a trauma, and the visual pictures as the writer seeks resolution.

Arriving at forgiveness and "letting go" of the trauma is often a challenge. Many clients need to grasp that "forgiveness" does not necessarily include reconciliation. It does require giving up one's right to revenge, and giving that revenge to the Lord (Rom 12:19). Restoring the relationship with a perpetrator of abuse should only occur with repentance, time and safety.

Moving on to wholeness is the goal. Robin Shapiro (2010) describes the last two stages as closure and reevaluation: "Closure, includes homework to monitor changes, expectations, and, if needed, bringing the client to a state of emotional equilibrium. If the trauma isn't completely cleared, flashbacks of old or even newer material may pop up between sessions." Finally, there is the stage of "reevaluation, which includes checking in at the next session to see if the client requires new processing for the previous target or associated behavior. Because EMDR wakes up material that's associated with the original trauma, your client may come to the next session with a new, but related target" (R. Shapiro, 2010, pp. 95-96).

Risk openness and trusting again (of God, self, others and circumstances). It is time to ask the Lord to give new dreams. Visualize Jesus with play, laughter, new dreams and goals, and all the fruits of the Spirit today.

Case Study

Melissa's background history and presenting symptoms are as follows:

- Wife, mother of three children, part-time nurse;
- PTSD, reoccurring depression and anxiety;
- Childhood physical and sexual abuse; teen promiscuity;
- One auto accident, where her mother was killed and she was severely injured;
- Second auto accident, where she was helpless to save her own daughter's life;
- Previous extensive grief work; however, feelings of PTSD remained;
- Strong Christian beliefs, with a close relationship with the Lord;
- Questioning God's willingness to protect her and her children;
- Strong social support of two friends, readily available;
- Husband less available emotionally;
- Husband overwhelmed by her depression and his added responsibilities for family;
- Parents emotionally distant but available to care for their children while she was in intensive therapy;

- Motivated, strong ego strength, and desperation to heal and function in the present; and
- Minimal success in use of psychotropic drugs, anti-anxiety drugs used as needed.

In the initial stage of the intensive therapy, Melissa created her imaginary "safe place" with "Jesus" (her term for the Lord, which felt safest). She was troubled as she pictured him as distant and unavailable. As she connected this picture to the relationship with her mother, father and husband, she began to find Jesus more "approachable." As she prayerfully asked the Lord to reveal to her any splits that existed, she described several: a terrified five-year-old; a playful, happy four-year-old; and a very angry unknown child hiding in a cave. There were also adult splits: a competent professional nurse, a helpless frightened adult and a negative protective mom. Only the playful child could feel trust and run to Jesus.

Self-care was discussed, and Melissa committed to leave all family and work problems behind, using this time for self-care and recovery. She quickly adapted to the use of tactile probes for the EMDR, and agreed to the projected process as presented.

The trauma therapy began with her visualizing the Lord and asking him where to begin. The picture of her car accident in which her mother died first came to mind. As she focused on it, she was asked to rate the degree of anxiety on a 0 to 10 scale, and immediately said 10+, showing visible signs of terror. Her belief was that she was helpless and they all would die.

The EMDR and visualization of the accident, with Jesus there beside her, continued for several sessions, until the anxiety was gone and she could say, "I'm alive and I'm not helpless." Melissa remained at the McDonald Therapy Center all day long. In between the double sessions, she journaled, drew, listened to Christian music and sobbed intensely. She also exercised by walking at the beach. She repeatedly retold the story, with every detail, both in therapy and over the phone with her two friends.

She made excellent progress, except for the missing anger. She returned to her "safe place" and asked Jesus where the anger was hidden, despite her reluctance to do this. A picture of her at age four emerged, when she was very angry and was beaten by her father and told, "Throw another fit and I'll kill you!" That was the last time Melissa was ever angry. EMDR and Christ-centered visualization then focused on this trauma, again rated "10" with the belief, "If I get angry I'll die." After several sessions, the terror and anxiety were gone, and Melissa was able to believe that appropriate anger is helpful and necessary. With encouragement and modeling, she was able to use our "anger room," releasing the intense anger toward her dad, as well as toward the driver who hit and killed her mom. Later she pictured the adult Melissa holding this precious four-year-old, telling her she is lovable, that the adult will teach her to handle her anger, and that she will love her even when she is angry.

A similar process occurred with the incidents when Melissa was sexually abused as a child. Details of the sexual abuse were targeted with the EMDR. The expression of anger came relatively easily, but the shame and feelings of being "dirty" persisted. She especially struggled with the knowledge that parts of the abuse had been enjoyable on most of the occasions, and thus it felt like it was "her fault." Through EMDR and picturing Jesus cleanse the sexually abused little girl, she began picturing this child now dressed in white. She also needed to understand and process her promiscuity as a teen and young adult, receiving the Lord's forgiveness for her poor choices.

The final incident involved the car accident when Melissa lay trapped in her car, helplessly watching her daughter scream and shortly die from the injuries, and helplessly begging the Lord to save them. The added layers of guilt and helplessness and responsibility as the driver of the car made this the most challenging and lengthy incident for Melissa to process. The most difficult cognitions to change were, "It's all my fault" and "God didn't care."

For the first time she admitted she was on the phone talking, thus somewhat preoccupied, and believed she may have been able to prevent the accident otherwise. She acknowledged the change that had occurred with her marriage following this accident, and vowing to never tell her husband. The terror of his discovering this truth was an additional feared trauma, a target for EMDR and visualization. Through days of prayerful search for direction, she eventually told her husband over the phone, at a time when he was meeting with their pastor, who already knew the information and agreed to help him process this. Melissa sought forgiveness from the Lord, picturing his love and forgiveness. With great difficulty, she finally chose to forgive herself.

Integration of the child parts occurred quite easily, after the treatment of the trauma and the Lord's healing and cleansing. They could then become part of the adult, after reassurances that the playfulness and the ability to be angry when necessary would not be lost. The integration of the adult parts became more complicated, with numerous issues arising, but was eventually complete.

It is now two years later. Melissa continued in weekly therapy in her home state for several months, reporting that the anxiety did not return. She chose to share the information about the physical and sexual abuse with her parents and reports that it was a neutral experience, as they listened but did not give much response. She and her husband sought marriage counseling, both reporting dramatic changes. Melissa is no longer depressed, nor is she suffering any of the symptoms of PTSD. They are beginning to dream and plan for new projects. Life is good—God is so very good—and hope has returned.

REFERENCES AND RECOMMENDED RESOURCES

Amen, D. (1998). *Change your brain, change your life.* New York: Time Books.

American Psychiatric Association. (2000). *Diagnostic and statistical manual of mental disorders* (4th ed., text revision). Washington, DC: Author.

Arbuthnott, K. D., Arbuthnott, D. W., & Rossiter, L. (2001). Guided imagery and memory: Implications for psychotherapists. *Journal of Counseling Psychology, 48*(2), 123-32.

Bremner, J. (1999). Does stress damage the brain? *Biological Psychiatry, 45*(7), 797-805.

Bruck, M., Ceci, S., Kulkofsky, S., Klemfuss, Z., & Sweeney, C. (2010). Children's testimony. In M. Rutter, D. Bishop, D. Pine, S. Scott, J. Stevenson, E. Taylor & A. Thapar (Eds.), *Rutter's child and adolescent psychiatry* (5th ed., pp. 81-94). Malden, MA: Blackwell.

Francati, V. V., Vermetten, E. E., & Bremner, J. D. (2007). Functional neuroimaging studies in posttraumatic stress disorder: Review of current methods and findings. *Depression & Anxiety, 24*(3), 202-18.

Gilbertson, M. W., Shenton, M. E., Ciszewski, A., Kasai, K., Lasko, N. B., Orr, S. P., & Pitman, R. K. (2002). Smaller hippocampal volume predicts pathologic vulnerability to psychological trauma. *Nature Neuroscience, 5*(11), 1242.

Glaser, R., Rice, J., Sheridan, J., Fertel, R., Stout, J., Speicher, C., Pinsky, D., Kotur, M., Post, A., and Beck, M. (1987). Stress-related immune suppression: Health implications. *Brain, Behavior, and Immunity, 1,* 7-20.

Lang, P. J. (1979). A bio-informational theory of emotional imagery. *Psychophysiology, 16,* 495-512.

Lansing, K., Amen, D. G., Hanks, C., & Rudy, L. (2005). High-resolution brain SPECT imaging and eye movement desensitization and reprocessing in police officers with PTSD. *The Journal of Neuropsychiatry and Clinical Neurosciences, 17*(4), 526-32.

Levin, P., Lazrove, S., & van der Kolk, B. (1999). What psychological testing and neuroimaging tell us about the treatment of posttraumatic stress disorder by Eye Movement Desensitization and Reprocessing. *Journal of Anxiety Disorders, 13*(1-2), 159-72.

Loftus, E., Doyle, J. M., & Dysert, J. (2008). *Eyewitness testimony: Civil & criminal* (4th ed.). Charlottesville, VA: Law Publishing.

McDonald, A. N. (1995). *Repressed memories: Can you trust them?* Grand Rapids: Revell.

Murphy, S., Nordin, S. M., & Cumming, J. (2008). Imagery in sport, exercise and dance. In T. Horn (Ed.), *Advances in sport and exercise psychology* (3rd ed., pp. 297-324). Champagne, IL: Human Kinetics.

O'Craven, K. M., & Kanwisher, N. N. (2000). Mental imagery of faces and placed activates corresponding stimulus-specific brain regions. *Journal of Cognitive Neuroscience, 12*(6), 1023.

Oh, D., & Choi, J. (2007). Changes in the regional cerebral perfusion after eye movement desensitization and reprocessing: A SPECT study of two cases. *Journal of EMDR Practice and Research, 1*(1), 24-30.

Rasolkhani-Kalhorn, T., & Harper, M. L. (2006). EMDR and low frequency stimulation of the brain. *Traumatology, 12*(1), 9-24.

Selye, H. (1976). *The stress of life*. New York: McGraw-Hill.

Shapiro, F. (2001). *Eye movement desensitization and reprocessing: Basic principles, protocols and procedures* (2nd ed.). New York: Guilford.

Shapiro, F., & Forrest, M. S. (2004). *EMDR: The breakthrough therapy for overcoming anxiety, stress, and trauma*. New York: Basic Books.

Shapiro, R. (2010). *The trauma treatment handbook*. New York: Norton & Company.

Van der Kolk, B. A. (2002). Posttraumatic therapy in the age of neuroscience. *Psychoanalytic Dialogues, 12*(3), 381.

Yehuda, R. (2001). Are glucocorticoids responsible for putative hippocampal damage in PTSD? How and when to decide. *Hippocampus, 11*, 85-90.

Young, W. P. (2007). *The shack*. Newbury Park, CA: Windblown Media.

16

The TRUTH Principle

Christian Cognitive Behavioral Therapy for Depression and Anxiety

Leslie Vernick

Murray and Lopez (1996) predict that by the year 2020, depression will be the second largest cause of disability for men and women of all ages. Christians are not immune to the stresses of life and the effects on one's mind, body and spirit. Depression and anxiety are often the result.

Individuals who present with these distressing symptoms hope to feel better. Yet Johnson and Johnson (1997) remind us as Christian caregivers that we have a greater purpose than simply symptom reduction. They write, "Christian counselors typically have counseling goals that are fundamentally distinct. Beyond mere alleviation of discomfort—often the sole focus of their secular counterparts—Christian counselors recognize their work as redemptive and restorative in character" (p. 52).

Knowing God More Deeply

Our role in coming alongside those who are suffering is to cast a vision for who God is and what he might be up to during this season of suffering. We want to help them find the Lord to be an ever-present help in times of trouble, and to learn to trust him, experience his wisdom in relationships and learn how to practice these biblical principles daily. We don't just want to tell them what's true, good and right, we want them to encounter the living God and learn how to live it (Vernick & Thurman, 2002).

The TRUTH Principle Applied

The TRUTH Principle (Vernick, 2003) is a Christ-centered counseling model that gives the Christian counselor a specific template to biblically assess a person and his present situation, as well as develop a clinically sound and scripturally solid road map for treatment and deeper discipleship; a journey where informational truth becomes transformational truth.

The TRUTH Principle uses a simple acronym—T-R-U-T-H—to define a five-step process that helps both counselor and counselee understand self, and self in relation to God, to others and to the world. It reveals current coping strategies that are utilized to handle life's problems as well as what changes are needed to heal and mature. The focus of each step of the TRUTH Principle is not primarily personal healing but greater love for God, awareness of self and Christlikeness (Rom 8:29). Yet in the process of seeing Christ and seeing self in a clearer way, healing is often the indirect outcome.

Briefly, the goal of each step is to help an individual:

T—Gain a new perspective on the **troubles** God allows in his/her life;

R—Come to better understand his/her **response** to those trials;

U—Discover the **underlying** idols, beliefs and/or lies that keep him/her stuck or hamper efforts to change;

T—Learn how to discern the **truth** of God's Word; and

H—Begin to develop a **heart's response** that will draw him/her closer to God in love and obedience.

These five steps are not linear in application but overlap, are cyclical and are holistic. Keep that in mind as I present a case vignette with each step of the model applied.

Donna is a fifty-five-year-old woman who came to counseling diagnosed with recurring major depression by her physician and is taking antidepressant medication. She reports a long history of depression and anxiety, "As far back as I can remember," with only short intervals of relief. She is married and has three adult daughters and one son, who is still in high school.

Donna describes her thirty-year marriage as unfulfilling. She reports feeling bored and disconnected from her husband. Her childhood was lonely. Her father left the family when she was eight, and her mother remarried several times. Donna remembers growing up feeling sad, alone and afraid.

Donna and her husband became Christians early in their marriage and as a result of their new faith, she thought things would change. She believed she would finally feel loved both by God and by her spouse. She hoped for peace and a joy that would transform her life. Yet as the years have gone by, nothing has changed in her marriage and the reality of her faith dims. She says, "I know what God says in my head, but I don't feel it in my heart."

Donna has been in counseling off and on for years with various pastors and Christian counselors. She and her husband tried marriage counseling but nothing has significantly changed. She reports suicidal thoughts from time to time but says she would never hurt herself. Donna is tired, hopeless and isn't sure counseling is going to make any difference. She says, "I don't know what else to do. I'm really tired of feeling this way."

The TRUTH Principle in Process

T: Trouble. In the initial session, the counselor's goal is to understand what the client sees as his or her presenting *trouble*. Because everyone comes to counseling having a need, it is important that we listen. In fact, the Scriptures call us to listen hard before answering someone's problem (Prov 18:13). Listening is important for several reasons. It helps the counselor see how the client articulates her life story as well as how she sees herself, God and others in her particular situation. It also helps us build rapport. The crucial ingredient for therapeutic success is a caring relationship (Sexton & Whiston, 1994). Listening and validating are essential for someone to feel heard and valued (Cormier & Cormier, 1997). The client will not be ready to hear until she feels fully heard.

As Donna did, most clients enter therapy primarily looking for relief from their trouble. They want you to fix them, something that may not be either possible or wise. Our job, however, is not only to be used by God to help people solve life's difficulties (which are valid treatment goals), but also to help them to see those difficulties as opportunities to be in God's classroom of holiness, wisdom and maturity. Suffering can be one of the teaching methods that God uses. Suffering can make us a better, stronger person (Rom 5:3-4). It is often our client's poor responses to suffering that causes them to experience greater emotional and relational pain (Vernick, 2009).

Helping Donna to see her struggles differently may involve questions such as: Can she begin to gain a vision for something greater than relief?

(Jas 1:2-4). Can she begin to grasp God's larger purposes in the midst of her suffering? How is God using these troubles to mature her? How is God wanting to help her develop greater trust, patience, perseverance, love, courage or forgiveness?

The following is an illustration of a condensed dialogue I had with Donna during several of our initial sessions implementing the first step of the model. I will add my own personal thoughts as to why I asked a certain question or did something therapeutically in italicized parenthesis so the reader can see why a therapist makes certain choices.

Therapist: It's so good to meet you. Tell me a little bit about yourself and why you've come.

Donna: I don't really know why I'm here. I've been to many counselors and nothing has changed. I'm not happy in my marriage. I've tried talking with my husband and I just don't think he gets it. He's a good guy, works hard, he's a good father, but emotionally he's just not there.

Therapist: That must be very lonely for you. Has it always felt this way or were there times where you felt more connected? (*Diagnostically I'm looking for exceptions to her experience.*)

Donna: It's always been this way. I feel bad complaining. I'm just never satisfied. What's wrong with me? I thought when we became Christians things would really be different. I've tried so hard to be the kind of wife I should be and do the right things. Don't get me wrong. I'm thankful God is in my life. If it weren't for him I'd probably leave my husband and have an affair or something. (*Diagnostically, I'm listening to her internal dialogue about the way she sees herself, life, God—things that will be explained more in the* R *step of the model.*)

Therapist: What would you like to get out of coming to see me? (*Diagnostically, I want to know if there is something specific she wants to work on—can we set some treatment goals?*)

Donna: I have no idea. My doctor thought I should come. (*Diagnostically, I'm observing a woman who is tired, perhaps a bit passive, giving up on hope, and needs me to give her a bigger picture.*)

Therapist: If counseling worked this time, what would be different in you? (*Diagnostically, I'm seeing if she is able to define what she wants. Therapeutically, I'm trying to gain treatment alliance and an agenda to work on.*)

Donna: I'd feel better. I'd know how to live in this marriage without feeling like I want to leave. I'd be able to trust God more.

Therapist: Those sound like great goals. For today, I'd like to leave you with one thought to ponder during the week. (*Therapeutically, I'm going to start with her goal to trust God more.*) Do you know the story of Hagar in Genesis? She too felt like an unloved woman. She was used by Sarai and Abram to birth a child for them because of Sarai's infertility problems. Of course that didn't solve the problem and Sarai ended up treating her very harshly. Hagar was so upset, she took the child and ran away and got lost in the desert. She felt scared and all alone, but it was in that place that God showed up and spoke something very special to her. [We go through the passages together.]

I'd like you to reread the story in Genesis 16 this week, and I'd like you to ponder Hagar's words, "You are the God who sees me" from Genesis 16:14.

If you could believe that God is the God who sees you right now in your desert, in your loveless marriage, in your loneliness and pain, how might you feel differently?

Donna: [With tears welling in her eyes] I'd think I'd have some hope and maybe feel loved and valued. (*Donna needs an emotional connection with God; she doesn't need more information about him.*)

R: Response. The next step of the TRUTH Principle is to look at our client's *response* to her troubles: her thoughts, feelings and reactions to life's stressors. What is the client's coping style? We also listen for statements that reveal the client's automatic thoughts. Freeman, Pretzer, Fleming and Simon (1991) state, "One of the major premises of the cognitive view of human functioning is that automatic thoughts shape both individual emotions and their actions in response to events." The psalmist concurs when he reflects, "My thoughts trouble me and I am distraught" (Ps 55:2). A. W. Tozer writes, "Thinking stirs feeling and feeling triggers action. That is the way we are made and we may as well accept it" (as cited in Wiersbe, 1978).

Thus far we've listened carefully and compassionately to Donna and reminded her of God's faithfulness even in her suffering. Meanwhile, during the *R* step of the model we are listening for what Donna says about herself and others. During Donna's first session I noted that she said, "I'm just never satisfied" and "What's wrong with me?" Persistently negative mindsets are linked to anxiety and depression, situations that cloud one's own thinking and their perception of others' positive thoughts.

While feelings are important, her responses to trouble and how she manages her feelings and thoughts are also important. For example:

Therapist: Donna, how did your job interview go this week?

Donna: Terrible. I'm sure I didn't get the job. It was over in thirty minutes, and it's been four days and I still haven't heard a word from them. I know they didn't like me. Why can't things ever go my way for a change? After I read that passage about Hagar, I thought God was there with me. I felt hopeful that I would get this job. I don't understand. I feel so discouraged.

Therapist: Donna, I hear you feel pretty discouraged over your interview, but may I show you a tool that would help you understand where your discouraged feelings are coming from?

Donna: Okay.

Therapist: You believe that your angry and discouraged feelings are a result of your short interview and the fact that they haven't called you back, but in reality they are coming from the *thoughts* you are having about your interview. Let's chart it out to look at what's happening more carefully.

Table 16.1.

Trouble/Situation	Automatic Thoughts	Feelings
Short job interview.	I know they didn't like me.	Worthless
They haven't called yet.	Things never go my way.	Discouraged
	Why can't I ever get a break?	Alone, abandoned
	God's not helping me.	Angry, scared

Therapist: Can you see that your thoughts about the situation are triggering your negative emotions?

Donna: But the interview *is* what triggered those thoughts.

Therapist: You're right. But here is the part I want you to really pay attention to. God understands the connection between what we think and how we feel. That's one reason why the Bible repeatedly warns us to pay attention to our thought life.

For example, let's read, Deuteronomy 9:4. It says, "After the LORD your God has driven them out before you, do not say to yourself, 'The LORD has brought me here to take possession of this land because of my righteousness.' No, it is on account of the wickedness of these nations that the LORD is going to drive them out before you." If we chart this verse to show the thought-feeling connection, we can see why God told the Israelites how to think rather than what not to feel.

Table 16.2.

Trouble/Situation	Automatic Thoughts	Feelings
Israel was to possess the land.	God did this because of my righteousness.	Proud

God knew that what we think about shapes how we feel. Instead of warning the Israelites not to feel proud, he told them how to perceive or think about the situation. When they thought truthfully, the appropriate feelings would be the result.

Table 16.3.

Trouble/Situation	Automatic Thoughts	Feelings
Israel was to possess the land.	God did this because of the wickedness of other nations.	Humble Grateful

So Donna, do you see that if you're not thinking truthfully, you will still feel the emotions that go with your thoughts?

Donna: You mean like if I'm watching a scary movie on television, I will still feel scared even though I know it's not real?

Therapist: Exactly. Our emotions match what our mind meditates on, true or not.

Donna: But the truth is, I didn't get the job.

Therapist: You're right you haven't gotten the job yet, or perhaps you won't get it at all. But let's look at what you're telling yourself about the interview. You're telling yourself you know they didn't like you. How do you know that? You're also telling yourself that God wasn't helping you. How do you know that?

Donna: I don't know for sure, but it's how I feel.

Therapist: Yes, but you're feeling that way because that's how you're thinking. But what if the things you're thinking aren't true? Since you don't know if they are true, is there another way of looking at the interview?

Donna: I don't know. Perhaps they haven't made a decision yet. Or maybe there was another candidate more qualified for the position or had more experience. Or someone's relative needed a job and so the boss felt obligated to give it to him.

Therapist: Excellent. See, Donna, you came up with several different ways to look at this situation other than that they didn't like you. If you thought about it in a different way, how do you imagine you would feel?

Donna: I guess I wouldn't have taken it so personally and felt so horrible, but I still wouldn't have been happy.

A trouble/thought/feeling journal can enhance client awareness. Can the client recognize automatic thoughts and their impact on emotions? Does the client recognize that negativity doesn't arise out of trouble, but out of thoughts about the situation/trouble? Sometimes emotions lie (Is 49:15; Lam 3:1-25). If there is no evidence that a thought is true, then, as I did with Donna, encourage the client to look for alternative ways of seeing the situation.

There will be times where the client is thinking truthfully or can't come up with an alternative way of thinking that makes sense to them.

Therapist: Donna, what if it's true, that they didn't like you? What does that mean?

Donna: That means I'm a loser. I'll never get out of this hole I'm in. My marriage stinks, I can't get a job. Nothing good will ever come my way. [Looking very depressed.]

Therapist: Let me chart out what you just said.

Table 16.4.

Trouble/Situation	Automatic Thoughts	Feelings
They don't like me.	I'm a loser.	Worthless
	I'll never get out of this hole I'm in.	Hurt, sad, depressed
	My marriage stinks.	Hopeless, helpless
	I can't get a job.	
	Nothing good will ever come my way.	

Therapist: So what you're telling yourself is that your entire sense of worth and future well-being rests on the evaluation of three people who interviewed you. Am I hearing you right? (*Therapeutically, I'm directly* *challenging the truthfulness of her thoughts as well as her person-centered idolatry. This moment is a crossroads in the therapeutic hour where we as therapist have to choose which road to go down. I could continue to press Donna more on her internal lie that she's a loser as well as point out the power she gives people to define who she is, or I could give her some new evidence that her thoughts are not true. Both paths are valid, and the therapist's knowledge of a client and the amount of time you've been working together would influence which path you take.)*

[As she let this sink in . . .] Let's turn to Mark 3. Here three different groups of people defined who Jesus was. His family said, "He's crazy." The religious leaders said, "He's demon possessed," and the crowd said, "He's a miracle worker." Which was the truth?

Donna: Neither. But how did Jesus not get upset by what people said about him?

Therapist: Good question. Jesus centered himself on God's definition of him, not on other people's definition. Who does God say you are?

Donna: I know what he says, I guess I don't believe him.

Therapist: And what's the result of believing the words of others over the words of God?

Donna: [Beginning to cry] I feel unloved, ugly, hopeless like always.

Therapist: Let's turn to Psalm 107:20. Read it.

Donna: "He sent out his word and healed them."

Therapist: I want you to write out what God says to you and about you this week. [I give her several passages such as Psalm 139 and/or Ephesians 1.] Donna, I want you to talk with him about what he tells you and why you don't believe his words. Be honest. Wrestle with God here. Your healing depends on it.

Therapeutically, it is important that we not simply take a client step by step through the process of identifying and refuting lies, but provide a context in which she can connect with God and come to trust his words over her own internal lies.

In this second step of the TRUTH Principle, we can create momentum toward healthier responses to life's troubles by assigning homework that implements a more godly and healthy response. "A well-designed behavioral experiment can be very effective, particularly when the client accepts the therapist's point of view intellectually but is not yet convinced 'on a gut level'" (Freeman et al., 1991, p. 77).

For example, a depressed person may lie in bed all day or sit staring out a window ruminating about all of her life troubles. Focusing on her thoughts or feelings may only intensify them. A more strategic approach may be to assign slight behavior changes like short daily walks or doing simple household chores that can result in a temporary mood shift (Tan, 2007). As she notices that doing something productive has some impact on her mood, her thoughts may become more positive as well.

U: Underlying idols and Unresolved relational wounds. The third step of the TRUTH Principle is where the counseling moves to a deeper level. Sometimes clients get stuck because, as they say, "I know that in my head, but I don't feel it in my heart." One can think true thoughts yet still unknowingly believe lies. Donna often tells me, "I know I'm not worthless, but that's how I feel."

In this step of the model we press to expose more of the *underlying* heart themes and false root beliefs that are the core of their idolatry. The Bible tells us that it's not only what we think that's important, but also our heart's desire that rules us; our functional gods or idols. Many people say they love God the most, yet evidence shows lesser loves rule our lives (2 Kings 17:40-41). We say God is enough but feel we need God plus more. Recognition of these usually hidden idolatries can result in a reorientation toward Christ and deeper healing.

Another factor influencing depression is *unresolved* relationship wounds. "Listening to depressed people over a number of years and their own explanations as to why they thought they were depressed, I've often discovered that beneath a person's depression was a past relationship wound that was affecting present functioning and/or a present relationship difficulty that was denied, unresolved, or not being addressed in a godly way" (Vernick, 2005, p. 9).

O'Connor (1997) writes, "Depression is both caused by and a cause of poorly functioning relationships" (p. 157). Men and women who are divorced or separated suffer the highest rates of depression. The condition of the marital relationship can predict depression rates, especially among women. The absence of an intimate, confiding relationship and the presence of marital conflict are related to depression in women. In fact, rates of depression were found to be the highest among unhappily married women. Many times women in abusive relationships are clinically depressed (Diseases and Disorders, n.d.).

The National Institute of Mental Health (NIMH) indicates that the highest rates for depression for both men and women are among those who are separated and divorced. The condition of a marital relationship is a significant factor in predicting depression, especially in women. The NIMH reports, "Lack of an intimate, confiding relationship, as well as overt marital disputes, has been shown to be related to depression in women" (National Institute of Health, 2007). In fact, rates of depression were shown to be highest among unhappily married women. Many times women in abusive marriages are clinically depressed.

The Bible affirms the importance of fellowship and relationship (Rom 12:10). The two greatest commandments God gives us have to do with loving connection (Mk 12:29-31). We are to love him first and to love others deeply from the heart (1 Thess 4:9, 10; 1 Pet 1:22). Desiring good relationships is a healthy thing. However, seeking something in a relationship that only God can give is not.

Donna: I'm so frustrated and hurt. Every time I try to engage my husband in a decent conversation he just wants to watch television. I'm so tired of begging him for attention. I don't know how I can live like this.

Therapist: Donna, I know this has been extremely trying for you. You long to have a better marriage, and what you want is a good thing. But you are at a crossroads here. You're going to have to decide what you want the most right now.

Donna: I don't understand. What do you mean?

Therapist: It's obvious that you're not going to get what you want from your husband. Maybe you never will. What does that mean for you?

Donna: That means I'm going to be unhappy the rest of my life. I can't get divorced. He's not going to change. What hope do I have?

Therapist: So your hope is in having your husband love you the way you want to be loved. Is that what you want the most?

Donna: Sure would feel good for a change.

Therapist: Temporarily, but a human love can never fill us up and make us happy. If your entire well-being rests on that, what happens when he fails, or can't, or doesn't want to love you like you desire? Then what?

Donna: Then I guess I'm right back where I started. Depressed, anxious, lonely and angry.

Part of the goal in this step of the TRUTH Principle is to help make the unknown known. Jesus says, "If your eye is clear, your whole body will be full of light" (Mt 6:22-23 NASB). Since the heart is automatically self-deceived, this process helps the client become more aware of her false loves, her other gods, the things that rule her. Tillich (1951) said, "Whatever concerns a man ultimately becomes god for him."

In the sanctification process, God seeks to transform a person's heart from a natural heart to a spiritual heart; to return us to our first love (Mk 12:30). People's legitimate desires typically cluster around the three themes of (1) security and comfort; (2) approval, admiration and affection; and (3) power and control. Ultimately how we act and live flows out of our hearts. Counseling is not just about restraint, but helping our clients develop a love for the right things like greater compassion toward others and love for God.

T: Truth. In this fourth step, *truth*, our therapeutic relationship must be solid enough to actively challenge our client's belief system about who God is and what he says is true, wise and good. Peck (1978) writes, "One of the roots of mental illness is invariably an interlocking system of lies we have been told and lies we have told ourselves" (p. 58). The apostle Paul confirms this when he says, "They exchanged the truth about God for a lie, and worshiped and served created things rather than the Creator" (Rom 1:25).

Secular psychology can lead only to despair and more confusion as there are hundreds of approaches, each with their own truth (Gilligan, 2001). In this model we share the truth of the gospel, showing our counselee how to know and experience the One who is true. Jesus doesn't just tell us the truth, he is the truth (Jn 8:32).

There is scientific evidence that mindfulness and meditation are helpful aids for individuals suffering with clinical depression and anxiety (Williams, Teasdale, Segal & Kabat-Zinn, 2007). To be attentive and aware of the present moment or, as Jesus asked his disciples to do, to be "watchful" (Mt 26:41) when they were getting drowsy, spiritually trains the eyes of our hearts not only to see the deeper things of God but to become more aware of him in our daily life; to have eyes to see and ears to hear. These are metaphors describing a spiritual attentiveness to the presence of God. Initial studies on forms of Christian meditation have yielded positive results (Carlson, Bacaseta & Simanton, 1988; Ferguson, Willemsen & Castañeto, 2010).

I assigned Donna Psalm 23:1 with instructions on how to be still and listen, as well as reflect on what God was saying to her. I chose this particular passage because of Donna's idolatry and her deeply held belief that God has denied something good from her—a satisfying marriage. If she is going to repent of her idolatry, she must begin by believing the truth and trusting God that he is her shepherd and knows best what she needs.

H: Heart's response. The last step of the model requires the movement of truth from head to heart. What is the client's heart's response to God and the truth of his Word, to her awareness of her idolatry, to becoming aware of her internal lies, false beliefs, immature responses and negative emotions? Typically we encounter three different types of responses.

1. The first is unbelief and/or rebellion. I will not believe God and I continue to choose my own way over God's way.
2. The second kind of response gets confused with biblical repentance because there is weeping and heartfelt sorrow, but it does not lead the person to genuine change. Rather it stays focused on the pain one is in because of the consequences of sin, or the blow to one's ego once a person becomes aware that they are not better than they are. See Hosea 7:14 and Matthew 27:3 for examples. It is important that self-hatred and wounded pride not be confused with biblical repentance.
3. True biblical repentance involves more than feeling sorry. It is a "change of mind that involves both a turning from sin and a turning to God" (Vine, 1984, p. 525). "Repentance means agreeing with God and yielding ourselves to his right to rule us. It leads us to make every effort to act accordingly in the daily details of our lives" (Vernick, 2003, p. 129). In true repentance, we dare to challenge our counselee with the question, "Are you going to yield yourself to God and God's perspective on things (true truth), or are you going to continue to cling to your own version of reality?"

Below is a sample dialogue with Donna after her homework assignment on Psalm 23:1.

Therapist: Donna, how did your homework go this week?

Donna: At first I felt a little weird, but after a few minutes I began to feel relaxed and I really liked focusing on one verse. I realized that I don't see

God as my shepherd. He's everyone else's shepherd but not mine. Putting the emphasis on certain key words helped me realize that.

Therapist: That's a really valuable insight you gained about yourself, Donna. How did you feel when you realized that? (*I'm looking to see what her heart response was to that awareness.*)

Donna: I felt really sad.

Therapist: What happened next? (*Still not sure whether she just wants God to be her shepherd or she now believes he IS her shepherd.*)

Donna: [Starting to cry] God told me, not with audible words, that he felt sad too. He told me that he was always my shepherd and felt sad that I didn't believe him. (*I allowed her time to sit with this awareness.*)

Therapist: What happened next?

Donna: Then I felt him saying to me, "You have everything you need even if you don't have everything you want."

Therapist: Wow, how did that feel?

Donna: It felt very special. Like God knew my situation at home. I didn't have to worry.

Therapist: How will those special words from God help you when you feel disappointed with your marriage?

Donna: I don't know yet, but I think it will help me be disappointed, but not despairing. God knows what I need and he has already given me that. I want to learn to trust him more.

This was a significant shift in Donna's heart. What she wanted the most wasn't the love from her husband but to know the love of God. Our goal in this step is not to simply remove the idol but rather to displace it with a stronger affection (Chalmers, 1855). Gary Thomas (1994) writes, "We cease from sin, not just because we're disciplined, but because we have found something better" (p. 61). This is truly transformational change.

Conclusion

Each of the five steps of the TRUTH Principle gives a counselor plenty of places for meaningful counseling interventions. They repeat themselves within each session, or the counselor may choose to focus on one particular step for a season when appropriate. Where God shows up within the model isn't always the same, but the counselor's goal is to listen for the Spirit's prompting and to provide opportunities where an encounter between the client and God is more likely to happen.

It is important to keep in mind that the TRUTH Principle isn't helping someone be morally good, but showing them how to walk out that long head-to-heart journey of change where he or she can be more yielded to God's Spirit and rule in his/her life. It provides practical steps to live out the words of Moses when he reminds the Israelites, "You can make this choice by loving the Lord your God, obeying him, and committing yourself firmly to him. This is the key to your life" (Deut 30:20 NLT).

References and Recommended Resources

Carlson, D. A., Bacaseta, P. E., & Simanton, D. A. (1988). A controlled evaluation of devotional meditation and progressive relaxation. *Journal of Psychology and Theology, 16,* 362-68.

Chalmers, T. (1855). *The Expulsive Power of a New Affection*. Edinburgh: Thomas Constable and Co.

Cormier, W., & Cormier, L. S. (1997). *Interviewing strategies for helpers: Fundamental skills and cognitive behavioral intervention* (3rd ed.). Pacific Grove, CA: Brooks/Cole Publishing.

Diseases and disorders—depression and what every woman should know. (n.d.). Retrieved January 19, 2013 from <www.mentalhealthcanada.com/ConditionsandDisordersDetail.asp?lang=e&category=63>.

Ferguson, J. K., Willemsen, E. W., Castañeto, M. V. (2010, June). Centering prayer as a healing response to everyday stress: A psychological and spiritual process. *Pastoral Psychology, 59*(3), 305-29.

Freeman, A., Pretzer, J., Fleming, B., & Simon, K. M. (1991). *Clinical applications of cognitive therapy*. New York: Plenum.

Gilligan, S. (2001). Getting to the core. *Family Therapy Networker, 25*(1), 20-22, 54-55.

Johnson, W. B., & Johnson, W. L. (1997). A wedding of faith and practice. *Christian Counseling Today, 5*(1), 15, 52-53.

Murray, C. J. L., & Lopez, A. D. (1996). *The global burden of disease: A comprehensive assessment of morality and disability from diseases, injuries, and risk factors in 1990 and projected through 2020*. Geneva, Switzerland: World Health Organization.

National Institute of Mental Health. (2007). Women and depression. Retrieved from <http://psychcentral.com/lib/2007/women-and-depression>.

O'Connor, R. (1997). *Undoing depression: What therapy doesn't teach you and medication can't give you*. New York: Little, Brown and Company.

Peck, S. (1978). *The road less traveled*. New York: Simon & Schuster.

Sexton, T. L., & Whiston, S. C. (1994). The status of the counseling relationship: An empirical review, theoretical implications, and research directions. *Counseling Psychologist, 22*, 6-78.

Tan, S.-Y. (2007). Use of prayer and Scripture in cognitive-behavioral therapy. *Journal of Psychology and Christianity, 26*(2), 101-11.

Thomas, G. (1994). *Seeking the face of God*. Nashville: Nelson.

Tillich, P. (1951). *Systematic theology: Vol. I*. Chicago: University of Chicago Press.

Vernick, L. (2003). *How to live right when your life goes wrong*. New York: Random House.

Vernick, L. (2005). *Defeating depression*. Eugene, OR: Harvest House.

Vernick, L. (2009). *Lord, I just want to be happy*. Eugene, OR: Harvest House.

Vernick, L., & Thurman, C. (2002). Change in process: Working from a biblical model of TRUTH in action. In T. Clinton & G. Ohlschlager (Eds.), *Competent Christian counseling: Foundations and practice of compassionate soul care*. Colorado Springs: WaterBrook.

Vine, W. E. (1984). Metanoia. In *The Expanded Vine's expository dictionary of New Testament words*. Bloomington, MN: Bethany House.

Wiersbe, W. (Comp.). (1978). *The best of A. W. Tozer*. Grand Rapids: Baker.

Williams, M., Teasdale, J., Segal, Z., & Kabat-Zinn, J. (2007). *The mindful way through depression: Freeing yourself from chronic unhappiness*. New York: Guilford.

17

God's Intervention in Sex Addiction

Mark R. Laaser

My Story

I must admit that one of the theme words of this book, *intervention,* causes me a bit of pause in that my own journey of recovery started with an intervention. The anxiety part of my memory has more to do with the fact that I don't think the people involved in that intervention had even prayed about what they were doing—they were just angry. In the midst of that storm, however, God did show up and I owe my life, my marriage and my ministry today to the fact that he did. Today, as a Christian counselor, the fact that we can rely on God to show up emboldens me to be more confrontational and direct with clients, particularly the sexual addicts with whom I work.

In early March of 1987, I had been living a life of sexual sin and depravity for twenty-five years. I had stolen my first pornographic magazine from a drugstore in 1961. That led to an ongoing and escalating pattern of looking at porn, masturbating and having sexual encounters with women. In those days I didn't even know the term *sexual addiction.* Yet I was living a lie and my life was very compartmentalized. On the outside I was a successful pastoral counselor, college professor and part-time Sunday preacher. My high school sweetheart and I had been married for fifteen years and we had three wonderful kids. On the inside, however, I struggled with lust and sexual fantasy. I was having regular sexual encounters with a number of women by that point in my addiction. One of those women finally reported me to the board of directors of the counseling center where I worked.

So, on March 17 of that year, the board "invited" me to a meeting. They were angry as they reported what they knew, and at that point they didn't even know the half of it. One by one they went around the room and told me how disappointed they were. Bottom line, I was fired from every job I had. I was to be given a two-week severance, and they seemed to be done with me. They didn't even want to hear from me and wouldn't let me talk. At that devastating moment, one of the members of the board stood up and came over to my chair. He was an orthopedic surgeon, and it was common knowledge that he was a recovering alcoholic. I will never forget his words as he towered over me as I slumped in my chair, "Mark, I think your sins with sex are no different than mine were with alcohol. If you'll trust me, I'll get you some help."

You see, because he was in recovery himself and "strangely" enough was the head of the state impaired physician committee, he had commonly dealt with doctors in trouble. He had heard of a new treatment program for sexual addiction in the Minneapolis area. He told me he would find out more about it and that he would come over that afternoon with information. Today, I know that this doctor was my angel in that room. He did find out. That afternoon, I was interviewed by the treatment center, and three days later I left for a treatment program that changed my life. I have now had twenty-five years of freedom and recovery from my sexual sins and addiction.

When I entered the doors of that treatment center, I truly thought that God was finished with me. Little did I know that he had only just begun. He continued to show up in my life. God showed up and through the power of the Holy Spirit, he comforted my wife, Debbie, enough to stay with me and brought help and support into her life. Today she is a partner in our ministry. God continues to show up in how he leads us in ministry. And, most importantly, he shows up every day in our counseling office and guides us in what to say to our clients. Perhaps the most important thing for me to say in this chapter is that we can intervene only in proportion to our ability to trust God to show up. It really helps me to have experienced that personally.

Step by Step

I have been blessed over the years of my practice in that virtually all of the men who seek my help are already Christians. In terms of intervention, it is more common that I am dealing with what James called "double-minded" men in his letter (Jas 1:8). James is referring to men who doubt, who are unstable and who have no integrity. They say they believe, but at least in part of their lives, they don't act accordingly.

The men that come to me are addicted primarily to sex and also to other behaviors and substances. Most commonly, since they are Christian, they have prayed for God to remove their sin and have been very disappointed by their own perceptions that he hasn't. The problem usually is that they want God to do all the work. They are like little children in wanting God to remove all future temptations. They certainly don't want to go to any trouble themselves. You see, it is their understanding about how God acts and their own selfish pride that create an agenda for God. When God doesn't "deliver" the way they want him to, they get angry with him.

Three questions. The first step in my process of working with them is to ask them a set of three spiritual questions in order to confront this double-mindedness. All are taken from John's Gospel and are based on conversations that Jesus had with people (M. Laaser, 2011a).

Do you want to get well? In John 5 Jesus talks to a man who is an invalid, who has come to the Pool of Bethesda to be healed. The man has been lying by the pool for thirty-eight years and has probably become quite used to his "role" of being sick. The Greek word that John uses here for invalid is *astheneia,* which means a weakness of body but also of soul. If this man hadn't become used to this role, or if he wasn't also weak of soul, why else would Jesus ask him, "Do you want to get well?" (Jn 5:6). I ask all the men I work with if they want to get well. They always say yes, and then we will have a conversation about why they have continued to choose their addiction. It is not uncommon for them to realize that they have been disappointed and angry with God. I tell them that it will only be when they are ready—body and soul—to cooperate with the power of God to heal them that he will.

For what are you thirsty? Next, we discuss the story of Jesus' conversation with a woman at Jacob's well in Samaria in John 4. Given the fact that all of the men I work with have been sexually unfaithful, this is a great story for them to look at because the woman is an outcast and has been shunned by "normal" women in her village of Sychar. The reason is that she is sexually promiscuous, having been married five times and currently living with another man.

This is a great story for the men who, in their sexual shame, might believe that Jesus would not have anything to do with them. In this story Jesus is breaking through three barriers, as Jewish men were not supposed to talk to women, Samaritans or the sexually unclean. I tell the men that if Jesus can talk to her, he can certainly talk to them. And Jesus tells her that anyone who drinks of the water of this well will always be thirsty but that anyone who drinks of the "living water" that he has to offer will never thirst (Jn 4:13-14). It is at this point that we can talk about the symbolism of this well being that of sexual sin. I ask them how many times they have drunk from the well of sexual fantasy, pornography, masturbation or affairs. It is at this point that we can talk about living water being pure water, and that it is only through sexual purity that they can have a real relationship with Christ.

For what are you willing to die? The third spiritual question is taken from the story of Lazarus in John 11. We know that Lazarus and his two sisters, Mary and Martha, were great friends of Jesus and yet, when the sisters send Jesus a message that their brother is sick, Jesus doesn't come right away, so Lazarus dies. Most of the men I work with have felt that they have sung "What a friend we have in Jesus" and sent him many messages, but that he hasn't come. They feel that they have died in that they have experienced many consequences of their sexual sin. I tell them that Jesus decided to let Lazarus die in order to make his resurrecting power known.

Then I ask them if there is anything about them that needs to die in order for Jesus' resurrecting power to be made known in them. Often it is their pride and anger that needs to die. Then I ask the central spiritual question, which is, "What are you willing to die for?" There is everything about their addiction that has been selfish, and there is everything about sexual purity that will need to be selfless. The obvious reminder is, of course, that Christ died for them. Are they willing to die for their spouses, children and others? It will only be through sacrifice that sexual purity can be obtained.

Support groups. The second step in the process is to persuade or counsel the men that they will need to be in support groups. In my experience, the Holy Spirit often shows up through the power of fellowship. I conduct counseling groups at our clinic with ten to fifteen men in each. We seek to go deep into difficult spiritual and emotional issues, and it is often the wisdom of other men speaking the truth of their own experience, quoting Scriptures to each other and reminding each other of the truth of God's Word that creates deep spiritual awareness in the men.

These groups also help the men create accountability with each other in that the encouragement and fellowship extends outside the group. These men regularly call each other, have face time (such as simply having coffee), and often serve as reminders of commitments made (M. Laaser, 2011c). Often the men will also choose to participate either in twelve-step or church-based support groups. There is no doubt that no man ever recovers alone. In my experience the presence of God through the power of the Holy Spirit will often "show up" in the power of these groups.

Capture every thought. The third step of the process is to teach men to control their thought life. Every sinful act begins with a thought. Paul teaches us, "We take captive every thought to make it obedient to Christ" (2 Cor 10:5). It is imperative that men know that God helps them in their thought life but that this doesn't usually mean he takes the thoughts away. Often men wish, pray and seek to beseech God to take away lustful thoughts. They will have usually worked to get sinful thoughts out of their lives. I have found that the harder we try to get rid of a thought, the stronger the thought becomes.

In my own recovery I have found that it is better to "allow" the thought to stay in my way and to do what you would do with a captive—interrogate it. What I've found is that every fantasy is actually a message from the person's soul. Fantasies, including even the most perverted sexual ones, are usually a man's attempt to get some deep needs or desires of the soul met (M. Laaser, 2011b).

Making a thought obedient to Christ will always mean that a man discovers how to get those deep needs met through his relationship with God. In one story, for example, Paul (not his real name) struggled with homosexual fantasies. He was preoccupied with thoughts of specific sexual acts with men. These became particularly vivid immediately after Paul's father died. Paul had never been very close to his dad and yet, of course, he grieved his death. I asked him, after some basic teaching about fantasies, what he thought the message from his soul was that the sexual fantasies were trying to tell him.

Paul said, "I think they mean I miss my dad." He also said that he missed that his dad had never really modeled to him how to be a man. Paul's quest was really to "participate" in real masculinity and to find men who would "comfort" him. He had sexualized that need years before when he became involved sexually with an older man. I asked him if he thought there was another part of the message. He said, "Yes, I think I still long for relationship with an older man." I encouraged him to initiate relationships with older men that he knew he could trust not to be sexual. His group encouraged him in this pursuit and, gradually, as he developed a network of older men who became mentors, his same-sex thoughts began to be much less powerful.

The second part of taking every thought captive is, after having recognized that the thoughts are often messages from the soul and that fantasies are a man's own creation, to ask God to help him turn them into thoughts of his vision. I believe that the Holy Spirit can help a man convert sinful thoughts and fantasies into a vision for God's calling, plan and purpose. Paul received what he thought was a vision about a calling God seemed to be giving him. While he felt excited about it, he couldn't imagine who might help him with it. However, on his next visit with one of the older men in his life, he mentioned the vision. As it turned out, this man had a friend who was the exact right fit to help Paul with his new venture. Today, Paul is pure, doesn't struggle with the sinful thoughts, and his vision for ministry that was, in fact, given to him by God is reaping many rewards and is prospering.

Healing of wounds and shameful core beliefs. The fourth step in my process involves individual healing from wounds and shameful core beliefs that most addicts have experienced. Limited research has indicated that a large percentage of sex addicts experienced some form of sexual abuse, physical abuse and/or emotional abuse as a child. In addition to being invaded in these ways, most were deprived of essential forms of love and nurturing. It is really the neglect or abandonment that drives the desires that can be manifested in fantasies. Sex addicts often experience core beliefs that they are bad and worthless, unlovable, that no one will meet their needs except for themselves, and that the main way they meet their own needs is through sex. In my experience it is common for sex addicts to suffer from all three of the unhealthy attachment styles described in psychological literature, playing a game of hopscotch between being avoidant, ambivalent/anxious and confused/disturbed about relationship (Clinton & Laaser, 2010).

When I have had a chance to assess the history of the men that I treat, I can usually make a better recommendation about longer term counseling that can address these wounds. This can include working with me or one of my staff counselors one-to-one and in group counseling. If the level of trauma is very significant and posttraumatic stress disorder is one of the diagnoses, I may recommend that they receive specialized counseling services such as Theophostic, EMDR, CBT, DBT and EFT. I have been accused of being very eclectic in my own approaches and my own referrals. This is, for me, a function of the fact that each individual is unique and I often seek to rely on the presence of the Holy Spirit to help guide me on which of the counseling approaches might be the most effective in certain situations.

Therapeutic Goals

I believe that it will be essential for a client to achieve two spiritual goals in the counseling journey of healing from trauma. First, he will come to an understanding of how he is stronger as a result of the pain and suffering through which he has worked. He will see the meaning in the pain. With James he will say, "I count it all joy when I experience trials" (Jas 1:2). There is a growing field of research that is empirically documenting this healing psychologically. It is called Post Traumatic Growth. Both Debbie and I are involved in research with the men I counsel and the women she counsels to also empirically demonstrate that this growth is evidenced by spiritual maturity.

Second, a person heals from trauma when he is able to forgive those who have hurt him. Forgiveness is an essential release of repressed or denied anger and resentment. For me, Christian counseling involves spiritual direction. There are times when I must confront a person that it is time; his journey has been long enough that going through an intentional process of forgiveness is in order. It is often during this work that we will witness the transforming presence of the Holy Spirit.

John is a wonderful example of this journey. He came to me a number of years ago because his girlfriend had discovered his acting out with pornography and prostitutes. Slowly, he was able to achieve sobriety from those behaviors by practicing the early steps that I have described above. John was willing to be pure. He came to understand that his desires were often based on a search for the nurturing his mother was never able to provide. And he longed to lead a life of service to his girlfriend, now his wife, and his children (from a previous marriage).

John participated in both one-on-one counseling and support groups. In the process of my work with him we discovered that a significant part of his trauma history was that he had been repeatedly abused as a fourteen- to seventeen-year-old young man by his local priest. As is often the case, I was the first person he told about this. I was successful in getting the archdiocese to pay for his counseling and treatment in exchange for an agreement not to sue. Gradually, I was able to direct his anger and grieving work, and then we transitioned to a more formal process of reconciliation. Eventually, John was able to talk to a priest friend of mine and, as he began to experience this priest as safe, was able to return to full communion in the church. John wrote a letter of forgiveness to the priest, even though the priest was dead. Today John would say that he is a much better man, father and husband for having struggled with this pain. He continues to be sexually pure.

Relational Transformation

Our practice is based on working with husbands who have sexually sinned, their wives, and the two of them as a couple. Some of the greatest acts of transformation have occurred when we see what has historically been called "restoration" and what we prefer to call "transformation." In transformation the couple experiences a new level of intimacy that they may never have known. We can see them restored to the purity of the early days of their relationship. We also work to see that this new level of intimacy is used to address some of the destructive issues and patterns that initially caused their problems.

It is obviously common for wives who have been betrayed to experience great sadness, anxiety and anger. They have a variety of reactions from self-blame to overt hostility toward their husbands. In the midst of all this pain, it is often the case that my wife and I find ourselves mightily praying in the middle of a session with the couple, *God, please show up. We have no idea how to move this couple past this crisis.*

Often in response to this prayer, God uses us as an example. Debbie went through all of these emotions in reaction to learning of my sexual addiction (D. Laaser, 2008). She was devastated, depressed, anxious about the future and angry with me. Yet through it all, she had a sense of peace. She felt great and difficult emotions, yet also felt that God was at work in our lives. It was that sense that allowed her to "hang on" long enough to get the support she needed and to be assured that I had found sexual purity and that I was "different." God led both of us to counselors who were effective, to support groups that were encouraging, and to friends who walked with us. Today we realize that God often uses our story as a sign of hope that restoration, transformation and reconciliation can occur. There have been countless people who have told us, "We have hope because of your story."

COUNSELING STRATEGIES

As trained counselors, we do have our specific strategies. One of them is based on our belief that relationships involving a sex addict won't be healed until the addict is able to get completely honest with his spouse. Addicts, out of their pain, have lied incessantly. They have believed the lie that "if you knew me, you would hate me and leave me." In our experience it is really the lies that have created more destruction in the marriage than the sexual sin has. As one wife once told us, "I can forgive my husband, but I need to know what I am forgiving." Even if the addict gets sober or pure, if he continues to lie, the spouse may have a very hard time healing. The ongoing lie might occur when the spouse asks the addict how he is feeling and he says, "Nothing." That is a lie.

We are, therefore, big believers in "full disclosure." Full disclosure involves working with counselors like us so that the timing is right and both spouses are fully prepared. If we attempt to do disclosure too soon, it might simply be an act of catharsis for the addict and might make him feel better. But if the spouse does not have enough support and isn't prepared, it can damage her greatly. We must also be very careful with the nature of specifics. We don't believe that crass specifics are helpful, such as the nature of sexual acts or words that were spoken with sexual partners. We do believe that it is important to tell the exact nature of activities: the extents, duration, money spent or lost, and any consequences experienced by the family.

If the addict has acted out with people that his wife knows, it is important for her to know these names as it may help inform her and help her make decisions about relationships in the future. We further believe that it is important for the addict to describe the nature of any and all sexual activities from birth to the present. This often gives the spouse the bigger picture of how the addiction developed even before their relationship started. This can take the pressure off the spouse, who sometimes believes that her inadequacies caused the addiction.

We have the addict prepare a time line of all of his sexual activities. It is sometimes helpful to do this in either five-year increments or in life stages—for example, preschool, grade school, middle school, high school, college and so on. Preparation for the spouse also involves meeting with my wife, Debbie, to ascertain the amount of support that she has from other women with whom she can talk both before and after the disclosure. What does she plan to do if she were to hear bombshell revelations that are really heard to process? What unanswered questions might she have that are based on whatever information she has been able to collect or what intuitions she may have experienced? Debbie is always working with the spouse to help her trust her own sense of reality. Because the sex addict has lied so frequently, the spouse can often feel crazy due to the incongruences between what she believes or knows to be true and what the addict has previously told her.

Over and over again, we have seen God show up in these disclosure sessions. While they are terribly anxiety producing, and anger and sadness are often felt, there is usually a sense of brokenness and humility on the part of the addict and a spirit of forgiveness and reconciliation on the part of the spouse. Healing hurts, and rebuilding trust will be a long road, and the experience of disclosure is the cornerstone of the building of a new relationship. It is quite remarkable to see an addict saying how sorry he is and even more remarkable to see a spouse say that now that she knows the truth she will be willing to move on to a place of forgiveness.

John and Karen came to us because Karen had discovered that John was having an affair. Obviously they were both devastated and on the brink of a separation and possibly a divorce. John worked with me and, in taking his history, I discovered that he had had not one but nine affairs and that he had regularly looked at pornography and masturbated. John went to our workshop, participated in one of our counseling groups and did regular one-on-one counseling with me. Likewise, Karen started one-on-one counseling with Debbie, attended a counseling group for wives and eventually went to one of our workshops for wives.

After a time, we felt that they were both ready for disclosure. Karen had not heard the extent of John's activities. While John's sharing was extremely painful and both of them cried many tears during it, we could see the movement of the Holy Spirit when Karen said, "John, I am very angry with you right now, and I want you to know that I appreciate the courage it took for you to get honest. Thank you for telling me. I have seen changes in you, and in time I will continue to pray that we can build a new relationship and that I can fully forgive you." And that is exactly what happened after John was sober for one year.

While there are many facets of how we help couples learn to have healthy relationships, one other of our usual strategies seems to really have remarkable results as God shows up: building a marriage from the ground up. Obviously, a sexual addict has become so neurochemically tolerant to the various neurochemicals of sexual arousal that he will need to detox for a time. There is only one way for that to happen, and that is for him to abstain from all sex for a time, even with his spouse. Also, it is quite common that an addict has so objectified his wife sexually that she has become little more than a physical body to him. We believe that marital sexuality is the expression of the covenant of marriage, which is a sacrament. Christ must be in it. We counsel couples to mutually agree to be abstinent for a time, and that during this time they should focus on their spiritual relationship. Paul offers us this encouragement in 1 Corinthians 7:5.

A period of abstinence should also be timed in such a way that both husband and wife find it both mutually agreeable and purposeful. We also want to make sure that both have an agreement to pursue spirituality together. This might be through a commitment to prayer, Bible study, church attendance, reading a devotional together or all of the above. Our experience tells us that this period of abstinence should be ninety days, though some couples have found benefit in a shorter period. The addict will really need to be participating in an accountability program in order to make this period of abstinence successful, and the wife will need support.

Both husband and wife will need to share core beliefs about the role of sex in a relationship; this is our time as counselors to help them learn God's plan for healthy sexuality. We have countless testimonies from hundreds of couples telling us that this one mutually agreed upon time is the one contract that transformed their marriage. Taking the stress of sex out allows for God to really work in the relationship and help the couple get his order of priorities straight. God is first, friendship is second, and sex is the expression of the first two in the "knowing" (Hebrew *yada)* that the couple will experience.

A Word of Encouragement

I hope that a short chapter like this will do two things: First, it should embolden you to feel comfortable working with sex addicts and with their spouses. As the founder of our field, Pat Carnes, has said, we are experiencing an epidemic of sexual immorality and addiction in our culture. Church leaders are falling daily. People in the pew are longing for leadership and moral example. Couples who have experienced sexual sin need hope.

Second, even though you may not have a lot of training in sexual addiction, I pray that you will invite the presence of the Holy Spirit into your counseling office in such a powerful way that even through your inadequacies, God will be at work. Remember, he is most strong where we are most weak. God bless you.

References and Recommended Resources

Clinton, T., & Laaser, M. (2010). *The quick-reference guide to sexuality and relationship counseling.* Grand Rapids: Baker Books.

Laaser, D. (2008). *Shattered vows.* Grand Rapids: Zondervan.

Laaser, M. (2004). *Healing the wounds of sexual addiction.* Grand Rapids: Zondervan.

Laaser, M. (2011a). *Becoming a man of valor.* Kansas City, KS: Beacon Hill.

Laaser, M. (2011b). *Taking every thought captive.* Kansas City, KS: Beacon Hill.

Laaser, M. (2011c). *The seven principles of highly accountable men.* Kansas City, KS: Beacon Hill.

Laaser, M., & Laaser, D. (2009). *The seven desires of every heart.* Grand Rapids: Zondervan.

Check out many other resources on our website: <www.faithfulandtrue.com>.

18

Human Nature Concerning Addiction Recovery Within Group Therapy

Myke Williams Dorsey

Human Nature and Addiction Recovery

There are variants in genes that turn down the function of dopamine signaling within the pleasure circuit. For people who carry these gene variants, their muted dopamine systems lead to blunted pleasure circuits, which in turn affects their pleasure-seeking activities. . . . Addiction is not fundamentally a moral failing—it's not a disease of weak-willed losers.

Dr. David Linden, *The Compass of Pleasure*

Addiction is medically classified as a human disease; however, spiritually speaking, it can be described as a cancer of the soul. In the mind, addiction is the product of pleasure center dynamics of the brain malfunctioning due to misuse, overstimulation and, at times, naturally occurring chemical imbalances. The fact that some individuals have genetic variants that mute dopamine signaling within the brain's pleasure circuits, encouraging them to practice more indulgent activities in order to gain satisfying experiences of pleasure, only underlines the fact that addiction begins in the mind, is reinforced by the body and is perpetuated because of perceptions, beliefs and ideations that again stem from the addict's mind, causing the individual a restlessness of spirit and disposition (Linden, 2011, p. 117). This is a psychological causality loop of mental processing that dances on the borderline between the conscious and the subconscious, ending with the brain's closed system of stimulus and response (Amen, 1998, pp. 171-72).

Addiction recovery must be approached in three specific dimensions: mind, body and spirit. For it is in these three aspects of the human condition that addiction has its foothold. Talk therapy alone will not be effective, nor will medications alone be a cure or even place the disease into remission; in addition to these factors, the individual must have an awakening take place within. This borders on the spiritual, the way the individual perceives and understands reality. One must have a reason bigger than a personal desire or even a cause or conviction. This is why the idea of a "God of my understanding" is a phrase so often used in Alcoholics Anonymous and other twelve-step programs. An authority greater than ourselves must be focused upon for humans to reach their greater potential beyond the likes of the animal kingdom. The prefrontal cortex and other portions of the brain that are unique to humans must be actively engaged in order for this to take place (Newberg & Waldman, 2009, p. 221).

Our human trait for creating that which does not exist yet through the power of our imagination enables us to exercise optimism, hope and inspiration. These are the elements that have historically empowered people to achieve accomplishments that were thought to be impossible. The Bible reflects this when the author of Hebrews 11:1 writes, "Now faith is the substance of things hoped for, the evidence of things not seen" (NKJV). The spiritual is in fact the human being using both the body and the mind to focus on abstract mental constructs associated with meaningful emotion-driven factors to focus on something significant, and as a result grasping what some might describe as miraculous.

When people use recreational drugs, they do so to escape a painful reality. Moving away from pain toward pleasure is instinctual for humans. Human nature's imperative to crave what feels good and to ignore later negative consequences directly associated with impulsive choices is a trick the mind will not soon grow weary of playing on itself. Doing this without regard for consequence often indicates that the individual is lacking the vital ingredient of hope. Without optimism we are not healthy.

All addiction begins with an empty spirit; there is an emptiness that the mind alone cannot fill. The "God-shaped hole" that Blaise Pascal wrote about is not only in the pages of dusty old philosophy books, but in the hearts of lonely people in local taverns, crack houses, keg parties and alleyways. Once a person's spirit is broken and the mind begins to look for an escape, the bait is set for the body to fall under the spell of chemical addiction. If the unfortunate fellow happens to have a genetic predisposition that favors biological addictive tendencies, he is in for a heinous internal civil war with the forces of nature within himself.

Addiction is one of the greatest evidences that modern humans are still in need of the spiritual. Science alone will not be enough to solve the dilemma of being at war with oneself. Addiction is a clear example as to why we as people need a spirituality that involves *the direct experience of God*. Wonder, awe, beauty—these are aspects of what we instinctively recognize as sacred. They fascinate us and give us pause. Each of us experienced this as small children, but as life marches perpetually forward we have this primal wonder smothered out of us with the demands of survival and growing older.

Arrested development is the golden thread of all addicts, rich, poor, educated or ignorant. Emotional maturity comes to a sudden halt when addiction begins. Every chance thereafter that the individual has an opportunity to grow emotionally and to deal with the challenges of life in a healthy manner, the choice is made to use the chemical or compulsive behavior to mask the emotional distress. The endorphin release brings the synthetic high to the individual, reinforcing the habit that makes their life unmanageable.

The frightening fact that many addicts enter the addiction cycle in early adolescence means that emotionally they stopped growing between the ages of twelve to fifteen. They are left with the emotional skill set of an early adolescent, even if they are forty or fifty years of age biologically. Nevertheless, with a subconscious drive for psychological homeostasis, the addict may develop reasoning skills that are more than adequate, in an attempt to overcompensate. This allows them to function well for a short period of time in their chosen profession and other practical endeavors. However, the emotional intelligence and social skills required to thrive in the workforce and other relationally complex environments quickly reveals the emotional inadequacies addicts struggle to cope with. This makes problem solving extremely difficult even when the addict is sober. They may have a very high intelligence quotient, but their lack of impulse control and their inability to objectively understand their intrapersonal emotional states of being remains a mystery to them. Interpersonal skills development happens only after the inner life path has been proactively chosen. This is why spirituality is a key component of recovery for addicts.

Healthy spirituality, no matter what approach one chooses, must have key universal elements that mold and shape the character of the individual into a more focused and mature human being. First, one must accept the fact that they cannot control the world; the universe is more powerful than the self. Second, one needs to recognize that life can be a wise teacher if we choose to view it objectively, observing the life lessons of others as well as our own. Third, it is our job to begin to understand ourselves by learning the difference between self-love and self-centeredness. Life does not owe us an explanation for why we are the way we are; it is up to us to go on the journey of self-discovery. Fourth, living in harmony with others is to our greatest advantage; practicing whatever it takes to learn how to be at peace with our neighbors and loved ones will free us up to pursue what matters most to us personally. Finally, we must learn how to live within our environment and to nurture it.

People are not in harmony with life when intoxicated, high, or acting out obsessions and/or compulsions. When this occurs the individual is under the influence of forces within the world that are leveraged against that person's natural imperative to survive and thrive. The power of choice is a common yet powerful tool that is all too often neglected in matters of this nature. In between stimulus and response there is a pause, and in that pause there is a choice, and within that choice lay the fruits of the promise—healing and wholeness.

Christian Counseling and the Twelve-Step Process: A Spiritual Methodology

Addiction is the human condition gone horribly wrong. A methodology designed specifically to navigate the unique pitfalls and characteristics of addiction had to be developed in order for spirituality to be properly cultivated and practiced with this hurting community of souls. It has been said that the twelve steps are a spiritual primer, but more to the point, they are a specific method for bringing a unique populous to a state of being where they can most effectively begin to live out their faith and have the seeds of truth fall on the good soil that Christ spoke about in the Gospels.

Beginning with having a sponsor, someone who has traversed the badlands of the soul, is of paramount importance. "It takes one to know one" is quite literal when dealing with the dynamics of addiction. A Christian therapist that is not an addict in recovery may have excellent skills, keen insight and an anointing from the Holy Spirit, but there is no substitute for experience. When a person has faced the gates of hell because of addiction, they speak the language of experience that newer people in recovery desperately need to hear. This again is why group work is so crucial. The twelve steps approach breaks up the fallow ground and weeds out the thorny distractions of life that keep the healing effects of the gospel from having maximum impact. These steps present spirituality in a format that anyone can use to develop a proper awareness of the inner life all humans possess. Nevertheless, the addiction cycle is a disease process that can be likened to a life-draining cyclone with the delusion of denial at the eye of the storm. Remove denial and the storm will begin to die down. The key is removing the mental fallacy that the individual is not an addict.

Success of all treatment depends upon the eradication of this life-decaying lie called denial. Unfortunately, denial is often at the center of the addict's ego integrity. The grip of denial is locked into the ego. The subconscious fear of cognitive dissonance is driving their irrational thinking concerning denying the reality that they are suffering under the influence of addiction. If the individual accepts the truth that they are in fact an addict, they are forced to face the deep pain of no longer excusing their actions by projecting that pain onto other people.

The concrete, black-and-white, zero-sum thinking of the self being all good or all bad, a totally misunderstood victim or a totally irresponsible wretch, is the emotional pattern of how addicts see themselves subconsciously. These are soul wounds that reach back into the core of the individual's view of the self. This is the primary reason why denial tends to have such a death grip on the individual. They truly believe that life as they have come to understand it will be destroyed by projecting pain and fear when facing these uncharted realms of reality. To them the experience of addiction is bad, but fear of the unknown is far worse. Like a cave dweller seeing shadows reflected on the wall from the fire light in Plato's classic story *The Allegory of the Cave*, they are terrified at being blinded by the truth of the light of day. For most addicts the pain of their addiction must become greater than the pain endured under the deception of denial for them to finally face the truth. It takes tremendous courage to face one's denial and surrender it to the truth. Let go of the ego and denial dissipates. This is where the paradoxical nature of spirituality plays a key role.

One must lose in order to win, die in order to live, surrender in order to succeed. Denial ends when surrender begins. This is a very necessary prerequisite; unless this choice is made, the twelve steps will afford the addict few lasting results, if any. Stopping the abuse of substances is only part of the issue, an external action only; the inner life reasons for choosing to abuse substances in the first place *must be addressed.* Even facing the horrible biological withdrawal symptoms and the synaptic gap that the brain experiences with the absence of the addictive chemical does not begin to account for why the addict started down the hellish path of addiction, nor does this brave action alleviate the need to truly understand why addiction was chosen over facing particular life's challenges.

Authentic surrender of a person's free will, a true vulnerability of spirit, can be a frightening prospect. After all, emotional vulnerability is often the precursor to the emotional wounding that caused the individual to retreat into masking their pain through the addictive process in the first place. The wounded soul learned the painful lesson that being vulnerable opens up the possibility of being hurt, which triggers the emotional hijacking in the brain's limbic system to choose one of the emotional survival instincts of fight, flight or freeze. This is why it is important to gently persuade an addict to surrender, to trust that emotionally fighting, fleeing or freezing up will not end their pain—only surrender will do this.

Nonetheless, the odyssey of surrender unfolds in stages. The symbol of a white chip in twelve-step circles means that one is choosing to surrender their will for that moment, by admitting they have a problem—initiating the ending of the delusion of denial. This is the silent side of the action that goes against the grain of addiction for the very first time. Before one can begin to walk the path of recovery, letting go of *internal* striving and *external* shucking and jiving has to happen. Prerecovery always begins with surrendering the human spirit *first.* Only after this can anyone truly begin to practice step one effectively through the twin principles of honesty and acceptance, which are the hallmarks of recovery.

Without both honesty and acceptance a person is not living a *recovery life*. This is a cornerstone of truth that all addicts must understand and live out, through both theory and practice being done together. If an individual attempts step one without deciding to do step zero, there will be *reservations,* and reservations always leave a doorway open to *using,* because the individual is still thinking in an addictive manner. Without step zero, true honesty and acceptance cannot happen. The person may not be abusing addictive substances, but again that only means that they are abstinent, not actually on the road to recovery. The root of why one is caught in the addiction cycle is still not being faced. The pain that is being avoided or masked by addiction has not been surrendered.

In group this must be thoroughly discussed with true feelings and frustrations expressed. This is tantamount to living out the first step of admitting powerlessness over dependencies and accepting that life had become unmanageable. The principle of the second step is found in a *hope* that a power greater than self-will could restore the addict to health. Christians believe that Jesus Christ can and will restore us to sanity, leading to the third step, which is making a decision to turn our human will and lives over to the Lord Jesus through *faith* in his life-giving sacrifice. These principles of hope and faith can be meditated upon and discussed at length, and more experienced people in recovery can be given an opportunity to share their wisdom with the group. At this point, inner courage can begin to be cultivated.

Once people in the group practice honesty and acceptance along with hope and faith, this produces the courage to make a searching and fearless moral inventory of the self. The fourth step is the synergy of the first three. A moral inventory is the spiritual microscope that will keep a person in recovery and out of the addiction cycle. Denial is the deadly alternative. Not choosing to make that *searching and fearless* moral inventory is a dangerous exit onto the road that leads to relapse. Plausible but untrue reasons (excuses) for questionable behavior is the essence of the delusion of denial. Group members should be frank with one another when it comes to denying the disease process, having discussions like: What crisis brought each of us to recovery? What situation led each of us to formally work step one? When did we first recognize addiction was a problem for us?

Group therapy process. These questions lead to further analysis of the addiction cycle and the health of the recovery process. Understanding, experiencing and evaluating the differences is a powerful psychoeducational component of group therapy. Reservations also need to be discussed openly in group. Examples of former reservations and relapse experiences need to be confessed by recovery members with longer clean-time and greater step-work development. Plain talk about where this type of thinking leads will reinforce the importance of earnestly following the twelve steps in order to recover a life worth living.

Having worked with addicts for years, as a minister first and then as a psychotherapist, I have noticed some common misconceptions that those in recovery confuse with their faith-walk with God. It is not uncommon for those struggling in the grasp of addiction to go to church and have an encounter with Christ. Hopefully the individual truly surrenders to God and begins a new life. If the leaders in the ministry are not fully trained on the unique conditions the new Christian faces with the addiction cycle, there will probably be challenges ahead that all involved are not fully prepared to handle effectively.

One of the challenges that I want to address at this time is the ambiguous nature of spiritual growth or sanctification that can be quite a challenge for the new believer who wrestles with addiction. I have had more than one individual tell me that they don't need that "twelve-step stuff"; all they need is the "one step" of following Jesus. The merits of the twelve-step approach or the idea that it is somehow a replacement for authentic faith is not the issue. The principles the twelve steps methodically present is the issue. Facing the difficult and often painful questions of introspection and choosing to make amends when needed along with other complex character-building necessities is one of the most challenging things an addict will ever do in his or her life.

Going to church and having no specific treatment plan for how to live a drug-free Christian life, where past actions are reconciled and relationships are restored, is not realistic. I have seen people recover from addiction by giving their lives over to Christ. However, with greater investigation I have also noticed the telltale aspects of these rare individuals going through a personalized form of the twelve-step process. Principles don't change, surrender, honesty, acceptance, hope, faith, courage—all the steps are represented. I am writing this because one of the main forms of reservations addicts tend to use when they come into the body of Christ is the fallacy that they can do what I call "hiding behind the cross." I believe in Galatians

2:20, that we were crucified with Christ and we no longer live, but it is Christ who lives in us. When we give our lives over to God we become brand-new, and the feeling can be both exciting and relieving. All the addictive actions are under the blood of Christ. The temptation to want to avoid the effects of past actions and to ignore the disease process of addiction can be difficult for a new believer to handle. This is why having a sponsor is so important.

In step five the work is to admit to God, ourselves and one other person the exact nature of our wrongs. The effects of doing this reinforce the new way of living life. This is how God renews the mind of the individual: putting the recovering individual in a place where he or she is entirely ready to have God remove all his or her defects of character, which is step number six. This commitment and perseverance leverages one to leave behind the wounds from the past and look forward to the future, free in Christ Jesus. This sixth step naturally leads into the seventh, which is humbly asking God to remove our shortcomings. This is the second time an individual encounters a further stage of surrender. In step zero, surrender had to be done in order to get on the path; here, to go to a deeper level of inner health, surrender is further experienced in a manner unavailable to the individual previously. Step seven fosters a sense of serenity not experienced before. The concept of "godliness with contentment is great gain" is a Bible way of saying this very thing (1 Tim 6:6 NKJV).

Making amends to all whom one has harmed is an important step of reconciliation. In step eight a personal list of people abused through one's addictive cycles is a significant way to psychologically, physically and emotionally let go of the past. Brotherly love and justice are the principles behind making amends where possible without further injury being done to others. This is the important ninth step: facing the facts that harm was caused by the addict, and making it right cuts at the root of self-centeredness, which is the core of addiction. Even though others often play a part in past misadventures, it is the one in recovery that needs to decide to own his or her behaviors regardless of what others do. This is a major part of taking one's life back from the tentacles of addiction. This is a still deeper aspect of surrender, bringing further clarity to one's life. The Christian knows to immediately allow Christ to have that aspect of his or her past and leave that sin under the blood of Jesus.

The final three steps are equivalent to what the average churchgoer needs to be doing on a regular basis: taking personal inventory of our lives, promptly admitting fault when mistaken and asking for forgiveness. Step ten is to improve our conscious contact with the God of our understanding through prayer and meditation, asking for his will and the power to do it. Commitment, humility, courage and faith—all are reflected in the principles found in step eleven. When one comes to this step he or she will realize that the final three steps are a mirror image of the first three. Steadfastness is what sums up this step in recovery. The culmination of all of this brings those in recovery to a spiritual awakening that can finally be genuine. Practicing these principles in all of one's life is the goal of step-work.

There is no better way for a person to reflect upon these principles than teaching them to others. Service is what the final step is all about; just as service is what the gospel is all about, loving God with all our being and loving our neighbors as ourselves. Principles are changeless, regardless of phraseology. God is interested in our motives, what is truly going on in our inner lives. The most effective way to discuss openly what is happening on the inside is in a trusted space designed for this specific purpose, a Christian therapy recovery group.

Case study. I once had a client who was convinced she was ready to end her time in therapy. We had worked together for over eighteen months and had made great progress concerning her addictive tendencies. She had two years of clean-time from her drug of choice, had completed a degree in school she had been working toward on and off for several years and had been asked to join the children's ministry team in her church. When I suggested she join a therapy group I was beginning, she resisted the idea. "Dr. Myke, I think I'm ready to end therapy. God has done so much in my life already, I don't even have any desire to use anymore. Last month we had an evangelist come to our church and he prayed over me and something happened, I can't explain it, but I just feel so different. I honestly think God healed me of my addiction."

Having been a traveling evangelist myself some years before I began my private practice as a Christian psychotherapist, I could understand my client's enthusiasm for what God had done in her life. I certainly did not want to discourage her faith in any manner; however, there were tendencies in her behavior that she was blissfully unaware of that others saw in her at first meeting. "You have done excellent work in our one-on-one sessions over the months we have counseled together, and I am excited to hear that God has truly done a work in your spirit in recent days. I have felt led of the Lord to begin this new therapy group for individuals who are in a similar place of life with their faith-walk and recovery process. I mention this to you because I have been in prayer about who should be asked to be in this group and you were one of the people that immediately came to mind. Would you prayerfully consider joining this group?" She was reluctant but said she would give the group a chance. When we met for a one-on-one session three months later, the change was notable.

"I thought I had it together, but boy was I wrong." She was smiling when she said this, and her affect indicated that she felt safe enough to chuckle at her change of perspective. "Okay, I think I'm seeing the fact that I have a little problem with being a control freak! Not only did the guys in the group let me know in no uncertain terms that I like running the show, but the children's minister let me know that I needed to put the brakes on when it came to bossing around the other helpers in kids church." She put her hand over her eyes in mock shame, but more than a little real embarrassment. "You know, I would have been really ticked off at the church if my therapy group hadn't told me the same thing just a few days before the church folks had their little come-to-Jesus meeting with me about my bossiness. I guess this group therapy is something God wants me to keep doing."

I was thankful to hear her make the connection. In the previous months we had done sessions together, this client had changed churches three times, all because of relational conflicts. This was the first time that she confessed that she played a part in the conflict and it had been resolved with little or no negative consequences. The group was a safe place to hear negative feedback and feel empowered to do something about it. Because others were quick to confess their struggles with being "control freaks," she felt like she was in good company and most importantly was not alone in working on this life challenge.

Another factor she brought up was her budding relationship with one of the other women in the group. The lady was close to her mother's age and had grown up in a city not too far from her hometown. With more than twelve years of clean-time and a prominent position in a local Christian school, this lady was a natural role model for the above mentioned client.

However, the chances of the two of them having ever met outside of group therapy were slim. They went to two very different types of churches and lived in two different townships. The group meeting happened to be located halfway between their homes, so both decided to join.

I am convinced that this was divine appointment due to the fact that the older woman had lost her daughter years earlier because of choices made in addiction and was able to share this painful truth with the younger girl. The possibility for safe family reenactment like this new relationship also helps clients with true altruism. Knowing that you were able to help another with significant realities of life is no small thing. Feelings of emptiness and low self-worth begin to fade when these types of relationships start to develop. These two women can assist one another in ways I never could help either of them. With their relationship built on open, honest communication in a trusted space, they each can learn how to nurture the other.

Final Concerns

Addiction and recovery is a very personal journey. The journey is an interior one. Facing personal fears, practicing impulse control, learning to delay gratification, completing the emotional growth that was avoided when the addiction began and learning how to truly love yourself takes quality time and consistency. What I have observed as a counselor is the dismaying reality that many on the road to recovery grow weary in their efforts and stop halfway through the process, remaining in a state of limbo between addiction and complete recovery. Often the client refuses to grow further because to do so requires a greater amount of inner surrender. They are not satisfied with where they are emotionally, but the perceived inner work to have a more fulfilling life is projected as too costly an effort. The risk of failure is simply more painful to deal with than the possibility of greater fulfillment. Continuing to build one's faith that life can be better is of utmost importance in situations such as this.

The greatest challenge of working with recovery is the sad fact that relapse is a common condition clients find themselves in. They may be doing well for a time and any one of life's many variables can send them right back over the edge. Not only must relapse prevention be discussed at length in group, but a proper procedure of what to do when relapse does occur must be discussed at length as well. How to handle the negative self-talk that will flood into the mind of the individual and how to make the right choice to get back up are so very important to address. Group support cannot be overemphasized at this point. Just as the people in the body of Christ need one another; those in the group need each other as well. This spirit must be fostered in the group, and it is the responsibility of the therapist to lead the charge.

Guarding against self-medication or choosing to randomly stop taking medications prescribed by a physician is also a topic to be discussed in group therapy. I have noticed that a number of people in the recovery community have various medical challenges, some of which are a result of the addictive lifestyle and for others traumatic events lead them to abuse prescription drugs, bringing them into the addiction cycle. In either case a close watch must be given to individuals in these conditions. The temptation to abuse chemicals given by a medical professional because of chronic pain or other medical needs means that these clients must be especially honest about their condition. This is the type of information that needs to be shared in group to help protect the sobriety of the ailing members who are at various stages of recovery.

Using one's emotions and nervous system as a measuring tool for feeling okay is not healthy thinking for people in recovery. I have had numerous clients who have stopped taking their prescribed medications, most notably serotonin re-uptake inhibitors (S.S.R.I.) because they felt better. What the client failed to understand and accept is that it was the medication that was allowing them to feel better. Without it, their mental health began to deteriorate, self-medication became too tempting and relapse was not far behind. Recognizing these traps is what group discussions are for.

Human nature may be a random number of stimulus and response events that happen throughout the life cycle of an individual, but the unique elements of personal experience mold and shape a person's mind into a unique kind of personality. In the Christian tradition it is the spark of life that God breathed into Adam that made him come to life. This aspect of the human spirit must be reached, renewed and reconciled to the Creator. Chemical addiction, codependencies, compulsions—God wants us to be free from these burdens. In order for this to happen we must surrender to God what he gave us in the beginning, our human spirit—that breathe of life. Once this has occurred, the renewal of the mind can begin healing the brain, the body and the spirit toward complete reconciliation of the human soul.

References and Recommended Resources

Amen, D. (1998). *Change your brain, change your life*. New York: Three Rivers Press.

Linden, D. (2011). *The compass of pleasure*. New York: Penguin.

Newberg, A., & Waldman, M. R. (2009). *How God changes your brain*. New York: Ballantine Books.

19

The Power of Christ in Transforming Unwanted Homosexual Behavior and Attractions

Julie Harren Hamilton
& Philip J. Henry

Jesus looked at them and said,
"With man this is impossible, but with God
all things are possible."

Matthew 19:26

Introduction

Two myths about homosexuality are popular in our culture: that people are born homosexual and that change of sexual orientation is not possible. Yet the research reveals the opposite. While most people do not *choose* their attractions, the research is also clear that people are not simply *born* homosexual. Researchers on both sides of the debate recognize that homosexuality is not simply a matter of biology. In fact, in 2008 the American Psychological Association (APA) updated its information on homosexuality in a document entitled "Answers to Your Questions for a Better Understanding of Sexual Orientation and Homosexuality." In an older document they had claimed that homosexuality was mostly biological in origin, but in this revised document, they admitted,

> There is no consensus among scientists about the exact reasons that an individual develops a heterosexual, bisexual, gay, or lesbian orientation. Although much research has examined the possible genetic, hormonal, developmental, social, and cultural influences on sexual orientation, no findings have emerged that permit scientists to conclude that sexual orientation is determined by any particular factor or factors. Many think that nature and nurture both play complex roles; most people experience little or no sense of choice about their sexual orientation. (APA, 2008, p. 2)

Further, twin studies make clear that people are not simply born gay. Studies of identical twins reveal concordance rates of 20 percent for male twins (Whitehead, 2010). In other words, if one twin is homosexual, only 20 percent of the time is the other twin also homosexual. Identical twins share the same biological makeup, yet the majority of the time if one twin is homosexual the other is heterosexual.

Common Factors Contributing to the Development of Homosexual Attractions

What, then, are some possible causes of homosexual attractions?[1] These feelings typically stem from a combination of temperamental factors and environmental factors that occur in a child's life. According to Whitehead and Whitehead (1999), "Human behavior is determined by both nature and nurture. Without genes, you can't act in the environment at all. But without the environment your genes have nothing on which to act" (p. 10). One way of understanding this combination might be expressed in the following equation:

> Genes + Brain Wiring + Prenatal Hormonal Exposure = Temperament
>
> Parents + Peers + Experiences = Environment
>
> Temperament + Environment = Homosexual Orientation
>
> (D. Blakeslee, personal communication, July 2007)

While environmental factors may include experiences of sexual abuse or other traumatic events, one theory is that a disruption in the development of gender identity is a very strong contributor to same-sex attractions (Moberly, 1983). Gender identity refers to a person's view of his or her own gender; that is, his or her sense of masculinity or femininity. Gender identity

[1]This section is excerpted from Harren, 2006.

is formed through the relationships that a child has with the same-sex parent and same-sex peers (Nicolosi & Nicolosi, 2001).

The process of gender identification begins approximately between age one and a half and three years. For boys, it is during this phase that they begin to move from their primary attachment with the mother to seeking out a deeper attachment with the father. For males, the relationship between a boy and his father is the initial source of developing a secure gender identity. Through the father-son relationship, a boy discovers what he needs to know about being male, including who he is as a boy, how boys think and behave. As the father spends time with the son, shows interest in the son, and gives the son affirmation and affection, the father imparts to the son a sense of masculinity. The boy begins to develop a sense of his own gender by understanding himself in relation to his father (Nicolosi & Nicolosi, 2001).

When the child reaches the age of five, he begins to face another task—that is, to begin to attach to same-sex peers. At this age, he starts school and begins to look to the other boys to answer the same questions that his dad has been answering. He looks to the other boys to discover how they think, how they behave, how they play and interact with one another. He seeks to be included, accepted and acknowledged. Through the relationships he forms with other boys, he continues to gain a sense of masculinity, discovering more about other boys and therefore more about himself as a boy (Nicolosi & Nicolosi, 2001).

During the early years of elementary school, children are not usually very interested in playing with members of the opposite sex. They desire to spend time with members of the same sex. This is a very necessary stage of development, because a person cannot be interested in the opposite sex or in others until he or she first understands himself or herself. Eventually, after many years of bonding with members of the same sex, the boy enters puberty. At this time he begins to turn his attention to the opposite sex. He becomes curious about the gender that is different from his own, the female gender. With the simultaneous emergence of puberty, this curiosity becomes a sexual interest and a desire for romantic connection with the opposite sex.

Male Homosexual Development

Conversely, for the child who will develop a homosexual orientation, this process does not happen. So, what happens in the development of gender identity that might lead a child to have same-sex attractions? Typically, for this child, something prevents him from attaching to the father. Either he does not have a father or a father figure, or he does not have a father whom he perceives as safe and/or welcoming. Of course, there are many children who grow up without fathers and yet do not develop a homosexual orientation. In addition, there are many children who have loving fathers, yet still become homosexually oriented. This is due to the fact that there are various factors that contribute to a homosexual orientation. Human development is very complex and includes events as well as perceptions about the events.

Perceptions are very important. Perceptions are more powerful than what actually happens, because perceptions become that person's reality. Perceptions are influenced by temperament. For example, a child with a more sensitive temperament might perceive rejection even when rejection is not intended. Temperament is the biological contributor; however, temperament alone is not enough to create a homosexual orientation. The temperament type must be met with the right environmental factors in order to produce same-sex attractions. Typically the child who will later develop same-sex attractions is naturally sensitive, observant, intelligent and sometimes more artistic than athletic. This child often tends to personalize and internalize experiences and observations (Nicolosi & Nicolosi, 2001; Nicolosi, 2009a).

So, if a child perceives that his father does not want a relationship with him, that child might try a few times to connect with his father but will eventually retract in self-protection. This is called defensive detachment. Upon sensing rejection, the boy chooses to reject the father in return. He detaches from the father and even what the father represents, which is masculinity (Moberly, 1983). Typically at this point, he will stay connected to the mother, continuing to receive feminine input. Usually he is also surrounded by other female figures, such as a sister, an aunt or a grandmother. So at a time when he is craving masculine input and seeking to understand himself in terms of his male identity, he instead experiences ongoing female connections and begins to develop a sense of the feminine.

By the time this child enters school, he often has a difficult time relating with other boys. Either he is just more comfortable with girls, who are more familiar to him, or he is intimidated by boys. Often this child sees himself as different from the other boys. So he may hold back from bonding with them. If he has developed any feminine mannerisms, he might also be rejected by the other boys and quite possibly even ridiculed. He is craving acceptance from boys and continues to need this acceptance, though the need goes unmet. The boy watches the other boys from afar, he longs to be noticed by them and included by them, yet he remains with girls, further gaining a sense of the feminine while deeply craving the masculine.

This child typically spends his elementary school years learning about femininity while craving to understand masculinity. Specifically, he desires to understand himself in terms of his own masculine identity. Yet he does not assimilate with the same-sex parent or same-sex peers, so he does not acquire a masculine identity. He associates with the feminine, which is his primary source of input. He does not develop a secure gender identity. So by the time this child reaches puberty, the craving for male input has grown and intensified. At this time in his life he is not curious about or interested in the opposite sex. He already knows all about the opposite sex—they are quite familiar to him. What he is craving to know about is his own gender. He still deeply longs to know about boys. He longs to experience connections with males. This emotional need, the need for same-sex love, which has gone unmet, now begins to take on a sexual form. His unsatisfied cravings for male love become romantic cravings with the emergence of puberty (Nicolosi & Nicolosi, 2001).

To this child, it feels very natural that he longs for male love. In fact, he typically thinks that he was born that way, having craved male love for as long as he can remember. Indeed, he has craved this love most of his life. However, initially it was not a sexual craving. Instead, it was an emotional craving, a legitimate need for nonsexual love, an emotional need that has become sexualized.

Female Homosexual Development

The female development of homosexuality is a bit more complex. As with the male development, there are a number of factors that can contribute. For some women who end up with same-sex attractions, the development is similar to the male development previously described. For others, negative perceptions regarding femininity may lead to an internal detachment from their own femininity. For example, if a girl watches her father abuse her mother, the girl might conclude that to be feminine is to be a victim or to be weak. At an early age she might make an unconscious decision to detach from her female identity. She might detach from her own gender in an effort to protect herself from the perceived harmful effects of being female (Hallman, 2008).

Sexual abuse is another factor that can contribute to a homosexual orientation for both men and women. Women who are sexually abused may come to see men as unsafe, and lesbianism becomes a way of protecting against further hurt from males. For some women there might be an emotional disconnection from the mother, and lesbianism becomes a search for motherly love. For other women, same-sex attractions may not initially be present, but may later develop as a result of entering into a nonsexual friendship that becomes emotionally dependent. An emotionally dependent relationship is one in which two people seek to have their needs met by one another. It is a relationship in which healthy boundaries are not in place (Rentzel, 1990). The absence of appropriate emotional boundaries can then lead to a violation of physical boundaries.

The Possibility of Change

For any of these reasons listed above, and in combination with other factors, same-sex attractions may develop. People who experience same-sex attractions often report having had those feelings for as long as they can remember, which makes sense given the developmental nature of such attractions starting in very early childhood. Having the attractions as long as they can remember leads many homosexuals to conclude that they were simply born that way. When misinformed people state that homosexual attractions are "a choice" it is not only offensive to homosexuals, but also inaccurate. Same-sex attractions are rarely, if ever, chosen, are usually cultivated over a long period of time and are not easily diminished. Change can happen to varying degrees, but as with most other developmental issues, it is not an easy process.

Can same-sex attractions really be changed? There are many people who find themselves attracted to members of the same sex and yet do not want those attractions. For those who are dissatisfied with their sexual orientation, it should be noted that change is indeed possible for some people. Research studies have revealed that change of sexual orientation does take place (see Spitzer, 2003; Byrd & Nicolosi, 2002; Jones & Yarhouse, 2007). It is not a quick or easy process, but as with any other therapeutic issue, varying degrees of change are achievable through therapy and other means. It is important to note that change may be different for each individual. For some change may mean a change in behavior or identity, and for others it may include change in attractions.

The inaccurate concept that homosexuality is solely biological is extremely misleading. Gay-affirming therapists tell their clients that homosexuality is biological and therefore unchangeable. These therapists encourage their clients to embrace a homosexual identity, even when such clients are seeking change of orientation. In doing so, therapists negate clients' rights to self-determination. Clients have the right to choose their own goals for therapy and should be allowed to pursue the path they desire. Clients should not be discouraged from pursuing change when change is what they seek. In order for clients to have the options made available to them, it is vital that therapists as well as clients become better educated on this issue.

THE REALITY OF CHANGE

The National Association for Research and Therapy of Homosexuality (NARTH) completed a landscape review of the literature, examining whether change is possible, if change attempts are harmful, and if there are any differences between heterosexuals and homosexuals, which might lead to a desire to seek change of orientation. The results of this review are presented in NARTH's peer-reviewed journal, *Journal of Human Sexuality*, volume 1 (NARTH, 2009). This landscape review presents over one hundred years of experiential evidence, clinical studies and research studies concluding that change is possible, that it is possible for men and women to diminish their unwanted homosexual attractions and develop their heterosexual potential. It also demonstrates that change attempts are *not* harmful and that there are greater levels of depression, anxiety, substance abuse, sexually transmitted diseases and suicide among homosexuals than heterosexuals. These issues might lead some homosexuals to seek change. The document contains six hundred references.

Beyond the documented evidence that change of sexual orientation is possible, it is also a simple reality of life that people can and do change in many areas of their lives. At the core of what it means to be human is the belief that humans possess the God-given ability to change. Further, brain plasticity studies increasingly point to our ability to change and to shape what and how we as humans think and choose our destiny. This could be called existential, biological, spiritual-based free will. Rollo May (2007) and Victor Frankl (2006) and others have talked about this choosing. Much of the existentialists' writings were a response to the reductionistic determinism of the behavioral and psychoanalytic community of that day. Today we face a politically driven determinism, which, although espousing freedom, does not allow for the simple act of client-driven "choice." This type of determinism must also be met with a call to true freedom. Choice should always be protected and made available to the client.

This must be addressed not only on a hypothetical basis but also on a pragmatic basis as the client encounters the "choices of therapy." The therapist must see that the client leaves therapy with this sense of choice and freedom firmly placed in their hands. If not, then the therapy has been a failure, no matter what other good has taken place. There is no instance in which a psychologist or therapist should inform the client that she/he cannot change or that she/he should change. Therapists should provide general information to clients, including information on statistics; however, licensed therapists are ethically prohibited from either personally discouraging change or coercively manipulating change. Therapists should provide ethical, informed, professional care to clients seeking help, without manipulating them or advocating a politically prescribed form of therapy. NARTH has published practice guidelines for providing psychological care for clients with unwanted homosexual attractions (see guidelines in addendum at end of chapter. See also NARTH, 2010).

There are many forms of therapy and/or ministry that are used successfully with this population, including: Reparative Therapy, Interpersonal Therapy, Eye Movement Desensitization and Reprocessing (EMDR), Inner Healing Ministry, Cognitive Behavioral Therapy, Family Therapy and others. Therapy is often aimed at the underlying issues, not simply the attractions (see, e.g., Hamilton & Henry, 2009).

Progression of Therapy

As with many other issues, therapy for unwanted homosexual attractions involves at least two phases of therapy, regardless of the therapeutic approach. In the initial stage, joining with the client and establishing both rapport and trust are essential. In addition, assisting the client with behavioral change is very important. Clients often benefit by implementing support and accountability into their lives. Once accountability is in place and the client has adequate support to assist with behavioral changes, the focus of therapy shifts to the deeper issues.

The deeper issues commonly include, but are not limited to, the following: shame-based identity/diminished sense of self, past traumas (including sexual abuse), parental abandonment, lack of attachment, peer rejection, emotional losses, unforgiveness, and an insecure gender identity (much of the therapeutic work is aimed at helping the client to develop a more solid and secure sense of self in regard to his or her gender). Therapy assists clients in making peace with their gender (many homosexuals are detached from their own gender), developing a healthy self-image (including body image), developing healthy views of both men and women, and working out their misunderstandings of God or problems in relationship with God.

Another key issue of therapy as it progresses is to discover the current foundations of the same-sex attractions and actions. In other words, "What are the functions associated with unwanted thoughts and behaviors?" More simply stated, "What do the same-sex attractions and actions do for the individual?" For instance, what part does same-sex attraction play in stabilizing the inner psychic world or maintaining homeostatic balance, or how do the thoughts and behaviors change the biology relating to stabilizing the neurotransmitters, perhaps warding off depression, for example? The questions can also be developmental or spiritual. What tasks is the individual avoiding or delaying? How does anger with God or with what he has given (parents, body, obstacles to overcome) influence choices and behavior? These are only a few of the host of questions that reveal the function of the same-sex attraction.

While the current functions of same-sex attraction appear to be difficult or impossible to assess or to detect, they are most readily seen by their absence rather than the overt functions. For example, for men, the function of homosexual pornography and habitual masturbation is difficult to detect in its overt form. However, abstinence in these areas reveals the underlying function, like water that recedes from a drying lake clearly showing the bottom. Once the function is detected, choices can be made to address these issues in a more healthy way or to ignore them. At least for the client, the choices are made with knowledge and on some understanding of the dynamics involved. For the therapist, the goals of therapy by necessity must address the revealed functions of the same-sex attractions for the therapy to be successful.

Approaches to dealing with these issues vary according to the treatment method employed by the therapist. Treatment methods commonly applied include EMDR, Interpersonal Therapy, Relationship-based therapies, Cognitive Behavioral Therapy, Family Therapy, Inner Healing ministry and many others. In the following section, some of the common approaches are introduced.

Reparative Therapy

Although *reparative therapy* is a term mistakenly used by uninformed media or laypersons to describe all therapies aimed at alleviating unwanted homosexual attractions, it is just one approach to treatment, among many other approaches to psychological care for unwanted homosexuality. Reparative Therapy is an approach that has been developed and championed by Dr. Joseph Nicolosi. In this approach, homosexual attractions are viewed as a reparative drive or an unconscious attempt to meet previously unmet same-sex needs of attention, approval and affection (Nicolosi, 2009a). Nicolosi describes the role of homosexual attractions in repairing the following self-states: inhibited assertion; shame (feeling worthless and insignificant, a state Nicolosi describes as central to the homosexual condition); and the Grey Zone (a state of being shut down or emotionally numb). Nicolosi describes compulsive homosexual behavior as a man's attempt to be more connected with his own gender—that part of himself from which he has disconnected. "The homosexual impulse is also an attempt to rediscover the free, expressive, open, powerful, gendered self that each man was created to claim. The intent of the impulse is 'reparative' in that its goal is gender affirmation; the man strives to be 'seen' by other men as an attractive male" (Nicolosi, 2009b, p. 33). He explains that the impulse to act out is reparative, but that the original conflict or the man's disconnection from himself is never resolved and only results in more distress (Nicolosi, 2009a).

One of Nicolosi's therapeutic tools, the Preceding Scenario, is very useful in the treatment of unwanted homosexual attractions. The concepts underlying this particular tool can be applied with other approaches to therapy as well. Nicolosi describes three stages or self-states that often unfold prior to a client acting out homosexually (Nicolosi, 2009a). Assertion is a self-state in which a client is feeling strong, confident, calm and secure, within himself and with his gender. However, if a client experiences a shame moment, he will move out of the state of assertion and into a shame state. A shame moment can include experiences of disapproval, rejection or fears of disappointing another. The shame may even result from the *anticipation* of rejection, not necessarily the direct experience of rejection. When a client moves from a self-state of assertion into a shame state, the result is what Nicolosi describes as the Grey Zone. The Grey Zone is a dull, flat or lifeless mood that follows a shame moment.

According to Nicolosi, the common way that clients move themselves out of the Grey Zone is through homosexual enactment. He explains that even the idea of homosexual enactment shifts the client into an energized self-state, and so this enactment becomes a seemingly easy solution to the loneliness and lifelessness of the Grey Zone. As the client considers acting out homosexually, he may feel a burst of energy or excitement that stands in stark contrast to the isolation and deadness of the Grey Zone (Nicolosi, 2009a).

Clients often defend against feeling their true emotions. The Grey Zone is a defense mechanism that clients use to avoid feeling the pain of the shame moment they encountered. Instead of feeling the pain and grieving in a healthy way, they move into this shut-down state of the Grey Zone (Nicolosi, 2009a). The goal in therapy is to assist the client in recognizing the shame moment that preceded the Grey Zone. Upon identifying the shame moment, the therapist assists the client in discovering the beliefs about himself that are contained in that shaming experience. With the help of the therapist he may discover that he is holding on to false beliefs. As he recognizes the faulty aspects of his beliefs, he is able to move naturally back into an assertive state. If, however, he realizes that the beliefs do have merit, the therapist helps him to look more compassionately at himself, often moving into grief work over the underlying issue. For example, if a client had a shame moment in which he felt incompetent in a sport, the therapist helps him identify the belief. If the belief is true, such as "I am not good at sports," the therapist helps him to see himself more compassionately—perhaps recognizing that no one ever took the time to teach him how to play sports. This recognition leads into grief work regarding the lack of the father's involvement or lack of peer inclusion.

Much of Nicolosi's Reparative Therapy involves grief work: helping the client to feel his emotions, to grieve and to reprocess with the therapist his earlier experiences. The client is encouraged to stay connected to the therapist while remembering and describing the past trauma and feeling his own emotions. This reprocessing is central to the healing process. Nicolosi has implemented his model of therapy for over twenty years, reporting very high success rates. Successful outcomes include not only the resolution of homosexual behaviors, diminished homosexual attractions and, in some cases, the emergence of heterosexual attractions; but also, an increased sense of self, greater confidence, a stronger sense of gender identity, a decrease in feelings of depression and an overall improved sense of well-being. Nicolosi also advocates for the use of EMDR in many cases.

EMDR

Many practitioners who assist clients in overcoming unwanted homosexual attractions have found EMDR to be an extremely effective approach for dealing with past traumas associated with the development of homosexual attractions (Carvalho, 2009). EMDR is used to help resolve past traumas, such as peer rejection, sexual abuse or parental wounding. EMDR is an approach to therapy that requires specific training and certification (see www.emdr.com).

The God-given ability of individuals to heal physically is obvious to anyone who has suffered a simple cut on the hand. Francis Shapiro (2001) and others hypothesize that healing of the brain can happen in much the same way as sorting out maladaptive-processed information happens, leaving only a scar.

> Our memory record of everything that has happened to us colors our daily lives. The information that helps us move on, learn from our mistakes, examine what has happened and hang on to the good part is adaptive information. We can even call it wisdom in many cases because our memories help us survive and live more fruitful lives. But we also misprocess memories that distort our thinking, that lie to us about what is happening, that contaminate our decisions, and that impair our ability to choose our responses and behaviors. This maladaptive information, and its pain, will continue to haunt us long after the events linked to the record should have faded. (Carvalho, 2009, p. 175)

Esly Carvalho (2009), a Christian therapist with nearly thirty years of experience, suggests that the traumas that underlie same-sex attractions and homosexual behavior may result from difficulty bonding with the same-sex parent, a violent parent, a physically or emotionally absent parent, sexual abuse, eroticization of emotional needs, problems with temperament and a host of traumas that may be unique to the individual.

According to Carvalho (2009), these difficulties are lessened with the help of EMDR in a manner similar to the way that EMDR addresses other issues. She explains that EMDR helps people to process disturbing information in a new way.

> The EMDR protocol asks that patients try to remember the first traumatic experience, called the touchstone memory, because it is often responsible for the structuring of traumatic behavior. For example, we can ask the patient to identify the first time they felt unwanted (SSA) and follow it to that event, structuring the protocol with the touchstone experience as its target. As we re-process the memory, and it is put into the past, it loses its power to harm in the present. The underlying pre-supposition is that as we heal the trauma which caused the psychosexual arrest in development, the normal psychosexual stages of development will be unblocked and have a chance to develop. Often this brings heterosexuality options with it, allowing new responses to emerge spontaneously and opening possibilities for behavior rehearsal that were previously unthinkable. (Carvalho, 2009, p. 185)

While not being a "magic cure," EMDR appears to be helpful for clients to process trauma and appears to aid in the removal of obstacles created by trauma. Working with God's natural healing processes in the brain is opening new doors for those seeking help for same-sex attraction that has its roots in trauma and despair.

Interpersonal Therapy

Interpersonal Therapy, developed by Harry Stack Sullivan, is another effective approach to treating men with unwanted homosexual attractions. Dr. Dean Byrd (2009) describes the use of Interpersonal Therapy in the following way:

> In summary, the interpersonal approach to psychological care of those with unwanted homosexual attractions focuses on the interpersonal nature of relationships, both historic and current. There is a strong emphasis on "re-

> doing" historical interpersonal relationships and developing healthy interpersonal relationships currently. Such relationships are characterized by mutuality, non-sexual intimacy, and security. (p. 68)

Byrd (2009) goes on to describe the use of Interpersonal Therapy for helping clients reprocess past traumas, developing new understandings of self and discovering new ways of relating interpersonally with others. Parents and, in particular, peers played a vital role in this unfolding developmental process that consisted of a "dance" between the child and key figures in the child's world. One of the key components here was the development of a gender identity. This gender identity forms the basis for sexual orientation (Evans, 1996). If the individual does not obtain proper alignment and connection with others, the lack of this foundation is seen in a compensatory use of same-sex attraction.

Simply stated, successful Interpersonal Therapy is based on new relationship experiences. The therapist is central to this process. Byrd (2009) writes,

> Considering the interpersonal nature of psychological care, it is important to understand that the therapist cannot be objective and neutral. Rather the therapist is critical to the establishment of an atmosphere which promotes interpersonal safety and security. The therapist simply facilitates the process of interpersonal learning, and this is achieved through a respectful, empathic dialogue as the therapist listens to the details of the patient's experiences, calling attention to the developmental processes and the interpersonal processes. (p. 68)

The therapy develops in three phases. In the *initial phase,* the therapist helps the client see the same-sex attractions within the context of relationships and helps them understand the developmental processes involved in the attractions. Exercises aimed at self-awareness are important during this phase, for it is not relationships or development in general that the client needs to understand, but his own unique dynamic process.

The *second phase* of Interpersonal Therapy for same-sex attraction is addressing shame. This shame is often accompanied by the aftermath of trauma and a deep sense of personal isolation and loneliness. Behavioral interventions include helping clients connect more deeply with others, helping to reduce shame and developing a growing awareness of the role the same-sex attraction plays in this process.

During the *third phase,* the client is asked to consider early relationships and wrestle with the impact these connections had on development. In particular, unmet needs are examined, particularly unmet needs associated with affection, attention, approval and affirmation. Consequent to interventions such as the one noted above, men are instructed to focus first on similarities with men and then on differences. With this new focus, there comes a cognitive ability to separate affection, approval, attention and affirmation from issues of sexuality.

More importantly, many men report a diminishing of homosexual attractions when nonerotic, intimate relationships are developed with admired men, almost as if buddies or chums who were noticeably absent during preadolescence now emerge. For some men, this is the first time for such relationships.

Within this growing "chumship," men experience a newly developing sense of self. From this vantage point, God, self and others can be viewed without the distorting stigmatism of relational myopathy. The developing awareness both of historical and current relational connection with others leads to practical relating within the give-and-take manner that desexualizes what is admired. Only then can the command to love God first and to love others as ourselves truly arise.

Female Same-Sex Attraction

Janelle Hallman (2008) has developed an approach to helping women overcome unwanted homosexual attractions. She emphasizes the importance of acceptance and attunement when working with this population. She focuses on the therapeutic relationship as the primary tool for helping women to work through issues of past hurt, emotional dependencies and gender identity. She describes with warmth and compassion the population to which she has dedicated her career. She emphasizes the importance of understanding some of the unique characteristics of this population in that they are deep thinkers, sensitive and delightful. She cautions therapists that these clients are often confrontational and may display defiance, defensiveness and even aggression. Therapists must be willing to be authentic, caring, nonjudgmental, warm and engaged, offering clients an opportunity to relate in a healthy way (Hallman, 2008).

Hallman (2009) summarizes her approach as follows:

> As mentioned earlier, to begin the work of therapy, I first make a genuine effort to *know, build trust and establish a real authentic and caring relationship with the unique woman sitting in my presence.* Second, I will attempt to help her identify and resolve hurts, bring clarity to innocent confusions or inner conflicts, confront false beliefs, determine her true beliefs, unravel unhealthy relational patterns and expose blocks to meaningful intimacy. This is how I would proceed in therapy with any client. (p. 164, italics original)

Mary Beth Patton (2009), who also works with lesbian women, describes three stages in her approach to treatment. In the first stage, Patton focuses on building trust and addressing issues of shame. She also uses the first stage of therapy to assess for mood disorders and/or personality disorders or traits. Two other tasks of this stage are educating the client on the roots and causes of their attractions as well as teaching good coping skills through the use of Dialectic Behavior Therapy. In the second stage of therapy, Patton assists clients through the grieving process, as they reflect on past losses. In the third stage of therapy, she helps the client to rediscover her strengths, her talents and new ways of relating to others. As these clients begin to grow, the issue of individuation is an important one. According to Patton (2009), "There is no guarantee that an individual who has addressed her issues will no longer deal with homosexual desires or that she will be happy in a heterosexual relationship. However, doing the work of individuating will allow her to be stronger and clearer about who she is and what her needs are, which makes for healthier, happier relationships and more satisfaction in life" (p. 130).

For further reading on approaches to female same-sex attractions see Hallman (2008), Hallman (2009) or Patton (2009).

Summary

The future for those seeking help for unwanted same-sex attractions is bright. There are a number of successful and efficacious therapies for those choosing to address unwanted homosexual attractions. Success, of course, will vary, as with any issue, but the possibility of change must be acknowledged, and the undying desire of clients to find freedom must be heard and respected.

Change is possible. It is not easy, and the level of change varies in degree among individuals, including change of identity, of behavior and, for some, change of attractions. Change may also include decreased depression, increased self-confidence, improved relating with both same and opposite sex, improved relating with God and resolution of past traumas. While various levels of change do occur, it is typically not achieved without sacrifice and without the help of the divine Healer. As the apostle Paul said in his letter to the church at Corinth, referencing "homosexual offenders" among others, "And that is what some of you were. But you were washed, you were sanctified, you were justified in the name of the Lord Jesus Christ and by the Spirit of our God" (1 Cor 6:11).

Therefore we would conclude for the homosexual struggler that it is in this Spirit, the Spirit of our wonderful and miracle-working God, that change is possible—a change that is impossible for a man or woman to achieve in his or her own strength. As you attach yourself to God, which is true faith, a true relationship will develop that is beyond a mere intellectual understanding of God. He will do in and for you what is impossible for you to realize on your own. He loves you more than you can imagine and wants to do his work in your life.

ADDENDUM

Practice Guidelines for the Treatment of Unwanted Same-Sex Attractions and Behaviors

In December 2008, at its annual strategic planning meeting, the National Association for Research and Therapy of Homosexuality (NARTH)'s board of directors formally accepted the following "Practice Guidelines for the Treatment of Unwanted Same-Sex Attractions and Behaviors." Their purpose is to educate and guide mental health professionals to provide competent, ethical and effective psychological care to those with unwanted homosexual attractions and behaviors.

Attitudes Toward Clients Who Seek Change

Guideline 1. *Clinicians are encouraged to recognize the complexity and limitations in understanding the etiology of same-sex attractions.*

Guideline 2. *Clinicians are encouraged to understand how their values, attitudes, and knowledge about homosexuality affect their assessment of and* *intervention with clients who present with unwanted same-sex attractions and behavior.*

Guideline 3. *Clinicians are encouraged to respect the value of clients' religious faith and refrain from making disparaging assumptions about their motivations for pursuing change-oriented interventions.*

Guideline 4. *Clinicians are encouraged to respect the dignity and self-determination of all their clients, including those who seek to change unwanted same-sex attractions and behavior.*

Treatment Considerations

Guideline 5. *At the outset of treatment, clinicians are encouraged to provide clients with information on change-oriented processes and intervention outcomes that is both accurate and sufficient for informed consent.*

Guideline 6. *Clinicians are encouraged to utilize accepted psychological approaches to psychotherapeutic interventions that minimize the risk of harm when applied to clients with unwanted same-sex attractions.*

Guideline 7. *Clinicians are encouraged to be knowledgeable about the psychological and behavioral conditions that often accompany same-sex attractions and to offer or refer clients for relevant treatment services to help clients manage these issues.*

Guideline 8. *Clinicians are encouraged to consider and understand the difficult pressures from culture, religion, and family that are confronted by clients with unwanted same-sex attractions.*

Guideline 9. *Clinicians are encouraged to recognize the special difficulties and risks that exist for youth who experience same-sex attractions.*

Education

Guideline 10. *Clinicians are encouraged to make reasonable efforts to familiarize themselves with relevant medical, mental health, spiritual, and religious resources that can support clients in their pursuit of change.*

Guideline 11. *Clinicians are encouraged to increase their knowledge and understanding of the literature relevant to clients who seek change, and to seek continuing education, training, supervision, and consultation that will improve their clinical work in this area.*

The Practice Guidelines are published in the *Journal of Human Sexuality* (NARTH, 2010). Used with permission.

References and Recommended Resources

American Psychological Association (APA) Committee on Lesbian, Gay, Bisexual, and Transgender Concerns. (2008). Answers to your questions for a better understanding of sexual orientation & homosexuality. Retrieved from <http://www.apa.org/topics/sexuality/sorientation.pdf>.

Byrd, A. D. (2009). Psychological care of men who present with unwanted homosexual attractions: An interpersonal approach. In J. H. Hamilton & P. Henry (Eds.), *Handbook of therapy for unwanted homosexual attractions: A guide to treatment* (pp. 53-88). Orlando: Xulon.

Byrd, A. D., & Nicolosi, J. (2002). A meta-analytic review of the treatment of homosexuality. *Psychological Reports, 90,* 1139-52.

Carvalho, E. R. (2009). Eye movement desensitization and reprocessing (EMDR) and unwanted same-sex attractions: New treatment option for change. In J. H. Hamilton & P. Henry (Eds.), *Handbook of therapy for unwanted homosexual attractions: A guide to treatment* (pp. 171-97). Orlando: Xulon.

Evans, F. B. (1996). *Harry Stack Sullivan.* New York: Routledge.

Frankl, V. (2006). *Man's search for meaning.* Boston: Beacon.

Hallman, J. (2008). *The heart of female same-sex attraction: A comprehensive counseling resource.* Downers Grove, IL: InterVarsity Press.

Hallman, J. (2009). The basics of therapy with women with unwanted same-sex attraction. In J. H. Hamilton & P. Henry (Eds.), *Handbook of therapy for unwanted homosexual attractions: A guide to treatment* (pp. 135-69). Orlando: Xulon.

Hamer, D., & Copeland, P. (1994). *The science of desire.* New York: Simon & Schuster.

Harren, J. (2006, November). *Homosexuality 101: What every therapist, parent, and homosexual should know.* Paper presented at the meeting of the National Association for Research and Therapy of Homosexuality, Orlando.

Jones, S. L., & Yarhouse, M. A. (2007). *Ex-gays: A longitudinal study of religious mediated change in sexual orientation.* Downers Grove, IL: InterVarsity Press.

May, R. (2007). *Love and will.* New York: Norton and Company.

Moberly, E. R. (1983). *Homosexuality: A new Christian ethic.* Cambridge: James Clarke.

National Association for Research and Therapy of Homosexuality (NARTH) Scientific Advisory Committee. (2009). What research shows: NARTH's response to the American Psychological Association's (APA) claims on homosexuality. *Journal of Human Sexuality, 1,* 1-128.

National Association for Research and Therapy of Homosexuality (NARTH), Task Force on Practice Guidelines for the Treatment of Unwanted Same-Sex Attractions and Behavior. (2010). Practice Guidelines for the Treatment of Unwanted Same-Sex Attractions and Behavior, *Journal of Human Sexuality, 2,* 5-65.

Nicolosi, J. (2009a). *Shame and attachment loss: The practical work of reparative therapy*. Downers Grove, IL: InterVarsity Press.

Nicolosi, J. (2009b) The meaning of same-sex attraction. In J. H. Hamilton & P. Henry (Eds.), *Handbook of therapy for unwanted homosexual attractions: A guide to treatment* (pp. 27-51). Orlando: Xulon.

Nicolosi, J., & Nicolosi, L. A. (2001). *Preventing homosexuality in today's youth.* Downers Grove, IL: InterVarsity Press.

Patton, M. B. (2009). Working with lesbian and bisexual women. In J. H. Hamilton & P. Henry (Eds.), *Handbook of therapy for unwanted homosexual attractions: A guide to treatment* (pp. 89-133). Orlando: Xulon.

Rentzel, L. T. (1990). *Emotional dependency.* Downers Grove, IL: InterVarsity Press.

Shapiro, F. (2001). *Eye movement desensitization and reprocessing: Basic principles, protocols and procedures* (2nd ed.). New York: Guilford.

Spitzer, R. L. (2003). Can some gay men and lesbians change their sexual orientation? 200 participants reporting a change from homosexual to heterosexual orientation. *Archives of Sexual Behavior*, 32(5), 403-17.

Stickgold, R. (2002). EMDR: A putative neurobiological mechanism of action. *Journal of Clinical Psychology*, 58(1), 61-75.

Whitehead, N. (2010, April). *Genetic influence on SSA significantly overestimated?* Retrieved from <http://www.mygenes.co.nz/kaminsky.html>.

Whitehead, N., & Whitehead, B. (1999). *My genes made me do it: A scientific look at sexual orientation.* Lafayette, LA: Huntington House.

Resources for Therapists

Hallman, J. (2008). *The heart of female same-sex attraction: A comprehensive counseling resource.* Downers Grove, IL: InterVarsity Press.

Hamilton, J., & Henry, P. (Eds.). (2009). *Handbook of therapy for unwanted homosexual attractions: A guide to treatment.* Orlando: Xulon.

Nicolosi, J. (2009). *Shame and attachment loss: The practical work of reparative therapy.* Downers Grove, IL: InterVarsity Press.

Many other resources on this topic are available through the NARTH bookstore:

<www.Shop.pilgrimageresources.com>.

Resources for Clients

For Men

Dallas, J. (2003). *Desires in conflict.* Eugene, OR: Harvest House.

For Women

Howard, J. (1991). *Out of Egypt: Leaving lesbianism behind.* Oxford, England: Monarch Books.

Rentzel, L. T. (1990). *Emotional dependency.* Downers Grove, IL: InterVarsity Press.

For Parents

Dallas, J. (2004). *When homosexuality hits home: What to do when a loved one says they're gay.* Eugene, OR: Harvest House.

Haley, M. (2004). *101 frequently asked questions about homosexuality.* Eugene, OR: Harvest House.

Nicolosi, J., & Nicolosi, L. A. (2002). *A parent's guide to preventing homosexuality.* Downers Grove, IL: InterVarsity Press.

Schmierer, D. (1998). *An ounce of prevention.* Nashville: Word.

For Wives

<www.wifeboat.com>.

General Information

Chambers, A. (2006). *God's grace and the homosexual next door: Reaching the heart of the gay men and women in your world.* Eugene, OR: Harvest House.

Dallas, J. (2007). *The gay gospel? How pro-gay advocates misread the Bible.* Eugene, OR: Harvest House.

Dallas, J., & Heche, N. (2010). *The complete Christian guide to understanding homosexuality: A biblical and compassionate response to same-sex attraction.* Eugene, OR: Harvest House.

Additional resources available at <www.exodusbooks.org>.

20

Flourish in Life Coaching

Integrating Faith and the Science of Human Flourishing

Catherine Hart Weber

We are hardwired to flourish, along with all of God's creation. That is why, since the beginning of my training as a therapist and then as a life coach and spiritual director, I have integrated the best practices in neuroscience, psychology and spiritual formation to enhance God's desire for our well-being and human flourishing. I aim for intentional living in my own life as well, and am continually reminded of how much this matters, in working with clients and in everyday life.

God's balance of flourishing in beauty through transforming love, goodness and redemption in Christ are his divine antidote to the languishing, vandalizing and brokenness in and around us. This is the hope we recognize in ourselves, those close to us and, of course, those who come to us for counseling and coaching.

The Pursuit of Beauty and Well-Being

A dear friend of mine who admires pottery came across a large bowl that particularly caught her eye at an art show. It was in an amazing shape of waves, and the beauty captured her heart. But, it was expensive. So she focused on the joy of another potter's three small pots formed together, symbolic of a three-fold cord unbroken.

The next day, however, she just couldn't get the beauty of the wave bowl off her mind. She had to go back and admire it once more. Maybe the artist would be willing to give her a discount? She had saved some Christmas money—for such a time as this.

The potter was flattered at her admiration of his work. They had a great conversation. As she turned to approach him about the beautiful wave bowl, her bag knocked a large vase behind her, which fell to the ground, shattering in small pieces.

She was in shock. How could this happen? She came to pursue and acquire beauty to boost her well-being, and now she was faced with brokenness—that was very expensive! Right then and there, something in her also shattered. She broke down crying, sobbing. It wasn't just about feeling bad for the loss of the art, or the huge cost. It was much more, much deeper.

You see, most of her life is about dealing with or paying for brokenness. She has lived with cancer for over twenty years, consistently for the last twelve years. The fifth round of chemo and treatment she is on costs thousands of dollars. Her life revolves around the damaging consequences of her broken body and other shattered things of life and the people around her.

But it just couldn't end this way. She couldn't just pay for more brokenness and walk away with no beauty. God has always provided a balance of beauty, goodness and wholeness in her life. She exemplifies flourishing fruitfulness. Each fresh new day she embraces answered prayers, deep relationship connections, and daily "love and kisses from God."

God showed up that day in power and beauty, as the potter offered to let her pay wholesale for the broken vase and the wave bowl. She offered to pray for him and his wife and left with a bag of shattered vase pieces as well as a beautiful wave bowl. As God had done so many times before, *he left her with the balance of beauty and wholeness, against the brokenness.*

Flourishing in Well-Being Matters

That's how life can be for us, for those coming to us for counseling or life coaching: keeping the balance of beauty and well-being with brokenness and languishing; embracing the balance of both our strengths and weaknesses, happiness and struggles. We teeter on the edge of freedom and fear, of flourishing and languishing. We don't want to deal only with broken pieces keeping us deprived, holding us back.

That's why Jesus came. His love and beauty set us free.

He brings light into our darkness. He makes beauty from ashes.

He promises his love, joy and peace—abundant life.

Only the Spirit of God can release us, open our eyes and hearts to see all that Christ is, what he provides for us through the cross. What he promises to do in us is goodness, beauty, wholeness—*shalom*.

Beauty matters. The beauty of Christ's transforming life in us matters. A flourishing, thriving, abundant life as a whole person . . . matters. Living out the vision of God's shalom, his love and beauty . . . matters.

We can't escape the pain, darkness, brokenness and vandalizing on this side of his kingdom. But we can open our lives to the Holy Spirit, holding on to our visions of God paying the price, transforming and empowering us now and finally making the whole of creation anew—with love, joy, peace, hope, wholeness and beauty.

Why I Developed Flourish in Life Coaching

In the early stages of the field of psychology, and also of Christian counseling, the emphasis was on curing mental illness, making the lives of all people more fulfilling, and identifying and nurturing gifts and talent. Over the years, however, the focus became more influenced by a medical model of psychological problems and how to remedy them. As a result, great strides were made in understanding and treating many psychological disorders.

However, it is only recently, with the burgeoning growth of strength-based therapy and Positive Psychology (Science of Well-Being and Human Flourishing) and neuroscience, that effort has gone toward research and interventions on resilience, prevention, increasing well-being, fulfillment and the strengths that make life worth living.

These new developments are dramatically changing the way therapists, coaches, mental health practitioners and leaders deal with the average person's life experience and aspirations. Research and interventions are focusing on a reemphasis of the importance of philosophy, theology, religion and the benefits of religious faith and spirituality in building resilience and cultivating positive spiritual character traits and emotions. Flourishing in well-being now matters. Character matters.

Rigorous research is now being conducted at top universities on the benefits of faith practice, character traits and emotions of the spiritual life, such as love, compassion, kindness, joy, happiness, gratitude, forgiveness, appreciation, prayer and the benefits of relationships. I believe we, as Christian counselors and coaches, would do well to revive, relearn and discover these breakthrough benefits to our own well-being and ability to flourish and be resilient, so we can pass this on to those we counsel and coach.

CHRISTIAN HUMAN FLOURISHING

Innately we know that God didn't create us to wither, just exist or get by. In my life and those I journey with in counseling, coaching, groups and retreats, I have recognized a longing for more than getting over our "issues," living in the hum-drum of the mundane and being overtaken by stresses and worries. We are hardwired with a desire to live more intentionally, to open up to the Spirit of God for more love, forgiveness, compassion, joy, gratitude, peace and hope—the spiritual virtues that bring lasting fulfillment and impact.

This longing to flourish is universal. God designed us for well-being—shalom—in all areas of our life systems: our body, brain, mind, emotions, spirit and relationships; in our marriages, as parents, at school, in our work and community, in our churches, with our money, and in all our daily experiences. We long to grow through hard times, live fully alive as our best and most authentic self, cultivating positive spiritual emotions like joy, gratitude and hope.

The big question is: "How do I do that?" In my quest for a response and solutions personally and professionally, I have integrated and developed biblically based interventions and practical guides for tending the soul.

Biblical Basis for Flourish Coaching

The righteous will flourish like a palm tree,
they will grow like a cedar of Lebanon;
planted in the house of the LORD,
they will flourish in the courts of our God.
They will still bear fruit in old age,
they will stay fresh and green [fresh and flourishing]. (Ps 92:12-14)

In the beginning, God created all things reflecting his beautiful harmony and wholeness—shalom. Then due to the fall, this earth and its people were and continue to be vandalized and broken. We languish. It's the story of our lives on earth. However, the rest of the story is about God's deep love for us, desiring and providing for our continual transformation and renewal to *flourish,* living fully alive in wholeness. To flourish is to be aware of his amazing grace and presence in the ordinary.

The "flourish" theme resonates with our souls, reaching a deep longing for practical transformation and hope. "This is what I want!" is often what I hear. Flourish Counseling and Coaching is about this redemptive journey back to shalom, "staying fresh and green" even in difficult times.

What Does It Mean to "Flourish"?

You flourish when you have a sense of well-being and can function positively in your personal and social life. You flourish when you experience high levels of emotional, psychological and social well-being. This includes a life of vigor, vitality, goodness, generativity and continuous growth. You are able to have close relationships and a meaningful and purposeful life. It is a life that has fulfillment, using your strengths to be creative, contributing in meaningful and productive ways. From a Christian perspective, the "fullness of life" and "the good life" is having God's life in us. Living fully alive in the "now." The journey includes becoming resilient through adversity, during struggles, sadness, sickness and loneliness. It means growing in our gifts and strengths, using them for the good of others, which nourishes and blesses others.

The Spirit of God is our partner on the journey, helping us develop both a spiritual and a psychological immune system, so to speak, to help us effectively deal with life challenges, conflict, stress, anxiety and depression. The pathways that we journey on and with our clients lead us toward thriving. Integrated well-being is the antidote; intentional lifestyle is the medicine; and charismatic, contemplative spirituality is the cure.

Integrated well-being is the antidote. You are created as a whole person, with all life systems designed to work together. Your spirit, mind, brain, emotions, body and relationships—all interact in a highly complex and harmonious way. Most of life involves these life systems:

- Love and relationship system
- Joy and gratitude system
- Peace and tranquility system
- Hope and resilience system

You cannot be spiritually healthy if you are not emotionally healthy. Your thoughts and emotions impact your physical health. When you live within this divine order of faith and science working together, you flourish.

Intentional lifestyle is the medicine. Daily habits and intentional life rhythms in all life systems determine the choices you make for growth, happiness, health and well-being. Seventy-five percent of stresses and modern diseases are preventable through lifestyle changes and choices. Intentional wellness living in all areas of life changes thoughts, daily habits—it changes your life.

Contemplative spirituality is the cure. In the midst of the busyness of life, with so many distractions and stressors, it is essential to stay centered and balanced, making time to slow down, be quiet and connect with God. Regular spiritual practices such as prayer, meditation, study of the Word, community, serving—ways that draw us close to God and others—help us be attuned to God's Holy Spirit and presence in our daily lives. Intentional sacred rhythms calm your mind, change your heart rate and brain states, providing joy and tranquility.

FAITH-BASED FLOURISH COACHING

Flourish in Life Coaching integrates cutting edge new research and interventions in neurobiology, faith-based positive psychology and contemplative Christian spirituality that can be integrated into any model of coaching or counseling. Flourish Growth Groups are also helpful for sharing life stories and the journey of discovery together.

The principles and themes outlined below can be woven into the ongoing coaching relationship, or approached as six-, seven- or twelve-week sessions.

Discover how to flourish: Transforming systems by asking powerful questions and creating honest inventories. The first session or initial phase of coaching includes basic assessment—powerful questions and questionnaires that can be used as you begin with your client on the coaching journey. This covers the foundations of understanding how we are designed to live in shalom—well-being in all life systems: body, mind, emotions, spirit and relationships.

Wellness inventories provide an opportunity to understand a whole-person model, assess overall health and wellness, as well as discern areas of flourishing and languishing. The wellness wheel, and other whole-person inventories can be used to help the client identify areas of strength and weakness, setting goals for where to change and grow.

Flourish in relationship with God: God attachment system, known by faith, prayer and spiritual practices. The most important human need in order to flourish is to be loved—not only by others, but especially by God. Our brains and hearts are hardwired for love. God's love changes everything. Our relationship with God and others is what life is all about. We grow and flourish in well-being through relationship attachments with God and one another.

In this session or phase of coaching, help clients become aware of their relationship with God, their God image, and how they can explore, receive and absorb God's love before they can truly love themselves and love others. Be sensitive to meet them where they are, and go at their pace, exploring what is most meaningful to them at this time.

Explore spiritual practices, intentional sacred life rhythms with your client such as: prayer, reading Scripture, sacred readings, biblical meditation, spending time in quiet appreciating the beauty of nature and reaching out to others. Loving God and loving others lights up our brains, sustains our health and well-being, and leads to longevity.

Flourish in relationships: Safe-haven relationships and the human attachment system, known by healthy relationship connections and small groups. Healthy attachments are based on who you are, and who you are becoming. God uses our relationships to help us grow and mature our character. Relationships are God's crucible for transformational change—for revealing himself to us as the ultimate safe-haven relationship. Learn and understand how to integrate attachment theory for effective relationship interventions and growth.

Explore clients' relationship attachment "wellness wheel," and other relationship assessments such as love languages, attachment styles and relationship skills for communicating, solving conflict and forgiveness. In what ways are they flourishing in relationships, and how can they be more intentional to grow in the health and balance of their relationships? Who do they do life with? What disconnections, unresolved conflict or unforgiveness is impacting their lives? Encourage resolution, connection with others individually face-to-face and in small groups.

Flourish in positive emotions of joy and gratitude: Pleasure and joy system, known by appreciation, thankfulness and positive emotions. Your joy system is more than feelings. It is a state of being that encompasses your brain, mind, heart and even the cells in your body. All these systems of your life are involved in the pursuit of pure pleasure and enjoyment of positive emotion, and are channeled through the brain's pleasure center. Damaging the pleasure center with overstimulation, abuse or neglect can interfere with the ability to experience joy and other positive emotions. In this phase, asses the emotional health of the clients and what drives their lives. What factors could be interfering with the health of their pleasure centers? In what ways could they create a healthier pleasure/joy system?

Nurturing a grateful heart is one of the primary pathways to a healthier body, a happier mind and relationships. The practice of gratitude can actually change the state of your brain, right down to your neurons. Anger and gratitude can't exist together. Gratitude leads to infusing daily life with happier moods, more optimism, better sleep, lower levels of chronic stress, fewer physical symptoms of illness and pain, and the ability to avoid emotions that cultivate bitterness, envy, stress and depression when faced with life challenges.

Gratitude and positive emotional vitality expand your mental ability, creativity and problem-solving skills. Gratitude and joy build physical health and good relationships that support you through life challenges. The benefits from counting your blessings are tangible both emotionally and physically. Joy and gratitude bring alive what is good in life and may be even more valuable in hard times. Mounds of research verify that through practical daily exercises, gratitude and joy can be cultivated as a contagious gateway to other positive emotions, creating an upward spiral effect, even facilitating forgiveness.

Explore some of these natural joy and gratitude boosters with your clients, such as counting your blessings, keeping a gratitude journal, writing thank-you notes and appreciation letters, and singing to praise and worship music.

Flourish in peace and tranquility: Stress and tranquility system, known by practicing relaxation and Christian meditation. "A plain and simple life is a full life," according to Proverbs 13:7 (*The Message*). You are created with the capacity to benefit from a peace and tranquility system. Your parasympathetic system stabilizes you with peace and tranquility after the sympathetic system responds to stress. This is your essential nature that needs to be guarded and cultivated. It is up to you, with the help of the Spirit of

God, to maintain this harmonious state, managing your stress response system, worries and other factors that interrupt this serenity.

Explore with your client the causes of stress, worry and anxiety. Explore methods for mental hygiene, healthy habits of the mind, how to cultivate a healthy stress-response system, how to relax the body and calm the mind, and practical antidotes to stress and worry such as mindfulness, meditation and living fully present to the now.

Flourish in hope and resilience during adversity: Hope and resilience system, known by surrender, building buffers, and life purpose and passion. Without hope and a vision for the future, you languish. Although you are created with an amazing capacity for resilience, to cope and bounce back, hope isn't innate. But the Bible reveals and now science proves you can learn to cultivate hope to equip you through struggles. You can even grow, develop character and become a better person through challenging times. Ultimate hope for all things in life is in God. He gives the desires of the heart, direction for each day and into tomorrow. He is your strength through struggles and the keeper of hope and the future.

Help clients learn ways to build their psychological and spiritual immune system, cultivating character and hope in the midst of life challenges. Walk alongside them as they learn to surrender their lives and goals, trusting God to reveal his plan for redemption, restoration and being fully alive in him.

Develop your flourish-in-life plan: Arrange your life to flourish, known by life planning and intentional living. The final phase of Flourish in Life Coaching helps clients learn how to create an intentional life plan, discovering God's life purpose and calling for the season of life they are in. Summarizing what clients have discovered regarding how they can grow and change in each life system, encourage them to develop therapeutic lifestyle changes in all areas of life.

Exercises to Foster Flourishing

- Healthy nutrition and plant-based diet
- Time outdoors in nature
- Cultivation of healthy relationships
- Restorative recreation
- Relaxation, rest, recuperation

- Weekly sabbath
- Vacations
- Sleep hygiene: Getting enough sleep at night, including REM sleep
- Stress-management techniques for lowering the stress-response system

Healthy Habits of the Mind and Heart

- Practice and participate in spiritual activities and faith beliefs.
- Make family and close friends a priority (staying close to your "tribe").
- Have close relationships to "do life with."
- Serve others by volunteering, contributing in practical ways.
- Be involved in the community.
- Participate in small groups.
- Belong to a healthy social network.
- Limit television, technology and digital use.
- Have purpose in life.
- Set goals with practical ways to reach them.
- Develop a one- to three-year life plan.

How Does God "Show Up"?

Emphasizing an integrative, whole-person perspective and being open to the fullness of the Spirit of God fosters reflection and provision for wellness in all life systems, spiritual growth and stronger relationships.

Those coming for counseling and coaching often feel vandalized, wilting, broken in some way, longing for renewal, transformation, to be their best most authentic self, living fully alive in God, experiencing the balance of beauty and goodness.

This approach is effective with those who have reflective insight ability, who want to grow, change, get breakthrough from living a stagnant unfulfilled life, or are dealing with mild stress, anxiety, depression or going through a change or life challenge.

Those who experience the Lord work in their lives through these principles report that it brought attention to areas in life that, due to neglect, contributed to languishing. Through reflection, assessments and prayer, they discover simple yet profound ways to focus more intentionally and practically during the day on connecting with the source of life, Jesus Christ.

Others note that they are finally able to put into words what they have been trying to articulate and have desired for a long time. They realize a deeper understanding to the words "life abundantly," being reminded that God did say that if we would seek him, we will find him. And through intentional living, pursuing pathways to thrive, they do.

The focus on living well as a whole person—physical, spiritual and emotional—is important, even as a mature Christian. When life gets out of balance, the coaching relationship can help guide focus on inviting the Spirit of God to reveal how to get back to the basics for wholeness and well-being. Integrating these principles also helps remind us that in order to give out we must become a vessel that is first filled with the Spirit, to bear the fruit of the Spirit. As we walk alongside clients to partner with God, developing a plan to live fully alive, maintain joy and balance during "dry" seasons, we can cultivate spiritual renewal by staying balanced as a whole person, growing in the beauty of transformation in Christ.

References and Recommended Resources

Integrating Christian Human Flourishing

Hart Weber, C. (2010). *Flourish: Discover the daily joy of abundant vibrant living.* Bloomington, MN: Bethany House.

Find information on Flourish In Life Coaching and training, retreat opportunities, reflection exercises, quizzes, free downloads and more at <www.flourishinlifeandrelationships.com>, or email drcatherine@howtoflourish.com.

Positive Psychology Coaching

Biswas-Diener, R. (2010). *Practicing positive psychology coaching: Assessment, activities and strategies for success.* Hoboken, NJ: Wiley.

Biswas-Diener, R., & Dean, B. (2007). *Positive psychology coaching: Putting the science of happiness to work for your clients.* Hoboken, NJ: Wiley.

Gratitude

Emmons, R. A. (2008). *Thanks! How the new science of gratitude can make you happier.* New York: Mariner.

Voskamp, A. (2011). *One thousand gifts: A dare to live fully right where you are.* Grand Rapids: Zondervan.

Neuroscience

Lipton, B. (2008). *Biology of belief.* New York: Hay House.

Thompson, C. (2010). *Anatomy of the soul.* Carol Stream, IL: SaltRiver.

Spiritual Formation

Boa, K. (2001). *Conformed to his image.* Grand Rapids: Zondervan.

Calhoun, A. A. (2005). *Spiritual disciplines handbook: Practices that transform us.* Downers Grove, IL: InterVarsity Press.

Foster, R. J. (1998). *Celebration of discipline: The path to spiritual growth.* New York: HarperCollins.

Willard, D. (2002). *Renovation of the heart: Putting on the character of Christ.* Colorado Springs: NavPress.

Stress and Anxiety

Hart, A. (1995). *Adrenaline and stress.* Nashville: Thomas Nelson.

Hart, A. (2001). *The anxiety cure.* Nashville: Thomas Nelson.

Hart, A. (2010). *Sleep, it does a family good.* Carol Stream, IL: Tyndale.

Part Four

TOWARD UNIVERSAL TRANSFORMATIONAL PRACTICE

21

Transformative Encounters

When God Steps In

David W. Appleby

And since the Sixteenth Century, when Science was born, the minds of men have been increasingly engaged in those specialized inquiries for which truncated thought is the correct method. It is, therefore, not in the least astonishing that they should have forgotten the evidence for the supernatural.

C. S. Lewis, *Miracles*

The Divine Encounter: A Vision Lost

This book sprang from the conviction that there are many pastors, Christian counselors and students who sincerely want to integrate their faith and their practice. Yet, somewhere along the way that vision was lost. Some took their faith into secular graduate counseling programs where the possibility was never considered. Some became believers after completing their secular counseling programs so they were unaware that such a thing could even be done. Some others were trained in a Christian seminary or institution where attempts were made to integrate a basic understanding of the Bible and theology into a graduate counseling program.

However, it is not difficult, especially for those pursuing professional practice, to guess which portion of the educational program would be emphasized. Modern counseling and clinical psychology has made tremendous strides in recent years as the field has focused upon empirically based secular theoretical development and therapeutic resources. Many Christian counselors, however, have not given much attention to learning about the resources available in Christianity. After all, having a firm understanding of redemption and sanctification isn't going to help you on the day of judgment when you are taking your licensure exam and need to know your way around the Diagnostic and Statistical Manual of Mental Disorders (DSM) and the challenges of clinical treatment planning.

Too many Christian counselors can attest to working toward licensure while losing part of the dream that drove them to graduate school in the first place: the vision of being God's helping hand in the lives of broken people. It is so easy to simply become another licensed clinician, working successfully within a counseling agency, or building a private practice and focusing on making a living. What was the driving force early in one's career can become a point of contention and discomfort in our professional practice.

We hope that this book may help you to "blow on the embers" of that fire, or at least return you to your original vision of being a trusted conduit of all things helpful in Christ. I know that, over the years, I have become a lot less psychological and a lot more spiritual in orientation. Over and over again God has made it abundantly clear that his way is best and that following it resulted in the most potent and long-lasting change in clients' lives.

Salvation: The Basis of Encounter

Every one of the authors in this book shares something in common. We each want our clients to encounter God in some meaningful way. We want to create an environment where such an encounter can occur because we believe that it will result in significant transformational change. Our interventions presume the fact that we are a "new creation" as a result of our being regenerated by Christ (2 Cor 5:17). Salvation empowers us for any future encounter. Salvation touches us on multiple levels. We have seen that it impacts our

- Identity: We are no longer who we were. We have changed ownership and gone from death to life, from walking in darkness to walking in light (Eph 5:8) and have become citizens of a new kingdom under the care and direction of a new King who is also our Father. We can now come into his presence unashamed because we know that he loves us.

- Cognition: We no longer think as we used to think. We have gone from "futile" thinking, those thoughts springing from senseless darkened hearts (Rom 1:21) to ones that can now know him, see his hand and hear his voice. We can now think his thoughts.
- Affect: We can now feel what our Savior feels. Ezekiel 36:26-27 says, "I will give you a new heart and put a new spirit in you; I will remove from you your heart of stone and give you a heart of flesh." With our new hearts of flesh the things that break his heart now break our hearts. The things that bring him joy also bring us joy.
- Relationships: We have been reoriented in a way that touches our core. Everything shifts. We discover that, while we still love and respect our parents and other family members, we now know that our primary connection is not to them, but to our heavenly Father, our brother Jesus and the rest of his family, our fellow believers. Revelation 2:17 speaks of us receiving a new name. With our adoption into God's family even the ties of blood and origin are transformed.
- Behavior: The psalmist, in Psalm 40:3, says that our God has "put a new song in my mouth, a hymn of praise to our God" that will cause many people to see and fear and put their trust in the Lord. This gift spills out of our hearts and changes how we act. People see that a change has taken place and are drawn to the One who brings transformation. Sanctification and growth in God changes what we do and what we say. We encounter God personally in the experience of salvation.

However, as Christian counselors, we need to remember that salvation is not the end, but the beginning of spiritual life. God's goal for us is that we become like his Son, Jesus. Ultimately everything that occurs in the life of a believer is working toward that goal, our transformation. Romans 8:28-30 says,

> And we know that in all things God works for the good of those who love him, who have been called according to his purpose. For those God foreknew he also predestined to be conformed to the image of his Son, that he might be the firstborn among many brothers and sisters. And those he predestined, he also called; those he called, he also justified; those he justified, he also glorified.

Sanctification is a lifelong developmental process that changes us to our core. We realize that we were created for fellowship with God, and that something fundamental to who we are is missing if that relationship is not established and promoted. There is more to life than all that surrounds us. Rather than giving ourselves to pleasure and power, we are called to be "in Christ" and to live a life in the Holy Spirit (Eph 1). We are challenged to "walk by the Spirit" (Gal 5:16); "be filled with the Spirit" (Eph 5:18); produce the "fruit of the Spirit" (Gal 5:22-23); "live by the Spirit" and "keep in step with the Spirit" (Gal 5:25); and exercise the "gifts" of the Spirit (Rom 12:6; 1 Cor 12:1). Paul points out in Romans 8:6 that the mind controlled by the Spirit is life and peace.

Life and peace is, to my way of thinking, what Christian counseling is all about. It is about helping clients develop a mind that is controlled by the Holy Spirit so that they can experience life and peace. That is what each of the interventional models covered in this book attempts to do, bring life and peace. As I read and reviewed each of these chapters, I noticed that a pattern began to emerge. Each of these authors seeks to reintroduce the client to God in some way. They want the client to discover who God really is. Each wants his or her clients to find out that God doesn't hate them; doesn't judge them or abandon them. Instead, he loves them, accepts them and is always with them. All their sins, along with the accompanying guilt and shame, have been placed on his Son, Jesus, on their behalf. Death has been defeated. Each of these authors, in his or her attempt to make this real for the client, sets the stage for an encounter with God. The interventional encounters described in this book fall into three broad categories: the propositional encounter, the imaginal encounter and the power encounter.

Transformative Interventional Encounters

Propositional encounters. A propositional encounter is one where the Holy Spirit meets you through an encounter with truth as revealed in the Scriptures. When Jesus was in the wilderness in Matthew 4 and Mark 1, he was tempted by Satan but consistently overcame him by quoting the Scriptures. Paul reminded Timothy of their importance in 2 Timothy 3:14-17 where he said:

> But as for you, continue in what you have learned and have become convinced of, because you know those from whom you learned it, and how from infancy you have known the Holy Scriptures, which are able to make you

> wise for salvation through faith in Christ Jesus. All Scripture is God-breathed and is useful for teaching, rebuking, correcting and training in righteousness, so that the servant of God may be thoroughly equipped for every good work.

In the propositional encounter there is God-generated awareness and acknowledgment that what God is saying is true and applicable to us. As Pastor Bill Johnson says, "Life doesn't come from revelation, it comes from the encounter brought about by the revelation" (Johnson, n.d.). We meet God through the Word, whether we are reading it, singing it or praying it. From the Scriptures we derive biblical principles—generalized truths that are logical extensions of the Word. One cannot be touched by the Word of God and not be transformed. Hebrews 4:12-13 says: "For the word of God is alive and active. Sharper than any double-edged sword, it penetrates even to dividing soul and spirit, joints and marrow; it judges the thoughts and attitudes of the heart. Nothing in all creation is hidden from God's sight. Everything is uncovered and laid bare before the eyes of him to whom we must give account."

One can see the power of the Word of God in a propositional encounter. Yet it is so much more than that. It is overwhelmingly personal. You can't discover the truth that someone loves you without it touching every part of who you are. Edward Welch's biblical counseling (chap. 5), Siang-Yang Tan's Christian model of spiritually oriented cognitive behavioral therapy (chap. 6) and Leslie Vernick's TRUTH Principle (chap. 16) would probably be the clearest examples of this kind of encounter.

Imaginal encounters. An imaginal encounter is envisioned truth. This is an encounter that is framed by the Scriptures, but is more experientially based. When questioned by his disciples as to why he was speaking to the people in parables, Jesus turns to them and describes a people who can neither hear nor understand because of their calloused hearts. They have closed their eyes and ears so that they won't have to encounter God and be turned away from their sin or experience healing. Jesus' disciples, however, are not in this category. Jesus says to them, "But blessed are your eyes because they see, and your ears because they hear" (Mt 13:13-17). As believers we can see and we can hear. In a similar passage the apostle Paul writes to the believers in the church of Ephesus that he is praying "that the eyes of your heart may be enlightened in order that you may know the hope to which he has called you, the riches of his glorious inheritance in his holy people, and his incomparably great power for us who believe" (Eph 1:18-19).

An example of an envisioned or imaginal encounter occurred over in Acts 10:9-16. The Scriptures say:

> About noon the following day as they were on their journey and approaching the city, Peter went up on the roof to pray. He became hungry and wanted something to eat, and while the meal was being prepared, he fell into a trance. He saw heaven opened and something like a large sheet being let down to earth by its four corners. It contained all kinds of four-footed animals, as well as reptiles and birds. Then a voice told him, "Get up, Peter. Kill and eat." "Surely not, Lord!" Peter replied. "I have never eaten anything impure or unclean." The voice spoke to him a second time, "Do not call anything impure that God has made clean." This happened three times, and immediately the sheet was taken back to heaven.

In this passage God used this encounter to address and correct Peter's attitude toward the Gentiles, whom he saw as unclean.

In the following verses God takes Peter to Cornelius the Centurion who had been instructed by an angel to seek him out for instruction. When Peter gets to Cornelius's house he finds out about Cornelius's own encounter, as described in Acts 10:30-33.

> Cornelius answered: "Four days ago I was in my house praying at this hour, at three in the afternoon. Suddenly a man in shining clothes stood before me and said, 'Cornelius, God has heard your prayer and remembered your gifts to the poor. Send to Joppa for Simon who is called Peter. He is a guest in the home of Simon the tanner, who lives by the sea.' So I sent for you immediately, and it was good of you to come. Now we are all here in the presence of God to listen to everything the Lord has commanded you to tell us."

The most famous encounter of this nature is found in the writings of John the Revelator who received the revelation of Jesus Christ. Revelation 1:1-3 says: "The revelation of Jesus Christ, which God gave him to show his servants what must soon take place. He made it known by sending his angel to his servant John, who testifies to everything he saw—that is, the word of God and the testimony of Jesus Christ."

This encounter happened as "On the Lord's Day I [John] was in the Spirit" (Rev 1:10). While no believer today is ever going to have a revelation such as this, God still wants to communicate with and reveal himself to his children on a personal level. He wants to show us that he loves us, that he is faithful to us and that he will never abandon us.

The imaginal encounter touches both our heads and our hearts largely through God-guided visualization. Models that focus upon prayer, meditation and imagining truth being expressed and applied to us in this manner would fit into this category. This reflects many of the models contained in this book. It usually involves both seeing God and knowing him (1 Jn 3:6). No one who has seen God or knows him like this can remain unchanged. This encounter is found in many of the models in this book.

Power encounter. The third category of encounter is the power encounter. This type is truly action based. It is the aggressive use of the power of God for the expanse of the kingdom of God in the lives of both believers and unbelievers. It has the potential to change clients' understanding of themselves, their perception of God and their relationships with others. It can also result in physical healing. Luke 10:17-20 says:

> The seventy-two returned with joy and said, "Lord, even the demons submit to us in your name." He replied, "I saw Satan fall like lightning from heaven. I have given you authority to trample on snakes and scorpions and to overcome all the power of the enemy; nothing will harm you. However, do not rejoice that the spirits submit to you, but rejoice that your names are written in heaven."

And in 2 Corinthians 10:3-5, we read: "For though we live in the world, we do not wage war as the world does. The weapons we fight with are not the weapons of the world. On the contrary, they have divine power to demolish strongholds. We demolish arguments and every pretension that sets itself up against the knowledge of God, and we take captive every thought to make it obedient to Christ."

All of these verses, and others, associate power encounters with confronting everything that would stand against God, whether cognitive strongholds, arguments, pretension, lies, demonic spirits and so on. They are also used for confronting and overcoming the power of demonic spirits.

Each of the interventional models in this book, if you look at their major defining characteristic, could best be described as fitting into one of these three types of encounters. However, most of the authors, including myself, would argue that their models are too broad to fit into only one category; most have elements that are also found in other categories. I think that this is true, especially since these models can be dynamic with their application varying from practitioner to practitioner based upon their level of training, experience, inclination, faith and biblical understanding.

Figure 21.1 demonstrates the interaction between the various encounters and how they flow into each other and, in turn, flow into and inform the various interventions. These interventions set the stage for a divine encounter and transformational change on some level.

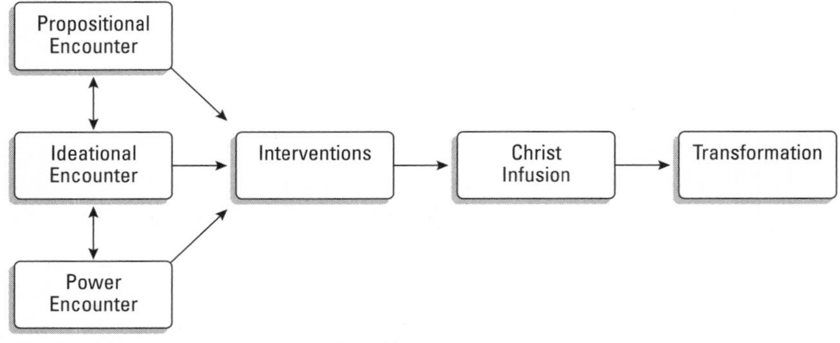

Figure 21.1. An encounter model for transformational change

Christ infusion in Christian-accommodative and Christian-derived models. In recent years we have witnessed another form of model analysis. What are often called religiously accommodative treatments that focus on specific religious approaches to treatment therapies have appeared (Worthington, Hook, Davis & McDaniel, 2011). Tan's model (chap. 6) of spiritually oriented cognitive behavioral therapy would be an example. Some of these are called Christian-accommodative models. These are well-respected, more Bible-based and empirically validated secular models that have been adjusted to accommodate and incorporate Christian content and practice. Accommodation can work well because many of the Christian counseling techniques that we seek to integrate into our secular models can be reframed in ways that allow them to be seen as accepted protocols. This accommodation also makes us Christian counselors somewhat more acceptable in the eyes of consumers, licensing boards and insurance companies. For the therapist trying to make a living doing counseling, there is much to be said for that.

Another group of models are called Christian-derived models. These models have Christian assumptions, beliefs and practices at their foundation and woven into their worldview (Johnson, Worthington, Hook & Aten, 2013). These models may also benefit from the knowledge and insight that psychology provides without compromising their godly foundation. Johnson (see foreword) noted that these models "are especially and uniquely reflective of Christian distinctives and . . . are therefore more likely to manifest particularly potent Christian treatment and less likely to be diluted by the secular assumptions of modern models of therapy." In short, Christian counseling tends to produce Christian outcomes (e.g., biblical worldview, godly behavior, etc.).

Johnson (see foreword) suggests that those models that hold on to their Christian distinctives are more likely to be powerful, in that they have not been diluted by secular assumptions that are inherent in modern models of therapy. Would it be safe to say that the more that our work looks like the work of secular counselors the less impact the truth of the gospel has? We cannot expect secular counseling to do more than what secular counseling is capable of doing. Some things only God can do. Royal (2012) says that "Christians simply cannot afford to have a worldview that rules out the supernatural."

Indeed, as Johnson points out in the foreword, "It may be that the most Christian-derived models had to be developed by those who were not trained and socialized by contemporary secular psychology."

Time for full disclosure. I do deliverance (exorcism). My world is full of broken people who have evil personalities deeply attached to their lives. These entities talk to them, compel them, drive them, torment them and seek to steal, kill and destroy them and their families. I live in a world full of divine impressions, Holy Spirit–directed nudges and spontaneous God-placed thoughts and pictures. In my work, I have to have a divine intervention if anything productive is going to take place.

Both the Christian-accommodative model and the Christian-derived model describe the perspective and expectations of the therapist. In the Christian-accommodative model we know what secular theory we will use and what elements of Christianity we want to accommodate. When we use the Christian-derived model we know that we are going to have an even stronger focus upon the Scriptures and the work of the Holy Spirit. Yet both models acknowledge that a miraculous encounter with the living God is possible and desirable. We all, regardless of whether we use a more clinical or more ministry-based model, want God to intervene and show himself to be the Lord of all.

As I reflected upon these two models I became aware that neither addresses the encounter with God in the moment. I call this emphasis upon the encounter in the moment Christ-infusion. I view it as the (theo)logical extension and experiential conclusion of both Christian-accomodative and Christian-derived models.

Christian counselors who adopt a Christian-accommodative or a Christian-derived model want God to step into the process and make it more than any purely secular model can be. We all want our work to be Christ-infused. We want our living God to be transformatively encountered by ourselves and by our clients in a moment in time. This "moment" may be propositional in nature and consist of many "mini-moments" as strongholds are pulled down and a client's whole perspective on life is changed over time. It can be imaginal in nature as God reveals his presence in a difficult time in the client's life through an image or vision. It can be a power encounter as God proves in a moment that he is indeed Lord over all. In all cases, this Christ-infused moment starts with God (through a supernatural intervention of the Holy Spirit), affects the client in time and is experienced holistically—touching the heart, head and spirit.

When I was a child it was my job to bring buckets of water from a spring that was down by the river up to our summer cottage. I was the "running water" for my family. The path to the spring was almost impossible to locate, especially at night, unless you knew it was there. That is the purpose of this book: to point to multiple paths where God can be encountered in transformative ways in Christian counseling. If we don't know a path exists, we can never expect to search it out.

Both Christian-accommodative and Christian-derived therapists want God to intervene. To see it happen, however, requires a shift in perspective. Not only do we have to know that Christ-infusion is a possibility, but we have to want it, be open to it, and expect to be God's instrument in the accomplishment of his purposes. We have to be intentional. John 5:19 says, "Very truly I tell you, the Son can do nothing by himself; he can do only what he sees his Father doing, because whatever the Father does the Son also does." To be most effective in our work, the same thing needs to be said of us.

In a very real way we are participants in the moment that God touches the client. Professional training is seen as supplementing the work of the Holy Spirit. The counselor says, as Zeider does in chapter seven, "Here I am, Lord; is there any part of my training that you can use to help this person?" In order to work at this level, we as counselors need to have a deep, intimate connection—an encounter, even—with the Spirit every time we work.

Christian counseling at its best requires the therapist to expect God to be an active participant in the therapeutic practice, inviting him to engage in a genuine conversation with him and with the client in the moment, to have an ongoing dialogue with the one who brings healing.

I know that I wrestle with this all the time. It is such a temptation to fall back upon years of experience rather than take the time to learn to pick out the voice of God for my client from all the other distractions that normally occupy my thoughts. I have to intentionally quiet my spirit to hear his voice and be prepared for his interjection of unexpected thoughts and images into my mind. I have to expect unknown things to be revealed to me and resist trying to lean on my own understanding (Prov 3:5) to "figure it all out." I have to be willing to use the gifts of the Holy Spirit—a whole toolbox of powerful tools that were given to the church for the purpose of strengthening both the church and the individual. I am sure that my fellow authors wrestle with similar challenges. Cookbook therapy is rarely Spirit-breathed, as God resists recipes and boxes. While we know that God will never violate his Word, we also know that he doesn't hesitate to violate "our understanding of His word" (Johnson, n.d.). Jesus said in John 3:5-8:

> Very truly I tell you, no one can enter the kingdom of God unless they are born of water and the Spirit. Flesh gives birth to flesh, but the Spirit gives birth to spirit. You should not be surprised at my saying, "You must be born again." The wind blows wherever it pleases. You hear its sound, but you cannot tell where it comes from or where it is going. So it is with everyone born of the Spirit.

I want my work to be Christ-infused, as do the other authors in this book. We have seen elements of it spread throughout all the chapters. All of my fellow authors have pushed themselves into unfamiliar territory and have thus experienced unexpected results.

Many of us, because of classwork required for licensing and the pressure of time, have found that our graduate programs, while strong in psychology and counseling, didn't teach us how to be open to God-directed transformative encounters, either in ourselves or in our clients. I never learned how to spend time standing in the presence of the Holy Spirit with my wet finger in the air trying to discern which way he was moving. I found that it was often much easier for me to just blow on my own finger and to choose my own direction.

As Christian counselors we are called to be better than that. We are called to experience a Christ-infused encounter of our own. Being Christian counselors allows us to move beyond what we learned in school and what is reinforced by our profession; we have access to the Spirit of the Living God, who is willing to interact with us for the benefit of his children. Taking some risks and stepping out in faith as the Spirit leads us can result in seeing people set free. We have to do this, however, in a clinically sensitive and ethically appropriate way: always aware of the needs and desires of our clients. One thing I know is the old saying: If we want to see things we've never seen, we have to be willing to go where we've never been. This was Jesus' task. It is also ours. Jesus said in Luke 4:18-19:

> The Spirit of the Lord is on me,
> because he has anointed me
> to proclaim good news to the poor.
> He has sent me to proclaim freedom for the prisoners
> and recovery of sight for the blind,
> to set the oppressed free,
> to proclaim the year of the Lord's favor.

References and Recommended Resources

Aten, J. D., McMinn, M. R., & Worthington, E. L., Jr. (2011). *Spiritually oriented interventions for counseling and psychotherapy.* Washington, DC: American Psychological Association.

Johnson, B. (n.d.). Bill Johnson Quotes. *Christian Quotes.* Retrieved from <https://sites.google.com/site/christianquotes2/home/projects>.

Johnson, E. L., Worthington, E. L., Jr., Hook, J. N., & Aten, J. D. (2013). Evidence-based practice in the light of the Christian tradition(s): Reflections and future directions. In Worthington, E. L., Jr., Johnson, E. L., Hook, J. N., & Aten, J. D. (Eds.), *Evidence-based practices for Christian counseling and psychotherapy.* Downers Grove, IL: InterVarsity Press.

Lewis, C. S. (1947). *Miracles.* New York: Macmillan.

Royal, K. (2012). Investigating the practice of Christian exorcism and the methods used to cast out demons. *Journal of Christian Ministry, 4.* Retrieved from <http://journalofchristianministry.org/article/view/10287/7073>.

Worthington, E. L., Jr., Hook, J. N., Davis, D. E., & McDaniel, M. A. (2011). Religion and spirituality. In J. C. Norcross (Ed.), *Psychotherapy relationships that work* (2nd ed., pp. 402-19). New York: Oxford University Press.

22

Toward a Universal Experiential Helping Model

George Ohlschlager

Doing [Christian counseling] is much about growing as a person. On our transformational model, the fully human person is one who is conformed to Christ's image of loving God and neighbor by means of union and being filled with the Holy Spirit. This person will have a true understanding of what it means to be whole, the paths and detours needed to be traveled, what the process will feel like, and the various means of grace that will assist one along the way.

John Coe and Todd Hall, *Psychology in the Spirit: Contours of a Transformational Psychology*

Christian counseling has perpetually searched for a comprehensive theory—a metatheory or overarching worldview that can integrate biblical wisdom, personality theory, developmental constructs, spiritual formation and especially what it means to live in Christ. Most important, a widely embraced metatheory could guide counseling practice in a dynamic way, a process becoming wedded to practice so that each realm helps shape the other as both theory and practice grow to maturity (see McMinn & Campbell, 2007, and Tan, 2011, for probably the best and most comprehensive Christian models to date). Christian counseling needs a metamodel that will help guide our helping efforts to the self-revealing I AM, especially as many of us try to sort our way through myriad counseling schools or differing theoretical perspectives.

Finally, a useful metamodel will be an empirical one—using clinical science to help Christian counselors devise and deliver more effective interventions. A Christian perspective on empirically supported treatments (ESTs) could be known as the BEST interventions—Biblically based, Empirically Supported Treatments. Such a model will not be slavish to empiricism or a naturalistic worldview, but will follow an orderly and natural path while remaining open to supernatural intervention, with methodologies constructed to allow for and observe those interventions in practice (for models and principles rooted in modern psychology, see Aten, McMinn & Worthington, 2011). While a few of the models in this book provide the validating research, most models still require empirical confirmation

In addition, we hope this metatheory will encourage churches to focus more attention on prevention and wellness and to incorporate the best of the positive psychology movement. Understanding how to promote healthy relationships and God-honoring psychospiritual behavior, and how to prevent the development of unhealthy and detrimental outcomes, would seem to have a profound future in the church. Such healthy and maturing processes should also be seen as fitting hand in glove with maintenance strategies that intend not only to maintain the gains made in psychotherapy, but also to build on them and flourish as sources of maturity beyond mere gain maintenance, as important as that is in psychotherapy.

THE TRANSFORMATIONAL INTERVENTION OF JESUS CHRIST

Jesus Christ, as always, is the master model on how to influence desired change, including change in just one session. The interpersonal context of calling his disciples was highlighted in John 1:10-11: "He was in the world, and though the world was made through him, the world did not recognize him. He came to that which was his own, but his own did not receive him." John reveals a serious disconnect between Jesus and his own people—the people he had come to die for and regenerate—and Nathanael's call is a key story of this social disconnect and how Jesus used one session to transform a true skeptic.

The call of Nathanael. John 1:35-51 tells of the call of Christ to his first disciples. The story of Philip and Nathanael (John 1:43-51) is the most detailed narrative. After Christ had challenged Philip to "Follow me," he sent Philip out to call Nathanael rather than calling him directly. Why this change of pattern by the Christ—a pattern of directly calling his disciples himself? It was likely due to the resistance and skepticism of Nathanael, which is very much like the resistance and skepticism that is normative in much counseling today. This is also the perfect example of Christ using his own network of disciples to effect action rather than assuming full responsibility himself.

A skeptical Judean. Jesus used Philip because Philip and Nathanael were good friends. Philip, likely displaying some excitement, told Nathanael, "We have found the one Moses wrote about in the Law . . . Jesus of Nazareth" (Jn 1:45). This must have attracted Nathanael, yet it also grated on his prejudice because he immediately responded with the disdain that many Jews felt about Nazareth and the cities outside of historic Judah, "Nazareth! Can anything good come from there?" Philip responded with hope and challenge, "Come and see" (Jn 1:46). Nathanael did come, but it is possible that he also came complaining and threatening to return home.

A righteous Israelite. When Jesus saw him from afar, he peered supernaturally into his heart to align himself with Nathanael's own self-perception. As Nathanael approached, Jesus stated, "Here truly is an Israelite in whom there is no deceit" (Jn 1:47). Now there was plenty of time for Jesus to challenge the prejudice and sin in the man—as we are perfect only in our own self-assessments—but right then Christ had a completely different purpose in mind, which was to overcome Nathanael's skepticism and win a disciple.

From skepticism to wonder. Jesus' words did drive part of Nathanael's skepticism away and got him oriented toward rather than away from Christ. Nathanael confirmed the accuracy of Jesus' statement by asking him, "How do you know me?" (Jn 1:48). He may have been on the edge of fear and hope, wondering if he was encountering the Messiah. Jesus fulfilled those hopes by telling him what was impossible to know for any other person but the God-man himself: "*I saw you* while you were still under the fig tree before Philip called you" (Jn 1:48, emphasis mine). Here was supernatural self-disclosure, not to arrogate praise to himself but to drive all skepticism and unbelief away and to establish a deeply rooted faith in a new disciple.

From wonder to profound faith. Nathanael then knew he was in the presence of God—and it hit him with the power of a lightning strike, for he exclaimed in genuine awe and worship, "Rabbi, you are the Son of God; you are the king of

Israel" (Jn 1:49). Nathanael was in the midst of a miraculous encounter, and all the disciples must have been in awe and wonder at what they were witnessing. Jesus, who was always ready to advance a teachable moment, told them they would see even greater things; that they would see heaven open and pour out grace and truth upon the earth in the form of angelic beings.

Amazing grace. It was an amazing encounter, a completely miraculous event whereby the God-man revealed the power of his godliness. Jesus created an atmosphere that transformed resistant skepticism into open seeking and then to worshipful awe. By aligning himself with the best self of Nathanael—an empathic, strength-based and solution-focused intervention for sure—Jesus made a disciple out of someone who earlier that day would have laughed at the thought.

Truth be told, the same Spirit that transformed Nathanael is now willing and able to overcome the most stubborn resistance in the clients we encounter. All he wants is an opportunity to reveal himself, to be invited into the counseling session. All he desires is for dyadic sessions to become triadic. In all that he does, he challenges our own faith to believe that such miracles are possible with those living today.

YIELDING TO SPIRITUAL FORMATION

Christian psychologist Larry Crabb (1998) emphasizes that the core issues behind most emotional problems are in fact spiritual. He warns that too many Christian counselors bypass true spirituality in their haste to solve problems that make people uncomfortable, even when God wants to use that discomfort to draw them to himself. He adds, "Counselors who value technique above conviction and theory above character will not adequately shepherd their clients" (p. 15). We would encourage explicit incorporation of shepherding roles into Christian counseling because the shepherd pursuing his sheep was a central metaphor in Christ's description of his care and comfort for those he loved (see Crabb, 1977; Egan, 2009).

Similarly, Christian psychologist Mark McMinn (1996) writes: "Unlike competence in psychology and theology, understanding spirituality does not lend itself to credentials. . . . Spiritual training is experiential and often private. It is rarely found in the classroom or represented by graduate degrees, but it is found in private hours of prayer and devotional reflection" (p. 11). McMinn goes on to point out that no matter how disciplined we become, we never can be fully spiritually competent. He adds: "Christian doctrine teaches that we are spiritually incompetent, in need of a Redeemer. The spiritual life directs us away from illusions of competence and causes us to confront our utter helplessness and dependence on our gracious God" (pp. 11-12).

The late Charles Colson (1989) has referred to the enveloping spiritual darkness of our time as the "New Dark Ages." The barbarians of spiritual neglect are again threatening the soul of our society in the unholy assault on religious liberty and client self-determination (see appendix), and without Christ we may not be able to withstand the assault. Without a solid spiritual foundation, society quickly turns to selfism, relativism and materialism. But such indulgence always leaves us empty and asking, "Isn't there anything more to life?"

Reviving the life of the Spirit. Scripture is clear on where to begin: "anyone who comes to him must believe that he exists and that he rewards those who earnestly seek him" (Heb 11:6). "Most Christians have lost the life of their heart, and with it, their romance with God," exclaim Curtis and Eldredge (1997, p. 10). No one escapes periods of living in a spiritual desert. None of us can avoid times where we are merely going through the motions religiously. "These people say they are mine. They honor me with their lips, but their hearts are far from me" (Is 29:13 NLT).

Feeling alone and isolated during a difficult time will break us of our self-sufficiency. It drives us to the only One who truly loves us. Jesus himself faced this—his rejection, arrest, trial and crucifixion would test the limits of his humanity. His disciples too would suffer isolation, persecution and even death in his absence. But Jesus offered them the wonderful gift of his comfort. He promised to send the Holy Spirit as their counselor (Greek *paraklētos* in Jn 16:5-15). He assured us that our own personal spiritual counselor would keep our relationship with Christ vital and real every day.

The experiential soul. The human soul is the living bridge between the material and spiritual realms of living, the arena in which God is encountered. Henry Ward Beecher referred to godly spirituality as "the quickening of the soul by the influence of the Divine Spirit" (1949, p. 783). Curtis and Eldredge (1997) call it a "sacred romance." They write, "This longing is the most powerful part of any human personality. It fuels our search for meaning, for wholeness, for a sense of being truly alive. However we may describe this deep desire, it is the most important thing about us, our heart of hearts, the passion of our lives. And the voice that calls us in this place is none other than the voice of God" (p. 7).

Living as a maturing Christian. We acknowledge that our "heart of hearts" is the place of transformed living, the place where we know God most intimately. In our heart of hearts we move from knowing facts about God to knowing him as one with whom we have a personal relationship. We learn of God both through general revelation (the creation) and through special revelation (the Scriptures). Through these mechanisms we learn about his reality, his attributes, his principles and his creative power. Second Timothy 3:16-17 says: "All scripture is given by inspiration of God, and is profitable for doctrine, for reproof, for correction, for instruction in righteousness: That the man of God may be perfect, thoroughly furnished unto all good works" (KJV). God has used this world as his Word to lay the foundation for possible transformation. However, it is in the encounter, in the infusion of Christ, where God's revelation becomes living and transformative. Hence, the expanded and ongoing schema for study, research and applied living in Christian counseling would reveal:

- Secular models of change—that are developed from naturalistic psychology with no spiritual or religious influence;
- Religious-accommodating models—that are developed by integrating principles of secular change with the various world religions (e.g., Buddhist, Muslim, Ba'hai);
- Christian-accommodating models—that are developed by integrating principles of secular change with Christian beliefs and principles (such as Tan's model of spiritually oriented cognitive behavioral therapy or Vernick's model of TRUTH therapy, in this book);
- Christian-derived models—that are developed with biblical assumptions and principles throughout, and are learned cognitively by study of the Scriptures (such as Sandford's model of inner healing or Welch's model of biblical counseling in this book); and
- Christ-infusion, whether found in either Christian-accomodating or Christ-derived models, is the experiential step of living in the moment with the Spirit of God—translating any model in which Christ may live by hearing his voice and seeing his way to the advance of God's kingdom.

Hearing and obeying God's voice in the moment is the fruit of God changing us from the inside out, making us ever more like Christ himself through experientially knowing God. Reflect on the "fire of love" that God created in the heart of Richard Rolle (1993), one of England's great spiritual leaders in the 1300s:

> I cannot tell you how surprised I was the first time I felt my heart begin to warm [during prayer]. It was real warmth too, not imaginary, and it felt as if it were actually on fire. I was astonished at the way the heat surged up and how this new sensation brought great and unexpected comfort. I had to keep feeling my breast to make sure there was no physical reason for it. But once I realized that it . . . was the gift of my Maker, I was absolutely delighted [by how] this spiritual flame fed into my soul. Before the infusion of this comfort, I had never thought that we exiles could possibly have known such warmth, so sweet was the devotion it kindled. It set my soul aglow as if a real fire were burning there. . . .
>
> But this eternal and overflowing love does not come when I am relaxing, nor do I feel this spiritual ardor when I am tired out . . . nor . . . when I am absorbed with worldly interests or engrossed in never-ending arguments. At times like these I catch myself growing cold; cold until once again I put away all things external, and make a real effort to stand in my Savior's presence; only then do I abide in this inner warmth. (pp. 160-61)

Similarly, four hundred years ago Teresa of Avila (1577/1993) overcame a disabling handicap and learned to keep her focus on the Creator. She described the power of her prayerful communion with the Trinity in a brilliant allegory of seven progressively higher dwelling places she envisioned in the "Interior Castle":

> When the soul is brought into [the seventh and highest] dwelling place, the Most Blessed Trinity, all three Persons, through an intellectual vision, is revealed to it through a certain representation of the truth. First there comes an enkindling in the spirit in the manner of a cloud of magnificent splendor; [and then] these Persons are distinct, and through an admirable knowledge the soul understands as a most profound truth that all Three Persons are one substance and one power and one knowledge and one God alone. Here all three Persons communicate . . . those words of the Lord in the Gospel: that He and the Father and the Holy Spirit will come to dwell with the soul that loves him and keeps his commandments. . . . You will not be able to enter the dwelling places through your own efforts . . . but the Lord of the castle himself brings you there. (p. 199)

These levels of spiritual experience, of transformational Christ-infusion, could become a worthy goal of all maturing Christians. More than seven hundred years ago, Rolle referred to this "comforting infusion" as a "spiritual flame" that kindled a "sweet" and "delightful devotion." It was called being "annihilated" by Teresa, the "self-forgetful" place by C. S. Lewis (1969) or the "illuminative way" by Groeschel (1983). Might we deem it the "spiritually forming" or "Christ-infusing way"? Tragically, it is often dismissed by Christians who have not known God with this level of intimacy or intensity. Haynes (1998) warns that "Christian clinicians who do not yet relate to concepts that aid souls more advanced than ourselves should be careful not to speak categorically against [what] we or others may need to turn to in the future. It could also be unfortunate to [misunderstand or stifle these kind of] spiritual interventions" (p. 51).

Yet in so much of modern-day living, when God speaks, we silence him by dismissing such spiritual experience as "mysticism" or distort his voice with outward activity. We go for counseling, join a small group, read a book or get religious. Curtis and Eldredge (1997) express it, "The voice in our heart dares to speak to us . . . 'listen to me—there is something missing in all this . . . You were made for something more [and] you know it'" (p. 2). It is this "sacred romance," to know and love God with all our hearts, that calls to us deep within.

Becoming attuned to heart life. It is more than God engaging our intellects. It is his passionate appeal to capture our hearts—to come alive in our heart of hearts. Counseling grounded upon Christ and his Word is oriented to believers who are putting on the "new self, which is being renewed in knowledge in the image of its Creator" (Col 3:10). It is this new self that, by becoming Christ-derived by study of the living Word, is drawn into deep communion with God himself, enabled to be Christ-infused and transformed.

Melding Head and Heart Together

As the head and heart of Christ live together *in one body*—mystically and realistically in the worldwide church, the body of Christ—so must head and heart be joined in transformational union by the one living organism of Christian counseling. Moreover, the dyad no longer accurately describes the counseling matrix. True Christian counseling must be triadic—joining client, therapist and the God who created and loves them both. We are advancing this triad of persons who engage in counseling by also committing to a tri-union that joins head and heart and the life that is poured out by a most gracious Father unto his children (this section uses and extends prior writings of the second author: Ohlschlager, 2006; Ohlschlager & Scalise, 2007; Clinton & Ohlschlager, 2002).

Using another metaphor, it is long past due that the right hand of inner healing in rational and cognitive Christian counseling be joined and celebrated with the left hand of emotion-focused change—we can no longer allow either hand to be ignorant of or condescending toward the other. As we have ranged across the fields of both hands in this book, it is now the task to form a more complete union of the elements that make up a transformational model of Christian care-giving.

Mind you, we are not advocating the union of biblical counselors with integrationists—as we no longer think in terms of that unfortunate binary dispute. Rather, we are advocating the union of two major approaches to Christian counseling contained in this book that have lived apart for far too long. These are the worlds of head and heart, arguably the most common spiritual complaint of clients, who deny the division that keeps what they believe in their hands from entering and affecting their hearts. These two worlds, when brought together, are like joining fire and fuse—the impact is truly explosive and the effect is transformational in the lives of those we serve.

Giving up our bipolar and selfish ways. We cannot, individually as counselors or corporately as churches, ministries and associations, live any longer in just one camp or the other, denying the power and losing the impact of joining these forces as one. As head or heart dies quickly without the other, we are dead spiritually and intellectually if we stay mired in just one of these models—dead without overcoming the prejudice and small-mindedness that keeps some of us arrogant, ignorant, afraid and apart.

Too many Christians—and too many Christian counselors—have and still take a bipolar view, an "either-or" approach to these two orientations. Too many either live in their heads, emotionally detached from life, or are pushed in every which way by their impulses and feelings. They are imbalanced by the way they live and stress the importance of just one side of this spiritual life, and by a one-sided approach to Christian counseling. It is tantamount to living with one hand tied behind one's back. When both hands are needed, it is foolish to fight with just one hand. Or haven't we learned that yet?

Final disclosure. I (G.O.) come from a professional counseling background—working for a quarter century, mostly as a California LCSW prior to my retirement from full-time clinical, mediation and supervisory practice in 1999. Now as a clinical and ethical consultant to the membership of the American Association of Christian Counselors, I work primarily to build up and defend the emerging profession-ministry of Christian counseling. While "praying the Scriptures" (in chap. 14) is Christian-derived and Christ-infused throughout, I did that practice only when needed (not in every case) and wholly within the larger Christian-accommodating context of doing cognitive behavioral and family systems therapies. Figure 22.1 shows the fullness of this comprehensive model.

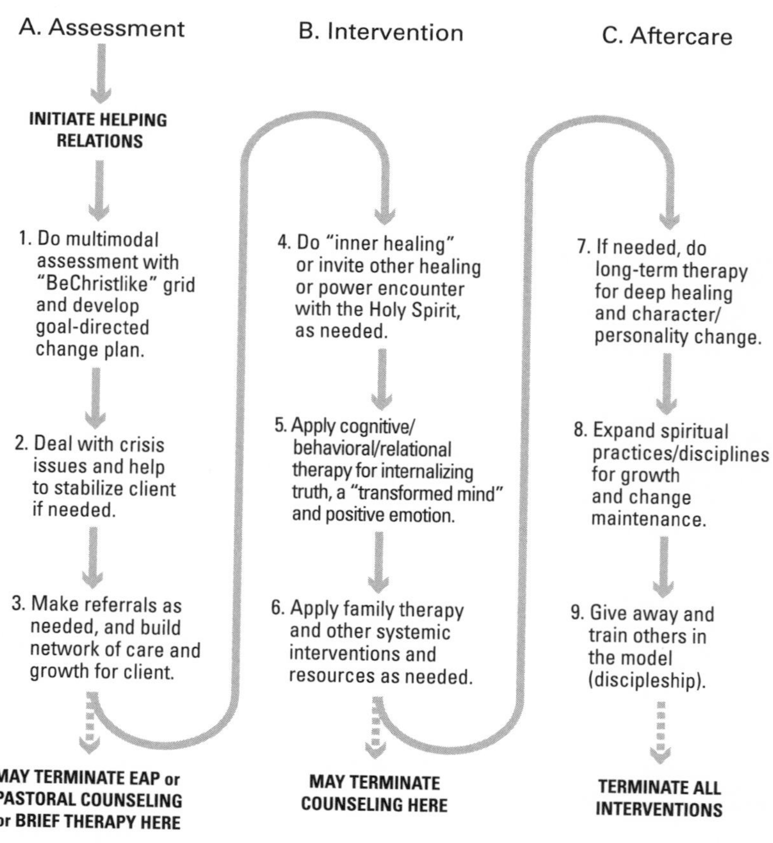
A Transformative Spiritual/Clinical Intervention Model
For Comprehensive Change, Growth and Discipleship
A. Assessment
B. Intervention
C. Aftercare
INITIATE HELPING RELATIONS
1. Do multimodal assessment with "BeChristlike" grid and develop goal-directed change plan.
2. Deal with crisis issues and help to stabilize client if needed.
3. Make referrals as needed, and build network of care and growth for client.
MAY TERMINATE EAP or PASTORAL COUNSELING or BRIEF THERAPY HERE
4. Do "inner healing" or invite other healing or power encounter with the Holy Spirit, as needed.
5. Apply cognitive/behavioral/relational therapy for internalizing truth, a "transformed mind" and positive emotion.
6. Apply family therapy and other systemic interventions and resources as needed.
MAY TERMINATE COUNSELING HERE
7. If needed, do long-term therapy for deep healing and character/personality change.
8. Expand spiritual practices/disciplines for growth and change maintenance.
9. Give away and train others in the model (discipleship).
TERMINATE ALL INTERVENTIONS

Figure 22.1. A model for transformative spiritual/clinical intervention

The right hand of Christian cognitive therapy. Constructively, much Christian counseling is now done as a religious/spiritual variant of cognitive behavioral therapy—especially with a depth emphasis on changing schemas and core beliefs. This seems to be the common preference of those who have been trained and practice professionally through one of the mental health disciplines. Assessing and renouncing faulty thinking—exposing the "lies" we still live by after regeneration and exchanging them with the truths of Scripture—is a central method of numerous models of Christian therapy now being practiced in Christian counseling. The best Christian therapists have incorporated Christ and the centrality of Christian maturity into the counseling goal and process. The best of these helpers have learned how to consistently merge client goals with the overarching goal of maturing sanctification in Christ, a dynamic we see present in so many of the models contained in this book.

Yet the best cognitive behavioral models are not enough. In the classic language of Carl Rogers, cognitive behavioral models are necessary but insufficient models for a fully orbed Christian counseling. Changed thinking and behavior, as good as that is, is still not enough—a changed heart is also required. In fact, it can be cogently argued from the Bible that changed thinking flows primarily from a transformed heart in the process of Christian maturity.

Russ Willingham, in his excellent book *Breaking Free* (1999), states this therapeutic truth so well in the context of sexual addiction treatment:

> No one is transformed by a purely cognitive approach, even if that approach is biblical. Healing of the self requires a spiritual-emotional attachment to a nurturing parenting figure. . . . Identity formation . . . comes about as the sexually broken person *learns to attach to Christ subsequent to conversion.* Contrary to popular evangelical belief, this doesn't happen solely through the accumulation of biblical facts or by religiously following the propositions and instructions of Scripture. This happens by interpersonal interaction with Christ, similar to the interaction between parent and child in a healthy family. . . . The processes are identical, yet obviously different, in that Christ will not literally take a person up in his lap and speak audibly into his ears. . . . *But a similar work must be accomplished by the indwelling Spirit, which is no less real.*
>
> In addition, since attempts to form a Christian identity are often based on the learning and memorization of biblical truths—largely an imper-

> sonal acquisition of facts—this also will not suffice. Please don't misunderstand me here, as I am dedicated to the study and learning of the Bible—God's revelation of Himself to us. *What I am opposed to is the mere learning of facts about God, and substituting that for a relationship, the intimate knowing of God. Far too many Christians, and most addicts, make this basic mistake.* (in Clinton, Hart & Ohlschalger, 2005, pp. 45-50; emphases mine)

The left hand of emotion-focused change. So then, do we forsake biblical counseling and cognitive therapy and turn wholesale to inner healing strategies or a dynamic twelve-step program? Not at all. Sole reliance on biblical memorization or charismatic interventions tends to rigidly program the uncontainable movement of the Holy Spirit, and often fails to attend to the ongoing challenge of therapeutic change in treatment as well as the aftercare dimensions of growth and maturity. There is often the false expectation that the dramatic healing encounter is all that is needed—that healing and maturing growth are included in the same touch. The hard work of discipleship or the ongoing challenge of spiritual formation and godly maturity revealed in the Bible is too often forsaken by a quick and easy approach that mirrors the "you can have it all and have it now" lie of the disbelieving culture.

However, we must incorporate inner healing and emotion-focused change—facilitating life-changing and transformational encounters with the risen Christ—into our Christian counseling regimen. "Signs and wonders" ministry not only is necessary for some who need a profoundly healing touch, but it is the growing currency for reaching a postmodern generation that is no longer moved by modernist approaches to the truth—empirical evidence and rational persuasion. Truth be told, critical aspects of biblical counseling, Christian cognitive therapy, emotionally focused therapy, and charismatic, inner healing therapies must all be incorporated into the construction of a new-century theory and practice for a robust and comprehensive Christian counseling. And all these elements exist in the comprehensive therapeutic program we deliver in this book and chapter.

TOWARD A COMPREHENSIVE CHRISTIAN CAREGIVING

We would suggest to you all a union of otherwise polarized forces, a "both-and" approach to life and to a larger call to comprehensive

Christian care-giving. To do so, there must be recognition that each side is necessary to the other—that head and heart must be joined in one organism to live, and that life is given to the united organism by God. Hence, it should be easy to see that each side is essential and necessary, but by itself is not sufficient for redemptive living—neither head nor heart can live on its own. We would encourage you to set both hands free, with right and left hands learning to work, to serve, to praise, to solve problems together. Understanding both head and heart and their union will come as you ponder their varied characteristics under our main metaphor of the body:

Table 22.1.

Head	Heart	One Body in Christ
Head knowledge	Heart-felt faith	God transformatively alive
Cognitive orientation	Emotionally centered	Whole and holistic
Rational/scientific	As the Spirit moves	Godly wisdom for all
Knowing God's truth	Experiencing God's love	Living out the truth-in-love
Changing beliefs/behavior	Being healed/transformed	Joy and peace made alive
God revealed	God encountered	God present and alive
Disciplined change	Miraculous change	Transformative change
Professional therapists	Lay counselors/recovery	Everyone a teacher/disciple
Practiced in clinics	Practiced in church	Lived out everywhere
Graduate training	Lay/recovery education	Life education/nonstop

Are you getting the picture? Does it make sense to you that joining head and heart together is the better way? Is it not true that if we are going to truly help our clients to bridge this division that we must bridge it first? These distinctives are not rigid, nor are the boundaries impermeable as many practitioners on both sides evince elements of the other side in their work—especially as they mature as therapists and grow wiser in their giftedness and their science. Nor are these differences present in Christian counseling alone. Much pastoral care and formational ministry in the church can be distinguished in similar ways:

Table 22.2.

Head Knowledge	Heart Life	Joined in Christ
Propositional truth	Experiential truth	Living in/with/for Christ
Explicit/language-based	Implicit/gut feeling	Giving intuitive wisdom
Prayer-focused	Praise-oriented	Living rhythm of prayer & praise
Individual	Relational/corporate	Person-embedded-in-church/society
Truth telling	Sharing love and joy	Speaking the truth in love
Proclamation	Realization	God is alive now and forever
Systematic theology	Experiential theology	Spiritual formation unto glory
Dispensational	Charismatic	Kingdom is alive now and forever

Embracing a Transformational Conclusion

God's transformative perspective will view these two streams as complementary and connected—they are not conflictual in the context of his kingdom; not complete without both views fully joined and influencing the other. A transformative view is the precursor to seeing the fullness of God and his kingdom design for the church. Both of these streams joined together represent the fullness of gospel transformation. Joining both of these aspects in pastoral care and spiritual formation has the same explosive impact as in Christian counseling. Lives are not merely changed, they are transformed. Christian helpers are not merely learning about God; they learn to know and to trust him intimately.

Finally, from both of us: We hope and pray that this book will prompt a transformational change for the better in your life, and in the lives of all those you serve.

References and Recommended Resources

Aten, J. D., McMinn, M. R., & Worthington, E. L., Jr. (2011). *Spiritually oriented interventions for counseling and psychotherapy.* Washington, DC: American Psychological Association.

Beecher, H. W. (1949). True religion. Quoted in S. Stuber & T. Clark, *Treasury of the Christian Faith.* New York: Association Press.

Clinton, T., Hart, A., & Ohlschlager, G. (2005). Caring for people God's way: Personal and emotional issues, addictions, grief, and trauma. Nashville: Thomas Nelson.

Clinton, T., & Ohlschlager, G. (2002). *Competent Christian counseling: Foundations and practice of compassionate soul care.* Colorado Springs: WaterBrook.

Colson, C. (1989). *Against the night.* Ann Arbor, MI: Servant.

Crabb, L. (1977). *Effective biblical counseling: A model for helping caring Christians become capable counselors.* Grand Rapids: Zondervan.

Crabb, L. (1998). *The safest place on earth.* Nashville: W Publishing Group.

Curtis, B., & Eldredge, J. (1997). *The sacred romance.* Nashville: Nelson.

Egan, G. (2009). *The skilled helper: A problem management and opportunity development approach to helping.* Pacific Grove, CA: Brooks/Cole.

Groeschel, B. J. (1983). *Spiritual passages: The psychology of spiritual development.* New York: Crossroads.

Haynes, L. (1998). Response to "Restoring the substance to the soul of psychology": Clinical and spiritual development applications. *Journal of Psychology and Theology, 26*(1), 44-53.

Lewis, C. S. (1969). *The screwtape letters.* New York: Macmillan.

McMinn, M. (1996). *Psychology, theology, and spirituality in Christian counseling.* Wheaton, IL: Tyndale.

McMinn, M., & Campbell, C. (2007). *Integrative psychotherapy: Toward a comprehensive Christian approach.* Downers Grove, IL: InterVarsity Press.

Ohlschlager, G. (2006). Embracing one metatheory: The head and heart of Christ—and of Christian counseling. *Christian Counseling Today, 14*(4), 8-11.

Ohlschlager, G., & Scalise, E. (2007). The 5 stages of competent Christian counseling: Toward a common factors/best practices process. *Christian Counseling Today, 15*(2), 19-24.

Rolle, R. (1993). The fire of love. In R. Foster & J. Smith, *Devotional classics: A Renovare resource for spiritual renewal.* San Francisco: HarperSanFrancisco.

Tan, S.-Y. (2011). *Counseling and psychotherapy: A Christian perspective.* Grand Rapids: Baker Academic.

Teresa of Avila. (1577/1993). Interior castle. In R. Foster & J. Smith, *Devotional classics: A Renovare resource for spiritual renewal.*

Willingham, R. (1999). *Breaking free: Understanding sexual addiction & the healing power of Jesus.* Downers Grove, IL: InterVarsity Press. Quoted in T. Clinton, A. Hart & G. Ohlschlager (2005). *Caring for people God's way: A new guide for Christian counseling.* Nashville: Thomas Nelson, pp. 49-50.

Worthington, E. L., Jr., Johnson, E. L., Hook, J. N., & Aten, J. D. (Eds.). (forthcoming). *Evidence-based practices for Christian counseling and psychotherapy.* Downers Grove, IL: InterVarsity Press.

APPENDIX

Keeping Christ in Christian Counseling

Recent and Developing Threats Eroding Precious Rights to Religious Freedom and Client Self-Determination

George Ohlschlager

At the beginning [1994] of our common work on behalf of the gospel, it did not seem likely that religious freedom would be one of our primary concerns. . . . We are now concerned—indeed, deeply concerned—that religious freedom is under renewed assault around the world. While the threats to freedom of faith, religious practice, and religious participation in public affairs in Islamist and communist states are widely recognized, grave threats to religious freedom have also emerged in the developed democracies. In the West, certain religious beliefs are now regarded as bigoted. Pastors are under threat, both cultural and legal, for preaching biblical truth. Christian social service and charitable agencies are forced to cease cooperation with the state because they will not bend their work to what Pope Benedict XVI has called the "dictatorship of relativism." . . . It is no exaggeration to see in these developments a movement to drive religious belief, and especially orthodox Christian religious and moral convictions, out of public life. . . . In the words of the World Evangelical Alliance, Christians are "the largest single group in the world . . . being denied human rights on the basis of their faith."

Evangelicals and Catholics Together (March 2012),
In Defense of Religious Freedom

A religion of the absence of God—a religion of humanity—is currently destroying and demoralizing the West. . . . This is not simply a fashion or opinion trend; it is a genuine large-scale project for governing the world.

PIERRE MANENT

Note to Reader: While the material of this book is essentially universal and timeless, the focus of this chapter is not—hence its placement in an appendix that sets it off from the rest of the book. This final chapter addresses the constellation of current events that reveal a growing threat to the freedom of Christian counselors—and to all Christian ministers, in fact—to practice Christ-centered ministry and intervention with those who come for help. This chapter reveals the growing threat to religious freedom and client self-determination in this new millennium, and what we must do to protect ours and our clients' precious rights before they are systematically taken from us.

The year 2012 may well become known as the most fateful ever in the over-400-year history of religious liberty in the new world. Surely for nearly 250 years, the US Constitution has protected religious freedom—protected the right to believe in God, however he is conceived—far beyond the protections afforded religion and the rights of conscience in most other countries on the planet. For more than two centuries, America has been a beacon of light, and the blessed home to millions of immigrants persecuted, abused and murdered for nothing more than the right to believe as they chose, and not according to the dictates of whatever regime is in power.

GOVERNMENT GIVETH AND GOVERNMENT TAKETH AWAY

Yet in January 2012 we have witnessed two of the three branches of our federal government either affirming these special rights or taking steps to kill them. In *Hosanna-Tabor v. EEOC,* the US Supreme Court reversed the primary federal agency on employment law by a unanimous 9-0 vote, upholding the fundamental right of religious organizations to hire and fire employees on the basis of their own religious beliefs. The high court respected what the EEOC did not—an historic and inviolate rule of judicial policy that all courts have always honored in America, and that all nine justices affirmed unanimously in making an important point. This long-standing rule holds that courts and all branches of government have no business—really, no ability or competence—to interfere with and muck around in the religious beliefs, practices, personnel and policies of churches and religious organizations. If the Court had ruled in favor of the EEOC, administrative control of the American church would have instantly transferred from the church to the state—with horrifying consequences.

Julea Ward case reversed on appeal. More good news came from the Sixth Circuit Court of Appeals, which reversed the Federal District Court judgment against Julea Ward and ordered a trial to be held regarding her expulsion from the graduate counseling program at Eastern Michigan University due to her strong religious beliefs regarding human sexuality. The Sixth Circuit Court, among other things, held that

> Ward's free-speech claim deserves to go to a jury. Although the university submits it dismissed Ward from the program because her request for a referral violated the ACA code of ethics, a reasonable jury could find otherwise—that the code of ethics contains no such bar and that the university deployed it as a pretext for punishing Ward's religious views and speech. The ACA code of ethics, in the first place, does not prohibit values-based referrals like the one Ward requested. (Ward v. Polite, et al., 2012)

Further on the Court reasoned incisively:

> No matter what the code of ethics means and no matter how it has been interpreted, the university defendants respond that the school had a different policy for practicum students—a "blanket rule" that they could not refer any clients. . . . But a reasonable jury could find that this was an after-the-fact invention. The university cannot point to any policy articulated in its course materials, the student handbook or anything else forbidding practicum students from making referrals. The student manual, to the contrary, includes a chapter dedicated to "Referrals" which says that students "may at times need to refer a client for additional counseling services outside the Counseling Clinic." . . . Worse, there are at least two settings where the university permits students—in practicum—to have a say over whom they counsel. The school permits students to request certain types of clients to counsel—what you might call a yes-referral policy—and the school will honor the request. . . . At the very least, it shows that the counseling department was willing to avoid unsuitable student-client matches in some instances. Why treat Ward differ-

> ently? That her conflict arose from religious convictions is not a good answer; that her conflict arose from religious convictions for which the department at times showed little tolerance is a worse answer. (Ward v. Polite, et al., 2012)

We are delighted that Ms. Ward will receive a new trial based on her substantial claims—claims that powerfully argue that the school treated her and her religious beliefs in a most discriminatory way (AACC delivered its first-ever amicus brief in support of Ms. Ward). And we are delighted that here is at least one applicable appellate case—the first of its kind, in fact—that stands up for the proposition that professional counselors, in training and in professional practice, have a right to integrate and incorporate our faith-based beliefs into our clinical decision making and practice. And especially in the white-hot realm of human sexuality, in a dispute about same sex issues.

Stripping away religious freedom. Just days after the Supreme Court ruling in *Hosanna-Tabor,* however—which some have called the most significant religious freedom case in over forty years—Health and Human Services chief, Kathleen Sebelius, allowed a rule to take effect that will effectively kill religious liberty in all healthcare transactions. She upheld a God-denying federal rule that will require all religious employers to deliver abortion and contraception services to all employees and service recipients as part of the new Obama healthcare law coming on-stream across the country. Many religious leaders are appalled by the deceptive and coercive tactics of the government to force these unwanted services—arrogantly defiant in the face of both the Christian commitment to life and, just a week earlier, the Supreme Court ruling in *Hosanna-Tabor.*

A gutless and useless conscience clause. The conscience clause exemption, a standard clause in American law that allows individuals and organizations to opt out due to their religious beliefs, is so specific and narrowly drawn in this rule that most churches and religious agencies will not qualify. Therefore, unless Congress overturns or the Supreme Court strikes down this draconian rule (and over a dozen lawsuits have been filed so far, including one by the University of Notre Dame), sometime in 2013 all religious universities, hospitals, social service and adoption agencies, charities, and relief organizations will be required to do what they consider to be the most rank form of evil that one can do—provide services that kill unborn life. To assert that a titanic clash of values and law is on the near horizon is surely gross understatement.

The Fifth Force as a Force for Good

So then, while this book is about the many wonderful ways that God shows up in Christian counseling, pastoral care and spiritual formation to bring transformational hope and healing, we have included this chapter to make our readers aware of the grave systemic threats we face—the challenge of keeping Christ alive and well in Christian counseling and ministry. It is to our good fortune, at a macropractice and systemic level of change, that a major development in counseling and psychotherapy early in this twenty-first century is strongly supportive of religious beliefs and spiritual practices. Described as the *fifth force* after the psychodynamic, behavioral, humanistic and multicultural influences, this developing trend calls for acknowledgment and respect for the role of spirituality and religious beliefs in all kinds of counseling and mental healthcare (Garzon, 2011).

Let God blow wind beneath our wings. This fifth force will need to be advanced with all diligence and godly power against the militant counterforce of God-dismissing secularism that is doing all it can to drive religion and spirituality—and by its close association, Christian counseling—from any and all influence in the public square. We are calling all ministers and counseling practitioners seeking to bring God's presence and power to their clients and parishioners to also bring a godly challenge to maintain our precious rights—especially the rights to religious freedom, to free religious speech and to free association with fellow believers. It is these precious First Amendment rights of religious liberty that have come under attack by forces determined to quash what we have for so long taken for granted in America.

The new science of religion and mental health. No doubt one major influence of this fifth force are the myriad positive correlations shown by literally thousands of empirical studies on the relationship of religion to mental health (see Koenig, King & Carson, 2012; Koenig, McCollough & Larson, 2001). This evidence directly counters the long-held bias against religion by many of the leading lights of psychotherapy, who held that religion was inherently pathological and superstitious, with terrible consequences to persons and society. Searching all the scientific studies of the nineteenth, twentieth and twenty-first centuries, empirical evidence was gathered from nearly three thousand studies that showed that good and healthy religion influenced these various human conditions and relationships:

1. greater overall well-being—80 out of 100 studies
2. greater hope and optimism—>80% of studies found
3. greater purpose and meaning in life—15 of 16 studies
4. greater self-esteem—16 of 29 studies, or 55%
5. better adaptation to bereavement—8 of 17 studies
6. greater social support—19 of 20 studies
7. lower rates of depression—60 of 93 studies, or 65%
8. fewer suicides—57 of 68 studies
9. less anxiety—80% of cohort studies, and 86% of clinical trials
10. less alcohol and drug abuse—76 of 86 studies, or 88%
11. less delinquency and crime—28 of 36 studies, or 78%
12. greater marital happiness and stability—35 of 38 studies, or 92%

America is a religious nation. Another major reason for the rise of this fifth force is the overwhelmingly religious/spiritual nature of the American populace. At the end of the last century, the Princeton Religious Research Center (1996) conducted an extensive survey on religious beliefs in America. Among its more salient findings were that

- 96% of American citizens believed in the existence of God or some kind of higher power;
- 90% believed in heaven, 73% believed in hell and 65% believed that the devil was real;
- 79% believed in miracles, mostly done as a positive healing and transforming force;
- 55% believed that the Bible was the inspired Word of God.

Moreover, within the past seven days of the study,

- 90% stated that they had prayed, some many times each day;
- 80% had read and/or meditated on the Bible; and
- 43% had attended services in a church or synagogue.

Client believers far outnumber secular therapists. To reframe and state it succinctly, *a clear majority of Americans believe in God in some way, and* *most of this majority want their religious beliefs and values to play a role—even a leading role—in any counseling efforts* (Garzon, 2011; Plante, 2009). Some would say this fifth force revolution is the first force that is being demanded and led by the clients—who believe at nearly twice the rate of their more skeptical and unbelieving therapists. This means that the professional community is reluctantly lagging behind the incessant demand that therapists respect and use the client's religious beliefs in the delivery of mental health services. Moreover, many religious believers are frustrated by this gap and are seeking answers from sources outside the community of professional counselors and therapists.

The Fifth Force Versus Secular Opposition

Although this fifth force is advancing at a brisk pace—with theories, interventions, ethics and research all pushing into a heretofore barren religious landscape in modern mental health practice—there remains a strong secular advocacy in our field that refuses to yield to and incorporate this fifth force. Fifth force advances are slamming up against the boundaries of secular beliefs and discovering strong opposition. This brittle atheistic ideology is rigidly convinced of its own "truth" and asserts its alien rights over the religious, constitutional, legal, ethical and moral rights inherent to religious belief and respect.

Religious freedom intersecting with client self-determination. We are convinced that this secularizing trend is exactly backwards—that the right to the integration of spirituality and religious faith in psychotherapy and mental health care can and should prevail in America. If instead this oppositional secular force prevails, then America will have devolved into the ranks of those mostly dictatorial nations that refuse to respect religious freedom and the rights of human conscience. Both religious freedom and client self-determination—and all manner of freedoms that today we take for granted—will dry up and die on the vine that would no longer be nourished by our constitutional genius and power. *What is at stake here is nothing less than the maintenance of our core constitutional rights to religious freedom intersecting with the cardinal counseling ethic of client self-determination* (see Clinton & Ohlschlager, 2002; Ohlschlager & Mosgofian, 1992).

Helping professions violating client self-determination. Furthermore, if secular forces prevail, the helping professions of America will have violated the foundational ethic of client self-determination that everyone learned in their first course in graduate school. This rule holds that the competent adult client has the inviolate right to have their wishes, values, beliefs and goals respected and supported in any and all counseling efforts (Egan, 2010; Ohlschlager, 2011). The violation of this rule is already being witnessed in a California legislator's proposed bill (SB 1172) in that state that attempts to criminalize any attempts to provide reparative or conversion therapy to anyone seeking to leave the gay way behind. This bill, which has already been passed by the California Senate, bars all such therapy to any minor and demands a draconian and fallacious consent requirement (see Ohlschlager, 2011) for any adult seeking change by reparative therapy (Shapiro, 2012).

The National Association for Research and Therapy of Homosexuality (NARTH) has come out strongly against passage of SB 1172, accurately arguing that it misrepresents the evidence of sexual orientation change efforts, tramples on the rights of parents in caring for their minor children, and usurps the role of mental health organizations and licensing boards in providing oversight. Christian counseling is the one field where these values intersect and clash on a daily basis. It is Christian counseling, especially, that must stand up for religious freedom—or watch the "Christ" being removed from Christian counseling with corrupt legislation like SB 1172. It is Christian counseling that must stand up for our clients to have their faith and values fully respected and incorporated into all counseling endeavors.

Additional Threats to Religious Freedom

While all Christian denominations are at risk, the Catholic church is on the point of religious institutions who are witnessing their ministry being lacerated by these multiple failures to respect religious freedom and client self-determination. The *Religious News Service* (Speciale, 2012) recently reported that emeritus Pope Benedict XVI warned a group of visiting US bishops in Rome that a "radical secularism" is gaining ground in American society and poses a "grave threat" to the Catholic church's freedom of expression in the public square. Catholics must be on guard to confront a "reductive secularism," Benedict said, which tries to "delegitimize the church's participation in public debate." The pontiff warned that America's "cherished" tradition of "religious freedom" is under threat as the nation's moral consensus has been "eroded" by "powerful new cultural currents" that not only run counter to "Judeo-Christian tradition, but (are) increasingly hostile to Christianity as such." This followed action by the National Conference of Catholic Bishops (NCCB), the main governing body of the Catholic Church in America, that just recently created the Ad Hoc Committee for Religious Liberty as a necessary resistance and counterweight to the various assaults on the church's religious freedom (Desmond, 2011).

Six specific assaults against the church. Against all churches, the year 2011 alone has witnessed (1) the already noted action by the US Department of Health and Human Services mandating that in the Obamacare health bill, birth control services be delivered in all employee health coverage in the United States; (2) churches working with the federal Migration and Refugee Services are now required to provide a full range of abortion and contraception to trafficking victims and unaccompanied minors; (3) the US Agency for International Development has mandated delivery of condoms and contraceptive services in all international relief programs; (4) the US Department of Justice has begun to legally label the federal Defense of Marriage Act's support for traditional marriage as "bigotry"; (5) support for traditional marriage is quickly becoming seen as being legally bigoted in those states that have passed laws in support of gay marriage (with Washington state becoming the seventh state to allow gay marriage just recently); and (6) Catholic adoption and foster care services have lost huge statewide placement contracts in California, Massachusetts and Illinois for refusing to place its children in gay and lesbian homes.

Facing up to the growing anti-Christian federal policy. Considering the wide-ranging scope of these actions—actions that will afflict all Protestant churches and ministries as well as the Catholic church—it is surely arguable that the Obama administration now supports a comprehensive and thoroughgoing secularization of American government, wiping out the delicate balance of church and state that has gone on since the founding of the USA. The current administration in Washington is quickly devolving into an anti-Christian, rights-stealing regime of the federal government—wielding power and acting in ways without precedent in the history of the United States. As stated by Kathryn Jean Lopez (2012) at the National Review Online:

> We live in a country that has long safeguarded religious freedom, believing it to be a good for the life of the nation. But current government policy suggests something else. President Obama and his administration have demonstrated a hostility to the free exercise of religion in the public square—except, that is, when it can be used to justify a policy dictated by the Left's ideology regarding the size and scope of government.

Archbishop Timothy Dolan of New York, president of the NCCB, speaking to and beyond his own church, asserted his concern about the "increasing number of federal government programs and policies that infringe upon the right of conscience of people of faith or otherwise harm the foundational principle of religious liberty. . . . Never before have we faced this kind of challenge to our ability to engage in the public square as people of faith and as a service provider. *If we do not act now, the consequences will be grave*" (Desmond, 2011; emphasis mine).

In the influential journal *First Things*, the Archbishop of Los Angeles, Jose Gomez, warned that in spite of religious freedom's first reference in the First Amendment—signaling its preeminence to the Founding Fathers—today both government and culture "express religious beliefs as only one of many private lifestyle options." Tragically religious liberty "is often 'trumped' in the face of challenges from competing rights and interests deemed to be more important." Gomez incisively argued that "our country's founders recognized that religious freedom is a right endowed by God, not a privilege granted by government. And they respected that what God has given, no one—not a court, a legislature, or any institution—can rightly deny" (Gomez, 2011).

BROADER THREATS TO CHRISTIAN COUNSELING

Examples also abound of militant secularists running roughshod over the beliefs and values of people who seek out Christian counseling. This brittle secular worldview, operating from a "freedom from religion" stance, intends to scrub clean all religious and spiritual influence from all law and any public policy views in the United States. This viewpoint sees religion as a form of antiscientific superstition—at best, a purely private system of beliefs and practices that have no right to spill over and influence law and policy in the public realms. Sadly, this radically bifurcated view of religion points falsely to a radical Islamism and the adoption of sharia law as a template of what will happen in the United States if a radical "theocratic Christian state" were allowed to rule. Not only does such radicalism appear nowhere in the mission statement of any church or religious organization in America, theocracy as such in radical Islam would be impossible to construct under our American Constitution.

Other examples of public trouble. Further examples have seen one lone federal judge recently overturn the votes of over seven million Californians, holding that Proposition 8's placement of one man/one woman marriage into the California constitution was invalid. Similarly, another lone federal judge in Massachusetts held that DOMA—the federal Defense of Marriage Act signed into law in 1996 by President Bill Clinton—was also illegal. The US Supreme Court just recently heard oral arguments on both of these cases. Closer to home, we have recently witnessed attempts in New Jersey to make CACREP programs the only gateway to LPC licensure. The California Association of Marriage and Family Therapists—by far the largest state association in America, with over 30,000 members—is still bloodied and embroiled by attempts to incorporate a gay-affirming stance into its ethics code. A number of psychology licensure boards have openly questioned whether "Christian counseling" should be banned among its psychologists as it is outside the "scope of practice" definition of psychology in its statutes. Other boards have attacked Christian counseling and faith-based practices from a confused church and state viewpoint, arguing for a "freedom from religion" stance that would negate any religious incorporation into mental healthcare (AACC Law & Ethics Committee, 2010).

The worst abuses are taking place in our secular graduate schools. This was exemplified by the two federal appellate court cases of plaintiff expulsion from secular graduate schools in Michigan and in Georgia. On appeal the Georgia woman lost her case, and the Michigan woman won hers. Yet these women were expelled—were told they had no place in the modern counseling professions of America—because they were Christians who believed in the Bible. Both of these schools considered biblical beliefs applied to human sexuality—especially to same-sex issues—to be "unethical," "toxic" and "immoral." These women were both challenged to participate in remediation programs that required them to embrace and publicly pronounce a gay-affirming ideology, essentially pressuring these two women to renounce their faith to do so.

The faculties and leadership of these secular graduate programs told these two women that it was not enough to tolerate and accept gay lifestyles, but they were required to become gay-affirming ideologues like themselves. Turning thousands of years of traditional morality on its head, persons with sincerely held Christian religious beliefs are now considered so terrible a risk that they are no longer welcome into the counseling professions of America as it is perceived by these unbelieving, secular leaders. Is this a harbinger of things to come? We believe that we have just begun to fight in the courtrooms and legislatures of America—a fight that will likely last a generation or more. Saddest of all, we could not honestly predict for you the outcome of this fight—whether the church and its rights will prevail and be protected, or whether the secular state and its anti-Christian views shall prevail.

Five Domains in Support of Christian Rights

There are five distinctive domains in the United States—domains of influential systemic power, foundations of knowledge and practice that support the right of integrating faith-based beliefs and practices into professional mental healthcare. These include biblical, sociocultural, clinical, empirical and legal-ethical domains.

Biblical supports. The Faith Factor Project of the AACC—a central linkage led by this author in AACC's multipronged effort to defend clients' religious freedom—is supported by the service call of the Great Commandment. We are called both to love God with all of our being (Deut 6:5; 11:1) and to love our neighbor as ourselves (Rom 13:8-10). This sacrificial love is the divine light of the love of Christ that attaches itself intimately to God and pours out life and sustenance to another for whom Christ has died. Second Corinthians 1:3-5 reveals: *"Blessed be the God and Father of our Lord Jesus Christ, the Father of mercies and God of all comfort, who comforts us in all our tribulation, that we may be able to comfort those who are in any trouble, with the comfort with which we ourselves are comforted by God. For as the sufferings of Christ abound in us, so our consolation also abounds through Christ"* (NKJV).

Empirical supports. Slowly, but steadily and surely, the scientific foundations of Christian counseling are strengthening. A joint Taskforce between Divisions 12 (Clinical Psychology) and 29 (Psychotherapy) of the American Psychological Association recently completed a meta-analysis of outcome studies that showed very positive support for Christian and Christian-accommodating therapies. They found that the rigor of the research designs were very strong and gave their hearty support to the integrity of this research (Norcross, 2011; Worthington et al., 2011).

As reviewed earlier, Duke psychiatrist Harold Koenig (Koenig, King & Carson, 2012; Koenig, McCollough & Larson, 2001) has reviewed over 3,000 empirical studies—every published scientific study from 1878 to 2010—on the relationship of faith to just about every health and mental health variable conceivable. He found that nearly 75%—three cases of every four—showed a positive relationship. A deep and active faith, in other words, translates to robust health, good mental health, and a long and satisfying life.

Clinical supports. While some Christian clients may support therapy being delivered by non-Christian therapists who are not hostile to the faith, many more are demanding that therapy be done by Christian counselors—especially counselors who have struggled and overcome the same issues that the client is facing. Client self-determination, reviewed earlier, is the cardinal clinical ethic that every mental health professional learned early in one's counseling training, and demands that client preferences on these core therapeutic issues be respected and followed. In fact, the best interpretation of the new ethical duties toward religious diversity among the secular MH professions yields a position that it is not enough to merely have some knowledge of the faith—while being an unbeliever yourself—but that Christian clients deserve a truly Christian counselor, one who has accepted Christ into his or her life and has struggled with many of the common struggles of those in the faith.

Sociocultural supports. Surrounding the fifth force influence of spirituality and religious faith in counseling and psychotherapy is the influence of biblical faith and morals in modern-day politics and public policy. This reflects the heightening contest between liberal, secularizing politics and religious values and more conservative influences in America. Moreover, the growing "faith gap" of a religious believing nation versus a nonbelieving mental health delivery force is an ongoing struggle in the challenge to match believing clients with believing counselors. We must build a strong hedge around Christian counseling—around all good Christian ministry—and our right to see our faith have blessed impact in the public square, or determined secularists will accomplish their objective to wipe away all religious influence on the laws and public policy of the nation.

Legal-ethical supports. If respected, there are three legal-ethical principles that are sufficient to defend and support our precious rights. The first principle is rooted in the Constitution itself—in the First Amendment of the Bill of Rights. These alien secular attacks on Christian counseling violate inherent religious freedoms, free speech and free association rights—values that should have priority place when they conflict with other important values. Second, these actions also violate core ethical duties to respect religious diversity—duties that have been strengthened in the recent revisions this past decade of every mental health ethics code. Also violated, third, is the long history in American case law that has shaped the protections of informed consent—law that codifies the cardinal counseling ethic of client self-determination. We seek your support in favor of God-honoring action at all three of these pressure points, knowing that God is with us as we advocate for godly strength in defense of this long-held but now fragile rights regime.

Professional Christian counseling connected to the church. A fourth legal objective will be statutory and systemic—to see Florida's alternative/exemption statute become law in every state in the Union (see Florida statutes, 2009). Christian counseling will be greatly empowered by opening an alternate practice front that ties Christian counseling more intimately to the church (rather than merely relying on the "benevolence" of state licensure). We will always contend for the right of professional Christian counselors to practice independently throughout America. But do note that from now on, we will also advocate for Christian counseling as a stand-alone, statutory-based practice-ministry of the church, expanding the historic and long-accepted "exemption" practice rule applied to pastoral counseling, and including complementary and alternative rights of choice.

Professional Christian counseling in the church in the twenty-first century. By this, professional Christian counseling will be enabled to deliver its ministry from a strong foundation in the church. Under church authority and protected by the legal exemption that all churches enjoy in America, professional counselors will be allowed to develop a fee-based practice, and to advertise as if they were in the professional roles that exist today. This will be a blessed twenty-first-century alternative practice form that will become increasingly attractive as state licensure boards become hostile and repressive to a Christ-centered way and role of professional delivery—a trend that we do not believe will abate.

Do Nothing or Take Action?

We must very soberly reflect on these things and gird ourselves for serious advocacy and action in the days and years to come. Remember that *Focus on the Family* is already being branded a "hate group" due to its historic and biblical defense of traditional one man/one woman marriage (Staver, 2011). The Obama Justice Department is already labeling support for traditional marriage as "bigotry"—a legal charge with very serious ramifications if it sticks. As a Christian counselor and marriage and family therapist advertising in the public sphere, you may already be targeted as a legal "bigot" by your own government, in league with powerful anti-Christian forces, simply because of your stand in support of the traditional and biblical foundations of marriage.

If we do nothing we will be rolled over—check that: we are being rolled over, and our precious religious freedom rights are already being trampled on—unless we stand up and say, "STOP! You can go no further" to this pernicious assault. Let us, instead, strengthen and stand together upon the five foundations that God has given us in protection and assertion of our precious rights. *And this must be a proactive and irenic stand,* not one that triggers our darker and defensive impulses as this wave of antireligious dogma attempts to sweep over us. Let us join together in faithful humility and godly strength, like our brethren have recently done in the Manhattan Declaration. Let us declare a new day—*a day where our allegiance to Christ is respected and welcomed* in the service we provide to others. We are compelled to stand and act against this atheistic thrust, and we must remain firm if this is to succeed on behalf of Christ and for our colleagues and clients.

This book is a comprehensive sampling of leading Christ-centered religious and spiritual interventions that we want to see protected in the United States and around the world. We hope you have found one or more interventions that you will make in future service to your clients, parishioners and directees. We plead with you to also join the movement to protect religious freedom and the right of conscience alongside your applied learning of these many ways of transformational change in the lives of those we serve. We believe that your advocacy for these precious systemic rights is every bit as important, if not more so, as your exercise of them.

It would be tragic to learn this hard-won lesson as a result of losing the right to practice our faith and exercise its necessary influence in the public square. And if we don't act assertively in defense of these rights, losing them seems more and more likely, requiring us to practice as "outlaws" if we practice at all. If we, instead, stand corporately and act in the power of God, we can stop this assault, or at least limit its damage.

For the sake of your clients and parishioners, and for the sake of America and the church, let's stand and gird ourselves for holy action on behalf of the God who stood alone on the cross for us.

References and Recommended Resources

AACC Law & Ethics Committee. (2010). *Data on ethical-legal complaints*. Forest, VA: AACC.

Clinton, T. C., & Ohlschlager, G. (2002). *Competent Christian counseling: Foundations and practice of compassionate soul care*. Colorado Springs: WaterBrook.

Desmond, J. F. (2011). Bishops fight threats to religious liberty: Catholic agencies required to provide abortion and contraception. *National Catholic Register*. Retrieved from <http://www.ncregister.com/site/print_article/30867/>.

Egan, G. (2010). *The skilled helper: A problem management and opportunity development approach to helping* (9th ed.). Belmont, CA: Brooks/Cole.

Evangelicals and Catholics Together. (March 2012). In defense of religious freedom. *First Things*. Retrieved from <www.firstthings.com/print/article/2012/02/in-defense-of-religious-freedom>.

Florida Statutes. (2009). Chapters 491.014 and 456.41.

Garzon, F. (2011). Spirituality in counseling. In T. Clinton & R. Hawkins (Eds.), *The popular encyclopedia of Christian counseling*. Eugene, OR: Harvest House.

Gomez, J. H. (2011, October 25). Defending our first freedom. *First Things*. Retrieved from <http://www.firstthings.com/print/onthesquare/2011/10/defending-our-first-freedom>.

Koenig, H. G., King, D., & Carson, V. (Eds.). (2012). *Handbook of religion and health* (2nd ed.). New York: Oxford University Press.

Koenig, H. G., McCollough, M. E., & Larson, D. B. (Eds.). (2001). *Handbook of religion and health*. New York: Oxford University Press.

Lopez, K. J. (2012, May 29). Losing America? *National Review Online*. Retrieved from <http://www.nationalreview.com/articles/299145/losing-america-kathryn-jean-lopez>.

Norcross, J. C. (Ed.). (2011). *Psychotherapy relations that work: Evidence-based responsiveness* (2nd ed.). New York: Oxford University Press.

Ohlschlager, G. (2011). *Advanced consent practice for change seeking, ego-dystonic homosexuals*. Paper presented at the 2011 AACC World Conference. Nashville, TN.

Ohlschlager, G., & Mosgofian, P. (2012/1992). *Law for the Christian counselor: A guidebook for clinicians and pastors.* Eugene, OR: Wipf & Stock.

Plante, T. G. (2009). *Spiritual practices in psychotherapy: Thirteen tools for enhancing psychological health.* Washington, DC: American Psychological Association.

Shapiro, L. (2012, May 13). Fight against gay "conversion therapy" gathers momentum. *The Huffington Post.* Retrieved from <http://www.huffingtonpost.com/2012/05/13/fight-against-gay-convers_n_1513043.html>.

Speciale, A. (2012, Jan 19). Pope warns U.S. bishops of "radical secularism." *Religious News Service.* Retrieved from <http://religionnews.com/faith/leaders-and-institutions/pope-warns-u.s.-bishops-of-radical-secularism>.

Staver, M. (2011). Christian counselors become targets of open hostility: Is this a harbinger of things to come? *Christian Counseling Today, 18*(4), 70-71.

Ward v. Polite, et al. (2012, Jan 27). *United States Court of Appeals for the Sixth Circuit,* No. 10-2100/2145. Eastern Michigan University.

Worthington, E. L., Jr., Hook, J. N., & Davis, D. E. (2011). Outcome research on Christian-focused treatment has come of age. *Christian Counseling Today, 18*(4), 18-22.

Worthington, E. L., Jr., Hook, J. N., Davis, D. E., & McDaniel, M. E. (2011). Religion and spirituality. *Journal of Clinical Psychology: In Session, 67,* 204-14.

Contributors

David W. Appleby, PhD, PhD is the founder and president of Spiritual Interventions, Inc., a nonprofit ministerial group serving Christian counseling and the church in critical areas of deliverance and spiritual warfare, and a pastoral counselor at Wyndhurst Counseling Center in Lynchburg, VA. He has taught psychology at Greenville College in Greenville, IL; was the director of the Counseling Center at St. Mary's College of Maryland; was associate and then senior pastor at Immanuel Church in Wilmington, DE; and was an associate professor in the Center for Counseling and Family Studies at Liberty University in Lynchburg, VA.

Dr. Appleby graduated with a BA in English from the University of Delaware, an MDiv from Denver Seminary, and an MA in Psychology, Counseling and Guidance and a PhD in College Student Personnel Administration from the University of Northern Colorado. He completed his second PhD from the University of Delaware in Family Studies with an emphasis in Fathering.

Dr. Appleby has been involved in the deliverance ministry for more than thirty years and has presented at professional conferences, churches and counseling centers on the role that deliverance plays in the counseling process. He and his deliverance teams work several times a week with individuals who come from all over the United States. His book *It's Only a Demon: A Model of Christian Deliverance* was published in 2009 by BMH Books. He has also had material on deliverance published in *Christian Counseling Today, Leadership Journal* and *Christianity Today* and other articles published in the field of Family Studies. He can be contacted at dappleby@spiritualinterventions.org.

George Ohlschlager, MA, MSW, JD serves as senior editor of *Hope Notes* and all other publications for the Center for Counseling and Health Resources (A Place of Hope). He is executive consultant to the American Association of Christian Counselors (AACC), and is also a clinical and forensic consultant with Spiritual Interventions, Inc., serving churches and Christian counseling worldwide. He is chairman of the AACC Law & Ethics Committee, and drafted and helped revise the AACC Christian Counseling Code of Ethics. From 2003 to 2008, George was senior editor and writer of *Christian Counseling Today*, AACC's flagship publication, and was cofounder and executive director of the International Board of Christian Counselors, the AACC-affiliated credentialing agency, from which he is credentialed as a Board Certified Christian Counselor. He was the cofounder, supervising clinician and mediator at the Redwood Family Institute in Northern California. He also teaches in the graduate counseling program at St. Petersburg Theological Seminary in Florida and the DMin program in Marriage and Family Therapy at Denver Seminary, and he consults with Liberty University in the conception/construction of a new School of Social Work. This is his tenth book as author, coauthor or editor. He has written and published over 330 articles, chapters, columns, codes, editorials, reviews, reports, monographs and legal briefs, and has made over 100 conference, seminar and webinar presentations in his many fields of interest.

George earned a BA in Psychology and Religious Studies with honors from Humboldt State University in California, an MA with high honors in Counseling Psychology and Biblical and Theological Studies from Trinity Evangelical Divinity School, an MSW and JD in Social Work and Law at the University of Iowa, and is now completing an interdisciplinary PhD in Counseling Psychology and Spiritual Formation at the International University for Graduate Studies (West Indies). He now serves worldwide as a writer, editor, and practice and ethics consultant, and can be contacted at goslager@aol.com.

Robin Caccese, BS, MT (ASCP) was a Sister of Christian Charity from 1964 to 1968. She trained as a Medical Technologist after receiving her BS degree in biology from Albright College. She began working part time at the *Journal of Christian Healing* and eventually became the managing editor. She also served as editor of the "InterACT" newsletter and founded Julian's House, a small publishing company that seeks to publish books, CDs and DVDs related to the integration of best medical practices and Christian healing.

Lydia Kim-van Daalen, PhD was born in the Netherlands, where she earned her BA in music therapy. She has earned an MDiv and PhD in Pastoral Theology/Christian Psychology from Southern Baptist Theological Seminary.

Myke Williams Dorsey, DMin is a middle school teacher for the Pinnellas County School District in St. Petersburg, Florida. He recently earned his D.Min. in pastoral counseling from St. Petersburg Theological Seminary. He and his wife Shay have two teen-aged daughters.

Aubrey L. Gartner, PhD (Virginia Commonwealth University) is currently a postdoctoral fellow at the Veteran Affairs Medical Center in Durham, NC. She served as student representative of Division 36, Society for the Psychology of Religion and Spirituality for three years as a graduate student at Virginia Commonwealth University, and has participated in numerous articles and book chapters.

Chelsea L. Greer, MS is a PhD student in Counseling Psychology (APA-accredited) at Virginia Commonwealth University. She studies forgiveness of in-group offenders within religious groups.

Julie Harren Hamilton, PhD is a licensed marriage and family therapist in private practice. She is a former assistant professor of Psychology in the Graduate Counseling Psychology program at Palm Beach Atlantic University (2004–2009). Dr. Hamilton served as president of the National Association for Research and Therapy of Homosexuality (NARTH), 2009–2011. She is also the coeditor of *The Handbook of Therapy for Unwanted Homosexual Attractions: A Guide to Treatment.*

Philip Henry, PhD earned his MDiv at Southwestern Baptist Theological Seminary, his MS at Chestnut Hill College and his PhD at Temple University. He has been on faculty at Temple University, Chestnut Hill College and Eastern University. He is currently a professor at Palm Beach Atlantic University, where he teaches in the graduate school. He is the author of *The Christian Therapist Notebook: Homework, Handouts and Activities for Use in Christian Counseling.*

Jan P. Hook, EdD is a licensed clinical professional counselor at the Arlington Center in Arlington Heights, IL. He has his EdD in Educational Psychology and Counseling from Northern Illinois University and MA in Counseling Psychology from Trinity International University, where he is also an adjunct professor. Jan is a clinical member and clinical supervisor with the American Association for Marriage and Family Therapy (AAMFT).

Joshua N. Hook, PhD is an assistant professor of Counseling Psychology at the University of North Texas. He has a PhD and MS in Counseling Psychology from Virginia Commonwealth University. His research interests include humility, religion/spirituality, forgiveness and sex addiction.

David J. Jennings, II, MS is a graduate student in the Counseling Psychology (APA-accredited) doctoral program at Virginia Commonwealth University in Richmond, VA. Before pursuing doctoral studies, he was a licensed professional counselor in private practice in Atlanta, GA. His major research interests are inspiration, forgiveness and relationships, and spirituality and counseling.

Eric L. Johnson, PhD is the Lawrence and Charlotte Hoover Professor of Pastoral Care at Southern Baptist Theological Seminary and director of the Society for Christian Psychology. He edited *Christianity and Psychology: Five Views* and has written *Foundations for Soul Care: A Christian Psychology Proposal.*

Mark Laaser, PhD holds a PhD in Religion and Psychology from the University of Iowa and an MDiv from Princeton Theological Seminary. He is an internationally known author and speaker and has written six books, including *Healing the Wounds of Sexual Addiction, Talking to Your Kids About Sex* and *The Pornography Trap*. He is also an adjunct faculty member at several graduate schools.

Yin Lin, MA (University of Delaware) is a second-year doctoral student in the Counseling Psychology (APA-accredited) program at Virginia Commonwealth University. She has published one article and one chapter in forgiveness.

Werner May is a psychologist, president of the IGNIS-Association of Christian Psychology–Germany (www.ignis.de) for twenty-five years, and president of the European Movement of Christian Anthropology, Psychology and Psychotherapy (www.emcapp.eu). He is the author of many books in the area of Christian counseling and education. His practical focus until 2003 was counseling foster families and adoptive families. He is the publisher of the web journal *Christian Psychology Around the World.* Download under www.emcapp.eu.

Arlys Norcross McDonald, PhD is a Christian clinical psychologist, specializing in trauma recovery for over thirty years. As a clinic owner and director, author, psychology professor and speaker for workshops, television and radio, she is an acknowledged leader in Christ-centered healing. She is an "expert witness" in the courts, and provides empathy and understanding through her personal journey of therapy for trauma.

Herman Riffel studied at Multnomah School of the Bible in Portland, OR; at Wheaton College in Wheaton, IL; and at the C. G. Jung Institute for Analytical Psychology in Zurich, Switzerland. He served as a Baptist pastor in Michigan and Illinois for twenty-five years. He has ministered to missionaries, taught at the Vatican and lectured to the Jung Society of Sydney, Australia. He has written *Christian Maturity and the Spirit's Power, The Voice of God, Learning to Recognize God's Voice, Dreams: Wisdom Within, Dream Interpretation: A Biblical Understanding* and *Dreams: Giants and Geniuses in the Making.*

Mark Sandford, MDiv graduated from Denver Seminary and is the spiritual director of Elijah House Ministries and the author of *Deliverance and Inner Healing.* He is also a well-known conference speaker.

Douglas Schoeninger, PhD is president of the Institute for Christian Healing in West Chester, PA, and editor of the *Journal of Christian Healing,* the official online journal of the Association of Christian Therapists (ACT). He has a PhD from the University of Wisconsin. He has studied with Carl Rogers, PhD; Ivan Nagy, MD; Barbara Krasner, PhD; Scott Walker, DC; and Theresa Dale, PhD.

J. Mark Shadoan, EdD is the clinical director of Light Counseling in Lynchburg, VA. He practices as a licensed clinical social worker. He received his MSW from Virginia Commonwealth University and his EdD from the University of Sarasota.

Edward M. Smith, DMin earned his graduate degrees from Southwestern Baptist Theological Seminary and Midwestern Baptist Theological Seminary. He spent seventeen years serving in local Southern Baptist Churches before starting Theophostic Prayer Ministries.

Siang-Yang Tan, PhD (McGill University) is professor of Psychology at the Graduate School of Psychology, Fuller Theological Seminary in Pasadena, CA, and senior pastor of First Evangelical Church Glendale, in Glendale, CA. He has published numerous articles and thirteen books, the latest of which is *Counseling and Psychotherapy: A Christian Perspective* (Baker Academic, 2011).

Leslie Vernick, DCSW is a popular speaker, author, licensed clinical social worker and coach. She has over twenty-five years of experience helping individuals and couples heal, rebuild or grow in their relationships. She is a guest lecturer at Westminster Seminary. In addition, she is the author of six books including *The Emotionally Destructive Relationship, How to Act Right When Your Spouse Acts Wrong* and her most recent, *Lord, I Just Want to Be Happy*. Contact Leslie at www.leslievernick.com.

Terry Wardle, DMin is professor of Practical Theology at Ashland Theological Seminary and president of Healing Care Ministries. He holds a DMin from Fuller Theological Seminary and has authored numerous books, including *Healing Care, Healing Prayer; Strong Winds, Crashing Waves; Draw Close to the Fire;* and *Untamed Christian, Unleashed Church.* Terry conducts frequent seminars on emotional healing for counselors, pastors, therapists and other caregivers.

Catherine Hart Weber, PhD received her MA in Theology and her PhD from Fuller Theological Seminary and Fuller Theological Seminary School of Psychology. Catherine is a licensed marriage and family therapist, counselor, coach and spiritual director in a private practice in Pasadena, CA. She has also been an adjunct professor at several universities including Fuller Theological Seminary and Denver Seminary. She is the author of *Flourish* and *Flourishing in Relationships.*

Julie Wegryn, MS, MAT, NCC is a licensed psychologist, a licensed professional counselor and a national certified counselor. Executive director of Christian Counseling and Therapy Associates of the Main Line, she obtained degrees from Douglas College of Rutgers University and The College of New Jersey. A certified teacher in Special Education and Vocational Rehabilitation, she obtained a degree in Counseling and Human Relations from Villanova University and completed the requirements to become a psychotherapist.

Edward T. Welch, PhD is a faculty member at the Christian Counseling & Educational Foundation (CCEF) and holds a PhD in Counseling Psychology with a Neuropsychology specialty from the University of Utah as well as a Master of Divinity degree from Biblical Theological Seminary. Ed has been counseling for over thirty years and has written many books and articles on biblical counseling, including *When People Are Big and God Is Small, Addictions: A Banquet in the Grave, Blame It on the Brain?, Depression* and *Running Scared.*

Everett L. Worthington Jr., PhD is a professor of Psychology at Virginia Commonwealth University. He has published about thirty books and over 300 articles and chapters mostly on forgiveness, religion and spirituality, and couples. His most popular book on forgiveness is *Forgiving and Reconciling* and on couple counseling is *Hope-Focused Marriage Counseling*—both through InterVarsity Press.

Charles Zeiders, PsyD is clinical director of Christian Counseling and Therapy Associates of the Main Line. He is a postdoctoral fellow of the University of Pennsylvania's Center for Cognitive Therapy, a member of the Department of Psychiatry of Bryn Mawr Hospital, and is adjunct instructor of Graduate Counseling at Eastern University and Pastoral and Theological Studies at Neumann University. He is the author of *The Clinical Christ: Scientific and Spiritual Explorations of the Transformative Psychology Called Christian Holism*. Dr. Zeiders's many publications may be obtained at www.drzeiders.com.